I'm NOT DEAD:

I'm ALIVE...without a body!

What's it like after <u>we</u> die?
Find out from these
amazing and genuine
conversations with loved ones
alive in the Spirit World

Channelled by French medium

BRIGITTE RIX

CON-PSY PUBLICATIONS

First Edition

© Brigitte Rix
2011

Published by
CON-PSY PUBLICATIONS

P.O.BOX 14,
GREENFORD,
MIDDLESEX, UB6 0UF.

ISBN 978 1 898680 57 4

Acknowledgements

My loving thanks to my mother, father and husband for their love, patience, support and understanding while they were on the Earth. Now they are in Spirit World, all my love, admiration and thanks, for having learnt to communicate to share their amazing discoveries and their joy at still being ALIVE in Afterlife!

My loving thanks to Grandma Léonie, in Spirit World too, for her affection and caring help 'behind the scenes'!

It is an honour for me to be the recipient of their revelations and to offer them to Mankind as evidence that EVERYBODY SURVIVES DEATH.

All my love and gratitude to my son Jim for his support and suggestions and my daughter Anne-France for her help, devotion, patience and artistic talent with the cover and my website.

Warmest and heartfelt thanks to my friends on Earth: Matt Gough, for conscientiously and enthusiastically devoting long hours checking the manuscript. Also Merle Holmes for reading it with great interest. And Jack Hunter, for all his kind help and support. Grateful thanks to my good friend, the great engineer, Ron Pearson, for his great backing and kindness and of course, my very dear friend, Stan Pattison, for his wonderful patience, understanding and caring support.

Finally, big thanks to my publisher, Candy Taylor of Con-Psy and Psychic World, for her help and work to ensure the publication of this book.

And my beautiful cats, Princess, Timmy and Lady for keeping my lap warm and watching over the computer mouse!

I'm NOT DEAD: I'm ALIVE...without a body! (Vol.1)

CONTENTS

CH 11.   476 - 526

Spirit warning - Floating above bed - Spirit 'video' of funeral - Dave speaks from Beyond

(Grandma one of my helpers - Mum helping new 'arrivals'- Dave's operation and last birthday - Time of death unsure until will to live is lost - Dave's last days and vision - Out of body shock - Medium's unexpected confirmation - Dave and others shown 'mental video' of his woodland burial - Dave communicates via Spirit intermediary: Describes his passing - Spirits' built-in "pattern-receiver-thought-processing-method" deciphers slow Earthly thoughts).

FINAL PAUSE FOR THOUGHT   526 - 527

***

Biographical INTRODUCTION
Understanding this book:
Who? What? When? Why? How?

"It's amazing! Whenever we lose <u>anything</u> you are likely to find it! You must have a gift!" How often throughout my childhood I heard Mum say this to me! I used to think I probably looked more carefully than the others. I knew nothing about sixth sense in those days.

I used to attend a French Catholic grammar school in Algiers, North Africa. I recall being about 15 years old when, during a Religious Education lesson, the teacher was going on at length about Hell, that 'terrible place filled with flames, gnashing of teeth and gnawing pain'. Suddenly I heard, very clearly, someone saying to me: *"Hell is not a <u>place</u>, it is a <u>state</u> of mind, a state of immense remorse."*

I nearly jumped out of my skin, as there was no one behind or near me and we were on the second floor! At that time I realised something strange had happened, yet I didn't really understand where the voice came from.

"You are a bit like Joan of Arc, you hear voices!" Mum joked when I told her about it, *"but what you heard <u>makes sense</u>, doesn't it? One can feel one is in 'Hell' even while still on Earth; If someone does something horrendous and realises, later on, how much harm this has caused to some-body else, they'll regret deeply that they cannot erase the bad deeds! So it will be far worse if they are in the Spirit World, as it would be difficult or impossible to make amends! Remorse gnaws at you day and night, that's why the Church talks of flames burning you, agonising pain etc; these are symbols, allegories, to explain what will befall nasty people"*. I soon forgot this small incident which was to be, without my realising it, a forerunner of the development which began twenty-four years later. Meanwhile, I was lucky to have parents who brought up

my three brothers and me well, teaching us to do good and avoid harming others, but without imposing religious dogmas. They believed in an Afterlife, though it was probably rather nebulous in their minds.

My Catholic school exposed me more to this religion, I did not know any other. Yet from a very young age, I felt frustrated to be obliged to learn things which seemed to me illogical and at times unfair. Why couldn't a baby 'see God' and only be able to go to 'limbo', simply because it had not been christened Catholic before dying? It was not its fault! Why were the Catholic Church and even some Popes involved in atrocious wars, such as the Wars of Religion in France, against the 'Protestants'. What about the horrors of torture during the Inquisition? What about the massacres of indigenous Indians of the Americas, on the pretext of imposing Christianity when in fact it was just a good excuse to steal their gold and precious stones.Why? Was that what their Jesus had taught?!

I used to pray dutifully, but I did not know exactly to whom I was praying. That invisible, all powerful 'God' did not seem able to prevent criminals from doing evil deeds...and nothing seemed to improve around us! Indeed, we used to live in Algeria during the 1954 - 62 so-called 'Independence War'. Yet we had Arab friends. Among others, an orphan, a young Arab teenager whom my father (who was a civil engineer and designed a large number of Algerian roads) had met during his trips around the country. Dad brought him back home! Mum must have had a shock but said nothing and quickly found ways to create a room to shelter and help "Abd" as we called him. Father, who had his office at home, introduced him to the other employees and trained him as a draughtsman too. The young man eventually earned an excellent salary and set up his own home in Algiers.

The majority of French people got on well with the

9

Arabs. It was politicians and a handful of hooligans and ex-convicts who triggered this 'war' for their own reasons and benefits, having received weapons from elsewhere. Nobody wanted to leave this beautiful country, which was one of France's 'départements'! Yet in 1962 General De Gaulle gave it away to the 'fellaghas' rebels, thus abandoning Algeria and all its crude oil wells and vineyards, among many things! As this gave a free hand to criminals, not only French people but also a very large number of Arabs too felt obliged to leave because they did not feel safe. Therefore we were forced to flee our country, huddled like sheep and packed like sardines on the deck of an overfilled ship. Our only luggage a suitcase in each hand. For our family it was destination Nice, where I was to spend only two years before setting off for England. Why England? Because ever since I was young I always had this inexplicable desire to go there. I studied for and obtained a degree in English at Nice University, including a compulsory one year stay in the South of England, as an 'assistante' to improve my language learning...and my fate was sealed. I met this kind and intelligent young man, a teacher of Russian, in the English school where I was making pupils practise conversation in French: Dave Rix, whose eyes were as soft and gentle as his voice. One year later, I asked for my position as 'assistante' to be renewed so I could remain at the side of this young linguist who could speak four languages and had asked me to marry him. I wanted to stay in this green and pleasant land. I was happy for England to be my new 'Motherland'. After I completed all my studies, we got married. Dave was posted to Leeds, in the North of England, where he became Director of the Russian section of The Nuffield Foundation Project which was in those days the spearhead of language audio-visual teaching. Then he was appointed Lecturer in Russian at the University of York where he became, over the years, Director of the very modern Language Teaching Centre.

We had two children: Jim (James Christopher) and Anne-France. Life was very busy. I too started teaching again eventually. It was for me the beginning of decades of teaching French in Higher Education, not only at Adult Education classes, but at the University of York. Then, as my reputation spread, also at Ripon &York St John College which became York St John University. Moreover, in 1989 Nestlé took over the famous York confectionery factory, Rowntree Macintosh. Nestlé's HQ being in French-speaking Switzerland with many branches in France (and the whole world), York staff had to become bilingual in double-quick time! So I was appointed to teach French at all levels, in all departments, from top executives to secretaries and receptionists! This went on for several years.

One thing lead to another and to the famous BBC Worldwide asking me to write one of their future publications for tourists, '*Get by in French*', published in 1998. Later, when the publishers Arnold/Hodder-Stoughton approached the University of York about a new series of language courses, I was asked to write the French course.

This overview of my teaching life and work is only to help you, the reader, understand who I am and show I have my feet firmly on the ground. On top of, or between, those years of language teaching, I also trained in, then taught, modern dance and 'Shape Up To Music'. Another experience came along later, when I became Fund Raising Organiser in Yorkshire for the Royal National Institute for the Blind.

As my children were growing up, I was then able to *discover another side of life* which I had not had much time to learn about while they were little. For a long while I had 'done some research' via reading, to try to solve a problem stirring within myself; there were far too many reports and stories of well-documented incidents experienced by intelligent and trustworthy people such as doctors, pilots, mathematicians etc, telling of their 'supernatural' experiences, their encounters with so-called 'ghosts'. These reliable people would not lie, therefore it must be true. Something existed which I felt had been kept secret from me, which was hidden from all of us, the Public! My quest for 'THE Truth' as I called it, had started!

I became acquainted with the wonderful knowledge of the Incas and the Mayas. I dived into dozens of books such as *'Supernature'* by Dr. Lyall Watson and Colin Wilson's work *'The Occult'*, as well as Dr. Carl Sagan's research and H.Bergson's works, also fascinating studies on telepathy by Russian scientists and F. Capra's *'Tao of Physics'*. I tried to grasp Albert Einstein's Quantum Theory in order to endeavour to find a link with what seemed to me, a very scientific idea particularly relating to physics; the fact that those so-called 'ghosts' or invisible spirits must be a kind of energy. After all, what did the celebrated scientist Lavoisier say? Basically: Nothing disappears and nothing creates itself out of nothing. Energy cannot be destroyed, it simply changes shape, that's all. I pondered on ultra-sounds which humans cannot hear, yet animals can! Therefore, the very fact we are no longer aware of something does not mean at all it does not exist!

It is obvious we are all made of energy, our thoughts and emotions are intangible energy, so, I told myself, they cannot disappear when the flesh body and flesh brain turn into dust! Where do they go?! Where indeed does that energy go, which was part of our personality, which was 'us'?

Finally, what definitely opened my eyes was my encounter, through reading, with authors such as F.Marion who had fantastic extrasensory gifts and was backed up by Dr Wiener of the London Institute for the Study of Parapsychological Phenomena. Then I read the psychiatrist Dr Raymond Moody's reports in his books on 'Life after Life', telling of 'near death experiences' had by several hundred people. They died temporarily during an accident or an operation, flew out of and above their physical body, left the room or the vehicle and could <u>prove</u> they had been witnesses of facts happening far beyond reach of their ears or eyes! Whatever their race, profession, religion or lack of, they all went towards a 'light', met somebody, often deceased loved ones and they all wanted to stay in this superb new world, but they were told they had to go back into their flesh body, for it was not yet their time to leave. The majority somehow felt they were asked: *"How did you use your Earth life? Did you learn anything? Did you show compassion towards others?"* Upon returning to Earth, they all realised they had experienced something extraordinary which changed their attitude and their life down here.

Then Doris Stokes appeared in my life, the wonderful medium who had filled the largest auditoriums in the world, whom I had the pleasure to watch at Leeds Town Hall (after reading her biography *'Voices in My Ear'*) proving beyond all doubt that the so-called dead are still alive!

Eventually I also discovered there was a Spiritualist Centre in York itself! I had reached my goal: THE Truth about the existence of Spirits. They <u>do exist</u>, they <u>can</u> communicate, they are people without a physical body, but their mental energy, their personality, their emotions, still live on with them. This awareness was not the end of my road but the beginning of an even more fascinating phase and of the rest of my life!

The year 1981 turned out to be very formative. Besides meetings at the Spiritualist Centre, I attended the amazing 'Silva Method' courses. They taught me superbly how to reach a calm and receptive state of mind, in order to <u>develop the sixth sense and use the latent abilities</u> we all have. Once in that state of inner peace, you can really <u>use your 'Thought Power'</u>. You learn to improve your health, stop pain, attract beneficial situations to you and finally to work at developing the gift of 'second sight': 'know', 'see' and 'sense' at a distance. Incredible but true! I was able to do this at the end of a 4-day course, me who thought I would be totally incapable of such a feat! I must add that José Silva's organisation generously offers to refund your course fee, if you can sincerely say you have not obtained any results, which happens extremely rarely from what I saw and heard!

I also found out that in 1930, the Kirlians, a Russian couple who were scientists, had invented a photographic method to prove the existence of the energy <u>field which emanates from everything living</u> and cannot be destroyed. Modern technology has at last made it possible to photograph and film, in colours, this energy field, also known as 'the aura,' which spreads out of and around our physical body and changes constantly with our emotions and our state of health. It has even been possible to take photos of this 'energy body' escaping from the physical body, at the time of death.

Among many others who took me on long journeys of discovery, Dr Richard Gerber's fascinating master piece, '*Vibrational Medicine*', enlightened my way through the most refined systems of Human Energy. All this fascinated me! There was I, who long ago would have loved to read Physics at University but disliked Maths too much, now beginning to discover Metaphysics, a science far more advanced than that taught by colleges! Feeling encouraged, I carried on developing this sixth sense, as I had the intense desire to learn THE Truth, learn everything there is to know and, it seemed, had been kept hidden from me. I also wanted to be eventually able to speak to scientists in the Hereafter, as I guessed their knowledge is far superior to some scientists' on Earth who refuse to have an open mind!

Do not think for a moment that I was and am gullible and 'swallow' everything and anything I see or hear, particularly at the Spiritualist Churches! Nay! Not I! Cartesian logic implanted in my French blood and my analytic mind, have always empowered me to approach any subject using good

common sense. Therefore I <u>observe with an open mind</u> but am ever ready to <u>analyse objectively</u>, in case there was another reason for the amazing demonstrations of evidence that death of the physical body does not kill the real person.

To be fair, of course, one must recognise that, as in all professions, some people are better than others. Moreover, mediums are human beings, so there may be days when they feel below par. But in the majority of cases, time after time, over months and years, not only other members of the congregations but myself and my own family and friends have had remarkable proof that our loved ones have survived and still live on - therefore <u>everyone survives</u> so-called 'death'! What is the link making the communication possible? Friendship, admiration, respect, affection, love. A medium cannot 'summon' someone from the Other Side; his/her task is to be the channel, the link, the telephone line between the two worlds and to transmit as precisely as possible information <u>provided by</u> the departed.

So, one does <u>not</u> 'wake up' the so-called dead. It is <u>they</u> <u>who choose</u> to come and communicate, the medium is only their telephone!

One must not forget that those 'departed' in fact still live on, they are alive in a world where telepathy is the means of communication, since there, one uses one's thought power and one can receive and read the thoughts of those around you. The operation is quite tricky, if you think about it somewhat. If those 'survivors' want to be able to convey some information to the Earth world, they must <u>learn to control their thoughts</u> <u>and direct them with clarity</u>, one at a time, towards the person they want to transmit them to. This implies necessarily an adjustment of vibrations! Moreover, the recipient must also be at least clairaudient, i.e hear clearly, but perhaps also clairvoyant (clear seeing) and clairsentient (clear sensing). So, twenty-four years after hearing a mysterious, supernatural voice during a

grammar school lesson defining 'Hell', there was I, now guided to develop this gift, shelved for so long! Various mediums told me:

"You have a guide (like everyone has; some call it 'guardian angel' but I could never grasp this idea of a being of light with feathered wings!) *who is waiting patiently for you to open the door of your mind to him"*. Easier said than done when one has a brain like mine, faster than a racing car - if I don't practise regularly the Silva Method exercises, as it often happens, I get very rusty, my busy life wins with all its worries, so the inner calm is choppy!

Around that time, I made the acquaintance of Kay R. who became a dear friend and who renewed her own skill at 'Automatic Writing' (an invisible hand guides the pen to form words). After many a conversation with her guide, via Kay's pen, one day I sighed: *"How I wish I could do this!"* Her guide replied: *"Get on with it! Relax, take a pen and try!"* Very surprised and most unsure whether I would be able to, I thought: *"It will take me at least 6 months...but let's try!"*

On that Monday, morning and evening , I sat quietly alone at home, after a short prayer just in case, asking for protection against any possible mischievous clown who may have wanted to play tricks on me, because I was new to this. I had a piece of paper and held a pencil on it, asking aloud: *"Anyone there wants to speak to me?"* Just in case, to prevent my brain possibly interfering and thus risking to influence what might come, I kept it busy by looking at the wall opposite me and repeating aloud: *"Wall, wall, big wall, plain wall..."* - I did not look at the paper.

The little zigzags beginning to appear? I ignored them, assuming it was probably blood pressure or muscle tension or some other anatomical reason! Throughout that week, twice a day, I repeated the experiment, determined to let the pen write on its own, **if** that was meant to happen! The zigzags changed shape but did not mean anything to me.

16

Five days later, on that Saturday morning, 29th January 1983, after my usual question I felt the pen move, without my looking at it, but I realised somehow it felt different. When I looked down, there was one single word: *"Yes"*. As I had not watched the pen, the letters had overlapped a little but it was very legible. It was far from the original little zigzags resembling an electro cardiogram! I was flabbergasted, excited and incredulous at the same time! *"Who are you?"* I asked, 'emptying my brain' as best as I could, thinking only of the bare wall facing me. The writing started again very slowly and carefully. <u>I had absolutely no idea</u> what was being written. When it stopped, I looked. There were several letters all linked up, in fact two words linked up. I deciphered: 'Silver Arrow'. A few moments of confusion, then I dimly remembered, one or two years earlier, a medium saying to me: *"Your guide calls himself Silver Arrow, though it does not necessarily mean he was an Indian. Names given can be symbolic too."*

Ah! So it was my guide at the other end of the pencil?! Yet I had <u>not</u> thought of him at all, nor of his name! I asked another question, I forget now, to which he answered "Yes". So, delighted, I very naively told myself I was going to be able to find out all sorts of information, acquire great knowledge, such as the origin of the world(!) etc. Therefore I asked and waited for the revelations! The pencil started off very slowly, wrote a bit more than before and stopped suddenly. I looked and read: *"Very tired, bye"*, followed by a downward stroke caused by the drop of the hand and the pencil. So much for the flood of great knowledge! *"Just a minute, please, please, stay a little longer?"* I begged, but despite my efforts to get the pencil going again, not a single zigzag, not a single letter! Not even a 'message from my subconscious', in case some people imagine that's what was communicating with me!

I dashed to Kay's to show her. She pointed out that I had pressed the pencil down too hard on the paper, which explained the slowness of the writing…and the burning up of my poor guide's energy! In fact it is better to use a ballpoint pen.

Of course that evening I tried to 'tune in' again. He came back more easily but was firm, though kind too. His answer to my requests about 'out of the ordinary facts' was: *"We shall teach you what <u>we</u> judge suitable, all in good time!"* (And he was right, for what they taught me over the years to come has been more and more complex, as my comprehension was able to expand and learn). Anyway, that week he also adapted his communication means; I soon <u>started hearing his thoughts</u> as they were written! He explained it was easier for him than manipulating the pen! At the beginning I panicked as I was wondering whether it might be the famous 'subconscious' interfering and I gave my communicator a hard time to prove to me it was and is indeed him!

After all these years, I know and can state categorically without any doubt whatsoever, that the various people who spoke and speak to me are indeed alive in the Hereafter, a fact confirmed many a time by numerous mediums who did not know anything about me.

A few weeks after crossing my 'Sound Barrier' by learning to successfully tune in to the Great Beyond, one day, unexpectedly, my conversation in English (as usual) with my guide changed suddenly...and I heard French spoken! I asked why it changed language. The voice replied: *"Because I always spoke French to you, my darling daughter and anyway I can't speak English!"*

As I had not realised there had been a switch of communicator, I was taken by surprise! Imagine the shock to speak to someone I actually knew well, my own Dad - this happening about 3 or 4 months after his departure from the Earth. That evening, he told me of the joyful welcome he had received when he arrived on the Other Side, his impressions, his sadness to be parted from us, but also his joy not to suffer

18

any longer, his regrets etc. I could hardly believe my ears, I was biting my fingers to check I was not dreaming. It seemed to amuse Dad. Our first conversation lasted a very long time! Mum was surprised but also moved to learn he had managed to communicate with me, all the more since he had asked me to pass on a (private) message to her.

Over the years to come, my conversations with my guide and helpers became more and more interesting, educational and revealing. From time to time, Dad would come in for a chat and share his 'discoveries', especially about physics, because it intrigues him, seen from another world! Not only in our correspondence but also when I went on holiday to my mum's in Nice, I made her discover and understand as well as possible what my 'Friends from Beyond' were teaching me. She seemed to accept it on the whole. Not only had she often had premonition dreams herself which turned out to be correct, but sixty years earlier she was very impressed by a lady who had the gift. This person made several detailed predictions for Mum's future, every one of which proved to turn out to be amazingly correct!

As I uncovered, discovered and learnt more myself about the Afterlife and developed my own psychic gifts, I was careful not to tell anyone about it (certainly not 'in passing' during small talk) apart from those who understood the subject. This for a good reason. Unless one has a lot of time to explain in factual details, with examples, the scientific side of communications with the World Beyond, and to reply to questions or 'objections', what's the point of risking being labelled 'mad' or 'a danger to the public for dealing with the devil', as some ignoramus could imagine it to be (especially if they've been brainwashed by a narrow minded religion!)? Moreover one does not know what other people picture in their mind if, for example, one talks of mediums or of hearing voices! Because they saw some stupid horror films, some imagine some idiocies and lies such as thinking a Spiritualist Church spends its time having 'frightening séances in the dark', or that horrendous apparitions come to 'attack' people, or that hearing voices means one is ready for the straight-jacket and the lunatic asylum! All this is completely wrong. How many people, gifted with a good sixth sense and with second sight, must have been and may still be nowadays, incarcerated by some doctors or psychiatrists who are either ignorant, or closing their mind to <u>the reality and facility of communication between the two worlds</u>!

On the other hand, people who know me well, professionally and in private too, will testify that I have my feet firmly on the ground. They think that I have some common sense, am sensible and reliable. I say this as modestly as I can, in order to explain why I realise I have a good <u>reputation as being level-headed</u>. People I know (even only on a professional level, without being 'friends') to whom I gradually reveal my other facet, are amazed *'not to have noticed before'* (noticed what?!) and are surprised I had said nothing on the subject throughout all these years! Basically, they all said to me: *"I believe you for I know you well. If anyone else talked to me of 'voices, visions' etc. I'd think she is potty! But I know you are so sensible, absolutely normal, in good physical and mental health, educated and you approach things in a rather methodical, rational and let's say 'scientific' way. So if <u>you</u> believe in all this and can do it, well...there must be something true in it! Tell me more"*. Of course, I must point out as well that Mum who is also down to earth, intelligent and with good sense, never had her head in the clouds, so she would have shaken me and told me off if she had suspected that I was 'losing my mind' or was filling it with nonsense! All the more since her motto was: *"Don't ever waste your time!"* Yet she never said it about my delving in After Life communication!

As can be understood by reading the chapters to follow, my guiding Friends from Beyond and my 'deceased' loved ones have indeed helped, warned, guided, taught and given me proof of their existence since we started communicating a quarter of a century ago. Now I do NOT BELIEVE in an Afterlife, I KNOW it exists!

An example my guide reminded of, in Sept. 1999: "*We are all here to help you help others learn as much as possible about our world. So, there is no reason why we could not give you good results, is there? You must trust us, of course, but you know we have given you beautiful and good proof of our sincerity towards you, whether to do with your Mum's departure or the details of her arrival or the very fact you wanted us to warn you etc…*".

How true!.. Indeed many years earlier, long before my Mum's sudden demise, I had sent a fervent prayer to the Spirit World, asking whether my guide could warn me when the fatal day I was to be deprived of her was approaching. I would indeed be eternally grateful, if it was possible to give me a clue that the end was near (as I live far away in UK). I also wished I could be helped to be near her at the time of her 'departure' - if possible several days before, so that she would know I was there! When I make wishes, I pile them on!

During one of my ensuing conversations with my guide, he announced, in those far-off days, that my request would be fulfilled, even though that day was certainly not yet on the horizon! So I replied: "*Just a minute! You are very kind to say this but…do not rush making promises, as I know that 'the Future' is very flexible and difficult to foresee. Besides, I'll have in writing what you have just told me…so I could reproach you if it did not happen as you said! Therefore you can go back on this promise now, I'll understand perfectly*". But he insisted and repeated his announcement. So, on the cover of that notepad I wrote: 'THE Promise!' not to lose track of it. ***Years later, in June 1999 everything happened as promised!***

In January 1999 as if by chance, in the course of a chat with the Spirit guide of E.C. (A good medium, then in trance), his guide implied I should do my utmost to go and spend some good time with my mum in France, as that would "do us both a lot of good"…and that the Spirit World was sending me plenty of healing energy as they wanted me strong for things to come. So I went to Nice (France) as soon as I finished teaching for the Easter break. I found Mum in better shape than she had been for a long time, as she had treatment for her thyroid in January; even my brother noticed it. Those weeks together in April/May were very pleasant, we chatted a lot and exchanged ideas. Then I had to return to the UK because of my teaching.

About 6 weeks later, on June 14th, via the excellent medium A.W, whom I happened to be consulting only about my job, Dad came to speak first and I received an unexpected piece of news, without my asking about Mum! He did not want to sadden me but he wanted *"to prepare me and warn me"*, he said, *"that the 'process' had started and was inevitable"* as far as Mum was concerned and he would be there to receive her. What a shock!

I asked if it was possible to get an idea when it might happen, as I lived so far away. The only response the medium got was being shown a wintry scene - a very snowy landscape. On the left, white trees, a path covered with snow. On the right, large drifts of snow blocking the door of a house. The description was very precise but I could not think of such a house. I reckoned since Nice (French Riviera) does not get this quantity of snow, it must mean 'in the middle of winter'. So because it was June then, I'd have 6 months to 'prepare' myself. After that, I was given other messages relating to my work etc.

Five days later, on June 19th, at dawn, I received a phone call from my brother in Nice. The night before, he had found Mum struck by a stroke and paralysed on the left side! I just had time to pack a case quickly, reserve seats on trains and the plane and shoot off to catch my flight to Nice! I was then able to spend a week on a chair at Mum's bedside at the clinic, taking no heed of any visiting time rules, disappearing just in time when doctors were due to visit. <u>Mum knew I was there, just as I had been promised</u> by my Spirit Guide! During what turned out to be her last days on Earth, the shameful inefficiency of some nurses of the L.II clinic (who on top of that went on strike all day long on the Thursday) resulted in them not noticing Mum was suffering! They were practically laughing at me when I drew their attention by saying I knew she was in pain! It's because I did insist so much, that on the Friday they realised at last, that Mum's bladder had been nearly completely paralysed and she had a very painful kidney infection! So a doctor had to give her a powerful painkiller. Eventually I was told they could not do anything for her and we should go home. Her blood pressure dropped next day, on that Saturday morning, June 26th, her fingers were blue. I was told she could still hear me despite the drug, if I spoke to her. Therefore I was telling Mum she'd soon go back home and would see her beloved cat and that I hoped she had heard what I said...when suddenly she opened her eyes, stared in front of her looking surprised and inquisitive, gave two sighs and she fell asleep for ever. I really was not expecting her to die there and then!

Yet ***as promised by my Guide***, *I was in fact also with my Mum right until the very last moment!*

I only understood the clue of the snow scene after leaving her bedroom, a few minutes after her 'death', when I let the staff see to her body (as Mum had donated her body to Science - I am also an Organ Donor). Instead of scurrying down the corridor as I had done, day and night, for a whole week, I stayed near her door and leant against the wall. That's when I saw the small painting on the wall near her bedroom. Until that day I had never had enough time to notice it as I was shooting past! It was the <u>very snowy scene</u> my Dad had <u>shown</u>

23

to the English medium 12 days earlier; the description was 100% correct! I was so flabbergasted that I spoke aloud (in English, whereas all week I had been speaking French!) repeating the words I remembered her saying. That picture was to show me Mum was not going to come out of this place alive, whereas over the years she had stayed in many different hospitals and had come out. It was me who had wrongly interpreted Dad's clue, thinking he was talking of 'winter'! *But my Friends from Beyond had kept their fantastic promise, made years earlier, to the very last detail!*

So, how did I come to write this book? The beauty and marvel of it all is that **I did not write it** myself! I only typed the manuscript of what had been said to me by my mum herself over several years, during our numerous full-length conversations! Nothing magic about that...except she started to dictate it about 26 hours **after** the **death** of her physical body, as she'd arrived in Spirit World, in Paradise, whatever the name given, in that very real world where we shall all go one day!! This book is the journal, the report of this 'new arrival' full of wonderment, enthusiasm and emotions; sadness to have 'abandoned' her family but also joy to find, in the Other World, loved ones and old friends again and never to be in pain again. Throughout her conversations with me and answering my questions without any hesitation, Mum describes how she left her physical body without even noticing she was doing so (" *I played a dirty trick on myself to 'die' without warning myself*" she jokes), how she learnt so quickly, to communicate with me still on Earth. Also the surprises she had, her astonishment and bewilderment at first, as it is a world where thoughts take shape in front of you, since the main 'tool' of the residents in the Hereafter is the Power of Thought. Then we follow her progress as she is determined to learn more and more, to adapt to her new life and to share with us her fantastic, mind-boggling discoveries! Several interesting communicators joined in too and, tragically

24

for us, eventually <u>my husband</u> (who left his flesh body a few years later) <u>described his own passing</u> and settling down too.

I made the error of not realising the extent and magnitude of what was going to be gradually revealed to me, nor the time it would take me to type it neatly on the computer. I started, unfortunately, quite late to get round to typing neatly (and translating into English!) those hundreds and hundreds of handwritten pages which I had written at high speed as I heard the words clairaudiently, some starting in 'Automatic Writing' at times! It is the firm but kind calls to order from my guide and even from Mum and Dad, which opened my eyes. My life was very hectic, then once more, struck by another tragedy in the family, but I had to organise myself better to dedicate some time to try to catch up with lost time.

Why so many efforts? Just to show my brothers that our Mum lives on and Dad too? No, not just for them, the revelations are too superb. <u>I had never read elsewhere, nor heard of, many of the facts</u> my communicators talk about, the extent of knowledge is so wide that I could not keep all this for us! I had to share it with all those who, like me 30 years earlier, look for 'the Truth'!

We shall ALL get out of our flesh body and we shall ALL go to the Spirit World, whether you believe in it or not! There is absolutely no doubt whatsoever. It has always been, still <u>is and will always be possible to communicate with those in the Hereafter.</u> In this beginning of the 21st century, these conversations with half a dozen people included here prove it once more. May you keep an open mind, so that you can enjoy the 'Truth'...it is an eternal gem.

***

CHAPTER 1
Out of the flesh - Reunions - Surprises - Ever changing décor - Communicating with Earthlings

(Medium's comments and questions ('BR') are in <u>italics</u>)

Sunday afternoon, 27th June 1999 -

I am in Nice, France, about 26 hours after my mum's 'departure' yesterday morning! Of course my heart is heavy but I am very calm, I am not sobbing. Just sadly resigned to the fact my darling mum is no longer here. I am pleased for her, as I know perfectly well she would never have wanted to be forced to remain paralysed after her unexpected stroke. That was what worried me most when I stayed at my mother's side in the Clinic Larcher II, Nice. She was not aware of the fact she was paralysed on one side. She was nearly 91, her quality of life would be awful for her who was so active mentally and physically.

So today I sit down to 'tune in' to my Spirit Guide and hopefully converse (in English) with him, as I have been doing for the past sixteen years; I hear Spirit communicators. I intend to ask them whether they have any news about my mother. In order to make sure I am well tuned in, I ask them to start answering in automatic writing, as I know how to let the pen write on its own, while I concentrate on something else to make absolutely sure I don't risk influencing it. To my great surprise I notice the reply is written in French, whereas, throughout all those past years, only my Dad used French to converse with me from the 'Other Side', as I prefer to speak English:

"Console yourself Darling, I arrived safely! I understood everything you told me and you were so right! Dad asked me to warn you straight away as he knew you would be unhappy. I am very comfortable, I am not suffering any longer and I have understood that everything you'd been telling me during all that time was true indeed. The pleasure to be here is spoilt by the sadness you must feel. I don't know how to make you understand I cannot free you from it, I am not expert enough! *(Although I know it is definitely not me, nor my 'subconscious' writing this, I find it difficult to believe it is Mum, already, so early after her passing. As I always take care to check and be wary before accepting anything, I wonder whether by any chance, it could be either Dad or some kind soul possibly pretending to be Mum, simply to soften the sadness we all feel obviously when bereaved? Therefore I direct my thoughts towards my guide, and even say it aloud, to reject such possible communication, but the voice comes back).*

You must not doubt, Sweetheart, I am indeed speaking to you myself, as I learnt quickly what to do, because I had promised you I'd communicate once in the Hereafter!

I am certain you know I did hear what you were telling me *(In the hospital bedroom, when I spoke to her, in case she could hear me in spite of the morphine, but I was absolutely unaware that when she opened her eyes it was going to be for the last time!)* and I saw some lights in front of me. I went towards them. Then <u>those lights suddenly were transformed into human shapes and I felt my dad and your dad</u> Nic! So I understood that indeed I had 'died'...and my life 'Upstairs' had started! I did not know what to do, they showed me the 'Thought System' to speak to you. All I want is to let you know I feel well and I am sure you'll realise that I have understood what you used to tell me. The problem is it feels as if there is a black wall between us. I am told the secret is to <u>pierce this 'wall' with my thoughts</u> for you to receive them. That's all. When I know more I'll tell you.

You are going to have a lot of work in the house, I did not have time to clean or tidy more, I am very sorry and apologise. You can throw away as much as you want, it will make some space! I was unable to say goodbye because those blasted doctors put me to sleep, but I know you'll be able to explain to the others that I wanted to say good bye to them too!

28

BR- (Pretending I do not understand) Which others? What do you mean? Touk, Mich and Françoise of course! *(Family members).* I know you have contacted Pierre but he won't have received it yet, I am told. I shall be ok here, don't worry about me, I am not ill anymore. You had warned me and you were right.

BR- What happened exactly? Were you in the bedroom, out of your body?

I was no longer in the room. I saw at once the two lights, that's what caught my attention. I did not know they came from the Hereafter until I realised these lights were Dad and my dad, but once I'd seen them *(the dads)* I understood everything! I don't think I was in the bedroom...well, I am not sure where I was.

I could not understand what I had to do at first, but now it's all right. I'd like to tell you lots of things, it will have to wait for later, I am tired of thinking! The big light surrounding us here is soft, <u>I am familiar with it, it is a light I had seen in my sleep</u>! To be more precise, I recognise it. I didn't know it would be what I would see here! People here are those I used to know, a lot of friends and family.

(It seems so incredible this is happening to me. I ask: "Who is really there? Give me your name, please!" Then I block all thoughts and let the pen write in 'Automatic'. The signature Suzanne Bondaletoff, with the 'd' slightly gothic as Mum used to write it, is signed twice, the second time more hesitantly).

I can't manage it anymore, it is hard to force one's thoughts through. I'll try again another time if you don't mind. I am so tired! I am not in pain any longer and I am not losing my memory anymore! I recognised my friends from near the harbour, Boulogne's harbour. They were old friends of my mum, yet they were there. Incredible...why them?!

It's so good to see my dear dad, he has not changed, I

29

recognised him. He has a little moustache as before and kissing me, he said: "At last you've arrived safe and sound. I told you I was always close to you, you see, it's true!" It's all a question of understanding, that's all. Hard to believe when one is on Earth, but I promise you I am going to learn a lot here, so that you can know about it even better, directly! I'll come back to talk to you. You'll learn personally.

BR- What can you see around you?

I am in a kind of room with curtains all around. My dad is here, Nic too, both smiling. They are pleased to see me. I wanted to speak to you, you see, so I asked them to show me before going any further. You'll be surprised when you realise it is me indeed speaking to you!

At the moment I am in a beautiful room with curtains, silk ones I think, it's really pretty. In this corner there is the 'black wall' as I call it, on which I must concentrate. I am in front of this wall, it's thick like a kind of big black cloud and I concentrate my thoughts to think about you and about what I want to say to you. I am like on a phone; I don't see you but I hear you. I have trouble concentrating without losing the link, it's difficult. I need to be guided but I know it reaches you because your "light shines" they say. That's what they say, I haven't got a clue what they are talking about! I'll come back in front of this wall another day and I'll try again. I hope you'll be able to have your 'proof' as you say. For the time being, believe me my darling, I feel so well here!

Well, I am unhappy because of the grief I give you by leaving you, but you seem to have understood I don't suffer anymore, so it's good for me isn't it?!

BR- Did you know I was at your side all the time in the hospital?

Oh yes, I knew you were there, not half! You did everything for me, I don't know how to thank you but I'll find a way somehow. You did not have to be there all night long but you did.

You are a treasure, as always. I was so thirsty, it was horrid...but now I feel good so don't worry. I do realise there will be so much to do at home, it bothers me, but I did not have the strength to finish off the sorting out. I must have left quite a lot of things untidy hey? It's so silly to die without knowing in advance, one could organise oneself better if one knew ahead of time!

You were quite right, everything, everything was correct! Thank you for warning me and helping me *(about the Afterlife)*. I was certain you were right, yet I had difficulty in believing everything, because there were things I was told differently at Jehovah Witnesses' meetings *(some were Mum's friends)*. They were very kind and I enjoyed going there but I now see the 'errors' they are making. Thanks for helping me!

*(This is why I was concerned: The Jehovah Witnesses tried to tell her that when you die, you go to a kind of pleasant 'black hole' where you 'sleep' for ages until the Trumpet of Judgement wakes you up! I used to argue strongly with Mum about this, telling her it would happen only **if** she really believed it, as firm <u>beliefs can create imaginary surroundings</u> when you arrive in the Hereafter! So, when I sat down today to get news from my guide, it was to find out whether the Jehovah Witnesses had influenced her mind).* Now Dad told me that we are to go to a park where we shall meet some people I am fond of. I'll see, all this is mysterious.

This unexpected stuff is also fun! I only had time to say: "Where is R-?" *(R- is the pet name my family gave me and which I wish to keep private)*. I want to tell her I am here". So they showed me this strange system, no telephone to hold, only this kind of thick wall which one puts on...er...into which one pushes one's head a little, it's dark all around..."Each thought must be firm, strong and unilateral" they tell me, "without thinking of anything else at the same time!"

BR- I was afraid you might believe you were in the 'black hole' Jehovah Witnesses speak about!

No! No Jehovah's black hole. I grabbed those lights 'with my hand' so to speak and I pulled towards me. I got the strength to get out of the heaviness around me. I felt as if I was so heavy and I <u>clung onto those lights by staring at them</u>, I felt I was pulled towards them. I managed to get right close to them...then I saw they were no longer lights but people ALIVE! And my dad and yours had...er...all in all 'become them', 'become themselves' - I was going to say 'appeared' but <u>they were already there as lights</u>, then they became solid in front of me!

BR – Marvellous! Can you try to give proof if you can, especially for Touky? For example moving your photo at home.

I heard what you said now, about the photo. Well, I'll try...but I don't know how, hey! I will have to ask. I have difficulty leaving you as I fear I will not know how to link up with you again another time. My darling children, you are all my beloved children and I am proud of you. I want to tell you not to be miserable because of me, as I don't have any pain anywhere, anymore. I feel 'light' and not 'damaged'! I had so many things wrong. At last I feel better. It's so good!

BR- Were you able to drink when you arrived?

No, no need to drink, that's over. I had to think of getting up towards the lights then I did not need to think of thirst or anything else, because I saw my dad and yours and understood everything, bang, at once. "Ha? So I must be dead! Phew that's good; all went well!" I thought.

Right, I must let go they say. I'll relax my concentration of mind as they say. I am giving you a big kiss and I thank you again. Also tell the others I love them so much and you too Sweetheart...bye bye.

BR- You had a secret word we'd agreed you'd use when you pass to the Other Side.

I'll tell you, it was 'ta ta' wasn't it?! Your loving mum.

(15.30hrs) Notes written straight after this amazing happening: "I feel and felt strangely calm since all this started. As I am a realist, I cannot help wanting to get confirmation elsewhere that it's all true (via a good medium for example). But as I read it again, I can see that it is genuine and I certainly did not write this myself nor is it my subconscious!"

29th June 1999 -*Afternoon. The first 8 words start on their own, then I begin to hear the rest in full flow, in French:*

I did what I could and did not want to harm anyone, that's the main thing isn't it! What matters is that one makes the effort. I am here to encourage you all.

BR- Who is writing and saying this?

Me, your Mum, why don't you recognise me? I am well now and like where I am. I have landed where I should and realised you were ever so right indeed! I would never have thought all this could be so true!

BR- Please remind me how it all happened?

I have already told you how I left my flesh body and went towards Dad's and Nic's lights...me who thought I was just going towards some lights, I only realised it was the two dads when the lights turned into living beings! I could not believe my eyes! My dad welcomed me first, as I told you, then Nic kissed me and said: "At last! Now I can explain everything to you!" I am calm and glad I got out of it without too many problems. I had trouble surviving those last days at the clinic, because I was suffering. I did not know what was wrong, I was in pain and no one was helping to relieve it! You tried, I do know that, but the doctors?...Well, it did not seem to work. It was worse I think! Anyway now I've left all that behind and am peaceful. You are grieving, I think, but I feel well and would like you to know it to help relieve your grief.

BR- Can you see us?

I only see what I think about for the time being, as I am concentrating on the thought of what I want to say, as they tell me to do. I don't know exactly how it works 'technically'. I know I must put my head in the dark corner of this room, that 'thick cloud'. The thought sets off towards you, arrives and when they think you have received it, they exclaim: "That's it! It's working". I was told expressly not to think of several things at the same time if I want it to work well.

BR-What clothes do you think you are wearing?

I've to admit I have not been concerned about clothes! I was so impressed by my painless arrival, the transformation of the lights into my dad and Dad Nic and all that, I did not think of myself! I suppose I can say I feel normal, I have brand new clothes and I 'shine' rather than look dull so to speak. It seems strange but I am far too busy 'absorbing' what I see and must understand. I must look at the surroundings, the landscape. It's like a dream, I see the landscape but it changes often without my noticing! "There are vibrations", they reply, when I ask why. Vibrations are electrical things which, apparently, make a difference to what is all around here. When I went out 'yesterday' and went with them to the park, the trees were so high, I can't guess at their height! Extraordinary! I could not believe such high ones existed! Yet the wind was not blowing.

BR- Did you say "the wind"?!

What I mean is the wind does not blow here, yet one feels nice and cool. I also saw the grey cat we used to have in Algiers and the tortoises! Do you remember the tortoises? Also my big cat 'Mimine' from when I was little and my little she-dog, Mum's really. I think animals can come and see you more quickly than people. Anyway, it's marvellous here. In fact I have only seen a few people so far. I was told a lot of friends and family were waiting. I only saw the Protte family - that means Uncle George and Ramie. Then there were people you

34

did not know, whom I used to know in Boulogne and Wimereux, who came back to say hello to me. That is really astonishing they come from so far back in time and yet they are here! Anyway, do not fall out with each other over the house and all that. It's not worth arguing about. You are lucky to be able to be together. I was alone, with no brother or sister.

So love each other and do not cry over my death. I did cry and grieve for my mum and even longer for my dad, but I did not know, like I know now, that they were fine and indeed still alive! I was a single child, there are three of you at home and Pierre, so don't fall out over details of what is for whom and where. These are only 'things' and you are not as mean as other people. Be kind to each other and do believe I love you all, even from here! I am not far, only the distance of a thought between you and I. It creates the link, so think of me and I think of you, that way we are not cut off! The pleasure to speak to you is immense, you have no idea Sweetheart!

When I think at one time I believed that the Jehovah Witnesses knew everything... I see now you did know more indeed! So I salute you and say 'bravo' as I would never have thought that everything you were telling me would turn out to be so true! You did very well to warn me or else I would have wasted my time elsewhere, I can see that. Well, I thank you once more, you are lucky to know all this, it must help you, mustn't it, now I am no longer near you? So make the most of your knowledge and let's make sure I don't go away from you, I mean I do not lose contact with you! I don't know why I would do that, but I am so scared I may forget one day how to link up!

BR- There is no reason why you could not any longer…

Yes I know. I want to be able to carry on doing it, so keep thinking of me and we'll be together.

BR- I spent all my life close to you, you bet I am not likely to forget you!

35

No, I know you won't, it's just a manner of speaking. I'll stop now as I am told you need to leave...(*Indeed my brother was due to come to fetch me and Mum's cat to go to the vet*) I'll come back when you want. I kiss you with all my love, Touky and Mich too, the cats and my grandchildren. Anyway, my children's mother feels ok here, she is whole in 'Spirit flesh', I could say! I'll see what I can learn and I'll tell you all about it. You are lucky to have someone here now, who can explain to you what goes on! Kissing you with all my love. Talk soon again. Your mum.

(Later on at 1am: After writing a few letters, I 'feel' someone wants to communicate with me, so I let the pen start...)

Get up early and go to bed early Darling. You are staying up far too late, you are overdoing it! You'll wear yourself out. I'd rather see you sleep than staying up.We are all here, near you, watching what you are doing, you are writing letters, it's good but it's not sensible. You are right to say we want to speak to you, it is to tell you off! So I can only advise you to go quickly to bed. The hours of beauty sleep are the ones before midnight!

BR- (I am always on my guard) Is it Mum? Or some kind Spirit helper wishing to give me some advice? (The reply comes in English: it means my own guide has popped in!)

One day you'll realise we did not play tricks on you! It is indeed your mother speaking to you, who comes to speak to you. She wants to practise. She knows you are not in bed, are not asleep and she wants to let you know 'you are not sensible', as she says. Now, please go to bed, because she is concerned and does not relax because of you! You need your sleep, she needs to relax!

1st July 1999 - *I settle down to see whether I may get some communication. The pen starts writing the first 6 words 'on its own' then I hear the rest. It's in French:*

Mum cannot come all the time. She needs to teach herself to link up on her own and to settle down. Let her become acclimatised and you'll see you'll be able to have her close more easily...*(I am surprised and assume it must be my dad speaking in French-but the next sentences are in English, so now my guide must have popped in!)* Many a times I have told you we try to help you. You needed help, we gave it to you. We brought your Mum near you twice and helped her to speak to you so that you are reassured about her settling down, but she does need to rest now and to look around, wander round, learn and observe. Therefore please do not call her yet, as it will distract her. She has a lot to learn and discover.

8th July 1999 - *Still in Nice. English is spoken, so it is my guide:*

Since you are with us, we can tell you your beloved mum is coping very well. She is not able to speak to you as she is resting mentally; she is making good use of her 'eternal time' as she says! She wishes to relax and think of nothing as she has been rather stressed lately. We know you wish to speak to her. Make the most of your time there *(in Nice)* to get on with your tasks, then when you get back home we'll give you more information. Patience is the key for the moment. She has suffered a lot and was in great pain. It wore her out mentally.

BR- Why did you let her suffer? I always prayed for her not to be allowed to suffer!

Listen, the help we gave her was tremendous, you'll never know the extent of it! We cannot show you what was done to soften her suffering, we could not remove everything but most of it was! Now you know this, we'll let you get on with your work.

BR- Was it really Mum speaking to me or was it one of you kindly pretending it was, to soften my sadness?

Why can't you believe what we told you? She was very lucky to reach you at her first go! She was tired but determined to let you know she was all right and safe and sound. Now she's done it, she is resting, a well-deserved rest indeed! We know you constantly want confirmation and double proof! We agree it can be rather tiresome and boring...but we do understand you. Because of Earthly life you have difficulties believing that everything coming from our world is true and real. That's why we are trying to reassure you. Yes, your mum communicated as soon as she left your world to come here. Yes, she was surprised and happy and relieved. As soon as she realised where she was, she wanted to let you know, because she said it would reduce your grief and we know this helped you, didn't it?

We send you a lot of help and you receive it, but you don't always realise it, not all the time anyway. It was essential <u>you</u> were told first, it was the only thing which mattered to your mum at that time. Now everything is fine, she only <u>needs to adapt to her new environment</u>. We know she has pretty and very pleasant surroundings, created by her own wishes for peace, tranquillity and rest. She will create for herself a world of her own when she knows how to. For now, her <u>surroundings were prepared for her by those who love her</u> and know what she needs for the time being.

The main thing is that she can have a long rest to recover from the hectic last years, full of worries and health problems. We'll let you know when she is ready to speak in great detail and you'll then be happy and will be able to communicate more often and you'll both feel good.

BR- I was concerned she could have been influenced by her Jehovah Witnesses friends who believe when one dies, one must remain in a kind of dark nothingness until the so-called Judgement day!

38

We know about this and there is no danger she would stay in this 'mental darkness', as you say. We've been watching her and she is fine. She will not imagine she is in that 'nothingness' because we have spoken to her, she saw all of us and she <u>knows</u> for certain where she is. She asked to have a rest but she knows it is not forever, nor until 'such and such a date'! She knows perfectly well she is only resting. We shall let her know what you've all been doing, so that she does not miss anything.

BR- Thank you for talking to me. I don't want to appear to expect you to be at my beck and call nor to be a bore...or disturb you if you are busy?

We are always close to you in mind and with love as you'd say. Your calling us never disturbs us. We do want to communicate with you any time you wish to do so. Our activities are varied; nothing can prevent us from accepting or force us to decline a call, or refuse to come close to someone we look after!

BR - May I dare ask who is 'we'?

There are several of us looking after you, you do know that! There is a main leader, as you may call him, but the whole group is devoted to your well-being and progress, so we are here for you whenever you need us. Therefore do not hesitate to call us, to think and to speak. We shall always respond and this is a promise, <u>like many promises made before which were kept</u>, do you remember?..

BR- Oh yes! I am very grateful you did keep them! I thank you ever so much!

We know...love is the key, isn't it? We've said everything there is to say for the time being so you can go and get on with your chores. We'll let you go. Goodbye as always with our loving thoughts.

17th July 1999 - *Mum's departed 3 weeks ago today. Am back in UK because of my pre-booked plane ticket. Once more the first words appear in 'Automatic Writing', in French. I notice the use of 'tu', the 'familiar' word for 'you' in French.*

Your mum guesses you must have a very strong desire to know what is happening to her and around her, but she hasn't got the strength to sort herself out in order to be able to explain everything. She says she would like to be able to tell you what she has discovered up to now, but she doesn't know everything so far of course and she would like to know much more.

When you are a newcomer, it's not easy to know where and what to start with! You are so shaken by everything you see and hear and finding again things and people who had been forgotten! The very fact of being alive is a bizarre shock, pleasant but bizarre! Therefore she must be allowed some time to get used to her new situation. Would you believe that she is carefully making notes of everything she does! She has not got out of the habit...

BR- Has she got some paper to write on?
Yes, she has paper and pen simply because she was used to it before, but it does not mean one is obliged to have paper etc here! It's the only way she knows how to make notes.

BR- Perhaps she and I could write a book using the facts and information she is taking down?
Of course you'll be able to do that! You'll have to talk to her about it, so that she makes sure she notes all her impressions.

BR- Who is speaking to me?
I have been speaking to you for quite a while but you did not realise it was me. I have been your dad, have you forgotten? Long ago I was your dad, you understand? I was also there to welcome Mum when she arrived. I had foreseen it was to happen as I had been warned. I was and am there all the time, so that Mum knows that since I am 'dead' then so is she, therefore everything is fine and there is no problem!

40

It was indeed great fun for me to surprise her when she arrived, as it was the first time I was doing it for someone I knew! Up to now I had only spoken to people I did not know.

If you want to carry on this conversation later tell me, otherwise I could tell you that on the day of her arrival, I had organised a big party with her friends of long ago - I knew there were people she had forgotten about, so it surprised her to see them again. Moreover, I asked her dad to explain to Mum how to communicate with you as it was something you would have wanted; also it should help you through the days after her departure.

So you see, we thought of you, Touk and Michou (*my brothers*) too of course, but I mean as far as understanding the Hereafter, it is you who knows more about it.

BR- What do you do? Talk to me about yourself, please?

At the moment I have a lot of work, welcoming here 'dead' people who had lost hope. It's essential to give them some hope again and it is hard. There is 'fishing for people' and fishing for fish. Fishing for people is the hardest because they are lost, but I take a great interest in seeing them eventually fall back on their feet one day. I'd like to speak to you a little longer if you have time. It's a great pleasure for me to converse with you as I'd like to reassure you about Mum. Yes, she suffered but she has already forgotten it, do you understand? She doesn't think about it any longer, that's what you must understand. She is no longer in pain and does not think about what she's been through, as she has so much to see and discover here that it keeps her busy!

BR- Please be there if I go to a good medium, to help me have some proof for my brothers to believe these conversations are true indeed!

I'll do my best when you go. Wait a little longer to see a medium, so that we have more to say to you and you'll see

41

you'll have 'proof' and things which will help you all. (*As I was sitting on a cliff in Scarborough (UK) it was beginning to get cold, I had to get back. Dad sensed it*) I think I must let you go as you are busy, but I'd like to be able to come back if you let me.

BR- I am very sorry, it's only because I am getting cold as the wind started blowing.

Go on, don't catch cold! I am nice and warm, really comfortable here, but you are not in 'Paradise', that's why. Go on. Talk to you later.

31st July 1999 - *Nearly 5 weeks after her departure. The pen writes the first words in French on its own:*

As soon as you spoke about it, Mum wanted to come close to you. Mum is here! It's Dad speaking by the way. Here is Mum now... Mum here, hello my Darling! I am talking to you as if I was phoning you, that way I know better what I am doing. I am so happy to be able to speak to you! You must be wondering what I am up to here. So there it is.

I met up with my and your Dad. I went elsewhere too, I travelled in the 'region'... err... where I am. I saw lots of people I used to know. You knew the Thiébauts, yes they are here. The Mirouzes and the neighbours across the road too, it's incredible, we met again as if we'd never lost touch! I saw some people I knew when I was little and animals too, my cats, my dog or rather my mum's dog and...<u>my parents had a little girl I knew nothing about</u>, would you believe! My parents had lost a little baby (I think possibly still-born?) and I never knew it, can you imagine, because they did not want to talk about it. That's really strange - me who thought I was an only child, in fact I was not really. I'll talk about everything if you wish. I am so happy to speak to you...

BR- How are you feeling?

It seems to me as if I have not aged - <u>I feel as I was at</u>

the time I knew the people I am meeting. I feel quite young, but not very young at times. It's weird, one does not think of one's age, one feels oneself. I saw lots of people. It's amazing how many I have known on Earth!

BR- Have you met Roger?

No, not seen Roger yet, I don't know why - perhaps I did not think of him. Your dad is very well of course, we are all well here! He is very smart and elegant, his little beard is trimmed neatly. He likes to look handsome. He's done his best to help me come here, he 'attracted' me with the energy of his love and affection, my dad did too. So between the two of them, they helped me come so easily that I nearly did not realise I'd gone away from you. I felt all strange when I saw them in front of me... It was such a kind of...er... shock and surprise and relief that I had not suffered more to 'die' as one says...but I don't feel 'dead'!

I wanted to tell you straight away as I was so flabber-gasted to be so-called 'dead' and not to have had difficulties getting there. Isn't it something weird and incredible to 'die' and yet not be really dead after all?

Yes I know you told me so lots of times. I must have believed it a little after all, you see, since all went well without me filling my mind with the Jehovah Witnesses' ideas about darkness etc!

(Remembering the pain I witnessed when Mum suffered when on Earth, I feel emotional) No, no, Darling, don't cry, certainly don't any more now! The suffering is over, nothing more could be done. No, I left because my body lost all its strength and I could not stay in it any longer, that's what I was told here. I thought you had understood that, Sweetheart. Don't be heartbroken about the last few days. It was only an end, it had to finish like that, otherwise it would have been awful.

BR- Did you realise you'd had a stroke and were paralysed for good?

43

No, I did not really know what had happened <u>until I was told here</u>. I thought I was simply 'ill', did not understand it was worse - paralysed! You can guess how panicky I would have been for all of you! You protected me right to the end, hey poor love. How worried you must have been for all of us, you and them and me. I am really sorry, but now it's all over I feel very, very well and happy.

BR- Where are you exactly?

At the moment I am in front of that 'thick wall' like before, because I wanted to speak to you as soon as I knew you were trying to contact me.

BR- How did you know that?

I knew because your thoughts came to me, I saw/<u>sensed your thoughts</u>. I said to myself: "This is R- wanting me, who thinks of me". I understood it. A little difficult to explain. So I did what had to be done to come here.

BR- What did you do?

I did as I was told before. I thought of the 'telephone room' as I call it and I found myself there at once! I had tried to walk earlier but I saw lots of people including Dad <u>not walking, but simply thinking and getting there</u>. So I said to myself: "Why not me?" I thought very hard: "I want to be with R- to speak to her" and there I was, landing in front of this 'black telephone wall'! I then thought of you and about what to say to you. I still have my dad and yours near me, as they guide me in what I do. I have lots of things to tell you. I'd like to say I love you my darling daughter, I have always loved you and shall always love you. I'd like you to understand that when I told you off and criticised it was to help you, at least I thought so! I was told you asked your 'guide' a question today?

BR- How do you know I did?

I was told it was to your guide. You asked something about a bracelet. I learnt you wanted to know whether I had bought you a new bracelet or given mine. I had bought one

Sweetheart. I sold mine later but at the beginning, as part of your wedding presents, I had bought a beautiful brand new bracelet for you and your chain too. That's why I had been so unhappy when you had not worn them at the wedding of some friends and elsewhere. I thought you did not like them whereas I'd paid a lot for them, you understand? No, you are not wearing my old bracelet, because I wanted the money for the roof and all that. That was my own business, nobody else's!

I've just felt you still doubt a little, hey? I felt a wave of doubt and I am afraid you may want to leave. I feel you in my head. I hear your voice, like on the telephone.

BR- Have you been to see things on Earth?

No, I have not tried yet to go and see on Earth because I don't know how to do it yet. I was told to wait a little longer in order to assimilate everything properly after the shock felt on arrival.

BR- What is there around you? Where do you see yourself?

I have my own place. It's a kind of lovely bedroom, but with lots of 'sunshine' outside and cool indoors. It's not really like a house, it is an area with lots of books…and cats, would you believe it! I've met up again with my old cats of long ago and I have others too. I am sitting here, very happy to have a rest and to look at my books on the shelf, saying to myself: "What's that book over there?" and the book arrives into my hand without me having to get up!

I can't tell you what fun all this is! It makes me feel like doing it just for the fun of it! I saw lots of books here. Recently I received a new one about where we are. We have a book looking like a 'geography map' in a way; it shows details of where I am, in colour photos - Of course! What else! They do everything the posh way here! There are so many parks, beaches and lots of beautiful places, but I don't really feel like going out at the moment. I feel more comfortable here, in my own 'den'.

45

BR- Where do you sleep?

At times I feel like sleeping, but I realise I am not really tired - it's more like a habit I think. I tell myself I am going to have a lie down and I think it's to sleep, but I am so interested by everything I see that I forget I wanted to sleep!

I am going to tell you this: I saw an animal I didn't know…a kind of flying tortoise and I thought I was dreaming! Then it turned into a flower, so when I saw that, I thought it was a joke or a magician's special trick you see! I don't know why it did that, I tried to understand but I have not yet grasped it. They told me why but I have not yet grasped it. It's blooming weird and irritating not to understand!

Would it be much trouble for you to come often to speak to me? I am so happy to have you on line! I need to feel I am helping you bear the departure and loss I have subjected you to. So if I speak to you, I tell myself I am helping you a little. You spoke to Touky today, I know because I saw it in your thoughts earlier. I have a kind of mental screen which is beginning to take shape, it shows what is taking place. It's so complicated, but sometimes I feel I see what is going on.

BR- Have you been taking a few notes?

I did not take a few notes, I took hundreds and thousands I think! Everything is so mind-boggling and amusing. You were right to say you wanted to be here yourself, it's a lot of fun to see all this! I see you are tired again, you must be going to bed too late. I don't want it to be because of me, hey!

BR- How do you know I am tired?

I saw your light disappear, it's what they tell me usually, but this time I saw it myself! I hear you when we communicate, but the light is something new! After saying "I don't see you", now I must say "I don't see your body, but I <u>feel you like a presence near me and I hear you in my head</u>".

BR- Do you have walls around you?

I have some walls of course but I don't walk through

46

them like a ghost does, at least I don't practise 'going through walls'...but no doubt after learning how to think about something and succeeding, I am sure there will be 'wall crossing' too...(*Unfortunately I finally fall asleep, after struggling to remain awake not to disappoint Mum and also because what she said was interesting*).

7th **August 1999** - *22.30hrs - The pen writes the first words. It's in French:*

Mum is here! Believe me Darling, it's me indeed once more. I am so pleased you have sat down to talk to me. I was wondering what I would do if you stopped coming. Once more, I am in front of my 'black phone' as I call it, as I realise it's so exciting for me to be able to do it, that you should have the experience too!

BR- You mean my dying and joining you?!

No! Not quite! But receiving news from Beyond. Well, actually it's true you'd had some before, but not from me until recently. I am here 'on the phone' and I'd like to tell you that I have understood that everything you told me before was so, so true, that you deserve a medal for having understood it so well! When I think I doubted a little! How silly I must have looked! I had proof of what you were talking about but of course it was not my own evidence I suppose.

BR- Are you eating nice things?

Not really. Would you believe I have not yet eaten since I arrived! No, not thought of eating, it's surprising! I assumed I wanted to sleep once and realised I did not really feel like it, it was more out of habit. Now you mention eating, no, I had no desire to eat. Did not think about it, with all I have to do and see here.

My 'day' starts we could say 'without really starting' as I don't have any night either, now I think about it. It's no longer like before, is it? What to say then? So I'll say 'a day'

47

but it is not really like a day, all right? Well, I must concentrate very often. By doing it, one learns to do it better and better and by doing it one finds one is able to do amazing things.

For example, apart from talking to you, which is an incredible and extraordinary skill, there is 'travelling by thought' - one thinks and one gets there, I have told you before haven't I? That's the new way to walk - you don't walk with your feet, you move forward simply by thinking it. It is possible to walk with your feet if you wished, but it's slower. I have done that just to see and because at times I am tired of thinking hard! It is <u>hard work to concentrate constantly</u>! I had no idea where I was to go, but the dads (in plural!) did their best to explain I could go where I wanted, but I had to concentrate on one thing at a time in order not to get myself confused at the beginning.

So to start with, <u>they made me do little exercises</u> like at school. I had to think of one object and make it come near me, like the book I told you about and lots of things like that. I have all the objects I may need, but if I wanted something else, all I have to do is think about it! I have learnt to do this quite well now and I congratulate myself! I knew it would not work if it was not done well, so I was right to do it correctly, you see!

I ended up 'building' myself a whole bedroom around me, with such pretty things that it's a 'sin' to own so many! I am joking, I wanted to say I feel spoilt to have all this. I have beautiful gold fountain pens which write superbly. I have books which are so wonderful you'd think you are dreaming; they cover all subjects one could wish for. They are like on Earth you know, they are real and solid but whatever they are made of is very <u>lightweight,</u> that's the amazing thing. When you carry them, they are not heavy, so it's not difficult to hold them. You see, there is no hassle here, not even the weight of a book!

After getting those books, paper and pens, I treated myself to a pretty dressing table would you believe! I mean like what one finds in a bedroom, with mirrors and drawers, it's so lovely, it's a pleasure to sit in front of it. I don't often look at myself but I <u>saw myself in its mirror, as a young woman</u>. That's what is so pleasant, not to feel old any longer! You had told me there was no need to feel old any longer, so I thought: "Why would I be old, now that I am in Paradise?!"

I '<u>visualised myself young</u>', opened my eyes and saw it in the mirrors; a young woman at the time of my first marriage. I had long brown hair and quite liked myself in those days you see! So it's really a pleasure to be able to return to that time. I no longer have hairpins in my hair like on the day of my wedding to Pierre's Dad anyway! They were such a nightmare!

But I want to point out I don't spend my time looking at myself in a mirror you know! I learnt that the body, here, is only a superficial body for pleasure, convenience, to simplify life. No need to worry about it and it won't ask for anything! Therefore no need for soups and vegetables, so there! I know you were a real treasure to bother making them and be concerned, it was for my own good - but now I don't need those and am jolly glad!

I've been told you are going to see your medium soon. You promised to do your best not to say anything about me to that lady and I know I have to go and speak to you via her or her guides - that's what I am told. My guides, or helpers as you say, are very kind people. I have only seen one person who I reckon is my guide but I wouldn't want to get it wrong. In fact I was told through a third party: "This highly evolved gentleman came today but he won't be there all the time, as you have your family for the time being. He'll come back to help you later." So I assumed it was a 'Guide' as you call them.

BR- Have you seen such beings as 'angels'?

Winged angels? No! I must admit I have not seen a single one!

So it's one in the eye for churches who believe in them isn't it?! It's incredible how different things are here! I have everything to learn. I must read as much as possible to understand everything more quickly, so that I can use my new knowledge and skills sooner. You'll benefit from it as I'll tell you about it straight away! That's why I am hastening to try to learn as much as possible to pass it onto you as I go along. That way we'll discover together that Hereafter you and I used to chat about so much, but before it was the other way round, wasn't it?

You must have been concerned about some of the stuff the Jehovah Witnesses preached about! I do understand why now, but I did not have any point of comparison, you see? I only knew what they said. Now it's different! They were very kind people. It's a pity I cannot go to their meetings and tell them to open their eyes more to what I am discovering here. Wouldn't it give them a shock if I appeared amongst them! It would be proof from Beyond, but they'd probably believe it's the 'devil' playing a trick on them, so...

About your visit (to the medium), I am told not to worry, as I asked: "Should I speak in English?" They replied: "No, it doesn't matter as we'll translate". But it is not impossible for me to speak directly to you, with her as an interpreter so to speak.

It's a new adventure all this, once more...we'll see. Anyway, don't worry, I shall be there in 'flesh and blood' we could say but it'd be incorrect wouldn't it?! I have so much to say, I don't know where to start or how to carry on.

You have understood I do not suffer any more haven't you? Really understood you must not, ever again, think of the hospital and the end of my life on Earth? That time must have been very hard for you and made you terribly unhappy, but I no longer have that in mind now, so I do not live it any longer, neither physically nor mentally. I have well and truly got rid of it, that's what matters, do you understand? One can get rid of

50

all those horrid things and delete them from one's memory in a way. One must not churn over worries one has not got! I also must explain something else to you as you must be wondering who are the people who speak to me?

BR- The two dads?

Yes, Dad 1 and 2, but I have also with me heaps of people I knew and whom you did not know. Madame de Lavignon, her sister and her daughter. They were my first friends in the days of my marriage to Pierre's dad. Also my school friends in the Boulogne era, my first 'fiancés' who had asked me in marriage...all those people reappear from time to time to say 'hello', they care about my well-being as a 'new arrival'...so I get lots of advice, tips and practice, to make sure I have understood what to do!

I did not know one had to 'work' so much here! I don't really mean work, but rather 'practise'. I've got to admit it's really a lot of fun to discover different things like that, really fun! Me who came to thinking one was going to 'sleep' in some kind of 'dark oblivion' for the rest of Eternity, until Armageddon and the Judgement day etc. It's a pity I can't explain to them it's not quite correct since I could communicate at once! It's frustrating! Me who had spent so much time teaching myself all that during their weekly lesson, with my little homework, like a good 'Jehovah Witness schoolgirl'! Ah, never mind...it doesn't matter, fortunately it did me no harm. I know now why you used to be so concerned! You were right, I'll repeat it once more!

So I wanted to tell you that my friends and acquaintances here are all those I used to know and have known more or less, but they don't spend their time with me. There are moments when I am free to be 'left in peace' you could say, but it would be unfair or unkind to say that, as they are so kind to take the trouble to come and see me, that I would be ungrateful to reproach them for it! I have a few hours of...do

51

we say 'hours' here? I don't think so, as I realise I have not looked at the time since I arrived here! I don't know how long I have been here, come to think of it. Which season was it when I 'died'? Summer I think...yes, it was summer, it was sunny and it was hot. It was June when I left for the hospital, I think...after that, it's rather blurred in my memory.

I have memories of pain and thirst, but I don't want to think about it, I delete them, I block them. Therefore I have no idea any longer about months and seasons, but it does not matter, here we don't bother with all that.

BR- What's the weather like where you are?

What's the weather like? Well, it's always fine, it's not difficult! There is no rain or fine weather in contrast, it's fine. Because I love the place where I am, I am pleased to see it like that. 'My place' as I call it, is not a 'French' or an 'English' place as you'd say. It isn't a bedroom or an office, it's a bit 'all in one'. I have walls but I don't really need walls. Would you believe if I want to go out of my den, I just say to myself: "I am going outside" and I find myself outside at once?! So I wonder what is the point of having walls?! I suppose it does give some shape to the room where I am...

BR- What does 'outside' look like?

Outside, well, it's either a street with shops, or fields, or parks, I think...because I have the impression it changes with my thoughts. Once I said to myself: "I'll go and see whether there is a town here" when I thought I was in the countryside and at once I saw a town, not very large, but big enough to call it a town. Another time I was thinking of the beauty of Nature...and that's what I saw outside! So, I reckon one must see what one is thinking about at the time. That is the kind of things one must get used to here! Therefore there is a lot to discover and it's really amusing and intriguing. I learnt not to ask myself too many questions anymore and accept these oddities.

I don't worry, I expect things may happen...I mean, I now guess that every time there will be things I am not expecting, and that's fine by me! I am quite happy about it, it makes a change to have interesting things to see and do.

BR- Do you still have your books?

The books? Yes, that's another strange thing. First, no heavy weight as I told you, when you take one it does not seem to have any weight. It does <u>look as if it is printed, yet when you read it</u>, often the words are printed, but <u>sometimes I realise I am seeing live, moving pictures instead,</u> do you understand what I mean? I see objects instead of words! That's why I thought that my imagination, being too active, must have created them...because 'the dads' told me one sees what one creates with one's mind and it's true, indeed! So I am getting used to seeing words disappear and some kind of 'films' appear instead! It's a little like having a portable TV isn't it! <u>You read a book...which turns into a television with a film about what you are reading!</u> Not a bad invention, I must admit! Quite quick to read too!

BR- With sound too?

With sound, yes! Now you are asking, I realise I get the sound too. One does not think about it while reading, as you are busy understanding what you read, then you think: "Ah! These are not words, they are pictures"...but it's interesting, so you don't worry about it! It suits me actually... I quickly learnt lots of things that way, and I enjoyed seeing them turn into <u>live pictures</u>.

BR- Is there a book you particularly liked?

A book I liked? I liked them all, those I read so far, as I saw what one can do with one's Thought Power, one's life here. That's what it is all about, not so much novels but instructions how to cope here when you arrive, do you understand?

I did grasp that if I paid attention, I would know how to cope better and better, faster and faster...and that way you too

53

could know more! Therefore, I am learning to teach you and teach me at the same time...not bad, hey? So I learnt what I've already told you: 'Walking' by just thinking about where I am going, having friends round me just by thinking of them, if I want to go outside, doing it without actually going through walls, but going out with my thought power and lots of things about 'the body without needs' etc.

But I did not explain what I had told you the other day: Why I had seen a kind of 'flying tortoise'! I had not understood, not well anyway and I told them.

BR- Who are 'them'?

'Them' is the dads. They told me: "You are going to make her panic, she won't know what you are talking about!" So I said: 'Write it down and I shall tell her'. That's what it says: "The object seen by Mum is not a real tortoise as you'd think of one on Earth. It has been <u>created by her thought</u> because she felt she was slow and heavy here, when she saw us moving about quickly. She had the impression she was 'as slow as a tortoise'! So, because she thought that, it created this kind of 'tortoise' ; but because Mum wished she could 'fly' like us, at once she saw a 'flying tortoise', do you understand? <u>Thoughts create everything here</u>, that's what she concocted without meaning to do it consciously. That is the mystery of the 'flying tortoise!"

Since then, I think I understand better, as I notice how incredibly powerful Thought is. If you don't control it, you have lots of things appearing right and left, because they 'crossed your mind', so to speak.

My thoughts are fast too, you see it's not just yours which are! Therefore I have heaps of bizarre surprises such as this, but I don't worry. No problem to get rid of it, all there is to do is think: "Throw it away! Into the bin!" or similar and it makes them disappear. That way there is no problem with tidying up you see! I am really glad, as my pet hate was the jumble I'd created and left at home, all those things and boxes with which Touky and Mich too reproached me!

So here, no problem, no boxes, no letters nor 'fraudulent mail orders' as Touky would say. Yes, poor lad, I wanted so much to be able to win for him those prize draw millions I was 'promised', but I never got them. It's so maddening, when you think there are people who win them, yet perhaps they already have millions of their own! It's not fair that life of money and work!

I feel guilty to have such a good time now, to have fun with my 'novelties' here and come to talk about it to help you write this book on the paranormal. It's really going to make your readers open their eyes wide, isn't it! When we tell them about 'flying tortoise', they'll say: "That woman is mad!" But now everything is explained...I suppose I'd better let you go.

BR- Anyway of giving 'special proof' to Touky?... Are you still there?

Yes, I have not left, I am still here. I heard what you said about proof for Touky etc. I am told: "We'll talk and think about it". I hope they'll manage it because I would not know how to do that kind of thing, of course. But we can be certain that one day we'll have this kind of proof. "Yes", they are saying. Ok we'll try, but don't think this happens automatically. There is a lot to do apparently, for that sort of thing to happen. So do not expect anything and only hope! But somehow we'll get him to understand it is me and not you who writes this!

Darling I am a little tired of concentrating, do you understand? I have been speaking into my 'black phone' with all my strength, so that it reaches you clearly, and I think it's been a success.

You are a treasure to come and speak to me, I am really sad to have let you down just like that, in the middle of your life, without being near you in the flesh - but do know I am with you in thoughts forever, you understand, forever. <u>All you</u>

have to do is speak to me and I shall hear you, because all I need to do is pay attention to the thought coming to my mind and recognise it as you calling or talking to me. I don't want you to cry as we have a good system now, you and me! We know how to speak to each other. I have learnt to speak with my 'black phone' and you already knew how to link up to the 'eternal line', so now all we have to do is use it!

My fatigue is not real you know, only an effort of concentration, it gets strengthened again after a few moments. But I'll let 'the receiver' go now (not really, it's only me who invents this to make things easy for me) and I'll let you sleep as I guess once more you are going to bed late, naughty you! No, I am not telling you off you know! It's too good to speak with you and to feel you near me, I am not cross with you.

BR- How do you hear me speak to you?

When you speak I hear it in my head, where my phone would be near the ear, but I don't really have a telephone you understand, I call it that for fun and also to manage better. Moreover I also sense you, like a presence but without seeing you. I know you have a house etc but I don't see it, I 'feel' it and hear you and have the impression I am speaking to you, like I used speak to you from my home in Nice to you in England. That way it's not too different for me. But it must be a shock for you I suppose, because you know I am so-called 'dead'. Me who thought it would be difficult to die! Really, I still can't get over how easy it was! I said it over and over again hundreds of times to people here: I can't get over it! They all laughed each time, it amuses them to see one is so happy not to have suffered more to get rid of one's flesh body. As for me, I am flabbergasted to find myself 'whole' yet to know my body must be dismembered I suppose, or something like that. So I don't say 'Long live Life' but 'Long live Death!' Ha ha! Darling, go to sleep, you are going to be tired tomorrow. Remember, the hours before midnight are 'beauty hours'.

Go and rest while I'll go and discover more things to tell you next time we'll phone each other...free of charge, hey! One more super thing here! (*00.30hrs*)

12th August 1999 - *20.55hrs. A few days after my sitting with A.W. who did <u>not</u> know at all Mum had been communicating with me. <u>I had kept this a secret from the outside world!</u>*

Thank you Sweetheart, I'd like to kiss you too. We'll manage it one day, don't worry! I have something new to tell you if you want. I've had some adventures here, you can't imagine! First I had to speak to you via your medium. I tried to have you told I was there and I was doing the writing with you. That was not that easy because she was not like I imagined. It was not going into her head as clearly as in yours. I suppose it's because she did not feel me like I hear you? I don't know. So I did as I was told here and I finally managed it.

I may have confused her a little because I thought of you looking after me and pampering me when I was unwell, as if you were my mother. Then I said that now I could think of you as my child which you have always been. I love that, I prefer that. I wanted to feel again the pleasure to love you like my little baby and I have 'felt it again' as I wished, it was great. Then I told myself it was silly not to want to see you like the grown-up woman you are now, as I have a lot of work for you now that I have discovered all those things here and there'll be more I reckon.

BR- Where are you at the moment?

I am here as usual, at my telephone table. I decided to bring you stuff to write a book, so that you can be known as having written an up-to-date book, since one cannot do better than having the latest news!

I am at my desk 'at home'. But I don't have a house as such, as 'my home' is restricted to a 'bedroom-office' combined into one room, for which I have nothing to do, because I don't need to tidy or clean since that's not the way things are here! I have quickly grasped that, as I was made to understand all I need is to have it tidy in my head and there is nothing else to do!

I then decided to have pretty things around me, so as not to have any sadness, or rather not too much sadness, for forsaking you all to your sad fate of Earthlings while I wallow in the voluptuous pleasures of the Hereafter! I am not into pleasures of the flesh but pleasures of the head and the Mind, but in a spiritual sense, because there is no longer any old head of flesh as you know.

There is so much to do here I'll need an eternity to discover what one can do with what is available. I don't have the time to be bored. I never get bored anyway, as you know well. I always hated hearing some people talk about 'killing time'...but I am off the subject, aren't I?! So to come back to what I want to tell you, there are quite a lot of people who do not understand that <u>death is not a tragedy but bliss</u>. I'd like to make this understood via your intermediary, if ever you publish this. I understood at once it meant I had 'died' when I arrived here, as I said before. As soon as I saw my dad and yours, I realised that everything you had tried to 'teach' me, absolutely everything you had explained about Spirit World was correct! You had understood but I had not quite grasped it! Now it's my turn: I understand and want to help you.

So, here is my story to publish if you fancy doing it and it will help you help people who need it, like I needed it. But what am I saying? I am certain it will be published and you'll get publicity for it, as I am told it will be helped. I am afraid I may get tired of concentrating if I keep talking about things other than what I intended, so I'll focus on the main point, ok?

The main point is that I still live, that's the principal! <u>I am alive</u>, am whole and am glad to be because I feel good in my new self, my new 'skin' as we'd say, but I don't have any skin to worry about. I see my 'body' as I was when I was younger. <u>I feel young, sometimes like a kid if I see my school friends</u>, but I have also other times when I have the impression to be young though not old (as I had enough of being old and ugly in Nice, I was disgusted to see myself so horrid in a mirror…). I am really pleased to have got rid of that nasty old wrinkled and scrawny body; during the last years it was so ugly! I wonder why I lasted so long in it. I wasted some time I could have had here, do you realise that? But it does not matter, now everything is back to normal. So, I am young, comfortably fairly young. I don't pay attention to my body as I told you. It's quite easy to understand that <u>if one thinks oneself young, one stays it forever</u>! Therefore I decided not to be concerned about that, I accepted to be in my thirties at times, or less if need be, but I am not worried about what I do or what my 'body' looks like. I am happy as I am because I keep myself busy with other things you see. I told myself: Why waste time with a body which does not exist really!

BR- Yet you do have a body?

Yes I know, I have a 'body' but I am now aware <u>it is a body I imagine, therefore it is not a real body, is it?!</u> So I ended up creating this one and that's it. I must tell you this: I made an inventory of my books I spoke to you about. I saw the totality is on the subject of where I am. I am sure someone is trying to make me learn very quickly what I can and must do here, how and why one can do it. Where I stumble is when the explanations have physics connotations, because physics and I don't see eye to eye. I don't always grasp what is explained to me, but the main thing is that I realise it can be done, and that's it!

Since my arrival here, I've learnt to stand for a long time without feeling tired, as I used to dread it at home in Nice, and wanted to be able to sleep, but now I have understood that in this world, <u>pain does not exist</u> so why bother imagining one is in pain or risk being! It would be stupid!

I also saw that the main room of my 'building', my

home is not really a room but is an area of Paradise, yes, a 'place of happiness'. I understood that if one feels happy and forgets the downside of things, one cannot be unhappy. If you settle there, in a good mood, with good positive ideas, the surroundings and <u>the décor reflect the feelings you have</u>. I tried several times and I saw it changes with my thoughts, like a chameleon alters its colour when it lands on a branch. So I thought: "I'll change myself into a butterfly" and I flew like a butterfly, in my thoughts of course, but I felt like a butterfly fluttering from flower to flower! I saw colours of flowers I had never seen before. It was so beautiful! Unbelievable! There were flowers of incredible beauty, I cannot find words or names to describe their wonderful colours.

This is to tell you I have a cosy den, where I create for myself a Paradise of happy thoughts and therefore of décor transformation. I am glad you seem to have understood I feel better here than on Earth, where I found myself trapped in a body giving me more and more trouble. Understand that I do not suffer any more, so do not cry for me! I am very sad, very, very sad to have abandoned you that way, but it's true that death must take place one day. Yet I have learnt so many things since I have been here. I must admit I enjoy discovering them!

I hope you won't be 'jealous' of my fun whereas you have chores and problems to cope with on Earth! I don't envy you...but I try not to think about it so as not to blacken my thoughts and my 'Thought Power', as well as my internal and external décor...since I am at the mercy of my thoughts! I repeat I am literally at the mercy of my thoughts, meaning if I think of something, it happens! So in a way, one is 'black-mailed' by one's thoughts: "If you think that, I'll make sure you'll get it!" says the 'thing'.

I think it's great fun but it could be irritating I suppose, if you kept changing your scenery. I told myself <u>I must control it in order not to get muddled up</u> and not be able to manage!

So, I have a beautiful room with golden silk curtains and I built myself a dressing table, just using my thought power...to see what I was like with my Spirit body. I saw myself surrounded with books when I arrived so I kept them since they look really interesting! I take care to jot down everything which happens to me, so that you can benefit from it.

My friends here are either people I knew before, on the Earth, or people I did not know but who had appeared in my dreams, yet I did not remember them then. But when I saw them again here, I knew at once who they were. That's what is weird - to remember who they are yet not to know them. I find it hard to grasp but that's how it is!

There is also the 'duration of Time'. As you said there was no Time, I wondered whether it was true and did some experiments. There are watches if one wants to make them, but if one doesn't think of watches, one does not see Time, so there is not any. You see people, you chat, you deal with all there is to discover and it looks as if all this happens, perhaps one after the other, but it is not a sensation of time, it feels simply like a series of small events or actions without you thinking 'It took me some time'. I suppose it makes life easier here. I do wish you were here as I would take you to see the animals I saw! There are cats everywhere if one loves them. I saw my cats again, and our cats and lots of cats belonging to other people! I learnt that cats love people who loved them, therefore they stay near you when you arrive, so that you can recognise them. It's kind of them. They are cats like those you know and the cats here are so affectionate. They lean against you and you feel their love when they purr. It's not just their purring noise, it is their love which comes out somehow, like a kind of light. It's a rather pleasant sensation of warmth, of 'love' to be more correct. I am sure you'll understand since you too love them so much, don't you! I saw Pierre's big dog who had disappeared. Also the dog we had in Hazebrouck - I saw it again because I was so fond of him.

I must admit the bear from Algiers zoo shocked me when he appeared. He showed me his paw, as he used to do it through the cage in Algiers and I've had him so close to me, safely, it's incredibly wonderful! He's changed as he is really handsome now, he has lost his thinness and the sadness of his eyes which he had in those days. I used to be so heartbroken for him when we went to feed him. It's incredible to be able to see him again too and he is so happy to see me! It's also amazing an animal remembers what one had done for him. He must have had some affection towards me or felt the affection I had for him, so he's shown himself here in all his splendour to 'thank' me and to 'reward' me, I suppose, to have tried to help him when he was miserable. There are lots of little animals too, but I have done other interesting things. Do you want to know what?

BR- Of course, if it does not tire you too much…

My mind does not get tired now, as I learnt not to try to think of too much at a time. I took some notes as I was discovering stuff, therefore I only need to look at them as I speak to you on my 'black wall phone'. That way I have no concentration problem.

Here is what I have to tell you as well: Would you believe the little (mahogany) desk from Algiers has followed me here?! I am sitting in front of it, I've tidied it. Also it is repaired and polished of course! I do not treat myself to a damaged piece of furniture when one can have one brand new at a good price! The price of really clear thoughts, that's all! So I have this small desk and a beautiful new pen, as I told you...and lots of sheets of paper since I also write to you as I speak to you. It helps me concentrate

I feel like writing this book for you, but it means we must both do it, you where you are and me where I am. Well, it will surely be of some use to someone won't it! I have my things around me and I am not alone.

BR- Which things?

My usual things to write, as I told you. It helps me concentrate while speaking to you. I write as I speak, in front of this invisible and weird 'black wall phone', but I don't worry about it, everything is so strange here that it no longer bothers me!

BR- Do the dads still come around?

They still do but, nowadays, usually when I think of them. They used to be here at the beginning, but they have understood I can manage and they are happy to pop in from time to time. I only need to think of them and to wish to see them and they'll be there! Everybody has understood I like to cope. I do not feel alone, I am glad to be where I am, without any pain, without any worries or hassle. All I have to do is look after myself and my activities, my discoveries, so I lose all sense of 'time' as people might say.

My parents are still 'at home' like before, but they too have understood there is no need to bother with material and worthless things, so they enjoy themselves like I do, playing with their discoveries and practising. They must have been doing it for a long time then...because they did not 'die' yesterday, did they?! But it must take time to discover and practise all those things. They showed me such possibilities as thought travel and crossing 'walls' which don't really exist. I don't know whether there are things they know how to do, which I have not yet encountered, but there is plenty of time, isn't there?! We aren't in a hurry over here! We don't bother with clocks and time limits, we only do what we feel like. My dad showed me where your dad is most of the time...

BR- What do you mean? My dad goes somewhere?

Yes, my dad took me to see your dad 'at work' as he says! It's not very bright, it's a rather dark place, where <u>he meets people who have not understood they have 'died'</u>. He speaks to them and makes them understand. I was shown from

63

a distance as there'd be difficulties if I went nearer. I don't know exactly why, but I saw I could not go closer. Dad was speaking to them and showing them things I could not see - after that they seemed to change their mind and were less unhappy.

Once more I understood that what you had told me was true! He was right when he used to speak to you and tell you he helped people- this is what he does. There are scores of people who need help, because they are trapped in their mind and don't know any longer where they are. That's why he needs to do this work.

BR- Are you going to do that too?

Not at the moment. I don't think I feel like doing it. Well, not now anyway, as I have enough to do to sort myself out, but I don't think I'll always be there, 'there' being the room where I see myself...*(Telephone interruption, unfortunately I had to answer it: I felt very guilty)*... One has to concentrate more when there is an interruption, that's what I am being told. You didn't do it on purpose I know, but you understand it is harder to link up once we've been cut off, so they came to help.

BR- Who? Our dads?

Yes, the dads. They are really kind, they felt I had problems to communicate again, so they joined me to tell me how to do it and now it's ok, isn't it?

BR- Yes. What happened your end when I interrupted our conversation?

I suddenly felt you had disappeared, as if I was talking to myself. No, not really. I suppose I felt there was no reaction from your thoughts.

BR- I am very sorry! Do you still need to go to the same 'black wall' to 'phone' me, as you call it?

I understood your question about the phone. My own 'black wall' is not the same 'black wall' I used at the beginning.

It's not the same 'room' as on the first day. I am in my own 'den-room', I have my own 'telephone corner' now. I don't know how they got it installed, I was just told it was there in a corner and I understood what to do because I had used it before.

BR- *Who are 'They'?*

'They' usually are the dads and my mum, but also often people who are here. My own corner is my invention, but outside there are things and people whom I did not invent of course, I am not able to do that! I can only think about things which concern me. So out there, there are people who pass by and pop in to say hello to me.

BR- *Strangers come in?*

No, I only see people I know more or less, but the outside has some good points too: You feel comfortable there and you can see people in the distance. Even if you don't really know them, you feel as if you do or should know them! But if I am alone it's never for long, there is always someone turning up to speak to me, to guide me, explain or ask how I am coping (*I had struggled against sleep but finally I dozed off! I woke up sad to have spoilt the conversation*).

16th August 1999 - *This evening we held our séance of physical mediumship experiments at E.C's, who is our trance medium. He did <u>not know at all</u> that my mum had been speaking to me for months! E.C only knew of her passing, that was all. After the 'usual experimental work' our communicator announced someone wished to speak to me, but he was trying to make this person understand she could not use the medium's voice, as one needs to be experienced to succeed, yet this person was insisting... Suddenly, absolutely <u>out of the blue,</u> a different voice albeit very faint and therefore not really comprehensible, was making great efforts to try to control E.C's vocal chords!.. After a few moments of whispers and guttural* *efforts, the deep booming voice of Buffalo, E.C's main guide, made itself heard, explaining my mother had been trying to talk to me, so he took over to help.*

17th August 1999 - *11h30 am. The day after the <u>unexpected </u>confirmation from 'Buffalo', all the more surprising since I had not even spoken of Mum that evening. Moreover, this is not the type of thing we do or receive during these <u>physics</u> experiment sessions! Now, after tuning in well and letting the pen start off the conversation, the first words appeared in French:*

Darling, do not ask me to bring you proof I am here indeed, hey! We worked hard enough 'last night' to prove it to you! I had tried to speak myself but I could not manage. I assumed since I could talk to you on the 'black phone', so I could speak to the medium too…but I was told 'it does not work like that'!

BR- Which medium? Ann W. or another one?

Last night at your house, in England. *(Note: Actually it is **not** at my house at all, it is and has always been at E.C's house; a fact <u>I</u> know, so it is not my 'subconscious' speaking! On the other hand Mum, to whom I had spoken of these séances when in Nice, did <u>not</u> know it was not at my house; I only ever spoke of 'my group'. The venue was of no importance).* There was a medium and I tried to make you all understand I was there but I had terrible difficulties making the 'telephone' work, as I call it… Even though I was thinking very hard, I could not manage to make my thoughts enter his head, it was as if it was made of concrete! For just a short moment, I was able to make a little noise I think, but I could not make it become words. I did not grasp the system. Apparently there is a difference but I don't understand why. I really wanted you to know I am near you, at all times, but I think you don't always know it. You helped me so much when you used to come to

Nice, each time. That's why I wanted so much to make you happy by letting you know I am here and not far from you. I was miserable not to succeed. Fortunately this kind, tall gentleman, a kind of Native American Indian, came to tell me I did not have the necessary strength. I think he said one needed practice, different language and amount of energy. Well, he was very kind! He got me to tell him what I wanted to say to you and he stated he passed it on to you. He seemed to know what he was doing. He was very reassuring and looked so kind. I think I had never seen a Native American Indian close up before! He did not look like a Native American Indian from cowboy films but more like a European-looking Indian. It was not very important, what mattered was that he'd succeeded to let you know I was there all the time and once more you asked if I knew how to speak to you and make you understand that I am there and I said: "Of course, I don't stop talking to her in writing and also in her head when I can manage it!" That's what you wanted to know wasn't it, that it was indeed me who 'wrote' to you in your head? I am sure that now we'll speak to each other even more, as there seemed to be a doubt at the beginning. I felt you weren't quite sure but **I** knew it was me and was wondering how to make you understand!

My 'Indian' appeared out of nowhere! He landed suddenly and started to take charge of my communication. I was at that 'black phone' as usual, but he shot up and meddled in my business I could say, though he did it very kindly. He explained you could not receive my message as there wasn't the necessary 'special energy'; what was needed was a different kind of energy from the one when I speak into your head. That's all he could say, but if I wanted to tell you something, he would see to it getting through the medium. So I said: "Oh yes. She does not know it is me near her who writes on her paper. I think sometimes she thinks it is someone else, as she doubts as I write along".

So he started to whisper something, eyes closed, the sound of his voice disappeared and after a few moments he said to me: "She has understood and she is very happy. She wanted to do a recording but could not, it was not the right sound for your voice, it did not reach her; but the main thing now is that she knows you are near her and she has perfectly understood. She did not ask for any other information after that, it was sufficient straight away".

So I thanked this gentleman I did not know. He didn't tell me his name, he'd only said: "I know what to do and why it is not working- I am going to help you, don't worry". That's it! After that he disappeared I think, I didn't see him anymore.

BR- Can you describe him?

He seemed to be tall and strong, with a big head...a large forehead, he has dark hair, black I think and a tanned complexion like a Native American Indian but not as dark. He wanted to speak to me in French but I said I spoke English too. Anyway he understood what I told him! Actually, I don't know whether I really spoke to him...I think it's probably more my thoughts he received as I don't remember making any conscious effort in one language or the other! But he let me know at once everything was all right and you were very happy I was there. As for me, I am delighted we spoke through them, that way you know I am really there!

We have succeeded you and I in carrying out our pact, haven't we, about conversations from the Hereafter to the Earth?! Incredible isn't it?! It takes time to get going and get used to it, it is weird indeed, but I have understood that all I have to do is to think very clear and simple thoughts, the rest happens on its own. So I thought: "Right, I am going to tell her I am here, close to her and I enjoy being able to make her write my words and my sentences. We'll create a good book together". Because this is what we have to do, isn't it? So that it's worth teaching others what I see from my angle, my world as a

68

'Spirit'. It's so weird to say this, me who thought I was all right in Nice! In fact I was not comfortable at all compared to now, where I can do everything I want, without any bodily problems!

I wanted to give you a better description of my surroundings; I had been a bit vague before, I think. I have so much to grasp and understand and discover. I would think I was going potty if I had not been warned by my darling daughter, then my dad and your dad! They taught me lots of things and I also have my 'books-films' which show me what I don't know. So, I am in my' den-bedroom' and I write to you as I speak to you but I speak in my 'corner phone'. My 'den-bedroom' is like the big room before, but it is my own telephone-corner here, a kind of 'dark wall' as I told you - we may as well think of it as a wall which is a large 'earpiece and mike' receiver I suppose. I write to you to concentrate my thoughts, I say them aloud and the 'wall' catches them and I know you've heard it, because the thought leaves and another one comes in. If you don't hear me, <u>the sound of my thoughts comes back to me like an echo!</u>

BR- Can you explain that again?

There I am, speaking to you and the sound of my voice comes back to me, so I know it did not get 'through the wall'. Now it's fine and you know I want to tell you heaps of things. There are lots of people outside.

BR- How is it, 'outside'?

Outside, it's a kind of big park-garden, with trees everywhere, such beautiful trees one could cry just looking at them… They are so beautiful, you'd never seen any like that on the Earth, neither have I!

Also people stroll around or hurry up, according to what they have on their mind I suppose; and there are animals everywhere, all kinds, but I look for the cats when I go there. I only go out when I feel like a change, because I feel so good in my den-room that I don't really want to get out of it. I got so used to staying at home in Nice, I suppose I got 'conditioned'. Dad tried to make me go out more but at the moment I want to be able to read those books packed with fascinating facts and I don't have time to go for a stroll like he says. Moreover I am not sure I'd find my way round on my own! (*Sadly, I doze off. Embarrassing, considering Mum's efforts to link up!*)

19ᵗʰ August 1999 - *The pen starts 'in Automatic Writing' with letters all joined up which I can't decipher, not knowing which language was used. So I ask for it to start again! It is in French:*

A victory is not celebrated without Champagne normally, yet we have not opened a bottle you and I! You could have some given to you because you successfully brought about the fact that we can communicate, by teaching me a lot when I was on Earth and by opening my mind to all this! I had trouble understanding everything that's all. There were things a little too complex for me so I felt a little lost, but I knew there must be some truth in it, because you believed in them so strongly and you did not seem to be potty! So I must have grasped a few seeds, mustn't I! I had only been doing my best to settle here as soon as I arrived. I had no time to lose as I knew I wanted to be able to have you at the other end of the 'phone', to explain all this stuff to you in good time. I did not want to risk losing the possibility to do it straight away.

I do feel really well here you know! You can't imagine how good it seems not to be in pain any more, not to worry about having to stand up or sit down, not to worry about money problems etc! It's all in the past for me in a way, because I know if I thought about this, it would bring back the pain in my back and legs. They told me very clearly it had to be avoided at all costs so as not to suffer again! You guess how careful I have been and am!

70

BR- Who explained that to you?

When I say 'they', it's usually Mum, Dad and your dad, but there are other people too and I am concerned I may never know who they are. There are so many who seem to appear without me knowing who they are. Most people I see are people I knew, but there are some I do not know. I feel silly at times not to recognise them when they seem to know me, but it does not seem to have any importance...because straight away we are on good terms. The result of the conversation is more important than details about the people who speak or discuss what has to be done. My 'home' does not look like a house I told you, it's more a 'niche' to make me feel I have a shelter, a 'den', but I know I can get out of it easily without even bothering walking, as I only need to think about getting out and I find myself elsewhere!

My personal idea of pleasure is to be sitting with my new books and have fun 'reading' them, if one can call that 'read' since the pictures unfold along as if one was watching a film! The colours are beautiful, very neat and there is neither overlapping nor any loss of pictures! There is always a theme in what I see. It teaches me all kinds of things that I have to understand to live quietly and peacefully here, without any worries or wondering how to do things. So I obey those ideas coming from a book-film because I know they are right. I've had enough proof since I have been here!

There is the same kind of ambience in my den as outside. I mean there is this enormously abundant 'light'... It is everywhere, it does not stop, it does not go off, it is everywhere in everything but it does not dazzle! I have trouble understanding where it comes from, why it is there. It is there, that's it and that is what is strange! I used to think light was to light up, but there is no night so there is no need to give out any light. I think the sun shines all the time but I don't think it is the real 'sun of the Earth', since first of all I don't actually see it, secondly it is not hot like it feels when on Earth. So I think this 'light' must be a kind of living being...or an energy enormously powerful since it never goes off! It took me some time to get used to it as I had never seen a place where a shadow is not a shadow!

BR- (puzzled) - What do you mean?!

The shadow of an object is not a shadow, it looks <u>more like another light around that object!</u> I saw things outside with a kind of 'sunlight', but I did not see any shadow. When I asked myself: "Why isn't there a shadow when there is so much light," the answer came at once in my head: "A shadow exists only on the Earth to help people find their way". So I understood there must be a system of possibly lots of lights and shadows in this different world. Personally I only see what I have in front of me for the time being and that's what I see, no shade but a lot of light, it's really pretty and pleasant.

At my writing table I don't need a lamp since I can see everything very clearly, but there are times when I ask myself questions like that, because one does wonder how they do it, how it happens. That's why I have so many books here, to try to understand what I have to absorb, to manage. There isn't just that, each person's lot is organised in a way.

BR- Lot? Do you mean 'role'?

Role is not the correct word, the correct word is 'lot'. It's as if one had drawn lots for what one has to do. Personally I used to think I'd have nothing to do...and there I am in the middle of having to explain things I don't yet understand well! There is so much to grasp, it's alarming!

At the end of a reading session I rest a little to 'absorb' it all. There is so much to assimilate, it'd be rather indigestible if one swallowed it all in one go! Yet it's fun to see things one had never seen before. It makes you wonder when all these new inventions will stop!

As far I am concerned I am really glad not to be hassled by anything. I can simply only learn if I want to, and there is nothing compulsory to do.

About the 'lot' I spoke of, I mean people are not obliged to do anything, but I think there is a kind of pattern they have to follow. I guess there must be one for me too, but I am not sure what. I reckon it's to advance towards a more complete understanding. We'll see... For the time being, for me, I have peace and quiet and that suits me. So you see, I've told you how I feel and why I want to speak to you. There is enough to fill a book and we have hardly started! It does not bother me too much if you 'accidentally break the link' between us. I do not suffer, so to speak. It is a little confusing to speak to oneself suddenly but it is not painful. I hear your questions in my head. I don't know how of course, but I feel it is you. Then if you 'leave', my questions or sentences no longer get through the 'wall' in front of me. It sends them back to me 'unsent' and I feel silly talking to myself! Apart from that it's not serious.

BR- Sorry, my stoppages are not a lack of interest you know, it's a need for sleep or telephone.

I do guess you probably go to bed late. You've done it so often , but I am quite content, selfishly, for you to speak to me, because it makes me <u>so</u> happy to have you 'on line' I could say, that I only think of that when I do it! I have things to tell you so it gives me pages and pages to write too!

BR- You are writing?

Yes, I write them down as I need my own book here! That way I have my own book of my experiences here as I become more and more a 'Spirit'! But I reckon there is so much time ahead of me, there won't be any need to hurry. To be 'dead' is not a catastrophe, that is true indeed!

<u>To be dead is not a 'true fact' because one is not dead</u>! One leads a superb and easy life, not worrying about any-thing, having fun and discovering tons of things, so why worry about 'being dead'? To have to endure a life on Earth is far less enjoyable than having an interesting life here like I have! If I

had to do it again, I would die again rather than live again on Earth! Yet I do not regret having had you all, because the four of you have been and are adorable children. I can only regret being obliged to abandon you. I did try to speak through the medium yesterday but I know it was difficult to make it happen.

BR- How did you know it was 'yesterday'?

Yesterday? Because I know it's...er...am not sure why but I do know, that's all! Perhaps you told me it was yesterday?

BR- Do you think of days where you are?

No, not really, I don't think of 'days'. I think of the moment I live, the moment I am in. So for me it's a new adventure, for you no doubt it's a nightmare (a good riddance? I don't know hey!). Poor Touky may perhaps think it sometimes. He had so many chores to do for me or because of me...but I know he did it out of love too so perhaps it balances out? Me who was constantly thinking of helping you all, I have now moved away! Unfair isn't it?! Anyway I have a lot of remorse having gone but I know we can re-establish things by talking to each other. So that's what we are doing!

BR- Do you remember Anne-France and Jim?

Of course I remember Anne-France! What a question! How could I forget her? You do have weird ideas sometimes! Why forget her? And Jim too! I know who they are but unfortunately I did not see them much nor write to them much, it was not easy. There are lots of things to learn regarding this system of communication here. One has to start gradually, step by step, "not to confuse the energies", as they say here! My 'energies' must be different from their own energies, whatever they are! I don't bother going into their physics, I am quite happy to do as I am shown and to get used to it. If it works, that's all that matters in my opinion! Yet I am really happy to have been able to make a noise the other day, even if it was not really a word! *(During E.C's trance)*. So I hope to succeed one day when I try again and I hope the kind Indian gentleman will

74

show me what to do with his 'energies', which he seems to be able to manipulate so easily! He was really friendly. I did like him when I saw him, even though at first I thought he was coming to interfere with my business, poor man! I realised I could not manage so I let him do it. He was quite right and he succeeded as you know! Have you got any questions for now?

BR- Is it my pen which writes 'automatically'? Is it you, a guide or?...

No, it's me who does it. I was told to think very, very hard and to concentrate and imagine the energy go into my pen. So I stare at my pen and send it all this thought energy... and I see it start writing!!

BR - Yours or mine?

My own pen. It writes on its own in a way. I see the letters taking shape on their own without me doing it. My hand does not form the letters, they do it themselves and I don't really know how, except that my thoughts are my tool if you like. I think, it writes, you receive! Try to understand anything in all that! Yet it does work! "All there was to do is think about it" just like Christopher Columbus said, didn't he? That's the story about the egg standing upright on one end, do you remember?

BR- Yes, his reply to the jealous courtiers.

That's correct, but the courtiers' jealousy did not discourage him. He held his own. He was quite right: all one has to do is to think about it, like here! Me? I am a new Christopher Columbus! I am only exploring the area I am in for the moment but for me it's a lot. I'll have time to do the rest later. There are only pleasures here, no dangers, no worries. What a Paradise indeed! That's what I wanted to tell you so far. I am not constantly at my desk, my thoughts go towards you all the time, because I know you want to speak to me, in your head, I feel you a lot. You have a very strong mind; your thoughts reach me quickly and easily. <u>When you are sad I feel it</u>. I want to remove your sadness by thinking of you lovingly.

BR- And your sons too I hope!

Of course indeed, I think of the lads too, there is no doubt about that! But I wanted to make you understand, that your mind being so strong, I can reach <u>you</u> easily. All the more since we have those books to write! How many books is that going to create I wonder? Probably a kind of encyclopaedia the way things are going! Can you imagine this, if you still live in 40 or 50 years time and you write everything I discover, there'll be enough to fill up town libraries just with our books from the Hereafter!! Yet there'll be people who won't believe it! What a pity indeed! When one sees how easy it is, I don't see why everybody does not do it, both from here and in your world on Earth.

I'll have the patience to wait if you cannot write all the time of course. You have your own things and life to deal with, but it is worse to think that if I write all this and my boys are not convinced, we are perhaps going to convince strangers but not them! It does sadden me not to be able to tell them myself directly. Who knows? Perhaps one day?

BR- Have you seen those I would call your 'guide' or 'helpers'?

Yes...I told you there were visitors and people I did not know on the Earth, but when I saw them here I realised I used to be acquainted with them before. I can't recall which 'before' but I am certain I recognised them and I was told: "Here are <u>those who have been looking after you since you left us to go and live your Earthly life.</u>" I did think they were joking but it was not a joke. It was clear that those people were beautiful souls since they took the trouble to look after me!
One came at once at the beginning when I saw my dad and your dad. He told me to go with them to the 'telephone room', but he did not have to say it using words, I understood the moment he opened his mouth and no sound came out...but the thought reached me! I had not noticed at the time, but afterwards,

76

thinking about it, I pieced facts together and thought to myself: "That one did not actually speak!" You know, at the beginning I was so flabbergasted to see all that, the dads and the others gradually and the telephone room and speaking to you...that I could not remember who was who or what or when, as I had all that bombarding my head! I had the impression of having several lives one on top of the other...yet it was the same life I suppose. There were people I did not know on Earth, yet I was certain I recognised them as if I had seen them before! So there is enough to make you go crazy you know! Fortunately they explained everything to me whenever I looked confused. I soon learnt to accept and not doubt, otherwise it does not work. One has to get used to it, that's all...

The Dolgouchine children came to see me, would you believe! I did not know they were here! So it gave me a shock to think they were already dead.

BR- Do you remember their names?

There was...Youra and Hélène. That's right, I remember now and they are here. They seem to know what they are doing so they must have been settled here a fair while I assume. *(Note: The Dolgouchine family were Russian, lived in Algiers too and were good friends of my Dad. Their children were about my age. So it is understandable that Mum is shocked and amazed that youngsters as old as her own children had 'died' before she did).*

All this is a very strange world, but fascinating! I see that with a little practice one can 'talk' to each other from thought to thought. This spiritual technology is wonderful! When I think I used to believe one could not do without the Bible. Now I am discovering things they never spoke of in the Jehovah Witnesses' Bible, I therefore know more than them, so there! They ought to have listened to me when I was telling them the world must certainly be older than what they say! Now I am going to send them a letter, to their big headquarters in America and teach them all that! Ah! If only I could, wouldn't it be great?!

It looks to me as if my parents have not changed! Dad still has his little moustache and his kind face I loved so much and Mum has elegant clothes and enjoys leading me up the garden path...

BR- In the garden?

No! I mean teasing me, pulling my leg, because she shows me things which disappear before I can touch them! All that has to do with stuff about energy, she tells me, so I can't wait to grasp everything in order to be able to do exactly what I want without any hesitation or need for explanation! My good books here will help me do that, I think.

If you had not seen your mum for a long time, you'd perhaps wonder how you would recognise her? But I recognised her at once. She had her smart going-out dress and she had not forgotten her indispensable hat! Her little dog has not changed either, he has his coat for outings too...it's handy, isn't it! They have their own beautiful house but I have not really been to see it. I spoke to them for a while about their house but they did not seem to want to go there. It was more me fishing out an invitation...

(Unfortunately I dozed off as it was nearly midnight).

23rd August 1999 - *The first two words start 'in Automatic' in English:*

'Mum' is in her usual room. She has a pen and paper ready, to speak to you. We are introducing the lady. We are pleased you try to make time for her as she is very impatient to have some communication with you and share her news! So be kind and do it often for her sake... *(Then immediate and sudden change of communicator as French is spoken)*

My little darling, at last! I wanted so much to speak to you. I was told you are not at home and I was wondering whether I'd manage to have you 'on line'. All this is better than a mobile isn't it! It reaches you anywhere!

I know you have to 'disappear' sometimes, it's a little disconcerting but it's better than not having you with me. I have a little more to tell you. If I have a pen, now I do not need to use my hand to make it write! All it has to do is to write <u>on its own if it is told to</u> follow my thought! I saw I was tiring myself in a way by thinking and using the pen to write. In fact all I need is to think and the book <u>writes itself</u> in front of me!

BR- Do you hold the pen?

Not even! I don't need to hold the pen now! It stops and starts on its own. I watch it work while I speak aloud in my head and it writes on its own! It's fun, isn't it! Incredible what one can find out here!

I had the honour to see again an elderly gentleman I used to know well when I was married to Pierre's Dad - Professor de Broglie. He had a high ranking at the University and had so much knowledge I admired him a lot. But he died a long time before 'Kap'*(The name she used to refer to her first husband, Professor André Giberton - he had been a captain)* or me, so we never saw each other again of course. Well, I was surprised to meet him and his wife again. I felt very touched to think he wanted to visit me after such a long time. I told myself he must have forgotten me…but he didn't seem to, as he spoke to me as if we'd only been parted a short while! He was very famous in those days and I was very proud to know him when I was young as you can imagine! He had invented or discovered lots of things I think, I can't remember - but he was well-known and I am really pleased to have met him again.

My friends in the 'New World' here, as I call it, had organised a kind of big reunion when I arrived. I have not really given you any details as I had all those exciting things to tell you. I had lost sight of lots of people when I left Boulogne and Paris but we all met again at that reunion! It felt like a lovely

79

soirée. I wanted to talk to you about it but I thought it would not have as much importance in your eyes as telling you that the books 'moved' and all those things I described. It must be far more interesting for you, more than names of people you don't know, that's why I did not mention it when it happened. To me it felt very kind and pleasant but it does not have the appeal of 'discovery' the rest has!

I've done lots of experiments with all my objects here. I made things using my thoughts as I was advised to do! I'd never had to do that before of course so I needed a lot of practice and training. Yet I did manage quite well and the dads congratulated me for what I achieved.

Just a short while ago, before starting to speak to you, I'd looked at a flower in my 'garden' outside, as I call it. I thought it would look pretty in the house, would brighten it... and suddenly it appeared near me, in a vase I had never seen before! So the vase must have created itself! Why and how, I have no idea, but it was there when the flower put itself in it!

BR- You did not like having flowers indoors, in Nice etc!

Yes, I know...I didn't have flowers in the house because I thought it was a pity to cut them and make them die, to have the hassle of having them indoors, watering them and picking up dead petals! But here there is no death, remember! There is only life, 'sunshine' and pleasure. So, pretty flowers can last all their life and after their life. Nowhere do I see wilted or dead flowers, so it's a pleasure to watch nature here. No gardening chores, only gardening for pleasure I think. Personally I don't do any, I had paid attention to this flower because I had looked at it from afar and admired it, then 'bang', it appeared near me: "Here you are, I am coming because you are thinking of me" it seemed to say! I was staggered but I am beginning to get used to all those magician tricks here. I am nearly blasé, one could say! No, not really because I am so amused and surprised by everything happening.

BR- My daughter Anne-France asked me whether you and Dad are getting on fine?

Your dad? Yes I do see him often and we get on well. I did not want to talk about the past, no, it was not worth it. All that is over and done with you see. Old stuff, ancient history from another world and another life isn't it! So why bring it back to the surface?

I preferred to have them showing me what they can do, your dad and mine, since they've been here for a long time, so that I can be up to date! I wanted to be able to do successfully what had to be done. Not only to speak to you and let you know I am in good form, but also not to fall behind the others who know how to cope here. It's a bit like learning a new language at top speed in order to make oneself understood! I wanted to see what there was around me, learn and tell you about it. That's all for the time being.

BR- Have you read all your books?

I have not 'read/seen' all my books, no! There are so many! There is enough material to read for years I reckon, but I've read a lot and learnt a lot, not always understood everything but if I don't understand, I can skip it until it becomes clearer. It's possible to understand the rest even if there are some things unclear here and there. At the moment I am on the chapter we could call 'The discovery of the Power of Thought and the manufacturing of things using Thought'. I had several examples of this myself; my dressing table, my pen, my flower near me etc. but I have to put the finishing touch to some small details! I think I understand the system. After all I managed to speak to you very quickly, didn't I! I am rather proud of it, it was something I did not know how to do and which you had not spoken to me about, I think- and I did it! So it must deserve a good mark, mustn't it?!

BR- Have you spoken of us (Touky, Michou and I) with Dad?

I must admit we have not really discussed it as I know he sees you, senses you and you are all in his heart. He told me he has often 'protected' or 'inspired' you (that's his words). So, I understood I didn't have much to teach him about you! On the other hand he taught me a lot about things here so that I can cope. Yes I've understood what you've just said. I'll try to speak to them about it now. Thanks for coming. I love you my darling daughter and I admire you for your constant courage, whatever the problems around you. I am near you every time you think of me, so we are not parted, are we?!

25th August 1999 *- 22.15hrs - When 'tuning in' I warn, mentally, that I risk falling asleep. The first word is in 'Automatic' in French then I hear the usual fast flow:*

Calm yourself Sweetheart, you have a lot to do and your thoughts are turbulent. I need you to be like a smooth sea, for me to able to speak to you. My thoughts are well organised, like tin soldiers in a row, one behind the other! I nearly forgot to tell you what happened after Dad and my dad welcomed me. I saw well-dressed people I felt I knew but I could not remember their names, yet their faces were familiar. I learnt later <u>they had been present when I had left</u> **for** <u>the Earth</u>! I thought they meant 'leaving the Earth'. No, it was indeed when I was born to go to the Earth, that those people were there to say goodbye, as if to a traveller, and these same people once more came to welcome me back, this time! My girl friends who used to live in Boulogne came to see me…*(Sadly my writing weakens: I struggle to shape the words as I am dozing off)* They had lots to tell me too. So I took my lovely wool blanket to make them sit on the grass in my garden and we chatted for hours I suppose…*(Unfortunately I give way to sleep).*

26th August 1999- *Mum left 2 months ago today.*
French is spoken:

My Darling you are kind to start again. Yes, I lost sight or rather 'sound' of you, last night as you call it.

BR- Does it mean anything to you, 'last night'?

Yes it's a bit like...last night. It's difficult to explain, as I don't sleep anymore, you see. It's weird not to have a need for sleep. Yet I did used to love it! But I am not tired anymore so why go to bed when there is so much to do and see here? I have a new 'system' to learn; I make lists for myself, of things to learn and of practice exercises, then if I succeed I give myself a good mark or two! That way it's more encouraging! I saw you starting to write with me one evening, as you say, then you disappeared from my 'wall of sound'. It came back! I understood you must have fallen asleep. Yes I know you'd said there was a risk you may disappear, that's why I understood. It's not serious since you are here now.

I saw a wave of ideas on my 'sound screen' as I call it, then they went away. The ideas I was sending you did not arrive when I sent them; they came back then disappeared, that's why I knew you did not receive them, but I still have them here. So I can start again if you wish. I was saying: I had a reunion with my friends when I arrived. We chatted outside on the grass, as they needed some fresh air and me too I suppose. My friends had brought a new picnic cloth and I thought we'd better sit on the grass to do that. I wanted to say there was no need to eat here but they seemed to think we did!..

So we settled down and chatted, nibbling what they had brought. Personally I was not very interested in food, as I knew (according to my good books) that this is all imagination! It looked like real cakes etc. but I knew that if we imagined them to be something else, they would change! So why bother?! I have lost the taste for eating you know. I am more interested in the stuff in my books and doing them, it's so much more fascinating! There are heaps to see and do!

BR- Who were those friends? French names?

I had school friends and others in my neighbourhood. You would not know them, so don't bother. I'd rather tell you what I saw 'this morning' as you'd say, but it is not really morning as there is no night. I popped across to my neighbours here, who are people I used to know in the days of my marriage to Pierre's dad. I did like them but had not seen them for a long time. I know they were called Roger and Lucie, but the funny thing is that <u>names are no longer important now</u>! People still call me Suzanne or other pet names, but I am not keen on it as I don't really like my first name, so I am not worried if they don't use a name for me.

I popped around to their 'house' and I saw they are much more advanced knowledge-wise than me! I admit they've been here much longer. I asked how one can see in a mirror something which does not exist in front of it! They replied: "The thing in the mirror is the reflection of your thought." So, let's say I think of a flower looking at the mirror. I'll see it <u>in it</u> but the flower won't be in front of the mirror! I tried it and it worked every time!

The silly thing is one cannot help wonder why and how, instead of accepting it. I did the experiment several times and had fun, but it's silly to waste one's time to do it more since after all, there is no need for a mirror for that, because all you have to do is think of something and it appears near you!

BR- Have you thought of me and I appeared?

I have not tried it but I suppose if I thought of you and you appeared it would be an image, an 'imagination of you', not the real you since you are still on Earth, aren't you! In a way I would love you to be here 'in flesh and blood' as we'd say (except it would not be 'flesh and blood'!) as we could have great fun together, discovering all these things and I

84

would not have to write them down! But if we did that, how would you publish it for other people, to inform others? We do have a job to do, you and I, it's obvious. I know we'll manage as we both want it. I want to teach you what is happening to me and you want not only to know it, but let others know it. So we are obliged to live on two separate levels, unfortunately...

I owe you more than I can ever repay to keep going, because if I did not have this to do with, and for, you, I think I would be feeling very, very miserable not to see you anymore and not have you near me. I must think of the possibility of convincing Touk and Mich (and perhaps even Pierre... but there it might be harder as I think his mind will have been blocked by the strange beliefs he has). As for me, I half believed in what my friends (who were Jehovah Witnesses) said, yet with a lot of reservations, though I did believe in several intelligent things they said. As for the rest, I can now see they must have misunderstood some points, even just the fact that one is not in a 'restful nothingness' on arrival in the Hereafter! Fortunately I had not 'brainwashed' myself with that, otherwise you and I would have never spoken to each other would we?! So it would have made you very unhappy, because of me and them!

Therefore the two of us did a good job when we were chatting all day long (when on Earth), it's helped me a lot, I understand that now!

You asked me why I was not receiving more visitors I think. I am comfortable here doing what I do, that's why I am left in peace. I am not unhappy as I do what I want you see. Pleasures of the mind are greater than the ones from the human body and my body does not bother me any longer now, so I don't think about it anymore.

I had a look around my 'bedroom-den': I saw all the titles of my books. They are fascinating and I tackled them, one after the other. I am still dealing with the experiments of thought and manufacturing of things. That's all. I saw lots of things happen near me just because I was thinking about them. I can make them stay by thinking about them again, let's say after a few seconds, or I can make them disappear by saying "good bye, that's enough, thanks, go away"!

At the beginning I jotted down a few notes so as not to forget what to do, but now I know how to do it. I am quite content with small things for the time being, but I don't know whether it wouldn't be possible to make big things appear. I am sure it is, after all it is only imagination!

I saw animals outside, lots of animals. I did not have time to make a list nor thought about doing it, but I told myself it might be interesting to do so.

BR- Did you make them appear yourself or were they already there?

They were there when I looked and had not particularly thought about it. I wanted to see my old cats, the ones from long ago, my dog (Mum's) but I had not tried to make others come.

BR- ('testing' her!) Did you see the bear from Algiers?

You ask me that?! I have already told you I had seen him, of course. He had obviously been very fond of me and me of him, as I used to bring him food, little treats of fish and other small things. But he always looked so ill and sad in his cage, in spite of the small pleasure I gave him, whereas here he is superb, handsome, big and strolls around safely. I had gone outside, he looked at me and recognised me because he approached me lifting his big paw towards me. He looked at me, 'kissed me with his eyes' I could say. I was not afraid, isn't it strange? To have an enormous bear in front of oneself and not be scared!

BR- He has a cage?

Oh no! No cage here of course! It is not a prison here, it's Paradise, remember! I don't know where he was, he just

86

appeared in front of me... We loved each other just by looking! Of course at the very beginning I had hesitated about approaching him. I suppose it was a reaction from a life on Earth, but I saw and felt he was not going to harm me, so I moved towards him and he touched me with his paw. I stroked his back...and he looked at me lovingly! It seems strange and silly to say that, but this is exactly what I felt when he looked at me. Then he strolled off further away and disappeared. I am not too sure as to where. He has perhaps a den not far, I didn't notice. I had thought of him when I was on Earth. I did not really think of him when I arrived here. I assume he knew I had arrived, I don't know. I would have understood if he had appeared because I had been thinking of him, but I had not! He seemed to come of his own accord, as if he knew I was here and he had to come and see me, I guess to say thank you or something like that... We are surrounded with kindness, it's incredible!

BR- You are and have been a person filled with kindness darling Mum, so your environment is full of kindness!

You are flattering me Sweetheart! I don't see myself as 'someone filled with kindness' as you say, but I understand what you are trying to say; one must be surrounded with the feelings one had on Earth.

BR- Do you see your dad? Has he appeared to you again?

My dad? I asked him whether he had interesting things to show me and he said: "Do one thing at a time, because if you want to learn too quickly before learning about the basic foundations, you are going to get muddled up and will perhaps even lose interest in doing it. So, first do everything your books teach you, then you'll be able to do things which would seem more complicated than they are, simply because you had not practised basic things". Therefore that's what I am doing - I obey my dad! I had always obeyed him when I was little, because I do love him so much.

I think he has not changed, but I know he has probably tried to show himself as I knew him during his days on Earth. I am quite happy to listen to him as he had taught me so much over there when I was little.

I have at last seen their 'home' by the way! But their house is not a real house you know. They are like me, they created for themselves a comfortable den to pretend they have 'a place of their own'- but they don't need a real brick house etc as they know they are not on Earth, so why bother? On the other hand, it helps to think one has one's own niche to withdraw from the 'crowd', though there isn't really a crowd here.

We only have people we are happy to see. Having a crowd of people one dislikes would be more like Hell than Paradise so, since I know I am in Paradise, I am not bothered by people I do not want to see! The fun side is those constant changes one can make happen. It could be terrifying if one did not know that it is one's thoughts creating all that! So it does help to learn to control your thoughts, not to have your surroundings, your décor changing all the time. I saw lots of surroundings zoom past one after the other, simply because I was thinking of them. For example I had a décor like a fortified castle, you know with wooden panels on the walls, a big fire in the fireplace, tapestries...because I liked castles, then I thought it looked dark! So I thought of a modern villa with windows and balconies, French windows on to the garden, the sea all around...and that's what I saw at once! Since these changes intrigued me I wondered: "What about if I changed all that into a forest, just to see whether it works?" And it did work! I found myself sitting on the grass in a forest full of trees!

I am telling you, it is really enough to drive you crazy, but only if you do not know you are doing an exercise with your thoughts! When you know that, you only need to see it as a bit of fun, a little exercise and a control to grasp, so I chose to keep my 'central point' as I call it, my corner, my den, call it what you like, in order to have a fixed place where I know what I am doing.

What is amusing is that there is never any dusting or tidying to do, unless you say to yourself: "I want to tidy this". It's so easy to look after, or rather not to have to look after it! It's ideal for me because I find tidying one more chore to do and I have escaped from chores by 'dying' as they say. My 'death'! I find that so 'funny' to speak of 'my death'! It looks like the title of a morbid poem! I do know that for you it must be so, so sad and for me it is too! Do not think I am not unhappy to have left you all without even kissing you one last time or saying something special as a farewell...

BR- I beg you, don't think about it anymore!

I appear to have fun, but it's only because what I am learning is amusing. I am studying it not only for me but <u>for you</u> too.

BR- I am not sure Touky and Mich understand all that. The Hereafter must seem to them like a single large room, a big magic box!

I too used to think the Great Beyond was a place where everyone knew everything, all of a sudden! So if that's what they believe, they are wrong but we can't reproach them. After all they have not come here yet, poor things! <u>When one comes here one is **not** omniscient and omnipotent</u>; one does not know everything nor can do everything - that is probably what they don't understand. I would love to be able to, as I've just told you; but it's not like that, the future is not visible, at least not for me! I only see what I see for the moment. I cannot see the future. I thought: "Will Touky succeed with his boat?" It's the first thing I wanted to see or try to see, but I could only see his boat. I did not see any 'chart of the future' nor any photos of the future. I don't understand what one should do, if one could do it. I think it's not possible for me, not yet anyway...

If I had more knowledge perhaps I could, so I am

going to learn and 'assimilate' as much as possible and we'll see afterwards... <u>It's not as easy as it seems from the Earth</u>, believe me! Up to now I've tried to do my best, as far as I can see I have moved forward. So as I go along, I hope to do better and better and perhaps help you or inspire you from here... I can't say more for the time being.

BR- Have you tried to think of your 'Guardian Angel' or ' main guide' to ask him to make himself known? Have you already seen him? (Silence for a few moments...then Mum speaks again, very excited and shaken, without 'catching her breath')

My thoughts went towards this kind person who must have been and must be my 'guardian angel'. I said: "Please make yourself known so that I can tell R- what I see and understand"...and the thought 'came back' in a millionth of a second: "I have never left you and am still here"... Then a tall 'Being of Light' appeared! I cannot tell you how surprised I was! I thought I was seeing a clothed man or a woman, the Being of Light seemed human in a way...but the 'light' was stronger than the body or the 'clothes', if you want to call them that. I can't believe it! He appeared for a split moment then disappeared! He must have sensed my thoughts to appear so quickly, but I could not grasp who he or she was without being even more dazzled. He popped in here then disappeared again, as noiselessly as he appeared! I say! It gave me a shock! He simply came because I thought of him, because you asked me to do it!

I told you what he told me...in thought I think. I don't recall hearing any voice, any sound! But the vision of his shape, his personality, his kindness, all that in one go! It's incredible! He appeared right in the middle of my bedroom-den, then disappeared without even moving in one direction or the other: he literally disappeared on the spot... I just can't believe it! No doubt he is from a more 'advanced' or 'evolved' place than me, he did not last long here, but I am only a new arrival. Perhaps it is harder for him to show himself as a body? I say 'he' because I think of a 'guardian angel' *(The French word is masculine)*. Yet I was <u>not</u> telling myself it had to be an 'angel', it could very well have been a person, like my dad; but you reminded me my dad was not dead when I was born so you were right. *(Mum remembers a conversation we had during her life in Nice. She used to say her dad must be her 'mentor' but I said a 'guide/ guardian angel' is with you from the moment you are born. On the other hand we can have 'helpers' during our life, who inspire us according to our needs).* There must have been someone else or some other Spirit first. Good gracious! What a beautiful apparition, a vision at my feet so to speak! He filled the room with his beautiful light then disappeared! I saw a large luminous form, in the shape of a light I think, of a body I assume? Yet it was not so much a human body as a luminous form and the importance of which was <u>not so much the shape as what was emanating from it</u>. It was only Beauty, Peace, Pure Love, a Beautiful Light...that's all I can say. Incredible! I had not thought of doing it, you gave me a good idea, you! But I still can't believe it...

You have more ideas than I have. Isn't it silly I had not thought of doing it? Yet I knew we must have a 'guardian angel' or 'guide' or something like that...

BR- It would be kind to send him your love and thank him now...

I am going to give him a kiss in my thoughts for all his good work during my life on Earth. He has been really kind, many a time, I know! He has got me out of many a problem, I remember... He's been really super, this 'angel'! I am going to tell him how much I love him for all his efforts and he deserves to be thanked, even rewarded... *(A few moments silence... I wait, wondering whether I have lost contact. Then Mum starts the conversation again, even more excited!)*

My poor darling children! I have no right to have so

much pleasure whilst you are struggling on Earth! I have just had, once more, an incredible experience! I did not know it was possible to do that!

Not only had I seen him, this brave guardian angel/ guide but I thanked him as you suggested...and he reappeared as a beautiful luminous 'Power of Kindness', which I could hardly bear without feeling nearly 'crushed' by this immense kindness! It's difficult to explain and describe. He reappeared instantaneously as soon as I thought of him...and, out of his Being, he made a light shoot up, stronger than the one he is made of... I felt this loving kindness wrap me up like a blanket, a cape... He 'kissed' me with that, I could say! He wrapped me up with the Kindness he consists of, I am sure! He is 'Kindness as a shape', it is not possible to say otherwise!

He did not stay long, he appeared and disappeared again. He had come back after you suggested I thanked him and he gave me an incredible shock showing himself in all his splendour of 'Love', 'Kindness,' 'Generosity', 'Purity'... Which word to choose?! I don't know how to describe him: A 'Being of Light' with indescribable forms, as he has not got shapes one thinks of when looking at him... because one does not look at him with one's eyes but with one's heart. I can only say he is filled with Kindness from head to foot, but he has not got any head or feet, I think! Yet I did not think of those details, it's just the luminosity and the beautiful shape and the Kindness I saw!

(I was interrupted and had to leave, so I apologised to Mum)

Thanks for coming. I'll talk to you again.

28th August 1999 - *On Scarborough cliffs, Yorkshire. The pen writes the first words in French. I realise it is my father:*

From the first moments of her arrival I knew Mum

would understand we were with her. That's why I tried to say to her at once: "Hello Darling, it's me... and your dad!" I saw she was flabbergasted but I enjoyed giving her that big surprise. I did what I had been taught to do before. <u>I had learnt to transform myself into a light, so that people find that easier to move forward in the darkness of their thoughts.</u>

  BR- How do you do that?

  I did what was needed. It's difficult to explain to you as you may not understand. I 'gather all my strength into one block', I 'gather myself ', if you like and I send this power towards the person. That power is an inner light, you know. That's why it is difficult to explain. <u>My thoughts gather into a very precise point, then I concentrate them into a very powerful force</u> and I <u>know</u> that it will become a light, I cannot explain more than that. This is what happens here when one does that. We always think of what we do here, so thought concentration is an engine, a motor, a rocket even, one could say! I only do that when I want to help people to get on the right track when they arrive from the Earth. They are all a little lost usually, so when they see a light they feel they have to go towards it.

  <u>Mum needed to leave her body</u> my little Darling, <u>because she had suffered. She was worn out, or rather her body was. So all she had to do was get out of it, to get rid of all that</u>. I did not want her to leave you of course, as I knew you would be unhappy, but I also knew she would be much happier here as she was not, over there...

  So when she appeared in her dream like a beautiful free soul, I saw her and said to her: "Why don't you stay now? It's better to be here than being unhappy on the Earth in a body which is suffering and not functioning correctly any longer!" That must have persuaded her, I think.

  I said to myself the best way to help her get out of her flesh body was to do what I do for others and to become a 'guiding light'. I did not make any effort to attract her, other than send affectionate, loving and encouraging thoughts. I knew my thoughts would reach her because <u>thoughts always do what they are told to do! They reach their goal every time!</u> So she looked towards us and came without any effort.

I only had to show myself as a normal man, like she knew me and that was enough for her to realise she was no longer on Earth, because she knew I was not either!

She exclaimed: "Good heavens! But... if you are here then I am dead too! Ah! That's good, it went well! I am glad", or something like that. So we showed her what to do to talk to you because she wanted to speak with you. A 'listening wall' we could call it...

BR- What is it?

The 'wall' she speaks of is the place where one concentrates to send one's thoughts and communicate. If she had nothing she would find it harder, I think.

BR- Is there a kind of telephone?

No, what she has is sufficient. It is <u>not</u> really necessary to be in front of a wall like that but <u>it makes it easier for her</u>, because she feels as if she is concentrating like one does when on a telephone.

BR- Is it made of ectoplasm or something like that?

We could make something like that with Energy etc, but I can assure you it is not necessary. All one has to do is to think of the person one speaks to.

BR- Do you use a "wall' too?

No, I am no longer in front of a wall. Before, yes. I used to think one needed one! But I realised the secret was to know how <u>to direct one's thoughts towards the person to whom you speak</u> and that's all there is to do! Once she could talk to you, she felt better and listened to us carefully.

BR - Who are 'us'?

My friends, her friends, her parents, we were all there

to welcome her from the start. We surrounded her with attention and love because she'd had a big shock to feel cut off so suddenly from the Earth and from you all. She was so afraid you'd be miserable and she was afraid to spend her time crying, because she knew she 'could no longer kiss you', as she said.

I know how it feels, because I too had that shock and it is very unpleasant. One realises suddenly one has disappeared from one world to go to another one, as far as and even further than Australia or America, because one can't come back from it as one could by boat or plane. So I too felt unhappy and lost, because normal life had been destroyed in a way. One is alone, without knowing what to do to remove the pain. But the parents, the friends, the people who come to support you, help you learn how to cope, so it is more pleasant to have all those people around you than being alone in an unknown place.

Also, here we are delighted to see her again! Personally I was pleased because I could at last talk to her properly, explain many a thing, help her, ask her for forgiveness and lots of things like that. Her dad was there too, he had lots to say to her as well! He too was impatient to see her again, after all the time we have been looking after her and watching over her! Poor Mum! She's been suffering for years. She should have come and enjoyed herself here much earlier really! But I know she was not quite ready to make that big step... That's why we had to wait for that day. You knew I was right didn't you, when I told you the winter snow scene would be a clue to make you understand... You did not realise straight away but in the end we understood each other, so that's what matters. You needed some proof, didn't you? I gave it to you. I hope that will be sufficient to convince you we have always been here to help you all and you in particular, to help you comprehend what goes on here.

95

I made an effort to admit to Mum that I regretted having made her unhappy sometimes, I did not really want to have to talk about it...but one cannot have a clear and pure mind if one does not get rid of one's detritus. Therefore I did and she said: "Amen. It's over, let's not talk about it anymore, it's old stuff and I don't want to think about it any longer!" So I felt better and I hope she will be happy here to teach herself all these new things she has to do. She 'made' herself her own place, where she feels comfortable and she is learning fast and well! We had prepared a comfortable place for her but as she thinks of what she'd like to have there, she makes it for herself. I think she does not need as much help as I assumed because she copes very well it seems. We see each other from time to time but she has a lot to do, so I leave her in peace as long as she does not ask something. That way she has some quiet and gets used to the new situation.

As for me, I deal with my own 'business' as we'd say. I do my 'people rescues' as usual and I have fun with my other occupations.

BR- Which ones?

They are studies of physics in this world. It is different from physics on Earth, because people on Earth don't have available to them the kind of things and knowledge we have here...

BR-Are you aware of my group, where we aim to make experiments like the famous Scole Experiment Group (in Norfolk, UK)? This is to help scientists, physicists from Hereafter, in their efforts to prove their existence; they aim to materialise objects, create photos in the dark on blank films, even manage to speak in 'direct voice, i.e without using a medium's vocal chords etc.

No, I am not really aware of this. I could find out more, perhaps get interested in it.

BR- Sorry, at the moment I am on a cliff by the sea-side, it's getting late and I'll have to go...I hope you won't be offended Dad!

I am not offended if you have to go...but I'd like to be able to speak to you soon.

BR- May I call you?

Of course you may call me, with great pleasure! We haven't spoken for such a long time. Bye my darling daughter. You are very kind and I love you. Your 'old' Dad.

***

CHAPTER 2
Fog of sorrow - Glimpses of Spirit physics: World of mind stuff - Discovering family secret

30th August 1999 - *I now know for sure it is Mum who speaks to me when she comes and I have been communicating with my guide for 19 years. Yet each time I 'tune in' in case someone in the Hereafter wanted to speak to me, I am still careful and do my best to ensure I am properly on-line! Today my guide has obviously decided to give me a lecture, since the first communication I receive is in English:*

Make sure the thoughts in your mind are good and pure and then you'll have no problem with linking to good and pure Spirits! Since you do that all the time anyway, then there is <u>no reason</u> why you should be concerned and worried about not getting a good link! We are all here to help you help others learn about our world. There isn't any reason why you shouldn't get good results from us, ok? You'll have to trust us of course, but we have given you good proof of our sincerity towards you in dealing with all sorts of subjects, whether helping the arrival of your mum or the details of her arrival or the fact that you wanted to be warned... We have done what we could, we did our best so that you were happy with all this.

So please stop worrying so much about 'bad communications'! We are here to help, not to upset or trick you. You are one of those who want to help us help the world, so why should we spoil our chances and your link with us? You know who we are, the usual group who cares about you and the work you do for the Earth people. All has been said before, as you are well aware!

We know who your mum is and where she is. She has settled very well in her 'belonging area', she belongs to a 'level' if you like, or an area of perfect peace of mind for her, as it is what she needs. She has suffered a lot before and now all her soul needs is peace and contentment and we try, all of us in this world, to help her find this contentment. She has learnt a lot before coming, as she must realise now. Otherwise she would not have settled so well. She is very happy with her new discoveries and the more she learns, the more she'll be able to achieve for her own progression, which is what matters most you know.

You'll have to consider her too. All is well to ask for details but she'll have to move on as she learns and progresses. You know she'll need to spread her wings, maybe not just now but she will have to, not so much as not communicating as learning to concentrate on her life here more than thinking of those on Earth. That's what she'll have to start doing one day, so don't be upset if she does not come close as often...

BR- Has she reached that stage now?

No, she has plenty to do now and it will be some time before she can do more or go further. That will be good for you as for her, because you'll still have a link, you know, it won't be broken off but it will be of another kind, you'll see. All will be revealed as it unfolds; you'll not be left in the dark wondering, so do not worry unduly in advance.

She is very pleased to be able to do her little exercises, because that's what she is here for. The world of our thoughts is so different from the world of the body, as you can gather. She is doing all right, we are pleased to see her progress and succeed. She is not lonely or sad, as she is surrounded with people who love her. She knows she can be sad if she wants to, but it would not lead to any progress or usefulness, instead it would get her down and not help matters one iota! So we may as well encourage her to go the other way, the light and happy way, away from the sadness and heaviness of heart as it impairs all progress. That's all we can say or want to say really. All is taking place as it should and all is going as well as it should. Nothing to worry about.

99

We won't keep you talking with us because you may want to have some conversation with your own loved ones of this life, i.e. your mum and dad. We have let them come close so that you can enjoy some more contact with them, since it is hard for those left behind on Earth, we know. It has been a long time for us here, but we know people like to have contact when they've left you recently. We understand. (*A very brief pause then the pen starts writing in Automatic. I notice it spells the first two words clearly in French then the rest comes as usual.*)

'AU REVOIR'*('goodbye')* I shan't say it for a long time! I am here indeed and have no intention of leaving soon!

BR- Who is speaking?

Me! I am your mum of course! Dad is here but he told me to talk first. I paid attention to what you were told. I saw your 'friends from here'. They are people who seem very interested in you and your life. I know they are there to help you because they came to explain they were going to speak to you first then I could join you.

BR- How did they tell you that?

I heard their thoughts. I learnt to concentrate on others' thoughts. They are very kind, it seems to me and <u>don't look like 'angels' but rather like 'normal people'</u> I'd say!

I have not encountered angels with wings here, you know! One does not see them like that. In fact one does not see any, I should say, as this is a place like one would see elsewhere but there are differences. That's what I tell you, the differences - the weird things and the problems one could have if one did not understand them.

BR- Can you explain?

Well, if you don't understand what to do with your ideas and thoughts, if you start 'thinking wildly', what happens is a big hotchpotch of problems because you end up not knowing what you are doing and what's going on. One needs some order in one's thoughts here, one must not get confused, otherwise one is faced with a big muddle, that's what one trains oneself to do you see. It seems strange to be obliged to learn to think, but I assume one must get used to it in the long run. I am just starting to do it you see. I have got used to a few things but there are plenty of others to learn, I can see that! But I think you seem to want to ask a question...

BR- To come back to my helpers and guides, how come you met them?

My friends showed me your friends. I have here a kind group of people I did not recognise at first, but they made me understand they are all acquaintances of mine 'from before', they said. "Before what?" I asked. "Before you left to go to live on Earth" they replied.

That's how I understood <u>I must have been here before going to the Earth!</u> Which I don't recall at all in fact! But I was told it is normal not to know it, as it would be too much to remember when one lives on Earth...

So I asked who they were. All together, in a 'joyful chorus' they replied: "We are your friends dear little one, your friends from here who looked after you when you were on Earth". As mentioned before, I no longer see people's mouths really speak. I 'sense' what they want to say, I can understand what they are thinking. That's how I made the acquaintance of those who looked after me, as they say, but there is still that handsome being who visited me that time. He must be far superior to these I assume, as he <u>practically did not look human, he was 'Light'</u>... He was Light and Kindness in one block! He was wonderful to see and feel, but he has not reappeared since. I think he must be using a lot of energy to appear? I don't know, anyway he was incredible to see!

It would have been a shock and a wonder for <u>you</u> to see him and meet him! What a pity you can't do it yet... Perhaps one day you'll be able to, who knows? But I did have the honour to experience this.

101

Now I'd like to tell you 'your friends from here' are people, in a group when I saw them, who approached me and told me who they were and they wanted to speak before me. They gestured for me to come nearer but I didn't have far to go as they seemed to 'think aloud'... Anyway that's the impression I had. They spoke to tell you not to worry, is that correct? Why do you seem to be concerned about who is talking to you? We are all here! I can promise you that and there are no 'baddies' on the horizon! Everyone is kind, caring, pleasant and sincere. It's Paradise thanks to this, I reckon! So they spoke to you and their thoughts reached you. Then I came to talk to you.

BR- How did they communicate? With the 'black wall'? They don't seem to bother too much with a black wall or my 'telephone-wall' as I call it... They began to think/speak at once without going anywhere else.

BR- Where are you?

I am in my room but I could not go any further as I wanted to speak to you soon. They said: "We'll speak to her first then you'll be able to afterwards". Then I ended up communicating with you myself. That's it! My friends here are near me when I feel alone, which is rare as I am so busy look-ing at all these books. I try to do what is suggested in them, so I am rarely 'alone' in the sense of 'lonely'! Dad comes too...

BR- Which one?

Mine and yours too of course. Mum is not far either. They have their business to see to, I don't think it is real 'business' but more 'activities' in the same way as I have mine. Yet I feel there is a difference; it must be because they have been here much longer so they must have learnt much more than I have during that time. I am allowed to know only what I can do for the time being... You'll see, I'll progress quickly so that you have something else to discover too! I can only tell you what I do, I can't show you unfortunately, which would be much more fun for you, because you would have the impressions and feelings it gives when one sees it oneself! Telling you a thing changes shape cannot be as detailed and exciting, come to think of it. It's much better to see it happen in front of you isn't it?!

My eyes are so good now! I no longer need glasses to read those books of course. I think I told you I don't bother much with this new body, which looks like a normal body but is neither hungry, thirsty nor in pain, so I do not pay attention to it! Good, isn't it?! I had enough of having to think about mine on Earth!

BR- Do you have clothes?

My clothes are no problem. I don't think of them really. I don't look in this mirror anymore as I got used to the idea of not bothering with this new body. Let it exist without being pampered! That way it allows me to concentrate on the interesting things offered by this place, this room and those 'films-books' as I call them. I feel peaceful mentally because the only effort I make is to think of what surrounds me. I know that if I thought of you in the same way as I used to think of you on Earth, I would worry a lot… and would make myself so sad that I could not concentrate on the 'work' I have to do here! There is plenty to do if one wants to keep busy, believe me! I have only been shown those books for the time being, it seems sufficient.

BR- Are there cats around you?

Cats? Oh yes of course, I've got some everywhere. I know I spoke about them before, to tell you they are there. You can well imagine I love having them around me, it reminds me of home with our cats... I am always scared of thinking of home as it makes me unhappy to think of what I left behind and not being able to help you more…

I am going to let Dad talk to you now, he's been waiting near me. We met again as you know, it felt good, which surprised me to tell you the truth, as I thought I would not have any more feeling or sensations- but in fact I was pleased to see him after all! So that's good, isn't it? Better this than the opposite! I wanted to make sure everything was all right before talking to him at length.

BR- What do you mean 'everything was all right'?

Everything was ok for him and for me and that we wouldn't argue any longer, but he told me he was sad to have made me cry. All that was a long time ago, so it's all in the past and I am glad! We don't think about it any longer.

BR- Do you want me to speak to you more often or do you reckon it's enough?

No, you speak often enough, it's fine. You can do it more if you like, but it won't be much use to your book if I don't have anything new to tell you, that's all. My Sweetheart, the link between us exists thanks to you and the 'work' you put in before, I assume. I would not have known how to reach you if you had not already been able to do it before and known how to communicate with the Hereafter! So you deserve all the congratulations, you helped make this communication possible through your previous work. All I did was speak to you in front of this 'wall' as I was told, you see!

BR- If you knew how strange it feels to me to speak to <u>*you*</u>*, because in fact it is quite easy! That's why I am careful and appear to doubt: I am sorry.*

I understand, you must find that simple yet weird. I suppose you are right to be wary of what you receive. One never knows, I guess... I am not used to doing it, so am not sure what you are talking about; but believe me, I am indeed your Mum, I am here indeed and I love you as always and even more perhaps because we are parted...without being completely apart!..

...Right, it's me now! Dad,yes?!

BR- Darling Dad, I want to ask you something: Could you tell me why you showed yourself to Ann.W, my medium, as if you were pacing a train station platform?

Yes, I'll answer your question about the station. I wanted your medium to understand that I was waiting for Mum, that I knew it would happen soon and I had to prepare myself and you for that journey… A journey is made in a train, a car, a plane, isn't it? So I showed this picture of train and station so that she understood the meaning symbolically. All I had to do was think of it. It was not difficult. I thought of a train arriving in a station...and people waiting on the platform. That's all. It was not complicated. The hardest was to know what to show you to give you some 'proof', as you wanted, of <u>when</u> Mum would leave you and your world. I had a bit of trouble doing it but I have some good friends here, some 'spiritual helpers'. They showed me what I had to see. I assume they had already done the groundwork, already seen where it would happen so I only had to repeat what I was shown…

I thought about what I was seeing, she understood it, repeated it and you received it…but a little distorted I gather.

BR- That's because I assumed the 'middle of winter' scene, of houses under very thick layers of snow, meant it would be in winter!

Well, finally you understood why I had shown you a winter landscape; it was there it would happen...that's all. Now we are all right together. Everything is fine here, no more problems.

I wanted to tell you a little more the other day, about my experiences here as I don't just do 'people rescues', I do some physics as I was telling you. So I discovered some interesting things. I have developed a system of studies of physics in this world, new for me and you too, though I have been here for some time now I reckon.

I have seen lots of weird things take place and I wanted to know why and how it happens. So they explained to me that thoughts of a man on Earth and thoughts of a being here are the same thing. It is 'Thought' and the thought of a being on Earth <u>cannot</u> be produced by the flesh brain, because the brain dies when the body dies! Therefore 'Thought' is neither linked to nor dependent on the brain. So it must exist somewhere else, mustn't it! That's what intrigued me and I wanted to delve deeper into this. At first when I tried I found it difficult, but now I've understood all one has to do is to look into the problem of light... No, not the 'problem' as it isn't a problem, let's say 'the fact'... The secret of light and thought and electricity, which make a whole here!

There isn't one thing which has not been created by one or several thoughts... So I wondered: "How does that happen?" I wanted to understand the physics behind all that. So here is how far I have got to for the time being, if you are interested or intrigued.

BR- Of course, go ahead! It's fascinating.

I see that light in the Earthly world is made by the light of the sun but not here of course. There is no sun... Therefore our 'light' must come from another source which I have not yet traced as such, but I know it exists. In my opinion it is not so much a source external to us all, than internal to us all and the objects here. So it seems to me that we produce that light which surrounds us, we cause it to exist with our thoughts, our ideas, our affections, our moments of joy and excitation when we discover all these new things! When one thinks a lot about it, one realises it must be true, because the more one thinks cheerfully, the more light one gets!

It changes, meaning it becomes stronger and more beautiful yet without dazzling... So for the time being (unless I get to another conclusion later!) I assume the internal light of the inhabitants of this world, creates the external light which surrounds them... Thereby I wonder whether the electricity we know on Earth may only be another aspect of this fact, somehow? Just musing!..

BR- (Astounded): Do you mean on Earth?

Yes, I think so. I do not know whether I am right as I

have to delve more into it!.. Perhaps I am wrong! I only see what I discover gradually. I learn as I think and as I think, step by step, I see ideas and facts taking place and taking shape and becoming possibilities... I don't know whether I am right, I am only thinking aloud! Progressively, as one thinks, one generates light, meaning electricity, that formidable force of positive and negative... The problem is not so much understanding where it is coming from, than understanding that <u>it exists in everything</u>. Also one must use it for doing good and not harm- the main point being that humanity must use it for good.

I am afraid I may not be able to explain better as I have not understood everything myself. I am only starting here... Anyway the '<u>light' we have here is indeed generated by the kindness and joy in people's 'heart' or more exactly their soul</u>. That's what makes everything so beautiful and good and gives you an impression of happiness as everything is goodness, 'made of goodness'.

I am not too sure about what happens on the Earth as all I did was assume that it may be like that. On the other hand I <u>know</u> that, here, this is what happens!

The substance everything is made of is the substance of 'Thought', so it is not really solid since Thought is not. It appears solid of course, but it isn't if one thinks about it. So one can change it, one can make objects change shape just by thinking about it, if one wants to and that's what is confusing at the beginning! Afterwards one learns to pay attention, be careful and not worry about it!

<u>Thought is 'light' in the sense of electricity, that is certain and it has the capacity to materialise here</u>, which you do not understand on Earth. To have what one wants just by thinking about it is incredible and handy! Thanks to this, one doesn't have any more problems! Yet you don't know how to do it on Earth!

The best thing to do is to wait for me to learn more I

think. I am just in the process of discovering all that and trying to understand it. I'll talk to you later, another time perhaps... I'll leave you now, I'll go and delve more into all this. So it's 'au revoir' from both of us and we'll talk soon, I hope!

6th September 1999 - *The pen forms the first two words in English:*

We are glad you have made the effort to sit today, when you are feeling more awake, because we find it difficult to talk to you if you are exhausted!

You have made a lot of efforts lately, we have noticed... but you must not rest on your laurels as you say, because this is not enough of course. You'll have to progress on the spiritual side as much as anyone else, you'll have to make greater efforts to be in line with what we need to do with you, which is to work for the good of mankind and the help needed there is enormous. So be prepared for more practice of quiet mind and peaceful heart.

We'll let you join your mum in a minute. You had a question about water and we have already asked you to drink more for two main reasons: You have a need for it in your body, you have been dehydrated for quite some time and you need to replenish it. We only know your body needs more water than it is getting and that's one of the reasons we asked you to drink more.

Secondly you have a need for better linking with us and this world and <u>the world of water has the same vibration as the world of Spirit</u>.

We know you think we are talking rubbish, but we'll tell you this: In the water you drink are particles you have no idea about. These particles have a velocity, such great speed of atoms that people don't know anything about it.

This is why <u>by drinking it, you ingest the fast particles which make you have, within you, some of the same vibrations</u>

108

as you would get in this world of ours, at the level we are speaking from. So be prepared to drink more so that the level of vibrations increases and helps you with your linking to us.

We know you feel it's not 'quite right' or 'weird', but we can tell you this with confidence and we'll make it be confirmed to you, so that you'll know we have every right to tell you so. You are hard work for us little lady...but the little lady has got every right to ask and check! Actually it's more sensible to do so, therefore we'll put up with it with understanding and love! We are at your service, Ma'am!

As we are about to leave you for your mum to come closer, we'll ask you to let her talk to you today before you ask any questions - she'll be more at ease that way. We haven't got the same level of vibrations as your mum of course, as we have been here much longer than she has. So we need to project our thoughts into your mind from where we are and that means we are not with her.

We know what you are saying, it's true in a way, she knows what we are saying at the moment because we let her know through you. She has to tune into your thoughts to be able to talk to you and you have to link up to her too. So, as she tunes in to your thoughts, she'll pick up what you have been told and therefore will know it. But she does not see us as a group of people standing there talking to you, as you can imagine.

That's all. Let her in now please... *(Suddenly: First three words in 'Automatic' and French is spoken)*

Yes my Darling. You've had a good conversation the two of you, people from 'Beyond' and you! I heard you chatting, that's how I know. I made a plan of what I want to tell you today, that way you won't miss anything!

First of all, number one: The 'work' I gave myself to do here. Not real work but rather a task I made myself do since I have been here. Secondly: The 'game' one can play with oneself by asking oneself trick questions and riddles, you'll see.

109

Thirdly: The prettiest things I see here at the moment and why I find them so pretty. Fourthly: People's 'business' - what they do here, not business in the sense of money but their activities. That's all for the time being. So now I'll explain in more detail.

First the work. Mine is very easy in a way, to learn as much as possible, as fast as possible. That's it! I do it gradually because to assimilate heaps of new things in one block is indigestible and hard to remember and understand! So I do my best to swallow one mouthful at a time and 'chew' well so to speak! I think I have told you lots about that before, about thought and its power, its force and what can be done with it… One never ceases to be amazed! Even though I have been doing it for some 'time' now, I still never stop being surprised by what happens and what one can do. I've reached the point of expecting the results with pleasure, because it's really fun to tell oneself one can make this or that exist just by thinking of it.

There is a new story I kept for a day when you had more time: I made a wall of gold in front of me!

BR - (Astonished) You made what?!

Yes, a wall made of gold because I'd told myself: "If I have some gold here, it will shine and will reflect everything". Gold is prettier than a mirror and it will shine, it would also have some value but not here of course! So, this gold wall is a golden panel with chiselled edges. I made it simply by looking ahead of me and saying to myself: "It would be great to make that" and it happened! I am surprised you are not excited by this idea!

BR- Sorry, it's just that it seems a bit weird and unexpected…

Why not? I did make a dressing table at the beginning and heaps of other things! Why not this? It is not particularly useful in a way, but it is so beautiful, it is a pleasure to look at and I see everything double!

BR- Why didn't you make a mirror?

A mirror? Hmm…yes, I thought of it. But gold is beautiful, it shines, it looks smart, do you understand? After all it is much more pleasant to look at this than a mirror! So you accept it now? I do have a beautiful 'horizon' in front of me with this, that's all!

BR- So it's used as a mirror?

Yes, that's right, it's like a mirror made of gold, but even better than a mirror, that's all. It also creates lighting effects when one moves and the rest looks much prettier! <u>I did this as an experiment</u> really, not so much to have a wall of gold…but I fell for it, so to speak! I liked it so much when I saw it arrive, that I kept it for myself, to enjoy having this beautiful object in front of me when I look at it. I assure you, the rest of the room looks even lovelier with that as a background.

I also made a garden very close by, which does not need to be weeded or anything else… All is needed is to look at the handsome trees and the lovely flowers and enjoy them, whereas on the Earth gardening is always work and chores! Here I have beautiful plants without having to touch them…

BR- Where?

I have them outside, in front of me, near my room (the walls of which I can get through, remember!)

BR- The walls are transparent?

No, they are not, but I assume if I wanted them to be transparent I could do it. It's cosier to have them as real walls, that way you feel 'at home' don't you? Then, when you want to go out, all you have to think is: "I am going out" and that's it, there you are! Really handy! So these are two of my latest activities, which give me pleasure at the same time as teaching me how to use this 'Thought' we are made of after all. That's what it seems to me…

BR- But you'd said you felt you had a body etc…

Yes, we are made out of Thought, but with a body of

pretend flesh, at least which looks like 'flesh', simply because it looks like the body one has just left! But I <u>know</u> it is not made of flesh. So it's great not to have to look after it any more, that was such a nuisance! I prefer this one. I have got it without having to deal with it. In fact I don't even think about it to be honest. I think 'me'- I don't think 'my body'- 'I want to go outside,' not 'my body wants to go outside'. You see what I mean? So, those are my useful games here, my work as a 'Beyondish' apprentice! It seems so strange talking of this and 'The Great Beyond', yet when one arrives here finally, one realises it has nothing to do with what churches teach and my 'Jehovah Witnesses' even less! No! I definitely would not want to return to Earth to do all that again... I feel far too comfortable here! But I want to pass to the second point.

The shock people get when they arrive here is not very different from the shock one feels when one gets lost somewhere, or has a knock on the head. It shakes you! This is part of the learning I guess, but it is a shock and it is <u>important to lessen it</u> as soon as possible. If you remain in a state of shock for too long, you become weaker and also you waste your time, don't you, since there is all this to learn!

I did my best to try to recover quickly and adapt, because I did not want to feel higgledy-piggledy and be a miserable and unhappy heap, as I know that if one doesn't adapt, one stagnates in one's misery like depressed people do!.. I had never, ever been depressed during all my Earthly life, so I was not going to start now, hey!

Well, I am going to tell you the other things I do, to enjoy myself. I go round this lovely garden, I see the animals I want to see and who are there. I am really happy in that place as it is very pleasant and useful since I feel good, so refreshed and regenerated.

The sun does not exist as a sun, but as a constant light, the origin of which one does not see and which seems to 'live' where one is! It is all around us and 'saturates' everything…and it does not dazzle, which is fantastic! I had already spoken of this, I think, but I can't stop marvelling at this beautiful light we never switch off and which seems to feed everything around! I believe it comes out of everything there - it seems to shine out of each thing but it does exist around them too! So I don't quite understand how this system can function!..

Anyway, it's gorgeous outside, I do like it. I come and go and I have fun looking at everything. The scenery and décor of this place have variations if one thinks differently! If I thought: "Oh, I'd like to see the sea here, at the end of this garden" I would see it! But I think the next person following me would not see it… I would have <u>my</u> sea, they would have their mountain or something like that. It changes because one thinks of it, you see, like everywhere and everything here!

That is the difficulty: not to change your thoughts constantly, otherwise you no longer know where you are!

Now, the third thing to tell you is the effect of the environment on you, here. When you feel good, you feel like doing some good and that is what is strange! You feel like sharing that feeling of well-being, it's something I have just discovered. I thought I was going to stay in, learning from all my books, but now I think I am beginning to feel like talking about it to those who know nothing about it. I talk to you of course, but <u>apparently there are some people here who do not know all that</u>. I can't understand how they don't, since all you need to do is think and you'll see things move or change! Perhaps they do not have the same strength of thought, or constancy, or fairly intense intentions? I don't know… Anyway, I pointed this out to someone I was speaking to and he asked me what I was talking about! So I threw myself into lots of explanations and he seemed to think what I was telling him was strange!

Therefore I'll probably have to become a teacher of all that here, instead of French or English! I don't know for sure but it's an impression I have... I know I like to share what I discover, so it will perhaps do some good to someone else who arrives here? I have no idea, we'll have to see.

Now the fourth point. But before that, I want to know whether you have any questions. Perhaps I got mixed up in the order of ideas and points? I wanted to let you know all those things...

BR- No, that's fine.

So, number four: People's occupations. I am going to carry on talking as I think, it will be better than writing I reckon. I know there are some people here whose task is to help others, to help each other and discover new things. I have not met so many of those because I have been so busy doing what I had to do, in order to get settled, understand and become acclimatised, as we say. But there are people with all sorts of occupations. You'll see gardeners, builders, shoe repairers if need be! People do what they feel like doing their own way, at their own pace, without rushing to earn some money, that's what I mean. They do it for the pleasure of doing it and that's what is surprising. They don't know they don't need to build something by hand, but if it makes them happy, well, they do it!

I saw it when I strolled around to have an idea of where I was. There was everything, like a little town this way, a village over there, then my dear trees, parks etc. elsewhere. That's why I reckon not everyone has understood what I have understood, or else not everyone wants to use their 'Thought Power' and prefers using their hands, that's my conclusion. Personally I prefer using my Thought; it's much faster and fun, also more perfect since one imagines things perfect, instead of having to bother putting finishing touches! So that's my recent discovery. I see it must make life difficult for you to assimilate all this, but I hope you'll get used to it. That way you'll have learnt something new, like I do all the time.

A little game I play to myself is to make myself guess

114

what there'll be further ahead before I get there, it works every time: "What will there be over there?" and before getting there I know it because I felt it or saw it... I learnt to do that with my good books/films. They explained you have to relax your thought and let yourself be guided by what is coming.

All that is amusing because one does not expect at all one thing or the other you see, one just wonders... If the answer comes before you arrive to the spot, then it is true indeed and you've succeeded. It makes you use remote viewing and telepathy and it's great fun, as you feel so clever to have managed it!

I really enjoy it every time. I made Dad have a go but, of course, he is good at it, because he knows how to do it since he's been here a long time!

BR- Which dad?

My dad. But yours can do it too, moreover he had a good sixth sense when he was on Earth, hadn't he?! Do you remember? So Dad and I have fun with these kinds of little games. It's amusing, just as if I was a kid and played with him once more...yet it's useful, as one must know how to use one's thoughts. It is an extremely essential tool and that's how one practises.

BR- Were you able to do it easily?

I could do it quickly, yes. I think there are people who will not know how to, because they had not learnt the other stuff I had 'studied' all kinds of little things and details which helped me to understand.

My Darling, I think that's all for the time being. I cope and I am glad to be able to. I do my best so that everything I do is useful and also to teach you something when I speak to you, so there it is! *(I ask Mum whether she remembered a young girl called N- to whom she gave lessons and whose acquaintance I was going to make).* The only thing I remember is she had bracelets which made a noise on the table as she was writing and it was getting on my nerves! That's all.

It's weird but I have the impression of looking at everything through thick fog! I don't remember details, it's more impressions...<u>the rest is vague</u>. It is irritating not to see things more clearly, I wonder why?

<u>I think it is because I am here and have been concentrating so much on my life here</u>. I can only tell you I love you my darling daughter, I kiss you and the boys too. So I'll leave you now. I am with you in a way: don't forget we talk to each other now and we'll see each other again... I'll wait for you!

7th September 1999 -

During the previous night I had a very vivid dream of being with Mum. Her face was much younger, beaming, strangely luminous, over which just a few wrinkles seemed to have been 'drawn' (!!). Yet I did recognise her. She stood in front of me, smiling - she looked in her forties. (As I type these lines several years later, I still see clearly in my mind, this 'apparition' which was very different from the vague and misty memories one usually has of a dream). I tune in, the pen writes six words automatically, in French:

We see each other during the night Darling. Your night is not a night for me but we see each other. We chat during your sleep but you don't remember it. You have not left me, nor me you. We speak to each other in writing for '<u>the</u>' book, but we meet during the night, hadn't you noticed?

BR- I had asked you last night whether you knew you were paralysed?

I was told I was when I came here. I had not really realised it when I was in hospital. I was in too much pain or too thirsty or both...so I had not paid attention to the rest. Fortunately, I suppose!

I am as usual 'at home', you come to visit, so to speak. I had been warned it was possible because <u>I had done the same</u>, they tell me, <u>when I used to sleep in Nice</u>. They

116

would teach me lots of things to help me manage without any problem. So I believe them since all went well for me eventually!

But when you come, it's a quick visit of a few minutes or moments. I see you, we kiss and hug, sit together very close and talk to each other. We have not got the time to say a lot, but we meet to be able to love each other. I think it's so that I don't feel completely cut off from you all and you can feel I love you. I have only seen those who want to come and see me. We meet only if we want to and think we can, I reckon… I did not know this before coming here. Otherwise you can imagine I would have visited my parents more often! As I told you, I write this for your book, to describe what is around me. I had not thought of mentioning we'd seen each other because it was to do with us, I suppose.

I am sorry Sweetheart, I should have thought about it. I am so busy trying to understand what is going on here and to explain it to you, trying to use words which make it comprehensible, that I had not thought of telling you about that. Yet you are right, it would have been better if I had remembered to do it. I only have one head…perhaps I need two! I know this won't look very convincing to Touky etc. but too bad, what can I do? I am only a beginner here and I see lots of people I had not seen for a long time, all those happenings are emotional shocks too. you know!

One could go crazy if one let oneself get caught in all this without understanding!

(I said I had made an appointment - in two months time as I could not get in earlier! - with the good medium B. N, hoping it will help give evidence to my brothers of my communications)

Yes I heard. You said you are going to see a medium on your dad's birthday and mine the day after. That will help us have a little birthday party, won't it?! I am pleased, we'll certainly be both there and we'll have fun all together, you'll see.

117

I hope your medium is good and will be able to understand what is being said! Ok, I'll have to let you go as you said you only had a few moments. Mum loves you.

22 September 1999 - *Mum's birthday - she would have been 91yrs old (yesterday Dad would have been 96). The pen writes the first words in French:*
   She looks rather sleepy that girl, I'll have to hurry up won't I?! Sweetheart, why are you, once more, a silly-billy? Why go to bed so late? Is it because we want to speak to you? So perhaps we should not do it...but you must not start so late in the evening, it's killing! You'll never get enough sleep and you'll feel so tired tomorrow...
   BR-Who is speaking? By the way your birthdays were yesterday and today.
   Me? I am Mum of course! I know <u>my birthday does not matter much now</u> I am no longer there... In fact <u>I am younger than my birthday would make me 'celebrate'</u>, because after all, what counts more, arriving in Paradise or arriving on the Earth, hey?
   But you know you must not be sad any longer, my darling daughter, because <u>sadness blocks the link between the two worlds</u> apparently.
   So neither you nor I are allowed to be sad since we want to be able to communicate with a peaceful mind, without having to worry about moments of unclear link. But I wanted to tell you something else, so I'll start in case we were interrupted. My dad told me recently <u>the substance used to make everything here is tangible stuff but it does not last long</u>, like in a dream...
   (That's a subject which promises to be fascinating, so to listen very carefully I relax even more... but at this late hour my eyes close of their own accord when I am too calm! It's exasperating but it's my fault).

118

24ᵗʰ September 1999 - *In the morning, for a change! Tuning in after my daughter Anne-France (who lives in the South of England) phoned A.W. for a 'distance sitting' over the phone. It would be incorrect to believe we spend our time chasing up mediums! Not at all! It's the first time for a very long time that A-F did this: she had a problem and was hoping the lady could 'see further' towards a solution. My pen starts in French:*

I am so pleased you are here at last Sweetheart, as I'd like to tell you what I was able to do. We all had a meeting with your medium and you know what she did - we spoke to your little darling, your Anne-France who seemed so unhappy! She sat down at a table while we spoke to her and she noted all that down. Personally I was glad to be able to tell her not to ruin her life for a man! She's suffered a lot I think, according to what I was told and I know men are not worth it, as I suffered because of them too during my Earthly life. I would not want to go through that again...

You know, I do not really know how to do that myself (give mediumistic messages) but <u>all I had to do is repeat what I was told to say</u>. We had people around us, they were the two dads and others, those who look after Anne-France. I saw them because they came especially to deal with this matter and give her some advice. They spoke to me and I was saying what I was told to say. I did see the medium's 'light' in my head, I don't know why it happens like that. I saw the lady in my mind's eye, she seemed to be very nice and I saw Anne-France's light. Because she was sad it was grey and dark; I learnt that's what one looks like when one is unhappy, so I wanted to tell her not to worry. We were all here around my desk and my 'black phone' wall. I translated their thoughts and advice. As I was repeating what I was told, I could see the lady's 'light' getting brighter and Anne-France's becoming less grey, yet not very cheerful.

I wanted so much to be able to kiss her, poor little thing, I didn't know how to say it! I was not speaking in French, I have at last learnt to not so much use words as try to use symbols or thoughts in pictures. I wanted to speak myself and I managed. I did not do the whole conversation, but let's say I had 'priority' in front of the 'phone wall'; that way I learnt how to do it you see. I suppose that's why they made me have a go to practise...

BR-What do you think of the whole business? Any more advice for AF?

You know what it's all about, so why ask me?! I repeat it again, I don't know much unless I am told. I learnt to think, to see people as 'light', light of their Souls I assume. I was told to think of Anne-France and I saw, as a vision, a girl in tears then a grey and black light in her place. She seemed very unhappy.

BR- Where did you see that?

Within my head. Then I was told she was going to speak to a medium, a 'person of great spiritual character' my helpers said, 'who has the gift to link up with us here'. So I pretended not to understand so that they tell me more! I saw a light in front of me and I said: "What is this?" Your friend's lady told me: "It's the medium".

BR- Which lady?!

The lady who looks after the soul of your friend the medium. She told me: "My medium is a good woman, one must concentrate to be able to reach her."

BR- How do you concentrate on someone you do not know?!

I tell you again that, around me, there are people who know what to do. They have perhaps put the picture in my head, I don't know. I saw a lady, then I saw a light in her place. She was beaming so I understood it was her, the medium, because I was told: "Focus on this and talk to her in your mind.

120

Tell her what we tell you to say, let her transmit it to the little one who is crying." So I did it, that's all. I cannot say all the advice came really from me, but I had my opinion though. I did what was needed so that we managed to help her.

BR- How did you know what the situation was about?

I keep telling you! I was told she had problems with her boyfriend and 'great love', that everything went wrong suddenly! That's why she had been crying for several days and why she wanted to speak to the medium! That is what we did to help her.

BR- Good, thanks a lot! What about you, your new life, all going well?

My life here seems to have changed a little bit, I've noticed. This incident is one more to show me I think, that we need to help Earth people in distress. You had told me Dad did it here after his arrival. I can see he's still doing it in a way, not all the time but from time to time. I would indeed like to be able to do it, if only I knew what to do! It does not appear to be difficult but it seems to really help people who are lost. I do not have a 'medium diploma' but I reckon that by speaking to people who don't know where they are (after their passing), it will help them.

Personally I was lucky to have a kind daughter who helped me a lot by trying to teach me where I would go and what would happen. I realise now that although I may not have understood everything, I still had grasped the essential!

So, I should perhaps do the same for those who arrive here, their mind filled with fear and terror, because apparently that is what prevents them from seeing where they really are! If we can convince them there is nothing more to fear, we are not wasting our time, nor them theirs, though here the word 'time' does not really seem to exist, does it! It depends on, and is relative to, what we do: we don't need dates here, though we know we have done one thing before another. Moreover I was told <u>the</u>

121

value of the action matters more than its 'duration'. It means if you help someone in distress, that's what counts, not how long it took and when it happened.

So, I was able to watch a little, from afar, what Dad did and I saw how Souls who arrive here panic-stricken and terrified, seem to run around right left and centre, as if to flee from something... Then he approaches them with a knowing look, says something to them which I can't hear from where I am, but it calms them down. I saw frightened children who had lost their mother or something like that. Dad spoke to them, they stopped, hugged him and huddled in his arms... He carried on talking to them, this seemed to have some effect on them as they calmed down and learnt gradually that their body had died but they themselves had not, not their soul. I don't think we actually say to them 'not your soul', as this is 'adult talk, isn't it! It's more like 'Jehovah Witness-speak'! That's why I decided to help him do that, because with a woman there, it might be better for some people.

BR- How will you know what to do?

One does not need big lectures for that you know! All that is needed is to have experienced fear or pain and to tell them it does not exist anymore here, then all will be well, I think. I have not tried yet, I'll discuss it with Dad and the others.

BR- Your dad does this work?

My dad no, I don't think so. I haven't seen him do that. I saw Dad Nic *(my dad)* doing it, he does a good job from what I see. I must admit he copes very well and I hope I'll also be able to! Yes! Me, the Samaritan from the Hereafter or Paradise! It sounds strange doesn't it?! I have the feeling I have just arrived and there I am, giving myself some work...but it is not really work I suppose - it's just to help people who are lost.

BR- What about tortured animals? Do they need help to find their way?

My friends from here say this to you: "You must not

worry about tortured animals because they don't believe they are still suffering. As soon as they come out of their body, they see a field or a garden or free space where they can run around and that's enough for them, because they do not see their murderer any longer.

Since they don't feel any pain any more, they think he must have gone away, so all is well now! We look after them and if need be, reassure them quickly".

Does that give you an explanation? I do think it must be true, considering once one is out of one's flesh body, one is no longer in pain, I know about that, don't I?! So I reckon I agree with all this. I saw animals here and they are all happy, not a single one looks unhappy. Whereas I have seen people arrive where Dad is and they are panic stricken, distraught, miserable...

As for me, I had the great pleasure not to be like that, hey! Ah! It was so good to feel free, without pain and with a body which is whole, lightweight and not old! It's impossible to explain this in words... It is unimaginable and infinitely wonderful and smashing! That's what I could say about it.

I also want to tell you something else: I have made another discovery. I had started speaking to you about it but you fell asleep (once more!..) because you were too sleepy... I am beginning to understand (but I am telling you and warning you it is only <u>beginning</u> to understand) a little that the stuff things are made of here is not the same stuff as on Earth. *(Note: Notice how this new subject comes quite naturally, without any hesitation, flowing at once from her previous topic, without me thinking of it or asking any question and it continues what had been interrupted on 22nd September!..)* They have a different texture in a way, if one looks at them closely. I mean, if for example I see a flower and look at it, it looks like a beautiful flower but the texture has a radiance in itself ... It seems to be made of 'light', not a big dazzling light but I could

123

say 'little drops of light'! It's weird and very pretty indeed, the effect is so interesting and unusual!

When I asked why and how it happens, I was told that <u>'the skin of things' here is not matter made of atoms, like on Earth, but rather of 'inside of atoms'</u>, that is to say light or electricity or something like that... I did not quite grasp everything but it is something similar. Because everything is made of the same stuff, there is a constant radiance out of all that is here. Yet it does not dazzle, because if it did, it would be unpleasant, wouldn't it? So there you are, it's something different but pleasant.

BR- Can you tell me more about it?

Yes, the stuff things are made of here, that's what I was telling you about. It's something weird which seems to be made of light, of radiance from atoms... They *(the Spirit friends)* are there around me anyway, as I don't know everything. So they tell me this stuff is not tangible, in the way that there are no atoms one could 'dissect', but there is still a structure, it's made of vibrations, radiance... That's what it looks like... Moreover if one thinks about something else, the first object may disappear! So for it to stay, one must <u>give it a more solid consistency. It is achieved by thinking of it strongly and intensely</u>, thinking of it more often than just a passing thought.

My 'belongings' are there because I created them, because I <u>wanted</u> them there, therefore I created them with more intensity than if they had been passing thoughts. Because I put some strength into it, that gave them some 'weight', meaning 'consistency' not 'heaviness', you understand? They exist because I wanted them to exist, but if I think of some things in passing and don't think about them afterwards, they disappear because I no longer think of them, so <u>they have no 'life', no 'matter' coming from my thoughts</u>...do you see what I mean?

All that is mind-boggling I know! You must be

wondering whether it is really true or whether I am raving! Yes, that's all I've grasped on that subject for the time being, but it's worth thinking about it and knowing it. It must have some repercussion on many a thing when one thinks about it as the basics I assume. Anyway, that was my first lecture in physics Madam! If you wish to find out more, you'll have to wait till I learn more than I know at the present moment!

BR- You are the 'teacher' who learns as she goes along!

Yes, I cannot be asked more than I know at present. Moreover I think these are things one must experience here, as talking about it can't have the same effect, I guess. I don't have much else to tell you now, except that I love you my daughter and I hope Touk and Mich will soon know I am talking to you, because I would like to reassure them.

BR - I need to type on the computer everything you told me, then send it to them... It does take so much time! Sorry! I should have done it as we went along, now it has accumulated...

I know. It will be all right, you'll see. I'll let you go now. Lots of hugs and kisses and I'll talk to you again soon? Have a good trip!

2nd October 1999 -

It's Mum once more. I am ready and delighted to speak to you at last. I have not had the opportunity for some time it seems, it must be several days I suppose. But don't panic if you cannot do it, as I know how busy you are and I don't want to have any remorse thinking I delayed you Darling. So only do it when you can.

BR- Do we still meet at night?

Yes indeed, we see each other at night, you do know that! No, it is not 'night time' for me, but 'night' for you.

125

BR- What happens?

We go together to a place where you feel comfort-able and which <u>allows you to join me.</u> I am told you are going to be there, so I go to that place and wait for you. You arrive, eyes wide open, not asleep! Yet <u>your body must be sleeping, but you, the Spirit, have come out of it</u> and you come to see me, speak to me and Dad too when he is there. He's got into the habit of coming too, from time to time, to catch up and know what's going on, what we are talking about etc. He looks so happy to see you again when he comes and you too. I think you have not seen each other often, but I want to speak to you frequently if I can, so I don't miss an opportunity!

You always wear an elegant dress when you come! Not always the same but you always appear elegant in my opinion and I see you have my bracelet and my chain with you. I was careful not to speak about it but you brought them automatically to show me you have not lost them!

You look absolutely normal to me, we kiss, hold hands and chat...and enjoy ourselves... You see what I can show you around me but <u>I cannot let you see everything I have in my own place, because they say you cannot reach that spot for the time being</u>. I don't see why but <u>I was told not to even try to take you there</u>, so I obeyed! You come where we receive people who come 'at night'. You come because you have a body which is asleep, so access to your Spirit is much easier, because you too want to talk to me, so we meet more easily.

I did everything I could to take you elsewhere, but they said: "NO!"

So...Amen! Anyway, where we see each other is very pretty too, you know. We are not complaining! There is a kind of garden with benches and flowers and animals, but they aren't all the ones I see usually. You saw certain animals but not all.

BR- What kind?

Oh, cats usually! But we don't pay much attention to them as we tend to talk about ourselves, you see.

BR- Do you show me how things appear and disappear etc?

I can only do what I am advised to do, so I don't do anything complicated. You don't have the same mind power as I am learning to have for example, <u>so it isn't possible to make you create or conjure away things like I am beginning to do</u>. Yet there are other aspects which interest us and it's mainly to be together, love each other, kissing and hugging. There are always things to say or discuss. You told me about your daughter's problems and her 'boyfriend troubles', you showed me your son and his non-existent job. You spoke about your cats and your job which does not appeal to you as much and your aspirations towards something more interesting and exciting... It gives me so much pleasure to be able to be up-to-date like that! I am not very good at concentrating my thoughts to manage to see what you all do on the Earth at the moment, so this replaces letters and phone calls. In fact it's better as I can see you instead of waiting for the mail!

I saw Touky sometimes, I gather he has more work. He appears to be optimistic, as usual, but I reckon he wants to please me by telling me everything is fine! He will probably not remember our conversation, I suppose, since you don't remember ours, you and I...

I hope he will get to understand, one day, that Dad and I have not forgotten you and have not turned our backs on our life on Earth, but have been obliged to leave it, this being 'a case of absolute necessity', as they would say in newspapers or political speeches! As for me, I was fed up with politics too! Everything on Earth had started disgusting me. I suppose that's why I must have wanted to leave it, in a way... Not to leave you, of course, but leave it, so as not to hear of those political and monetary troubles...and battles and wars and problems everywhere! Me? I wanted peace, as you know, I have always wanted it! That's why I wrote my sketch: '*Peace, please!* 'Do you remember?

But it's not that which made me come here, I assume. My body had aged so much that I ended up not recognising myself any longer in the mirror!

On the day of my stroke, when I fell on the bed, I had seen my mum and dad, you know! But I had not understood it was them...

BR (Stunned) - Really? I say! I did not know that at all!

I had suddenly turned round and had seen my mum and my dad in the dining room near the sofa, but my memory was a bit strange in those days and I told myself I was imagining things! But when I saw them again here, they confirmed they had come to warn me, to see me, to give me relief if they could...

I had not understood properly of course, because I was struggling with that blasted telephone which had fallen down, so I had forgotten all that once I saw you in the hospital! You seemed really sad not to be able to help me more, I know, poor Sweetheart. When I think I was reproaching you for not giving me more water! You must have felt tortured by those reproaches, I suppose... I did not really mean to reproach you for that. It was simply that I was so, so terribly thirsty I could not stand it anymore! But it's over now, I don't want to think about it again. It was atrocious but there are certainly more atrocious deaths than this, so I have nothing to complain about! I have not suffered as much as people or animals who have been tortured or cut up alive, have I! So why complain about what I had, when one knows there is far worse in the world of Humans on Earth!

I do have some peace at last! Peace, it's worth suffering a little to obtain it I reckon and my peace will be eternal,

I hope! So I don't have anything to complain about: I am really comfortable and feel happy all the more since I can talk to you.

I saw Michou but he seemed bothered by something. I only saw him quickly. I cannot 'order' those visits you know, they arrive without me knowing. I am told: "Come here, there are some visitors" and that's when I see you...and Touky and Mich rarely.

BR- So you saw Michou during 'the night'?

Yes indeed! I saw him. He does not seem to come over often though, I don't know why. On the other hand <u>we cannot control that from here</u>. I think it is you people who come when you want to, we can only receive you joyfully when you do, but there will be other opportunities, I am sure!

(A short silence then...) My friends here are those who welcomed me when I first arrived. I saw people from my younger days and some from later life but whom I am very fond of. I have seen lots of folks since who only pop in some-times but who are always ready to help me or explain things to me.

BR- People you knew on Earth?

People I 'recognise again', let's say! Perhaps from before or from elsewhere? From a life before? Who knows? I only know that I do recognise them but I don't always manage to understand why I do!

BR- Don't you ask?

Oh yes indeed, I do ask, as you can guess! But am not always given a full answer, that's what's strange. I often get a reply which only provides me with a few things. It's as if I am not supposed to know the rest! I assume I am perhaps not capable enough to grasp the explanations, for the time being anyway. If they explain more, you'll know it, don't worry! I won't 'abandon' you either.

So these friends show me many a thing and explain lots of stuff. I did some experiments with them and they encourage me not to lose heart and try to do better. I tell them I

129

want to be able to do everything so that I can tell you and also have a comfortable life here myself; I don't want to be in pain again or to have worries! So I make them tell me everything I can do to facilitate this!

BR- Have you still got your gold wall?

My gold wall was only a creative exercise, you know! Gold is pretty indeed but it was not for the gold, it was for the fun of achieving what was in my eyes a 'feat'! I did laugh a lot when I saw I could do that, without having to create it using a hammer or something! Well, it lasted a short while, then I became bored with it. Yes it was there, but I ended up not paying attention to it any longer, so it vanished gradually...

The exciting thing at the moment is the news of my new 'vocation'. I want to have some peace of course but it does not mean I want to do nothing. I always have interesting things to do here. So I asked what I can do to explain what I learn to others. This is because I am stunned there are people around me who have not understood how easy it is to change one's environment and what fun it is! Why deprive oneself of it?! I'll see whether I can start to explain it to someone who has just arrived recently and who wants to know what I am talking about. It is a gentleman who died of a long illness; he did his best to settle here but he does not seem to have understood everything I have grasped until now. Not that I know it all, but there are simple things he could at least tackle.

BR- Did you know him before?

No, I didn't know him, but he seems really nice and a little puzzled by what's here, so I'll probably lend him one of my books, to talk to him about it, then we'll have fun creating things to teach him how to cope here. It looks to me he seems not to have 'landed' properly, a little as if he was in a mental fog, but I am going to speak to him.

BR- Have you already done it?

No, not yet, I'll go to him. He does not really live in a house, he does seem to know he does not need a house as such, but he has a limited understanding of what he can do with his thoughts.

BR- Hasn't he got any family to help him?

I only know what I see. If he has a family they probably have not told him much, because he looked dumbfounded when I told him about my flower and its apparition in my room, with a vase on top of that! So, there is no doubt quite a lot to teach him!

BR (Jokingly) - You could perhaps teach some English while you are at it!

No doubt he does not need to be taught English. But he certainly needs to learn to think like one can think here, and that's more complicated than usual, but much more fun!

BR- What language do you speak?

I have at last understood that <u>ideas one has in one's head are not always words</u>. We think them as words sometimes, but we also think of many <u>things which are only pictures or impressions</u> and when we want to convey something abstract, it is difficult to turn it into a picture so we can use a word.

When we speak to one another here, we can think and converse by exchanging thoughts without having to open our mouth, you see, but thoughts are not always very clear when one is not used to it, so we use words too from time to time. It's a little like using a telephone and a telegram at the same time or a fax. I no longer know how to send a fax now, but I remember it was handy to be able to despatch a whole letter in one go, in seconds. Well, it's like that here, when we speak to each other by thinking and the other person does the same, no need to slow down to form words. Oh! I can speak French of course, but I have not had the opportunity to speak English, I suppose I could...

BR- What went on when I had the sitting with (the medium) B.N?

I was there, you can guess and your dad too. He wished to be present too so as not to miss an opportunity to speak to you, but also he wanted to make sure I was not doing anything 'silly' when I came near the lady whom you spoke to! All I was doing was saying aloud what I was thinking. I did not really need my 'telephone' but I had the feeling I had something in my hand, a kind of microphone or loudspeaker or something like that and I was careful to speak clearly.

<u>I saw where you were because I was shown it like on a cinema screen</u>: A room with objects all around and furniture, you sat facing each other, the lady was with her back to me and I was looking at you. I insisted to be very near to be sure you knew I was there. I had asked to be able to speak directly in her ear, but there were 'technical reasons', I'd say, why I could not do it that way. So they showed me a different way - a 'mike' a...

(I relaxed even more to make sure I grasped well what was dictated at full speed. But concentrating on all those previous pages was very soporific and fatigue made me doze off! So frustrating when it is so interesting!)

18th October 1999 *- I hear French spoken to me. I realise it's Mum:*

A bird does not fall off his nest or perch when he sleeps because he hangs on and is not that sleepy and worn out that he does not know what he is doing... You do not sleep enough, that's what slows you down for many a thing on the level of spiritual work.

BR- Touky would like some proof which only you and him know of!

I am quite happy to find something, unfortunately for the time being I don't see what he is talking about! At the

132

moment I am still busy with my thoughts and my power of thought. I don't have much to do as far as 'work' is concerned but I suppose I am not supposed to work. I have done enough in my life! I have been able to have a good rest since I have been here. I have also made the acquaintance of lots of new people, people I knew long ago, so I saw them again and that felt like making a new acquaintance (or acquaintances) as I didn't know much about them since their departure or since the last time we'd met. Sometimes it went back to a very, very long time!

I also met some new people from this present world, who have taught me things I did not know or made me practise lots of stuff. So I find it interesting and fun and it makes me spend my 'time' usefully - but time here is of no importance. I've had no need for a clock since I have been here, therefore you see, we can do without one! *(I feel emotional and Mum notices)* You will see me again one day Darling, there is no need to cry. You will see me again when you come here too and it's not for now, I am sure, but we meet during your night, you know. You may not remember but I know I see you and we speak to each other.

BR- What about?

About all I do here, about what you want to do with your life. You'll see, it will soon be better. No, I am not predicting, I cannot, but there are a lot of people here on this spiritual side of the world, who look after you and guide you and you will know what to do for best, you'll see.

I don't want you to think you are wasting your time or your life, because you are not! You have a task on Earth and that's why you are there. I have done mine and it's over, thank goodness, because I feel so well here that I wonder why I had not stayed, instead of going to the Earth!

<u>We were destined to be parent/child</u> you see. Now it's done, I am free from my Earthly worries and have so many

133

interesting things to do here that I am jolly glad not to be 'down there' any longer!

My mum has often come to see me with my dad. She keeps doing so of course, that's still the same. We have a link with those we love and have loved, but I don't 'need' them. I am happy they come but I don't have to be guided step by step. For the time being there are not many things I don't know how to do, but no doubt new ones I don't know will come!

My experiences are the same as earlier, but it's mainly to reinforce the power of thought, so that everything is clearer, neat and without ambiguity. I had tried not to get mixed up at the beginning, because it can happen easily. One must think of only one thing at a time and that's what is the hardest! This is because thoughts can be so fast and so muddled up. If one does not separate them, they can become a shambles of objects and events if you are not careful! The person you think of appears, the object appears, the place you think of pops up in front of you! There is enough to lose one's way in all that, it's rather crazy! So that's what I had to learn to separate little by little. Yes, I manage much better but it takes time and practice. I do have time for it, haven't I, there are no limits!

BR- Do you still have your room?

Yes, of course I still have my 'room' as a landmark but it is not what's important. I wander round this place and meet people all the time, whom I can talk to or ask what I want to know. There is no urgency, one takes one's time and it's pleasant.

I did the inventory of my books, did I tell you? They are all so fascinating! They have lots of photos and 'text-films' which are mind-boggling and smashing! It's enough to want to remain deeply immersed in them for hours and centuries, I think! They cover everything but it is <u>mainly to make me understand what is happening here</u>.

Your dad is there as well when he has time, because

he does useful things too. We all do useful things of course, that's why we are happy here as everything is of use, interesting and there is no need to worry. I am afraid this will seem very selfish to you, but know that my heart aches at the thought of having left you so suddenly, without any notice, abandoning you with a lot of work...so I feel guilty on that score.

BR- No, it's not you, it's your body which was worn out and gave up...

Yes I know, but I abandoned you in a way, without really meaning to of course. So I was told here to avoid thinking of it, as long as I am not strong enough to have the strength to do it without being very, very miserable. If I am unhappy, all I do is <u>darken my surroundings and my life here</u> and that does not help you in any way. Therefore I may as well deal with what I do here, settle well and not deviate from that, as long as I don't know how to help you with your lives. You still have your mum you know, you have not lost her, she is there and loves you all. We shall meet again one day my Darling and you'll see everything will be fine then.

21st October 1999 - *Nearly 4 months within 5 days, since Mum's departure. The pen writes 4 letters, which could be a name? I am not sure yet which language will be used though! Then English is spoken, so it's my guide:*

You've been wanting to talk to your mum, to be able to say goodbye before she stops communicating with the Earth world, while she has a trip to our higher realms to be able to understand what it's all about. You have the possibility to communicate once more, we mean now, but you'll have to understand that her state of mind is that of a person who is in a very heightened level of thinking. She has wanted to understand so much and so quickly that we have to let her move on, to be able to understand more at an earlier stage than usual. She is so eager to learn, we can't quench her thirst for knowledge!

That's why she'll go with her loved ones to better and higher places for a while, to learn what is to be learnt, then she will be able to have new links with you.

BR- What do you mean by 'new'?

New in the sense that when she talks to you again, there will be renewed energy and knowledge. There will be more facts, more knowledge, more understanding of what she is doing here and why. She'll be transmitting much more interesting things to you probably. You'll understand each other. There will not be things you can't comprehend enough. That will be for her to explain how she's seen and sensed and understood them. So there'll be a lot of exchanges of thoughts and love at the same time. You'll see, you will be able to grasp, don't worry. The love link is so strong that nothing could break it and there will be again opportunities to talk to each other. All will be well. All is explained now so that you have no pain or fear in your heart.

BR- Sorry I wasted time doubting at the beginning…

You had to doubt a little because you are a human and have truth in your heart and mind. You don't want anything to be false after putting your heart into something.

BR- Who wrote earlier what looks like 'leon'?

(I let the pen write, not thinking about anything myself. It starts in 'Automatic', replying with one word in French to my great surprise, then it adds 4 others after which I hear the rest all in French)

L é o n i e - The first word (*Léon*) is simply the name of the man who has always wanted to be near his daughter. He has not left her side once during her life on Earth. She's always loved him and he wanted to be able to have the joy of seeing her and helping her when she needed it. She's often had problems in her life but he was always there to help her and she knew it.

We know you think of us as <u>your grandparents</u> but we

136

are more than that. <u>We are the parents of the one who gave you life</u> and that's why we are talking to you! The first name was LEON, the second one tried to make itself be recognised as LEONIE but writing it was not easy... We tried to give you something different to soften the sadness you may feel for no longer being able to talk to your Mum for a while.

BR- *What a kind thought! Why do you use 'vous' instead of 'tu' to say 'you'?*

We do not dare to say 'tu' as we have never spoken to you before, have we? It is the first time we do and are not really used to it. I was the first one to speak to let you know I am Léon's wife and your mum's mother. Also I do want to talk to you to get to know you, so that you are not too sad to be parted from her.

BR- *Is Mum still there or has she already 'left' on her trip to higher levels?*

She's popped in to be near you, she is going to speak to you of course. We are not so heartless as to deprive you of your dear mum. But we wanted to make your acquaintance, let's say 'officially'!

I met you when you were very young, but you did not have the same shape as you have now, did you! My friends from here used to let me know everything you were doing as you grew up and how much intensity you put into everything you did and do. I paid attention to that as I was very interested and amused. I am the same, we are from the same mould! We have the same traits of intensity, namely a woman never goes out without being well dressed and a lady does not behave like a trollop. Having said that, I know you have always done, or tried to do, your best and that is what I admire in you my little lady. Also <u>I thank you for the love you have given my daughter, your mum. May I offer you my congratulations, and my condolences for the loss of your Mum on Earth.</u> You do know that the love one has for someone never goes out. The only aim of life on Earth is to meet again beyond all that and come back to the state of 'Spirit' one was before. So my little lady, I thank you for doing your best, because you did help your mum, without always realising to what extent you did, but it was worth it.

We did not want to leave you without having at last made your acquaintance. Her pallor caused by having to leave you to go and learn more made us understand that if we gave you another exciting little experience, it would help you bear the second departure of your beloved mum. She is not meant to go far you know. She will only remain silent for a short time then you will meet her again soon to start again your conversations.

It is not a question of years on your Earth, but several weeks, that's all! By then you will have learnt many a thing which will help you understand what she will come back to tell you. She will have new information and that will fascinate you. 'Novelty' is never ending here! Always, always new stuff, it's smashing, like she says. My daughter is our Suzanne but we also called her 'Suzon' or 'Zann'...yet we can no longer use those pet names, as she has grown up a lot and lived as an adult, she does not feel 'babyish'!

I must confess something: My 'little girl' is not the only daughter I had! She was not the 'only child' she thought she was. I did not have the courage to reveal it to her once she was old enough for us to explain it to her... She had not really lost a brother or a sister herself. She did not know what it was because the baby was born quite a long time before her! It was not a healthy child and she did not last long... That's why I had never wanted to speak about her again... My first daughter did not have a name. I did not want to talk about it to anyone… <u>The desire to live on Earth had disappeared as soon as she arrived and her wish to return to where she had lived before, that is to say the eternity of Spirit World, made her leave her flesh body</u>. But she made us suffer the sadness of the death of a first baby.

It was terrible for us and shook us so much that when

138

Suzon was born, I could not do anything else than love and pamper her and protect her, so that nothing happened to her. She was perhaps a little spoilt, but she was lucky to have us and not have lost her life, so she was worth it.

Personally I never recovered from that death, but I had promised myself to say nothing and never said anything all my life on Earth... It's only now that I am able to talk about it, because Suzanne is with us and knows everything. It feels good to be able to open my heart and no longer hide anything...

She must have had a shock when she was shown my other daughter, as she believed she was an only child! Never had anyone opened their mouth on that matter! We had promised ourselves to never mention it again, that's why silence was kept so carefully...Why for such a long time? I suppose in the end it was no longer important for other people afterwards. For me yes, it was. I always had the sadness within me of having lost my young baby, my little baby. I am sure Suzon would have understood if I had told her. She would have been sympathetic and would have liked to know she'd had a sister, but there we are...one does not always do what people want or expect!

So the mystery of the little sister is clarified, I hope, I cannot do better than telling you myself, that way you'll know what I am talking about. The same thing has been explained to my Suzanne when she came here - we've all had a big family reunion!

BR- Am sorry if I had some doubts...

Oh yes, we know you doubted and doubted, time and again! There is no doubt that you have doubted! Anyway, no more doubts I hope? Finally you are the one who can make the next step, by researching proof of what I told you.

Now we must let your little mum speak, as she has not been able to say one word because I chatted like an old woman! I am no longer old but I had a rather long chitchat,

139

I think... Anyway, if it can help you understand there is only truth in this world where I live and where your mum arrived, there will be more happiness in your heart, joy too I hope.

As soon as she comes back from her 'expedition' for extraordinary knowledge, she will not have to struggle against your doubts, but will have been accepted as she is, a very kind young woman (again!) who wants only to learn about her new life and help those she had to leave against her will.

She has no regret whatsoever to no longer be in her old body, but she cries out of sadness in her heart every time she thinks of you all and she starts to worry again about you. Therefore we decided to make her have this experience so that the final result is better. <u>The solution to her problem: Not to worry any longer so much for your lives so that she can enjoy being here</u> and not become a wreck and in floods of tears each time she thought of it all. We had to give her a lecture many a time in order to get it into her mind. She was so afraid for you and your unhappiness, on top of the pain to have seen her disappear from your lives. We'll have to work hard on you all too.

BR- Touky especially, I reckon.

Yes, we know. He has not had much luck lately, poor man. Everything seems to go wrong. He constantly has problems which appear endless. It will have to stop one day, otherwise he too will end up finding himself here with us!...

(A short silence)... Yes my Sweetheart, now it's me again... There is so much to learn here. They want to make me attend a 'Training course about the Hereafter', can you imagine!.. Me who thought I was going to have a cushy, quiet time in my room-den, there they are, taking me on a ramble into the Great Beyond and its unknown corners!

I don't think it is going to be unpleasant at all, but I know we have been warned that our book will have to wait a little, as I have to buck myself up, get some mental strength in order to be able to tackle the thoughts I wish to have about

140

you… I hardly dare to speak to you or think of you (other than dictating this) as it makes me remember Algiers and Nice and I melt into tears again! The pain is too sharp and deep to have left you so quickly, so suddenly, the worst being without saying goodbye to you…without even knowing that I was leaving! I played myself a nasty trick because I could at least have warned myself I was due to go away!

Yes I know, you are going to 'doubt' again what <u>my</u> mum told you, but you'll see you'll be able to check it up and it will be more than any other proof that you may have had, won't it! I cannot do more myself. I was very surprised indeed to see that young child, who quickly showed herself also as an adult woman, telling me she was my sister, but I could not get it you know, I could not believe it either! So we both have difficulties accepting it!

As usual you have a great need to sleep, so go quickly Sweetheart. Don't worry about me, we'll talk again and we'll have a lot of time together, you'll see. So 'night night', my little Darling. Do get your sleep so as not to be worn out the next day. And prepare yourself well for a big, big surprise when you have the proof that everything I told you is really true, then we'll see who was right, won't we! Goodnight 'my little lady' as my mum calls you...and have lovely dreams of me and you and everybody together. Ta ta! Your Mum loves you forever.

***

CHAPTER 3
Introspection therapy trip - Past lives - Visible light of kindness versus mental dark zones

30th October 1999 - *My guide talks to me, in English as usual, about the 'spiritual work' that I would like and could do. Then, when I ask the question here below, I am surprised the answer is suddenly in French:*

BR- Could you give me some news about Mum? Please do not disturb her! Just explain to me where she is, how she is faring etc...

Everything is well with your mum. She has not gone away, she is neither far nor gone for a long time.

BR- Is that you Mum?

It's not your mum who is speaking but your dad who was waiting for you, to be able to tell you something! Yes, me indeed, I am Dad! I'm going to tell you quickly a few things, so that you have some news about Mum.

She is well and has no time to lose where she is as she constantly has new things to do and see. She has not left her room in a way, but she's <u>had her way of seeing things transformed by a new attitude</u> towards her life here. She is not so afraid of no longer being able to see you and love you. She was filled with that sadness and fear which ate her up. She was hiding it when she talked to you...but she was hurting so much that it was a great pity to see her like that. She used to cry often when we did not see her, because she thought no one knew, but she had tears in her eyes so often that we could see she was miserable to have left you and was not recovering from it. <u>Explaining</u> to her that <u>crying</u>, did not solve things, did not remove her desire nor need, you know. So the other solution was to 'send' her to a world of rest where she feels freer, more healed.

BR- Can you explain in more details?

We'd need so many explanations which are impossible to grasp, to make you understand! It's going to be hard. What must be understood is that life here is not really lived day by day, but from one moment to the other. She needs mental rest and to forget the worries she had on Earth, in order to be able to settle here fully, without that terrible pain that separation causes. Pain must leave her Inner Self, not because we remove it for her, but because <u>she removes it herself</u>.

13th November 1999 -

The pen starts writing the first words in English, so it must be my guide:

You will hear from your mum again but not just yet. She needs a rest, a break and new 'training'. She is not asleep as you'd call it, but <u>she needs healing of the mind, as the sorrow of having left you is still very strong and makes her very unhappy.</u> So she has to be looked after in a way you may not understand.

BR- Try to explain, please…

She has a lot of sorrow in her heart and her heart is the centre point of her Being. So we need to soothe that area by sending a lot of energy in her whole 'Soul body' to help her recover. She loves and loved talking to you, but you need to understand that <u>the suddenness of the parting has left her in a kind of shock.</u> She has been excited by her new arrival here and the lack of pain, but she has also been and is suffering from the loss of her life amongst you all, who mattered so much to her.

She needs to feel she can help you, but at the moment feels she can't, because she is cut off from you all except through you - and the brothers don't really know for sure you have a good link with her. They probably think you may be a bit mad or something like that! As you get some good proof

143

they will recover from this wrong attitude, this way of thinking, but at the moment that does not help your mum, who has lost the ones she loves most and can't quite come to terms with the separation.

We said she needed to learn more because from where she is, life on Earth is a long way away and from where she will be when we have finished. She will have understood, we hope, that you all have a life to live which she cannot control or help in the usual Earthly way, but she can help in a new, different and unusual way. She'll have to learn a lot to be able to cope. (*Unfortunately my eyes closed themselves, against my will…*).

26th November 1999 - *5 months and 12 hours since Mum's passing. I settle down to listen in the hope of receiving some communication; yet I don't know whether anyone will come and talk to me, nor who. The pen starts to write on its own in English, then I hear the rest:*

Even if we were able to, we couldn't tell you exactly how far your mum has gone into her progress towards fitter emotional health, because it cannot be measured in grams or percentage. But we can tell you she is feeling much better already. She has understood there is no point in crying here and she is much calmer and resigned as to wanting to live here happily. She knows she has a task ahead to work with you if you want to and if she wants to, which she does wish to do. That's this book, the famous 'Book of Truths from Beyond'.

So you'll soon be attacking that again, but there'll be times when she needs a break now and then, for her spirits to rise, enlighten and refresh. Then she'll come back to you even more refreshed and enlightened to take your knowledge a step further. That's how it will go for her and for you , so that in the end you'll have produced a fascinating account of one life in the world beyond yours, yet a <u>world so close to yours in spite</u>

144

of appearances. Maybe we'll make the world of Humans comprehend this fact a little better after finishing this work of art, which the book will be. We are looking forward to seeing the result on your paper.

14th December 1999 - *My guide has a few words to say:*

Only a matter of weeks now before you can resume your conversations with your mother and you'll certainly feel a difference when she does, because she will have opened her mental horizons and also her spiritual ones. So, you'll be aware of a transformation in as much as she'll be more profound in her ways of expressing herself. You may think it is not the same person...but it will be, except that the knowledge she will have gained will have enlightened her way of thinking and talking.

BR- Does Mum receive my thoughts exactly as I send them or just a general loving, caring feeling?

As soon as you think a thought, we receive it here. We don't shelter her from your thoughts, we let you do what you want. If you wish to send some loving thoughts to your mum, you can rest assured she receives them. We do not separate thoughts into explanations or caring. If you care enough to send a thought, we get the whole as you sent it and the conversation is continued. You just need to think it and we get it here.

7th January 2000 - *The pen starts on its own, in French:*

Mum here Darling! Yes it's me indeed. I am back and really pleased about it as you waited for quite a long time, didn't you? Let me reassure you it is true I am not playing any tricks. I was not far, I had not gone 'elsewhere' in a way but I visited my 'inner feelings'. I had to grasp what we do on Earth and in 'After Earth life', so it took me some time. I see there will no doubt be a lot to learn, but it was interesting.

BR- Were you alone?

No, I wasn't. The family were there but also my 'spiritual helpers', as we call them. They are people and beings whose level of spiritual knowledge is very advanced; they guided me as I was progressing. I first had to 'face myself' and analyse myself, ask myself who and what I am, why I exist! It took me some time to do it as it's a bizarre thing to have to do. One realises one is no longer a body nor the person one was on Earth during that last period, but a spiritual being on its way towards Infinity in order to improve itself!

Personally it had always seemed weird to me why anyone would bother to do such things! But I now understand that once the flesh body is destroyed, we are left with a 'false spirit body' which is nevertheless the 'Self'. When one thinks about it, one never has a visible Self as it is an inner Self; how one feels, who one thinks one is. I saw myself very differently from what I imagined I was! I am certainly not a saint, not at all! But I perceived myself as if with a new pair of eyes and without worrying because I had to study myself.

One point one must acknowledge is that <u>we have an inner life much more active than we realise</u>. It's absolutely essential to pay attention to it and look into it, because that is what steers us. It is the voice of our 'conscience' or the thought one has with every gesture or decision made. The inner life is what counts, it's the only thing which matters! One becomes aware of it by listening to and analysing oneself, by sensing what one must do.

I decided not to bother much about my surroundings because they really are not that important. It's pleasant to have a home but not essential. Now I prefer to have the freedom to stroll around according to how I feel at the time, as tying oneself down to one particular place is limiting. One must not create restrictions for oneself if one wants to discover more! I know you must be surprised to hear me say this. Yet I have learnt lots

146

of things. I've realised I wasted ever so much time on Earth with all that studying of the Bible, as my friends here explained to me that in Spirit World there is no religion, nor belief in one 'tradition' or another! All we live on is the 'local' air, I mean we don't need to search elsewhere to find Truth. Truth is all around us. When I think I used to believe I had to read all those pages and do all those 'exercises' to reach it! Now I got to it without realising... I had understood one lived on but in a different way; yet I did not know that the pure life of a being is the life of what is called 'god'. The 'God' so much spoken about is ***not a benevolent Being but a way of living which is pure because it is caring and loving*** all the time. The very fact of being lovingly kind is to be 'God' yourself. It is the sign of kindness within oneself.

It is wanting to be kind-hearted and caring for the sake of it, not for 'scoring points' in order to go to Paradise! Personally I live there now so I don't have to 'score points', but since my arrival I saw that the 'air' around us is that eternal shining light which has a strange facet. I was going to say it has 'an attitude' but it sounds weird to say that. The 'air' of our environment is not oxygen etc. it is Kindness, I was going to say 'liquefied Kindness' but no, it has not turned into liquid! So let's say 'aired' or 'aerified' Kindness?! I am making up this word as it is impossible to find words to explain it!.. There are times one can feel happy without knowing why, simply by breathing in what surrounds you.

BR - Breathing in?

I suppose it's not the right word, as indeed breathing is not something we think about here! But do you see what I mean?

BR- Absorbing?

Yes that's it, absorbing. We absorb the 'air', the 'atmosphere' which surrounds us, saturates us and we feel so happy and good within. There is enough to ponder about all this for years!

147

BR- In what way did this help you?

The main gain from this immersion within myself was to discover who I am. That is to say I am no longer the little old lady or a mum (yet I still am yours, don't worry!), but mainly a living being alive in the real life of Paradise, as it is usually called, but let's say, it is the proper and real place to live, not the Earth! <u>The Earth is only there for a temporary stay</u>, then we'll all meet here again without any problem. At the beginning I had difficulty in seeing myself as anything but what I used to know on Earth - me as the mother of my four children. But I had some 'lessons on inner probing' as they call it. I then saw they were right; one feels oneself all throughout life, whatever the situation one is in or whatever one does.

BR- That analysis and those discoveries must confuse you?

No, it does not confuse me because I know I am your mum <u>too</u>, not '<u>only</u>' your mum. That is pleasant as well, believe me, I don't regret it! But it broadens my horizon as, following that, I am no longer obliged to think like a mother but like a Being from this world, that is a Being who has been alive for a long time and has seen other lives apparently!

BR- Have you seen a previous life?

No, not yet. I have not seen other lives but it was explained to me. It would not be worth living only one life if you did not experience the other happenings other lives bring! So that's it. I have found myself again I could say, or I have redis-covered myself as I had forgotten I had lived elsewhere! I did not know I have a wider range and scope within my Soul and Spirit and Thought and inner life than I ever knew! So this is what I have been doing lately. That's why I was told not to chat with you for a while, in order to give me the mental space to do all those exercises. I did not go anywhere else than where I actually was, but I <u>learnt to focus within</u> rather than without. This is why I had the impression of travelling 'elsewhere' because I no longer was in my bedroom-den, but within my thoughts as 'a unique person' instead of 'a many labelled person', as they call it!

BR- Who are 'they'?

The people who helped me do it. I did not have them there all the time but they would guide me now and then with questions and suggestions. Thus I learnt to do a kind of psychoanalysis! I had always thought that sort of stuff was hare-brained...yet I have had to do it too! We do get surprises here, don't we?!

The sadness which filled me when I realised I was here and you were over there has not disappeared! I am still very sad not to be near you as before. But because I did this kind of introspection of my Soul and so on, it helps me understand that I don't need to be miserable, I shan't have to suffer from it forever as we shall all meet up again! After all, I did find my own dad eventually and yours too, didn't I? That demonstrated to me that, though my sadness is real and painful, it is only temporary, since I can easily come close to you by thinking of you and it does you some good even if you are not aware I am doing it! When you feel better or have less problems because I have helped you, I shall feel better as I'll know it's me who gave you a hand!

I still have a lot to do to assimilate all this, you understand, as it's still a shock to be separated from my loved ones, even though they are only a thought away! My bedroom-den no longer has the same importance it used to have.

BR- It's a pity!

It is in a way and in another way it is good. I feel more liberated, I can feel happy to get out of it and not feel obliged to have a rest or stay in it. I feel lighter and freer and that's great.

BR- Sorry for stopping your psycho-analysis! Have you got more to do?

149

I was not told I was to do more but there is always more to discover here...so I wouldn't be surprised if I was made to do something else!

BR- About your sister: I tried to write to Boulogne's archives but there doesn't seem to be anything there. I am disappointed and confused as I want to find the real facts. Can you hear me?

Of course, I am here! The situation is strange indeed! As far as I am concerned, seen from here the situation is: When I arrived I saw a young woman who told me she had been my little sister, yet I had never known her as she'd died before my arrival on Earth! Why isn't she in the archives? I don't understand. I'll go and see what happened and ask Mum and Dad for more details...

(I am struggling to stay awake... Suddenly my guide pops in, speaking in English)

Make the most of your night now to get refreshed. You need your rest. May you be blessed for all your efforts. We shall discuss this another time. *(1am)*

26th January 2000 - *Midnight- The pen starts the first word- In English:*

Understanding the laws of Nature and Truth is quite a feat in itself. We need to explain to you quite a few things for you to be able to grasp what happened. My friend please listen, I am the voice for those who care for you. We have been trying to put together a plan for you to have 'the proof of all proof' for your Mum's book and yours to be published and believed in. We have been working very hard because it is not something which can be concocted overnight, whether in this world or in yours. We know you have been very disappointed by the news that the baby's birth or death do not seem to have been recorded....we know you wanted it badly. The Truth is nonetheless the Truth. The baby <u>was</u> born, the baby was loved but the baby died. That baby was a little girl who had not wanted to stay on Earth longer than that, because she had her own reasons for going back to where she came from. That does not help you but we cannot change what had happened. She was born to Earth life and has known it shortly but was not to stay there. That's why you had not heard of her, yet she <u>has</u> been there!

BR- Who was the mother?

The mother of the baby <u>had her own reasons for not telling people</u> about her new loss, but she was sad inside and was so happy to find her again when she came here herself. We know who she is, you too, you have been told. You know the mother of that baby was the mother of your mother. That's why that baby would have been your aunt, but you never knew her because you had never been told about her!

If we told you we have found a way to help you prove to your brothers you have been talking to your mum, would you believe us? We want so much to help you there. We've tried to find out why the results of that birth and death were not recorded. We only know you have already tried, but we don't know why they have not found it. Perhaps there'll be another place where records could have been kept? You'll have to believe us when we say the baby <u>was </u>born and did die. Many people want the Truth, no one more than us, so do not doubt us please. The baby was born at full term and was a 'proper baby' as such, not a 'failed baby', not a still-born or miscarriage. We do not know why this has not been recorded. There might have been some records destroyed by the war?

(Suddenly French is spoken! It's Mum) A person in danger is someone without faith. You must believe those who help you, even if you do not see them! There is no risk of getting people who are not there to help you but want to trick you, so do not fear this! No, your subconscious is not involved either! All we need is your mind in a quiet state instead of being a

choppy sea. You have no need to be concerned about 'bad spirits' or other unwelcome interventions, as I am told you are very well protected and surrounded. You have quite a lot to do and will do them - they say you have a good 'life plan'. You will do a good job of that book of ours, but we haven't worked at it lately, have we, so we'll have to get back to it! We kept quiet because you appeared confused and bothered by that disappointment about the baby's date of birth etc. Personally I only know what I am told here.

My mum explained to me I had a little sister who died a short time after her birth as her body did not hold out. She did not live long. I know you would like to know more, yet I don't know what I can do for that. I did see that young woman speak to me, telling me she was a sister I had never known, but I must confess I did not quite believe it at first! She smiled and kindly said: "Don't worry, I know what you are thinking and it's normal. I would have done the same." Such a kind smile! I only saw her briefly on my arrival, as everyone was around me and I could not get over it! I cannot say she looked like my mum or dad or me. Yet she did look kind and pleasant. I had not realised the hugeness of this discovery until you discussed it, wanting to find (Earthly) proof which would indeed be very good for Touky and Michou...but I don't know where we shall find them. You can still try and look elsewhere perhaps? My Mum is not near me, I'll have to catch up with her.

BR- Have you already asked her?

No, I did not really spend much time on that, as I had so many other things to accept and put up with! Your thoughts would not have reached me so quickly on the first days if I had not focused my efforts on our communications. My mum did not particularly wish to talk about it and I did not think of asking many questions. My dad did not dare to discuss it as he knew Mum was not keen to speak of it... I know they wanted to give you a surprise by bringing their news and Mum chatted with you for the first time in her life here!

BR- Didn't she see me when on Earth?

Yes she did, when you were very young but she had never communicated like this before, so it gave her a lot of pleasure and amused her! She was not used to doing that. Yet I hear she managed very well. I don't know exactly what she told you so I'll have to ask her.

I do feel like telling you what I have been doing lately, have you got time for it? You should sleep of course, but I shall be selfish and will carry on talking until you feel tired, so as not to lose the opportunity to have you 'on the phone'!

My activities are very varied. I do some mental sport, one could say! I saw myself face on, sideways, upside down, inside out, from all angles! It's incredible to have to do this you know! It is useful <u>because if one doesn't know oneself well, one cannot understand how one reacts and therefore how one creates reality around oneself!</u> This is what they showed me lately. Whereas before I kept wanting to go back near you to help you if I could, I since learnt why I had trouble concentrating. It was because I wanted to be here too much, but I felt obliged to help you as you have chores on Earth. However, I was shown that the <u>mother of her children is not the mother of their Destiny and worrying about them risked creating a shadow around them.</u> If I dread something for you, my thoughts surround you and you are bathed in doubts and anxiety. These could crystallise themselves into a reality, so of course I did not want that for you, me who wants you all to be happy and free from problems!

That is my latest news. I am a 'reformed' mum who has understood that to love and help her darling children, what she has to do is not worry about them. On the contrary she must only think of happy times, good possibilities, everything going well rather than wondering whether everything is going wrong or not well! I must admit it does make sense, if one can communicate by Thought why wouldn't negative thoughts

153

harm? That's my daily lesson, until it's really gone into my head!

BR- Did you receive my thoughts the other day, about the joke I was reading?

Er...no, I don't think so?

BR- You know how Parisians are often the butt of jokes. It's the one about the Parisian who'd gone to the countryside. He walks past a strawberry field. He says to the peasant who was there: "How beautiful your strawberries are! They look delicious! What do you put on them?"

- The farmer replies: "Just manure".

- Really?, says the Parisian, surprised. 'In Paris we put sugar and cream on them!"

Ha ha! I say, that's funny! I'll go and tell it to my dad and yours! Fancy that, we can tell each other jokes between the Earth and the Hereafter! So do not be sad not to see me, I am only a thought away, that means near you. I no longer need to worry about myself for anything. I feel super, marvellously in good shape. My children will always be in my heart and my mind. I shall never forget you my darlings. Go to sleep now, we'll meet up tonight. I'll wait for you. *(01.40hr)*

7th February 2000 - *The pen starts the first words - It's in English so it's my guide:*

Very many people want the Truth of all Truths. It is not always easy to get because of the human factors. If you have no physical proof like papers and photos, you as Humans can't seem to accept it. We have been trying to find out what happened to your mother's sister's records of life on Earth. There seem to be none so far, but that does not mean there had not been any. We know you are desperate for that to happen as we understand it would be good proof for your brothers etc. to realise we do exist in this world. But there has been no trace as far as we know.

154

BR- How do you know where to go?

We know of places where records are kept. We know of names of people who have been there. We make sure we link up to those minds and those papers.

BR- How can you read papers?

Lots of papers have been read by 'Spirits' (as you call us) over the years. It only takes us a moment to go through a paper to see what's written. We focus our mind on it and imprint it with what the paper says and we remember it that way. It soaks in, so to speak.

The lady in question has told us she has no recollection of this time because she had suffered so much of the trauma, she wanted it put behind and forgotten. Make your mind go blank to try to receive your grandmother's thoughts. You'll find you may be able to pick more facts? The result of your search has started forming itself because you want it so badly. We'll try harder and harder again and you need to have that faith and that desire inside you to keep it going. We can do only so much from here and you'll have to do the rest from your end. We know it will be difficult but we also know that the power of a wanting Mind is the best tool there is. You are desperate for that result. Make it happen by wanting it even more so that we can make progress and you too. We know that a Mind in need, a Mind in which a great desire is burning, can only succeed in its search. So make sure you scream for it inside and we'll do the same.

BR- Surely you or 'specialised Spirits' could delve into her Mind and kind of hypnotise her to retrieve facts?

An overall view of our world is difficult to grasp from your world but you have not gone wrong entirely. You say we could delve into the lady's Mind to fish out the facts. We have done so already and she has let us do so. We know she has indeed lost a little one when she was young herself. She had not wanted to remember all her life because it had been so

155

painful and miserable. She is now aware that you need to know, not for curiosity or slander but to help others, including your own brothers. So she will help us more she says, now she knows you must have more proof and we will work on it more, but you'll have to be patient for a while. We know it seems a long time to you!

Make your mind a restful place so that the love of those close to you here is received fully, that way the bond will be even closer and the link stronger. When the link is stronger the facts will be clearer. One last thing from all of us: The love we have for you will never go or die as you know; that love for you will show itself in your life as little events will take place to make it easier and to show you your Spirit Friends (as you call us) are there forever and ever.

Make the world a better place for all those who suffer. Make your aim one goal, as you have the touch of gold when you work with us. One mind, one goal. Make your mind an arrow going to one main goal and you will succeed. Sleep well and may your heart show you the way to the goal of your destiny. You'll find it, we'll help you.

26th February 2000 - *0.30hrs - 8 months since Mum left. Having had a little sleep earlier, I now feel refreshed. The pen starts writing slowly but clearly in French, the letters are linked up:*

How are you my Dearest, it's Mum…(*Then I cannot manage to understand the next words, to my great despair! I try to tell Mum but I still don't understand. So I send, mentally, a cry for help to my guide, hoping he can clear up the 'line'. He responds, in English*)

Make sure your mind is clear of clutter and pay attention to the fact that you are tired and not up to communicating. Your mind <u>is</u> tired. You've had a rest but your mind has been so active all week, you've reached the point it cannot stand still! Make it a 'task' to keep still inside, so that the period of reflection is a period of stillness and the minds of your loved ones can reflect upon it. You have made her try to talk to you but there has been interference from the fuzz, the fogginess in your mind's stillness. There is no stillness in fact and that's what causes the trouble! You have the willingness but not the tool. <u>The tool of a still mind is the secret of communication with us</u>. We can't talk to a crowd or a noisy room, we can only talk to a quiet, receptive mind. Many people try to communicate but don't understand that we need a good recipient for our communications and that makes it complicated.

BR- Yet I hear you talking to me!

We know you hear us but she has had trouble trying to get through because you have been 'in the way'. Receive better and you'll hear better...*(Suddenly French is spoken, it's Mum)*

Yes I hear you. You are going to tell me off for not talking to you earlier but I could not manage to hear you and understand you. I tried to write with your hand *(Automatic Writing)* to make you understand I was there and it's better now. I waited a long time to have you 'on the black phone', as it feels as if we have not chatted for a very long while... Now it's ok, I want to make the most of it! I saw lots of other people since I arrived and told you many things, but I have met even more people! They are so pleased to see me and are so kind... Also they explained lots of stuff to me. I want to tell you about it if we can manage. I tried to make a journey using my mind since you last listened to me. I wanted to go and see Touky and Michou and I tried. It is not that easy when one is not used to it but I wanted to practise.

One has to concentrate very hard on the person and one sees them in one's thoughts, telling oneself: "I want to go there now!" On opening one's eyes again, one sees where they are, or at least one senses them near. That's what has to be practised to get used to it - not to let go of the thought of that person one has in mind and hang on to it.

I managed it, more or less, I think... I saw Touky in his boat, he had a tool in his hand. I pretended to be there myself in order to really hang on to the picture of this visit - I told myself I was on the boat and I wanted to be able to see him better. I did everything I could, that is I concentrated hard on him. He had a tool in his hand, I don't remember what and he was working with it. He thought he was alone but I was there indeed! I reckon he did not realise it. I wanted to speak to him but I don't think he could hear me...

When I went that time, I only saw his thoughts and this picture of him at work; but I was told that if I manage to do it often I shall be able to see him in more details and remember better. I tried once or twice more but did not always succeed. I'll have to have a go more often. Of course I was sad not to be able to speak to him, but I knew straight away it would not work the first time, so my sadness is only temporary. I must try again to practise until it works properly.

He probably won't have a mind as open as yours and he might not see me, but I must try to find a way to let him know I still exist, so I have to have another go! At first he seemed to be squatted but I am not sure: He looked busy and I could not see more details because I was not very good at concentrating long enough to grasp what was going on around him... Sweetheart, I heard your 'distress call', you had difficulties hearing me because your thoughts are not calm. You need to relax more, that would help the communication. My own thoughts are calm here because I don't have any worries fortunately, but I feel you still have some and I am sad for you.

BR- Please send us your kind positive thoughts!

Yes I know, I do it all the time. I love you so much I can't help wanting to help you more and that's what is so frustrating... I am going to attend relaxation classes like you I think, as I am not as calm as I should be to be 'perfect' here! I have moments when I feel happy because I do not suffer any more and have no more worries, but I also have times when I forget I must not worry about you and I do it... which does not help things here, does it! So it causes problems with my surroundings... I see everything dismal and the 'sun' of my surroundings becomes all grey, which reminds me I did something silly! So you see, I am learning to calm down but it does not always work! On the other hand I really had fun with the 'practical exercises' as I call them, the tests one can do here. It's always very fascinating, always very useful and always very true... As you always told me, you will say! But it's correct, everything we do here is so good and so pure. How could one imagine it is wrong to be in this world and talk about it! <u>I cannot see how some people dare to speak ill of our communication with the Earth. It's dreadful this is so 'blackened'</u>!

I had a few 'lessons' here or there with specialists who helped me to do things I could not do well... Always to do with the Mind and manipulation of Thought or one's own attitude. <u>That is how one progresses</u> they explained to me. <u>By understanding oneself, by seeing what one does well or not, with such or such a way of thinking</u>. If one does not succeed at once, it does not matter, there is no exam at the end! Me who hated exams... I always had a headache before tests so now I don't risk getting one, do I?! *(I give Mum some news about the family)*.

I heard what you've just said, you spoke of your kids and brothers, yes. I felt rather than heard, it's weird isn't it?! Indeed I sensed what you were saying...yet it was a 'feeling of pictures' and I 'saw' what you were telling me. About Anne-France's car accident - it's a good job she was not injured or killed (though it would not have been terrible for her to come here, I would have been welcoming her, as you can guess!). Also you talked of your brothers, your Jim and all that. Yes, it's so good to get some news that way! I don't know whether I would be able to do the same and put images in your head so that you see where I am and what I do. It would be great wouldn't it?!

BR- What about Dad? Your parents?

My dad has not often got any free time because he works as an 'angel helper' as I call it. He helps those with problems; he gets them to understand what they must do to cope with their problems.

BR- People where you are or on Earth?

Yes, people from here, not those on Earth of course! He teaches them to open their mind, to see themselves as 'a large quantity instead of a small quantity', if you see what I mean. There is so much to understand about oneself here, it's incredible! He has understood all that himself of course, so he passes it on to others! He has always been a good teacher, I am not surprised he can do that. I shall never forget how much he helped me when I was little, with learning to read etc...

BR- Do you see your mum? Has she spoken of your sister? If I had some clear details I could perhaps find some proof in archives?

My mum? Yes, it's a problem as I can't get to know exactly what happened! Yet it should be easy, shouldn't it! I only see her from time to time, she has her own occupations too. She helps Dad in his 'guardian angel of angels' job, as I call it and I am busy myself...

Yet she accepted to admit there had been a baby before me!.. It's not a 'he' but a 'she', as it's a girl. I don't know why she died. I am quite happy to try again and to tell them we need details to help you have some proof. It does not look important seen from here I think, you know, but I understand what you mean.

BR- Could she have had the baby before her marriage?...

Mum is not the kind of woman who would have done 'anything naughty' before getting married, as you can guess! So don't go and offend her by asking her that! But I don't know why

160

she does not talk about it. Perhaps because she would have to make a big effort to see herself again in that situation of long ago?

BR- Couldn't you ask your dad, or your sister?

Darling, I don't know what to tell you regarding that matter. I can only try to do what you suggest, so that we obtain some details which can help you trace where, when and who she was. That's all I can try to get...

BR- Do you see my dad?

Your dad? He always looks busy and he is. He has his 'work' of rescuing Souls arriving here and he has also other activities. Amongst others, he is interested in the physics of this environment, why and how everything functions, but personally I find that too complicated!

BR- I want to apologise for not talking to you more often, it does not mean I forget you or no longer love you! I love you so much, Darling Mum!

There is no question of me imagining you forget me or don't love me, my poor Darling! I know how busy you are and I do not doubt for a moment you do wish to speak to me and write our book! So don't fret, it does not matter if we can't talk for some time. We'll catch up the next time! It feels so good to speak to you, I don't want to be selfish and ask we do it all the time... On the other hand, there may be nothing else to say after a few minutes if we did it all the time! So there may as well be intervals, it makes things more interesting when one has something to talk about! But I love you as much as before and perhaps more, if that's possible!

BR- Do you still have your 'room'?

My 'room-den' still exists of course, it's my point of reference and my 'niche'. However I don't live in it all the time. I have other places where I go - gardens, pretty and pleasant places, rooms, places where we meet which are interesting, where one does not pay attention to the décor but more to what we do there, if you understand that?

161

BR- I do understand. Have you and I met again at night?

At night your body sleeps, you must be exhausted indeed! And your mind is tired too, so you sleep most of the time! We have met sometimes and I did love those moments because we see each other so well, we feel so close to each other; but it only happens sometimes, when your mind is freer to come here. I do not know when you are going to come... It's only at the last moment I am told you are there! You 'appear' so to speak, so we meet and it's ever so good! Good night Sweetheart, go and sleep quickly, you do need it indeed. I love you, I don't forget you!

26th March 2000 - *9 months since Mum left us. The pen writes in French:*

Mum here Darling, I am no longer in flesh and blood, yet I am very near you and you don't realise it! <u>I come close to you in thought, it's very simple. All I have to do is think of you and I am there</u>... I see myself near you. I am not always sure where you are, as far as a physical place is concerned, but I feel you are there and I am near you.

BR- Do you know you've been gone for 9 months?

No, I must admit now I don't have any notion of duration of my absence. I have been here for quite some time I reckon, but I feel as if it is a long time... I realise I am really familiar with my environment now and I am well used to it. I no longer have that impression that everything is brand new, different and weird. On the contrary, it feels good to know where one is and not to suffer any more. That's the main thing: not to have any chores, not to worry about what will or won't happen, not to be afraid to fall and to suffer once more! Therefore I enjoy being here and do not worry any more.

BR- Good! I am delighted, you deserve it indeed... Are other people interested in what happens on the Earth?

The situation of people on Earth is sometimes a great topic of discussion here. Yes, I noticed a lot of people are concerned about what is taking place on the Earth, in general and in particular. The other people I meet don't always have someone on Earth whom they love- yet it worries them, in a way, to see what is going on in the world. I understand people being concerned, but when one has just left it, it feels good not to have to worry any longer. That's why it seemed strange to me that they bother to spoil their 'paradise' with that!

Yet come to think of it, it is very kind of them to want to help those left behind, because after all, we in this world, are very lucky to be here! It's you poor unhappy things who have to struggle with your problems of wars and battles etc...I do see now that it seems unfair not to like other races; it does not mean I understand everything in that subject, but I know it is not right not to want to have a neighbour who is an Arab or any other nationality...

Personally I could not help thinking like that, because we did lose everything after the war in Algeria, the house and all that!.. But I know now that wars are only one way for populations to reduce themselves and to avoid starting again the same thing another time, if one has understood the lesson it gives you!.. Yet people don't seem to learn!

BR- How did you learn all this?

I learnt it because they proved to me here, that I was wrong not to want to think good of Arabs and other invaders. Personally I used to think I was right, but at the bottom of my heart, in a way, I knew it was not quite fair, because I did like that poor Messaouda for example *(A middle-aged Arab neighbour who used to come and help Mum with housework)* and I know she would not have harmed me. But as a whole, people and politics are horrible! So I had to learn to see all that in a different way now... I know you were angry with me when I wanted to be racist and you thought I was a 'disgrace', you

163

were ashamed of me...yes, I knew you were not pleased... As for me, I only knew what I was feeling and thinking at the time.

A man on Earth has the right to choose his point of view. But *if he chooses in such a way that his decision harms others, he harms himself,* do you see? That is what they made me understand and I wanted to make sure you knew it too, so that you do not make the same mistake.

BR- But you have always been kind, you have never hurt other people!

No, I have not harmed anyone as far as I know, but I would have been glad to 'strangle' all the Arabs who made us lose Algiers and the rest! So I was not as 'saintly' as you think, you see! But I have learnt since, that my 'virtue' was not 'not to harm certain people yet want to kill others'! That was not a virtue! I only wanted to do some good to those whom I deemed deserved it in my eyes... That was my error apparently. I can see it now, but it had to be demonstrated to me, as I really thought I was right! My point of view now is: If one wants to do some good, one must do it to everybody, without any concern about race or other things and that is the hardest... My ideas are gradually changing now... Me and women with straight hair, do you remember? Yes, I hated that! I am not sure why...

BR- Perhaps because you had curly hair yourself when you were little?

Yes, perhaps it's because I had curly hair in my younger days but I don't know whether it's that... My ideas have changed now!

The history of France was very interesting, I still like it you know, I have not forgotten what I taught myself, but I understand better why you told me it was not of much use... *(Indeed I made such a remark once, just in passing though as kindly as possible! I feel guilty now to see she remembers!)* I got a bit upset when you said that, I think - well, I was not really, but a little saddened perhaps. Yet you do understand I used to

164

love it and I was surprised you did not grasp I thought it was important! Perhaps I shan't remember all the dates and all that now, but the main thing is to remember that Mankind's history is not <u>one</u> story but lots of stories added one to the others and linked together. That's what made it fascinating, because the facts of some people became the facts of others; they 'played games' against each other in a way, a kind of tennis match, the ball going from one side to the other, some do such and such and it affects the others.

BR- What's the format of your discussions with your friends? (I lose my concentration for a brief moment, but Mum comes back online)

It's me, yes I am here. Sorry... I am online again. So your question was: What's the format of those discussions? I don't think we would call them discussions, it's more by exchanging ideas with people here that I learnt to open my mind... More towards a 'universal acceptance' let's say, than accepting philosophical, political or religious theories. I mean we don't sit down to discuss such subjects with parties for or against, but rather to exchange ideas. Those who have been here longer than I have began to make me understand that I may not be correct to 'incarcerate myself ' into certain ideas.

BR- Who?

These are good people from the four corners of the world, we'd say. Some of them 'died' a long time ago and it feels really strange you know, to tell myself I talk to some 'old dead'! Then I tell myself I too am an 'old dead woman', except that I was old indeed when I 'died'! I find it funny because I am what we used to call 'dead' whereas I feel so good to be in a 'dead person's skin'! I am quite happy staying in it! I've done everything I could to know whether I had to reincarnate one day but they did not give me an answer on that subject...

BR- Who are 'they'?

'They' are people I speak to when we meet. My hope to

see you all again is very strong and really comforting you know. I told you I had trouble at the beginning not to worry about you all after abandoning you. Well I still do in a way of course, because I want everything to go well for you all, but I learnt I must think of you in a different way, so I try to only think in a positive and 'fruitful' way.

We all know now we shall see again those we love. We know it for sure and we do not doubt it, because after all, we have indeed met those we loved who had gone before us haven't we?! So we know we'll see again all the others left behind, like you and the boys. I for one can't wait to have the pleasure to be all together once more, that way we'll be able to talk to each other so easily, like I do here with the dads and my mum and my new friends. I don't only have old friends, I made some new acquaintances by questioning people, by accepting to discover new things. So there I am, spending my new life discovering new stuff or 'reinforcing' my knowledge of concepts I knew at the bottom of my heart to be true but I had not taken the time or the trouble to delve deeper into it.

BR- Are there courses or lectures, or is it your parents?

No, not really courses or conferences, but rather discussions, in passing, with my new acquaintances, then we think about it later. My parents aren't always there, no I don't always have discussions with them. It's rather people from here, I mean <u>other</u> people, as I am from here too and so are Mum and Dad of course. We talk and we help each other that way. I suppose it's more. They help me and I learn to open my mind, as you would say…

BR- When I cry thinking of you, does it sadden you?

<u>If you cry, my Darling, it saddens me automatically</u>, as you can guess! <u>I cannot 'not sense' you</u>…

BR- It must surround you with 'greyness' then?

No, not so much greyness as my feeling sad for you and wanting to console you. So <u>it changes my thought focus, what I</u>

was thinking about, in order to concentrate on your sadness and try to remove it. I mean I think of you with love and try to wipe off your tears and the sadness in your heart and soul.
(I am suddenly interrupted, then tune in again).

...Am still online, not got cut off! I was telling you it feels funny to speak of 'people from here' since I am part of it too! I know Earth people think people from the Hereafter have powers superior to theirs, at least often. Unfortunately I personally don't have any, I warn you. I am only me, as I was before. I can only love you as much or more if possible, but that's all. In fact it's difficult to imagine myself being able to do all sorts of impossible things: I mean personally I cannot predict your future on my own for example, I would not know how to do it.

I did ask to be shown, but it does not work like that. I had been warned I would not be able to do it, or not yet anyway. But it makes one feel like being able to, when one knows you are alone trying to cope on your own and me here so far in a way, without being able to help you - it's maddening! Yet I am told I must not fret! It's frustrating when one thinks of it, so it's better not to think. Simply concentrate on loving you, hoping all will be well constantly, in order to help you that way.

Sweetheart, if we could talk night and day I would do it, you know, but you would not last long at that rate. I am going to let you sleep but I'd like to reassure you that we do meet at night, very often you know. I see you, you see me, we love each other, we talk, we understand each other, we exchange ideas and that's all that matters. I show you where we are when we meet, the meeting area, a pleasant place so that Earth people can come and talk with us here and meet each other again but without getting lost.

BR- What do you mean?

If they went further in this world, they would get lost. They would not know how to behave or find their way round; it's got to be more like the Earth than like here for them to cope

167

better, so I come to join you here. We meet, we feel happy together, that's what it is for: To feel good together, to warm our hearts by seeing each other again. The heart of the Soul of course!

I am only going to tell you one more thing: I learnt to no longer be frightened of heights and be dizzy! I never liked heights and I had vertigo at the edge of cliffs etc... Well, here, no, I suppose it's because I don't have a solid flesh body. I 'flew' from one place to the other, with the dads at first and now I can, from time to time, do it by myself: I go somewhere simply by thinking about it, it would give me vertigo if I had not been cured of it! Before (on Earth) it was not possible, now it is! When one is in the air without noticing it because one thinks of something else, one would risk feeling giddy and to have a shock too! So it does help...

BR- Can you give me some news of my Dad? Your parents?

Nic, still the same, has lots of new interesting activities in physics. My parents? Doing their own things. Dad helped me a lot at the beginning. He still comes from time to time but he does what he has to do too, so we meet when we think of it, without any obligation.

BR- I do need to try to have names and dates about your sister. It's about 100 years ago... Archives are hard to obtain...

Yes I heard you. I'll try again. My mum does not like talking about it because it is old and ancient stuff and she has met her again here, but we need to know, don't we?! To help the boys. So I'll talk to her again about it. I give you a big kiss before letting you go to sleep. Thanks for coming.

21st April 2000 - *00.15am. I link up just in case. It starts in 'Automatic', in French:*

Mum would like to speak to you, it's easier in your head than to make the pen move.

168

BR- How do you do it?!
I hold it by the end and I push it.
BR- Which one, yours or mine?
Yours. I feel there is a pen in my hand, I <u>imagine</u> there is. I think of you and I 'see-sense' a pen and I make it move... I'd like to tell you that you are not sensible to stay up so late once more! I've fixed it for my friends here to give me lessons on everything there is to learn, in order to be able to discover it as soon as possible. When I have a discussion with them, I always have loads of questions; it helps me understand better what life here is about. Better, of course, is to live here, that way one knows what they are talking about! There is so much to say and discover! I am going to make you understand something:

There is within oneself a Being who is 'human' in one way but 'divine' in another. The hardest is to understand the 'divine'. If one ponders a little, one realises that human life would not have existed if there had not been a 'divine' contribution, that is to say, from outside, by 'someone superior'. That's what is hard to grasp for good when one is on Earth. I remember trying to understand all that but it was not easy and nothing seemed true. The experience of love for one another is a weak comparison to the love given to us by the 'God' some talk so much of...

(I succumb to sleep, embarrassed once more!)

23rd April 2000 - *The first word is in French and in 'Automatic':*
How can we prove our existence to you if not by speaking to you? We cannot do more than that, I think.
BR- Who is there?
I am Dad, darling!
BR- Mum's dad?
No, yours. I am your dad. I heard your requests and I

feel you wish so much we could help you find proof of the existence of Mum's sister. Yes she is here, I have seen her. It was at the same time as when Mum arrived but I didn't know her before. She came to welcome Mum to surprise her…and it was indeed a surprise!

I don't know how we are going to 'prove' it to you all! Archives are not always correct as facts are often missing. I don't know what one needs to do for that.

BR- Ask my grandmother please?

I can't really bother her with this, I'll get Mum to do it… That lady is not always near me, I don't really know her well, yet her daughter was your Mum… I'll see whether I can do more.

As far as I am concerned, I ended up settling down in a more interesting place. I make 'trips' one could say, to new and different places. I have acquired another kind of knowledge, different from the things I learnt before. We all have tasks to do here, that's what is interesting to start with. Then <u>one has to get to know oneself</u> and it is weird indeed to discover who you really are when you think you are otherwise.

BR- What did you discover?

Me!.. It's rather personal you know, but one sees oneself more as an eternal Soul than as someone with a certain gender or job.

BR- You don't feel like my dad, then?

No, I still am your Dad, but I also feel that this is only one facet of my personality, and that I must have a larger vision and outlook and go further in my understanding of things.

The Earth is made up of so many things, yet it is still the Earth, as a 'ball.' <u>I am made of so many things and yet I am not 'just your dad'</u>, I have a more important aspect if you like - or rather I could say, a wider span than being a father at such date or in such era! This is not to diminish my importance as your dad, but to explain to you <u>I have other sides too</u>.

BR- Can you explain, please?

My personality is not just one person now. I understand that I have lived before this life when you have known me and I shall live others if I choose to do so. I saw I had lived before and this taught me that what I did in that life was only one part of many other aspects which I am made of, which are 'me'. My darling daughter, this is difficult to explain, I have trouble putting it into words.

BR- That's ok. Are you aware of our physical mediumship experimental group?

My friends in this world taught me there are people who do the experiments you speak of. I know you go there but I have not gone myself, because one needs to be in a special state of mind to get closer to them. It's hard to explain. It's a mixture of understanding and knowledge and desire to take part in experiments and be able to bring something to their researches.

BR- Do you know what they're aiming at?

No, I am not sure what they want to achieve exactly. I suppose it has to do with materialising objects or similar, making things visible. I don't know what that group does, I have no idea about the final results. We'll see!

BR- You don't seem very excited by all that!

Sweetheart, I am not really knowledgeable in that field.

BR- (A little surprised) Who is speaking to me?

Me! I am your dad of course, I have not changed!

BR- I thought you were deep into studies of physics…

A little at a time, not everything in one go! I looked at and examined interesting facts which have to do with physics yes, but I am not an expert regarding everything to do with physics! My life here is not difficult, all I have to do is enjoy what I see and do, there is always lots to discover.

BR- Did you create for yourself or do you feel in a particular place?

A 'place' is not necessary, is no longer necessary when one has settled properly here. One knows one no longer needs to look after one's body, so one does not bother about one place or the other, one only concentrates on what one does for fun. To be interested in or to teach oneself more, is not necessarily done in one place or the other, you understand? People who surround me are those whom I speak to and whom I share my discoveries and interests with. I have lots of such friends.

BR- Are they members of your family?

I have more new friends here who deal with all this than members of my own family, but I did see them and do see them from time to time. They are busy with what they want to or need to do. I deal with my own pursuits, they with theirs and we see one another from time to time when we think of each other, but that does not mean we no longer love each other. We are in different worlds, we have so much to discover or deal with...

BR- Do you still rescue lost Souls? (But to my great surprise, Dad does not reply to this, he must be following the thread of his own thoughts!)

The world I live in here is the real world. You only realise it once you are well settled here! There is no comparison with life on Earth where everything is so hard and difficult to do. Here we can do what we want simply by thinking of it, that's what is wonderful! Why have to struggle on Earth? It's incredible one could want to go back to it, isn't it! We feel so well here...*(Those last lines sound so much like what Mum often says, I wonder whether by any chance she is 'online' now)*

BR- Is it still you speaking Dad?

Of course it's me Dad! Why do you think I am no longer here? I am. I wanted to tell you something else. Last time we spoke, I told you I had done some research in physics and that's probably what you were talking about. I have not suddenly become a 'physicist' but I am interested in what goes on related to physics. Well, I think I have indeed understood that the <u>light here is</u> not sunlight or electric light, but <u>vibrations of sheer Kindness</u>. That's why the dark zones, where those who have been nasty live, are deprived of this light because <u>it does not emanate from them</u> of course, since they are not kind enough in their heart, as long as they do not regret what they did.

That is why I have understood that <u>kindness and compassion have a light of their own. That is what illuminates here as long as one thinks that way</u>. If one started becoming nasty (it would not happen of course, but I say 'if ') we would have dark 'clouds' all around us and 'darkness' if we carried on.

BR- How can an emotion become a light?

One does not really know how it changes. I don't, I can only see the result. It is incredible how the light becomes even more beautiful when a superior Being comes near us!

BR - Who are those superior Beings?

I had the opportunity to meet someone like that. It's difficult to grasp I suppose, but they are people who have knowledge far, far superior to ours, to mine and who are so kind when they speak to you...they have infinite patience!

BR- Can you describe them?

I see them when they come, because they want to tell me or tell us something important. They appear 'normal', <u>but I know they are what I call 'superior' because the light changes as soon as they approach</u>.

BR- Where do they come from?

We realise they are <u>from elsewhere,</u> that is to say <u>levels of Thought better and superior to ours</u>, but I have never asked them where they came from, because it is not the sort of thing one is concerned about, you know! We are too pleased they want to explain something to us which we may have not understood properly.

BR - What kind of things?

I made some mistakes at the beginning. For example, I did not know how one had to look after others before oneself, or what to do to travel by thought. All that was explained to me by total strangers who appeared at the right moment to tell me what to do. So I thought you may like to know all this. For me it was new and I am still excited about it, because it took me some time to realise that mysterious light was internal in a way, shining outwards from within according to the emotions and the way of thinking and feeling. Very interesting, don't you think so?

Mum is well, she copes very well where she is. She has created a life for herself, learning a lot and she is happy to occupy herself that way!

BR- Did you all help her?

Yes, we worked at it here, all those who looked after her. She had a great need for resting and healing her Soul, because she was suffering from no longer being with you all and was worrying, in fact was terribly worried!

But we showed her that one's attitude of mind here must be different from the attitude one has on Earth. We grasp sooner or later it is useless to fret, as one has not got the means to change anything whatsoever for you the way we could perhaps do it on Earth, for example to do with money. Whereas here everything is different, one has to concentrate on the positive side. If the positive side is full of love and affection it will reach you and that way will help you a lot to change things so that they are more comfortable and favourable for you. So poor Mum had to learn to do that as quickly as possible, not to give way to despair for having 'abandoned you to your fate' as she kept saying.

Her communications with you were good except you had trouble believing it was her... I kept telling her there was no need to worry, that you would believe in it and that she

174

should be glad you paid attention to what you received! But she dreaded you may stop talking to her for fear of receiving 'nonsense' from someone pretending it was her. She was often frightened you may decide not to talk to her anymore, but she seems calmer about this now... *(I was disturbed therefore interrupted.)*

8th May 2000 - A *short silence then I hear the words, in French. It's Mum:*

The help we get here is amazing. As soon as I need to know or understand anything, all I have to do is think about it. Help arrives in the shape of someone who is knowledgeable in that field. It's fantastic, all I need is to think of it! I followed the efforts made by someone trying to understand something and I saw that's what he did, and realised it worked for me too.

BR- Who comes?

All kinds of people, not always the same ones. All they need is to have some knowledge of what we think about and they come to help, it's wonderful! The other day I wanted to know what to do when ideas I had were not materialising 'as I was used to'! (Fancy that!..)

Well, all I had to do was wonder about it and the 'apparition' who came explained **the intensity of my thought had diminished,** the thought had only crossed my mind slightly, **I had not thought intensely, therefore it had reduced the current which is necessary for the creation of what I wanted to see appear.**

That's why we must really put our heart into it, then we can see our efforts rewarded. It is simple but putting in some mental effort is essential.

The necessary effort here was to create something I really did want to create. It was more important than lots of passing, volatile, thoughts. A mental effort creates when one thinks of something really very, very hard from the bottom of one's heart, with lots of inner wishes. One absolutely must want it.

Personally I only have wishes to learn more in order to speak to you about it and to help you. I don't want anything for myself as I don't really need anything here, as you can guess, now that my body doesn't cause me any more hassle. That means if I think of something it's to learn more, so I don't need to be concerned about everyday things. I simply want to know more, understand more and be able to do more, so as not to depend upon others here and not to abandon you without helping you as much as I can. My life had one single aim you know - only look after the four of you. Therefore I find it very difficult not to have to do it any longer. When I was told I must no longer worry, just like that, I thought they were mad! How can you stop fretting for those you loved all their lives and all your life and 'not worry any more', especially when you have just left them so suddenly!

As you know, I didn't realise I was going to leave so quickly and so early... I would indeed have liked to see you again a bit longer and speak to you and say goodbye or something like that...

On the other hand I suppose it would be harder to know one is dying and one is going to leave without being able to come back physically... Come to think of it, I am not sure whether it would have been such a good idea after all, hey! For you too, it would have been harder I assume? I don't know...

Anyway, now I live just to learn more, understand more and do what is needed to progress here, make myself understood, make them understand I have only one aim - to help you and not need others to do it. I want to do it by myself. For that, apparently one needs to 'study' a lot! One cannot simply make money or good health materialise in a flash! One must be taught how to manipulate Thought and that's what I must learn to do very quickly or as best as possible.

BR- Touky has some clients, I think…

But it's not enough to have some clients! What is needed is stability, regularity and the necessary quantity of clients and money. So I am working at it. At least I am working on learning to help create all that. No doubt it will take time, but I will not let distance between us spoil the possibility of helping you.

My despair was when I realised I would not see you all again for a long time… It hurt a lot as I wanted to tell you once more how much I love you and I could not… I wanted all of you to succeed and I could not make it happen any more than before! I had so much hope for you, so many wishes... I always want everything to go well for you all.

So, if I have become an 'angel' since I am now a 'Hereafter-ese', at first I reckoned I'd be able to manage it…but it will take longer than I thought, I can see that now! That's why I work relentlessly to achieve something before you are all 90 years old and join me here!

BR- Please don't worry Darling Mum!

I want to see you happy and reproach myself for having gone too early.

BR- Do you see your mum and your sister?

Mum? Yes I see her from time to time, when she is not busy with her own pursuits. My sister no, I don't know exactly where she is.

BR- Ask her to come? To explain and prove her existence?

I've already said that to Mum, but there is something which seems to prevent her from remembering…

BR- It's important…can you ask for her to be helped?

I did try already, but I'll try again. I understand you have good reasons to want to succeed. We do have quite a lot of work you and I, haven't we?! Having to convince Touky, that will take time- Pierre even more, I think!

BR- It will help Humanity too! I beg you, ask your mum!

I am quite happy to do it! We'll have another go.

BR- Think of your sister with affection, call her, and your mum...

The first try was not a success. When I tried to make Mum remember, she seemed to be unwilling to talk about it! I know she came to speak to you but she did not appear willing to give any details!.. I too wanted some. After all, I never had a sister and as soon as I arrived here, I was suddenly introduced to one! It was incredible, I could not believe my eyes! But after this initial shock there were not many explanations. As I was too busy getting settled, I did not ask for more. When I have grasped the details, I'll be the first one to talk to you about it.

An important detail not to be missed is that the 'Solemn Communion' or 'Confirmation'*(Catholic ceremony for 12 year old girls who usually wore elaborate white dresses!)* was a farce as far as I was concerned! I did not want to take part in it as I knew it was rubbish. I thought one cannot go to communion dressed like that, one should be dressed more like a nun - but because saying that upset everyone and Catholics in particular, I stopped arguing... I had lovely clothes of course, because Mum always made sure I was elegant and well-dressed. But the dress itself did not look spiritual, there were silk and lace and pearls and all sorts of things far too posh to be like a 'Sister'! As far as I was concerned, to make some religious vows I wanted to look like a nun rather than a bride! But no one wanted to listen to me!

Ah well, it does not matter now you know. I just happen to remember it, so I told you. I also always wanted a talking doll, that's why I had bought one for Cécile *(her other grand-daughter, Touky's child)*, because my dolls did not talk really. They may have made a noise but did not talk.

<u>My childhood memories are coming back to the surface from time to time, it's strange!</u> I often have moments when I remember things on Earth, when I was little, I don't know why it comes. Thinking about it feels both good and funny because

178

I <u>see myself again, mentally, like a little girl!</u> So I live that again and wonder what I used to think in those days.

The 'solemn Communion' was one of those memories... weird, isn't it! I used to see others make a fuss and show off, it exasperated me. I know we probably made some fuss too, but if we did I did not realise it. Yet I thought all that dressing up idiotic, as usual. Children do not always appreciate what parents do for them, do they?! I was possibly like that too? My mum exerted herself to make sure I had elegant outfits, yet I really did not care at all about it, especially when I was younger. One does not feel at ease in clothes one has to take care of!

BR- It must teach you something to live all that again?

I don't know yet what, nor why it happens from time to time and it is becoming more and more vivid.

BR- It seems to be like the beginning of 'a film of your life'?

My life as a film? Yes I suppose, it has begun. From my being little, so it may be that, we'll have to see how it develops, won't we!

One thing is certain: <u>Death does you good!!</u> One becomes younger, one feels free, one is not in pain anymore, one has some time for oneself; one can learn interesting things and one is not afraid of suffering or dying! So, what is there better than being 'dead', hey? My life has only one regret - not to have had better health during the last years when I could have gone out more or not suffer. I would have liked to be more solid on my legs and not be in pain or have worries like I had. That spoilt the pleasure of living. It's probably why my body gave up.

But my Self 'inside it' did not want to leave, you know. I did not want to abandon you at all, it never crossed my mind. I was sometimes upset by what went on and I was sad and panicky, but never, ever did I think I was going to abandon you so suddenly, without any warning! So please, do not think I no longer wanted to be with you, because that is not true!

I love you all from the bottom of my heart and adore you all my little darlings. I shall never forget you and will never leave you, if at all possible. I'll try to do everything I can from here to love you, help you and teach you things. That way at least I shall have the impression I have not betrayed or abandoned you. I know you don't think I have but me, I feel as if I have done so, without doing it on purpose of course!

BR- Don't worry! It's bad for you! Do you feel my loving thoughts for you?

Your thoughts are coming towards me like lovely warm water on one's face when one has a wash, do you understand? It feels good, really good, I assure you! I guess it's your thoughts because I feel suddenly so good and well, without knowing why. Since you've just told me, I know it is coming from you, so that's the sensation it gives, it really feels great.

Sweetheart please don't cry for me anymore. You must have shed enough tears like that. I am indeed well, I assure you, believe me. I don't want you to tear your Soul apart.

BR- Oh! Sorry, you must have felt my tears...I am just upset for you because you sound so unhappy to have had to leave us.

I did not feel your tears, fortunately, but I do not want you to shed any, as there is no longer any reason for you to do so.

BR- Yes there is, you are not there anymore!

Yes I am, I am near you! I have been speaking to you for quite a while, haven't I? Therefore I am here! And I shall be even more, as I learn how to communicate and help you better. So you see we are not parted, all you have to do is take up your pen and we are together.

BR- I know... Have you got any idea of Time: Present? Past?

Time does not flow like it does on Earth. The 'direction'

of activities is in a way a lot of things at the same time, instead of one after the other. When I think of something I do things at the same time, it's very weird!

I must concentrate on one thing at a time but often we realise <u>that our thoughts scatter and divide themselves into other thoughts which create things and events</u>!.. Yes it's hard to explain, especially since I hardly manage to grasp it myself. When you concentrate on something the thought wants to see that happen, but it can also 'disengage itself' from that direction and split itself accidentally. Because of that, one has several situations being created at the same time!

BR- Can you give me an example?

For example <u>I wanted to think of a useful action to do in order to help you, and there were one hundred actions coming to my mind... They all created themselves in front of me, as situations which I lived and I had to try to find my way round all that</u>! It was not easy at all!

BR- Really one hundred actions?

Well, perhaps not a hundred...but lots and lots! That's why I told you it's terrifying when one doesn't control one's thoughts, as it creates whatever one thinks about!

BR- But surely your 'arrival', your meeting with your sister, must feel like past actions?

Yes, I know it was 'before now' and I have done other things since, therefore there is a kind of 'Past' that way. But there are times when everything is Present, like those cranky situations which hang on to a roaming thought. That's when you don't know what's going on, what to do to get out of it!

Darling, once more you stayed up for me. I thank you ever so much. I feel guilty because you'll be tired. Thanks a lot for wanting to talk with me, we were all happy to be near you.

BR- Who are 'we'?

Me and the people who help me, also my dad and your

181

dad. We also think of you when you think of us and we send you our warmest thoughts. Thousand kisses from your Mum who will always love you.

26th May 2000 -

Mum is here and we can chat if you wish Sweetheart. Let me talk to you, as I must focus on each word and sentence and I cannot do two things at the same time. I must concentrate hard to be able to send the thought into your head and that's difficult to do. I must not lose the thread of my thoughts... Afterwards, it's easier once the flow is steady. I'd like to say you have nothing to fear when you speak to me or write. It is indeed me who talks to you, it's not anyone pretending to do so. There are times when it is harder to link up to each other, but that does not mean it is not me.

Of course I feel good, I am not unwell as before. I can't stop marvelling about this! It is wonderful not to feel old, worn out and in a bad state. That's the main thing for me. The rest has been interesting since I came here. You know some of it, bits I told you about. There are others I cannot explain easily as it is difficult to make you understand things which do not exist on Earth!

We have here a <u>system of news conveyed by thought</u>: When <u>we want to speak to each other or make ourselves heard, we call the person with our thought</u>...

My memory has improved now. I don't need to make people repeat things as much (*as she used to do, during her last Earthly years*). Everything is fine here - that's the main thing and that it's fine for you all too. I think of you nearly all the time as I devote my time to learning to communicate better, to explain and understand how to do difficult things, because I want to be able to talk to you, to help you and to make you discover what I can do here, what one can have if one puts all one's strength into it. So I'd like to say to you: Don't be afraid to <u>have big and beautiful ideas, because all is needed for them to happen is to want them</u> if you put enough mental power into it!

I have seen extraordinary things here, amazing when one thinks they took place simply by the use of Thought.
I would have liked to explain better but it is so complicated to understand. The best is to do it and see the results. I have at last overcome, I think, my hatred of writing without knowing what I was going to say. I hated not to have in mind what I wanted to say…

Now I'll let you have a rest. Your Soul is tired, I feel you are tired and I am not going to manage to hold on to my concentration. With all my love.

***

CHAPTER 4
Shocking revelations - Future probabilities - Role of Spirit guides - Trips into historical events

28th May 2000 - *0.10h - This afternoon I had a session with the medium A.McI. from Edinburgh College of Parapsychology who was in York. She knew nothing of all my Spirit communications, yet Dad and Mum came to speak to me via her mediumship to confirm Mum had a little sister who passed over very young! Now back home, I tune in. The pen writes the first words in French:*

We had told you the sister existed, didn't we! She (your medium) transmitted our message correctly. We had a bit of difficulty to make her understand it was not somebody still alive or who had lived a long time but she finally understood.

I wanted her to manage to let you know what you wanted, so that you stop worrying and wondering whether we played tricks on you.

You see, all you have to do is write and talk to us, we reply, it's not difficult, is it?! We are both here, your dad and your mum, as we were together when the medium came to join us with her mind and her Spirit.

BR- How did your communication with the medium take place?

We saw a faint light looking like a person but it was not as solid. We knew it was your lady, as you said you would want to use a medium for the communication, for us to communicate our information. All we had to do was think what we wanted and make it go into her head.

BR- How do you do that?

All it takes is to think hard and direct it towards that person. It seems to get into their head. So that's what we did. She received it quite well, there were one or two other details which we did not manage to make her say. The name which she was giving you (*she'd heard something like 'Lyon'*) had nothing to do with the town in France, but with my Dad, Léon (*a name the Scottish lady's mind would not have been aware of and which would have sounded like that French town to her*), that's what you've finally understood. I was beginning to despair when I saw you going down the 'wrong track', but Dad said: "It does not matter, we'll carry on and we'll manage it eventually".

It took her some time to tell you that there was a sister belonging to your mum whom you never knew, neither did she, but you were to discover her. I said we had to show a baby, otherwise she would not have told you correctly.

There had been a little baby long before me. The mother had not got married in church because she was engaged to another man who was due to marry her, but he did not do it because he changed his mind! That's what caused immense grief. The baby died not long after its birth, so it was buried and never spoken of again! As for me, I had never known all that, because my parents would not have talked about it, as you can imagine!

We do know my Mum had been ill when she was young and she had been unhappy at one time, but I had never known why or how. It's only when I arrived here I ended up discovering all this!

Personally it did not bother me at all and I would not have made a fuss of it, but you wanted so much to know why, when, where!.. So I had to push my mum to try to make her explain to me what had happened and that's what she told me, very timidly!

I who used to think I was always afraid of my mother! This time she was 'frightened' of me in a way! She did look very embarrassed indeed, yet all that happened a very long time ago and we don't get concerned about such detail here... So, to find our way round all this and have some proof one

185

would need to go where Mum and Dad got married, perhaps there is something about it? There must have been some paper-work to report the fact the little girl was born and died? I don't know whether my dad had acknowledged her or whether she had been registered under Mum's name. She looked really upset when I made her talk about it, so I did not try to push more...

I wanted to know what to talk to you about today if I was asked *(during the sitting with the medium)* but there was so much to explain, it was difficult to transmit it via a medium, you see. I have told you as much as I know, I think.

My dad said he was aware of this matter, but he had never said anything to anybody. It possibly could be that the family where Mum lived when she was expecting the little one have some details somewhere? I guess I'll never know who they were - I reckon Mum has had enough bringing all this to the surface, but we can always hope she will perhaps tell me more another time?

This is to explain to you there were some things I could not manage to get transmitted via your medium. Mum had the girl <u>before</u> being married to my dad. So it caused a 'scandal' but Dad had been told as he was kind and understanding and in those days one did not play tricks on men...

He understood she had made a mistake without being a 'loose woman' because of it, so he did not hesitate to marry her. But the child had been sent away elsewhere and that's why it will be difficult to trace her.

My family never spoke about it so I don't see how I am going to help you with names, but I still want to try now that we have opened the 'Pandora's Box'... <u>We have revealed secrets until now unknown to all of us, including me</u>, can you imagine!

BR-It's fantastic!

I would never have known I had a sister if I had not

first died! So it's fortunate I died...or so-called 'died', because here one does not feel dead, I can assure you! I felt less alive on Earth than I feel here!

But to come back to the little sister: As far as I know, she had not been baptised, but one never knows... If someone adopted her, perhaps they will have done it, I don't know. She'd been sent far away, discreetly and unobtrusively. My mum suffered because she was wondering where her child was. I think it's only when she came back here and saw her, that she's known the little one had not lived long and had died of a disease, I don't know what. So they quickly closed that chapter as you can imagine, but in her head she must have suffered all her life to have had a little girl and not have known her... Perhaps that's why she used to spoil me with all those dresses and hats and other things!

I could not understand why I did not have brothers or sisters! She had me with Dad to please him, but she must have always regretted what she had been forced to do before him, that is to get rid of a baby she had not really wanted obviously but who, once born, must have made her regret to be obliged to abandon her. She had a lot of sorrow in her life because of that and I had never known!

I do feel rather guilty to have thought she had been selfish not to give me a brother or a sister! You see, I was wrong, without knowing of course. My poor mum... How much she must have suffered and felt unwell with all those nasty tongues around her! When one thinks of it, what harm is there to be married or not when you expect a kid, hey? I can't see why there is so much fuss and yet that's what is going on.

Mum has said nothing else for the time being. She's let me know she had enough remembering those hard times, but I am not losing hope, we are perhaps going to talk about it again if she knows more... It could happen or it could not happen! She needs to want to talk about it, but I cannot force her. Also it's occurred a long time ago, you know... One forgets one's life on Earth here, I mean if one has lived here for a long while.

So this is a little present for you, you wanted to know more, I had promised to try to get some information and there it is! I can't see how that is going to help you prove that to Touky or Michou, because they will say these are not 'historical facts' of course. But at least for you who <u>knows</u> that I do speak to you and it is me indeed, well, there you are! We both know that my mum had a baby a very long time ago whom <u>neither you nor I had a clue about, until today</u>! It was perhaps worth dying just to uncover that, don't you think?

Since we had a chat, I had time to think a little about all this and told myself that if I had known (when on Earth) that I had a sister somewhere, I would have wanted to do some research... That is what I could reproach my poor mum with. On the other hand the poor woman had been obliged to do something against her will, so we cannot resent her for it.

Moreover I am not sure that the sister would have necessarily been to my liking! After all, it was not the same father, so she might not have the same family tastes or traits or characteristics. There would have only been my mum as a link and similarity. Therefore I don't really know whether, yes or no, I would have wanted to know about her!

But I do understand now why you wanted so much to trace her, because Touky could not have rejected a proof on an official paper... It does not mean she does not exist, but it will mean there will be much more research than before. As long as we don't get a name you will have problems, I suppose... I'll have to convince Mum to sacrifice herself once more and help us prove it to the outside world. Then there would be some undeniable proof! One convinced man is worth ten half-certain! Thank you for your trust and your research and for wanting to prove it to the boys. I would like so much for them to know and understand I am here, I was going to say 'in flesh and bone' but, of course not, I am really here without flesh nor bone, thank goodness! My flesh and my bones made me suffer enough when I was on Earth!

I felt sometimes like throwing myself into the fish pond to end it all…but I was saying to myself that I would probably swim instinctively to get out of it! So, it would not solve anything, except putting myself in very dirty water! Therefore I stayed to the final day.

That's the end of my story for today Sweetheart. I am sure you've stayed up late once more, but I hope that was worth it to learn all those facts and that one day we'll know more, to be able to help you convince those who doubt.

I do believe in it now because I am here and 'whole', happy not to suffer any more but unhappy to be no longer near you. Your mum does not always know everything, you see! A mum who did not know she had a sister, does not know much, does she!

BR- Try to get a year, a first name and surname, a town or village?

Only one detail comes to light at the moment: The date was <u>not</u> just before her marriage, but a long time before, I think. Therefore years passed between this sister's birth and Mum and Dad's wedding. I really don't know where we are going to find all that. This detail has just reached me 'by pigeon post', I mean by thought flying from one person to the other.

My Mum must have sent it to me. I hope she will send me others! We are working on it, don't worry. Now we have started, we may as well finish brilliantly if we can. You'll see, we'll probably manage it or at least not far from it. Having said this, I'll let you sleep and kiss you as I always do when I think of you and the boys of course. I would so much like them to know I am still alive. They don't seem to understand it, do they?! I am indeed alive, alive, alive! I no longer have a painful body and old parts and wrinkles or live in a bad state! Long live the new ME in Spirit! Now go and sleep Darling. Your mum who will always love you until we meet again one day...and you too will have a big surprise on arrival!

12th June 2000 - *The pen writes the first two words in Automatic, the letters being all linked up, then I hear the rest straight away. It's in French:*

Léonie Moleux did not know what she was doing the day she let herself be seduced by that handsome young man whom she loved so much! She wanted to know what love was, she wanted to please her young gentleman and she knew her parents would disapprove, but she did not have the strength nor the courage to push him away the day he came too close and afterwards it was too late!.. She would have liked to suggest an abortion but she did not know how to go about it, nor what to do and the shame to have to talk about it left her full of remorse for what had happened. She wanted to understand why he 'dropped' her soon after, but she never really did know. Perhaps he never had any intention of marrying her, who knows!

The only true and certain thing is he did seduce her, loved her, made her believe he would always love her...then broke off with her and that is what hurt her most - not knowing why. Yet they seemed so good together. But one is never sure of what goes on in the head of a man one does not know very well, so that's what happened...

The result was a disgrace for the family, a shame, because a respectable and well-brought up young girl would not get herself pregnant without getting married first. But the worse, or the 'second worse' thing was having to abandon this little baby who had not asked to be created - that is what broke her heart. Yet she never forgot that little girl, she did love her but could not show her how much she did, as the baby had been taken away straight after the birth. When the child died not long afterwards, the joy of the birth and the death were no longer mixed up.

BR- Pardon? I did not grasp this: Could you explain it please?

They had become one single huge sorrow. The birth had been a joy in spite of everything because a little baby is always adorable, especially when it is one's own… Then the separation, then the necessary abandonment… Afterwards, the death! Why that death? Why was she born if she was to die? Why did she make me live those hours of agony, reproaches, remorse, then she disappeared, therefore doing so twice in my life!

I cannot understand it, yet it must have been for a reason, which I still do not know! So the life I had afterwards was completely aimed at trying to erase those atrocious memories which were <u>burning my inner core</u>. I was never able to forget her, I did not really want to forget her. I could not because if I did, I had the impression of being unfaithful to her and rejecting her.

I did not have a daughter yet I had one in my heart! She lived all her life in my life, even when she was dead! As for me? I killed myself little by little with those regrets and remorse, I reckon… That is why I did not really want to talk about it. Yet I wanted to help you understand what happened, so that you could 'have some proof' as you say. I do understand that if you were able to find where she has been and where she died and was buried, one would have extraordinary <u>evidence which would help you prove we all exist here</u> and that <u>you succeeded in communicating something which had never been known during your mum's life and your own</u> up to now.

At the beginning I was told nothing, then finally I managed to learn she had been sent to live in the countryside, so that I would not happen to meet her or have to hear about her! But I did want to know! She had been adopted by an old lady who liked kids and felt sorry for her.

I never bumped into her because she might have been afraid I'd want to take the baby away from her, but she let me know the little one had died - she had been very ill...then died of a disease, am not too sure which... What was tearing my heart apart was I was never able to see her again! I know you wanted a name. I tried to have it, up to now I was unsuccessful but I'll perhaps be able to research more if I am allowed, because after all it is for a good reason!

BR- Hoping she has not reincarnated!..

Let us suppose she has not, indeed...I have already asked around to be told those details. Let's come to an agreement my little lady: I promise you to try more, now I have found the courage to talk to you about it.

I know you find it normal to try to do some research...but for me it has been very painful to bring back to mind all those memories which had hurt me very, very much all my life!.. I am glad to have managed to do it now. I did not think I would have the strength and thank you for making me do it...

BR- I am so sorry to make you suffer! You know why I am seeking answers.

I know your intentions are good. Yes, we all know here that you have in mind this idea that the date of birth and identity of the little one would be irrefutable proof of the existence of our world, a world superior to the one on Earth. I admit I had not thought of this before...as I had my own grief to get over. But she was born, then left and came back here and I too am here, why do I worry so much?

You are not wrong to say I should not suffer, since she is near me if I want to see her. So we'll work more at it. I cannot promise you we'll find out all the details, you know! It will probably be difficult to gather all this! But at least the best we could do is to find out her surname, place of birth and the name given to her once I was parted from her. Please put my name in gold letters in your heart so that the love you send me gives me wings in my new task. I will need it you know! I don't think it will be easy, but I promise you I'll do my best... (*A few moments of silence then return of the usual rapid flow*)...The woman who looked after her was an old farmer's wife who had a few cows in the countryside. She had a good heart and accepted to take my baby, yet I did not want to let her go there, as it would be too far for me to be able to go to see her, but my own mother did not want me to see her! She wanted me to get rid of this 'stain to my honour', as she called it!

I did not see any stain, only an accident and a misfortune as I had no intention of doing anything wrong. It had happened by accident rather suddenly yet I ended up being reproached with it all my life...and I blamed myself all that time.

I have just heard that this old lady took pity on me and had promised me to let me know what she could so that I would not be completely cut off from my daughter, but it did not last long since soon after, the little one died of that disease the name of which I no longer recall.

My daughter died fairly quickly of it and I was unable to go and see her as she was already ill before I heard of it, then when she died, I was not informed until afterwards. So I never knew when she was buried. I think she was as she had been christened. The nice lady had given her a lovely christening because, she told me, she wanted "to make sure God's law was applied more from the heart than Man's law".

BR- So you've been told she has indeed been baptised?

Yes, she was christened but I don't know where nor when, that's the trouble and people's names are not clear yet. I think her name was a bit strange. I'll have to work at it more to find a way out of all those bits of information. One fact is certain: My baby did not live long. Now I have to go and ask for more details. I don't think I can do that at once…I'll have to work at it you understand, I must approach those who were involved in this. I hope this has not complicated your life or your mind!

BR- We are a 'chain of women'… I have the honour to receive this painful secret but it will create and bring some joy…

Of course, we are a 'list of strong women', we have the courage of our opinions and to tackle difficult tasks but, let's hope, feasible!

I am now going to let you sleep. My daughter Suzanne reminds me you spend your time going to bed late and do not sleep enough, so I don't want to be guilty of depriving you of more sleep! I give you a big kiss, my little lady, like I would have wanted to be able to do when I was on Earth. I am sure you and I would have got on very well.

BR- What would you like me to call you?

My surname was Leclercq, like your mum, but my mum called me Léonie and that's what stayed with me all my life. So you may call me 'Grandma Léonie' if you wish, would that make you happy?

BR- Would that please you? That's what matters!

Personally I am so happy to have managed to throw off the pain and terror of those days of the past, to have been able to get rid of the dread I had at that time, that I would accept anything!

BR- Have you still been having remorse for what I reckon to be some 55 years since you left the Earth?!

My remorse has never left me, whatever I did to get rid of it and even though I met up with my first born!.. I knew she would survive in the Hereafter because I believed in it, but I did not know whether I would see her easily and whether she would forgive me for abandoning her! She did, at once, so I wanted to forget the past in order to live only the present here.

BR- Many thanks for all you did. Will you be able to come back and talk with me?

No need to ask! I'll come back as soon as I have some information to help you. I don't know to what extent we'll succeed but if we don't try we'll never know! You go to sleep and I'll go to work!

(Suddenly change of communicator!) Your mum gives you a big goodnight kiss, Sweetheart. Go to sleep quickly. I love you as always.

BR- Many thanks for convincing your mum to reveal her secret!

I did not do much actually, it is her who had to make all the efforts, but we are really happy to have obtained those results up to now. We'll see what we can do afterwards. Lots of kisses, goodnight!

19th June 2000 *- Very late in the evening, in Sorento, Italy. Just in case, I try to link up. The first 4 words are in French:* Where did you go? *Unfortunately my eyes closed themselves and I fell fast asleep!*

21st June 2000 *- 22hrs. I try again, after a guided visit of Pompeii then climbing up to Vesuvius's crater! Throughout my childhood Mum used to say that 'one day' we would go to Pompeii, as a family, but it never happened. I used to day-dream about going there. So, on the first anniversary of Mum's passing I decided to do just that. The pen writes the first 4 words on its own and in French:*

A lady (in my world) told me you went somewhere very different today and that you wished to tell me about it... Yes Darling, it's me, I am very happy to have a chat. Where did you go?! So far I don't know, I was only told you went 'somewhere special' but I am not sure where, that's the problem. I could not think what she was talking about.

195

Another person told me you were going to fulfil one of your dreams, so I see it should be important. Do tell me, where did you go?! *(I explained)* Ah! That's why it seemed special, I didn't really know what she was talking about, because she was not telling me, but now I understand!

It is really good indeed, I am pleased for you that you were able to go; it is so interesting and amazing! I don't think there is anywhere in the world which is so astonishing and so well preserved. Now I do understand!

BR- How are the searches about your sister going on?

We asked my grandmother *(Therefore the grandmother of the little sister and mother of the poor pregnant lady)* to help you with all those facts. They are so important so we need to have them absolutely correct, don't we! Therefore I made my Grandmother understand we need very precise details so that it is possible to check them and present them to Touky, Mich and Pierre and the rest of the world! Unfortunately, up to now, I did not manage to make her tell me who took charge of the little girl! We did ask her not to make any mistake, but at the moment she does not want to make the effort...

BR- Why not?

I cannot understand why either, but that's how it is. My grandmother always appeared awkward to deal with, that's why I used to be a bit scared of her...but now I would like her to realise we need her help and those details.

BR- Would it be possible to ask your sister or your grandfather?

My sister took some time to settle here because she was a little baby when she passed over and she did not know what it was all about. She had not really wanted to be born but decided to do it, then changed her mind because the circumstances were not good. That's all she remembers I think.

BR- Does she know her name?

<u>A name means nothing here</u>, you know, so no, it is not

what she would remember. All we have to do now is to turn towards my grandma and hope she will do us the honour to accept to think back to that time in her life which she had found shocking and terrifying. I reckon she must have blocked it out of her mind so as not to think about it...

BR- *(Struggling to stay awake) Thanks Mum, but sorry, I am dozing off...*

1st **July 2000** - *21.00hrs. The pen writes the first 8 words in French, conscientiously. It's Grandma Léonie:*

The only detail about my mother is that we were all together on the terrible day when she came to fetch my baby.

I remember being in a large dining room with wooden chairs and the baby was asleep in a little wicker basket. Then the old lady came, she kissed me to console me because I was crying so much... She explained she would look after her and there was nothing to fear, I would soon recover from the shock...and all sorts of things like that. But I did not want or could not hear anything, as I was thinking of only one thing: I was not going to see my baby any more and that was tearing me apart. Then she left fairly quickly and we never saw her again!

She had chosen to come, rather than the other way round, as we would have had to go to her home and that would have revealed who she was and where she lived! We were at home I think. But I had the baby elsewhere! I had 'gone on holiday' for a long time...then I came back and we had all that organised by my parents, I am sure! I did not want to do anything, have nothing to do with that. I was too ashamed and too frightened and in too much grief. I never recovered, do you understand? I never forgave myself for doing this to a poor little defenceless thing, but it had to be done 'for the honour' and to be sensible; one could not keep a baby without there being a father and a mother, moreover the cost of bringing it up was to be considered too.

197

The worst was the 'stain to the honour' as my parents kept repeating to me and I was too young to resist or know what else to do! Those who knew where she lived did not want and never wanted to tell me, so that I did not risk going and getting my baby back! Such a cruel, really cruel thing! You have no idea how much I suffered to know that they knew and would not tell me! I wanted to find out, you know, I asked, I begged, but I was told to go to bed or to shut up or go to work, but not a single word was said as to 'who' or 'where'. So eventually I ended up resigning myself not to find out and accept not to talk about it... But I was 'talking about it' within myself, I was torturing myself wondering how she was.

I had some brief news when she was ill. A little too late unfortunately as she had been ill for some time when I found out. Then she died and I only learnt of it later on.

BR- How did you get to know?

The old lady had a lady friend in town who came near my home one day, and I saw her in the street. I was not really acquainted with her but she said very quickly: "You know there is a lady with a baby, in the countryside...she asked me to inform you the baby is quite ill at the moment. That's all I can tell you. She wanted you to know in case you were allowed to go and see her". After that she left in a hurry and I was out of my mind with grief. It woke up all my fears and horrors, I did not want to live where I lived, I wanted to live where she was, but I was not allowed nor had the means in those days, to leave without a penny and without knowing what I was getting myself into. So I did what I was told to do: Nothing! My daughter was dying, died and they all did nothing! Not a single gesture, nothing whatsoever...because 'the honour of the family had to be saved'!

As for me, my life was ruined, at least within me... Outwards I was a well-brought up, polite young lady, but within I was suffering so much I fell ill, I wanted to die or kill myself, but for that too I did not know what to do! Anyway, it would not have been the solution.

BR- Do you know how old she was when she died?

She must have died a few months later, I think. I was never told anything about that either! The same friend of the old lady was crying as she gave me the news later. She seemed to know whom and what it was about. She had tears in her eyes when she told me the old lady had done her best to look after the little one, but the doctors said she would not last very long. Indeed she passed away, in a way as fast as she had come - by accident, without anyone wanting this to happen in both cases. It was hopeless. I started crying hysterically and my mother was furious because the old lady said it without consulting her first!

I did not care, I wanted my baby...and throughout my whole life I wanted to see my baby! She only appeared to me the day 'I died' myself; in 1947 I think or perhaps later, I can't remember... I know she looked beautiful when she appeared. It was the picture of the baby which came first, then it changed into this beautiful young woman who said to me: 'I am your eldest daughter!' When she said 'eldest' I understood at once, as I only had one other daughter afterwards. So it made me so happy to see her that I cried with joy this time!

But I am going off the subject of your research. I wanted to know more details about the old lady and the little one. My mum does not contact me anymore as we had a lot of anger and arguments between us, all that because of that birth outside wedlock! Perhaps I should try and find her again, but I am not too sure where at the moment. We all have our 'work' here, our activities, our intentions and interests, that is what separates people gradually, so I'll have to work hard to find her again.

BR- Try to convince your first daughter or your guide, or those who welcomed her when she died herself?

The grandchildren of that old lady lived much longer

you know, I learnt that later! I heard she had children who had children themselves and they lived quite a long time; in fact I think they would be your age. It's when they came in... *(I did not catch what she said so asked her to repeat)*...I meant to say: This lady had taken them to town from time to time and they must have known who I was I suppose, because I met them once! But it was much later, when the 'whole business' was all over and they told me she too had died. It gave me a shock because after all, she had been kind to help me in that very difficult situation and had wanted to help me a little by letting me know what was going on.

I must have looked shocked when they told me, because they seemed very pleased with my 'interest and kindness towards them', as they said. I never saw them again after that, but that's how I learnt she too had gone out of my life. So I did not have a point of contact any more.

BR- Did you ask them the name of the village?

No...I did not...I was not thinking of it any longer. I mean I was not thinking any more of going to find my little girl, like I did before, since she had died. It took me a very, very long time to recover from all those emotions and pains, you know. My health was never good after that, I can assure you...

Then I was made to meet the one who was to become your mum's dad, the young Léon Leclercq, who was very kind, elegant and likeable. I did like him a lot and found him pleasant... and that's how we eventually got married. I had explained to him what had happened in my gloomy past, so that he did not get a shock one day if ever anyone told him by chance! But he was able to understand I had not been a disgustingly loose woman. Straight away he wanted to console me, reassure me and tell me he loved me as I was then and not for what may have happened years ago. So we got married and that subject was forgotten, between us anyway. But I never forgot...and here we are now.

BR- Do you know how old you were?

My date of birth is very distant now, I can't remember it, but I was less than 18 years old when the big mistake of my life took place. I think around 17 or something like that. I was afraid to become a spinster, I wanted to get married! I had met this handsome young man who appeared to be so respectable, so kind, so loving... Then one evening we met secretly...and I made the mistake to let him love me 'his way', as he said. That is what caused the destruction of my happiness... I wanted to kill him in my heart, I remember that! He had destroyed me when he rejected me and changed his mind about us getting married...and I've never known why! Perhaps he had weird ideas or he enjoyed seducing women and running away! Anyway, he abandoned me and disappeared. I think he never knew or wanted to know what happened. All this is so long ago...it's not important any more.

My own mother had been so shocked when she heard of my pregnancy she had an attack of I can't recall what. She made herself ill. The shock, I reckon. She had to face all those problems, poor thing! I suppose I should forgive her, because after all she only did what looked right in those days, come to think of it. She wanted to spare me the shame of a birth without an 'official father', but I could only see my own sorrow, not my mum's nor my dad's either who must have been unhappy too I guess!

They must have managed to get some information very discreetly, so that no one knew... otherwise the 'Big Secret' would be revealed and 'the honour of the family would have been tarnished' after all that!

I don't know how they did it, but they obviously succeeded very well, otherwise there would have been some rumours and some shocks...

So, there we are my dear grandaughter. I call you 'my granddaughter' with pleasure because I did not really have the

201

pleasure to know you well on Earth. We did not look alike, I did not have the same lifestyle as you, but you did manage to understand one lives on in the Hereafter as you call it and that's what is really interesting, isn't it?!

They do not teach that correctly at catechism and Sunday school, do they? I remember going to <u>catechism</u>. It <u>had been one of the reasons for my terror</u>...because I knew that all those terrible things, which one does not speak about, had a 'taste of sin' we would have said! So I was torturing myself even more! Not only the honour of my family had been in danger but, on top of that, the 'sins' had been committed! That is certain 'hell' for the sinner, isn't it!

Fortunately, <u>no hell for me when I arrived here</u>! Only my daughter, my friends and my animals, because I had had a lot of animals, you know. My cats and dogs gave me a lot of pleasure in life, more than people did, so I do understand you well on that subject! You adore them too, don't you!

But to come back to my main topic: Mum and Dad did their best, I can see that now. I had not wanted to think about all that again, you understand? I did not want to bring back to memory that story as it had hurt me far too much and my little one was here, as an adult so to speak, therefore it did not matter... All I could do was forget it...

BR- You must have seen your mother again as she must have died before you. Wasn't she there to welcome you?

My mother died before me of course - she was older than me! But I had always wanted to avoid them because I had been too miserable after what had happened! Since I have been here I have not really had the opportunity to speak to them about it. We saw each other again, yes, but I did not try to see them much or to talk about all that. I wanted it to be forgotten, that's all. She was there.

BR- Had you given a name to your baby?

My baby had been named by the old lady. I had not

been allowed to name her so as not to get attached to her. All I was to do was to give her birth then forget her, that's all!

BR- Didn't your parents suggest an abortion?

My Little Lady, an abortion is to kill! We do not kill in our family! My mother was a Catholic and would never have considered such an act, even if the 'honour of the family was tarnished'! She had friends all over the place and was able to find the woman who would be able to look after this little being, who had done nothing wrong yet could not live with us... That's what religion, society and customs of the time created - misery all my life.

On the other hand, my little Suzanne was a delight. She was always kind and well-behaved and I loved her a lot. Yet she never had the little sister she would have wanted to have (or little brother as she invented once!)...but I did not want any more children. I couldn't start creating little ones when I'd had one I had not been able to love and pamper. My first one had suffered far from me, she died far from me, how could I create others? One was sufficient, because I got married and it would have looked strange not to have children when we were a young couple...but one was enough! *(I am interrupted by my young cat Timmy catching a bird!)*

6th July 2000 - *The pen writes the first 8 words laboriously on its own, in French, before the usual fast flow. It's Grandma:*

The 'old' lady tells me her baby was buried in a little cemetery near her village... She had wanted to help me out of kindness, because she took pity on me and this poor little baby who had never done anything wrong, so I had to agree. Anyway I had no choice but when she let me know she was dead, I did not want to know where, it was too painful. The name of that little village was well known at the time, it appeared small but was large.

BR- In which region?

The region is not far from Boulogne, I think? There was a little village where cows and orchards were usual. I feel you are not too sure...*(I ask some questions but do not jot them down)* How do you want me to get to know all that? It won't be easy! The old lady is here now. She kindly accepted to join me when I called her in my heart, with all my strength, because she knew it was important we speak. I am told she's made a big effort to come as she comes from a different world in a way (*Meaning from a higher, more evolved mental and spiritual dimension because she has progressed*). She learnt via intermediaries I needed her once more! She told me her little town was a village in the middle of the countryside with a small castle or manor. She had to make a lot of efforts to remember as all that was very 'distant'! I think it will be difficult to find out all these details, but I am going to keep asking her... Their family name started with a B, like Bal...ard? Bal...aud? *(The pen tries to spell it on its own - It is perfectly understandable it is very difficult to remember dates and names etc. Once in the Hereafter, people's Earthly names and status have no importance, one is known for the person one is 'within'. Moreover, after some 100 years or so spent in Spirit World, where this lady has progressed to a more evolved mental and spiritual state and been used to communicate telepathically, to try to suddenly look back and concentrate on man-made Earthly labels such as names is terribly difficult for her!).*

BR- What about the baby?

She had a lovely little name because she was cute, the lady tells me. I'd like to find out more about everything if you don't mind... She tells me that the power of her love for the little girl brought some facts back to her memory but she needs more about the baby, she'll think about it a bit more... It's so far back in time, you understand, so buried in her memory... So much happened since we were parted, I suppose it must be nearly a century. You told me your mum is nearly 91 years old, that's very old isn't it?

I did not live that long on Earth but it was better I came back here, at least I was able to meet again my husband and my first little girl. That's what helped me recover emotionally - to see them so quickly as soon as I arrived.

The poor lady who adopted my little girl had feared I may want to take her away one day! But it could not have happened anyway as I had no idea where she was and I was not allowed to ask, so… She came to see me here, looking as she was when I knew her. I suppose she has changed since, but it would have thrown me, so she is very kind to have wanted to show herself as she used to be, that way it was easier for me. That's what she told me when she arrived without any warning, she appeared on my door step so to speak! She said: "Hello! I am your friend of yesteryear!

BR- Did you ask her name?

I did not need to as I recognised her at once, to my great surprise! She knew you wanted to know all those things. She admitted it gave her a lot of difficulties and that she had trouble remembering all that because it was 'past' and her 'present' is so different from the Earthly world that she has forgotten a lot about it…

She points out to me her small house was surrounded with orchards, beautiful trees which made her happy as she loved greenery. The first time she saw it, she thought it was paradise because she absolutely loved that countryside. "That little girl gave me a lot of joy" says my lady, "it gave me great pleasure to have her. I remember her, so little, so sweet. But she was in pain when she was ill, she cried a lot, she bled, she coughed…she was very ill. I did not know what to do to make her comfortable. She ended up getting so weak that I was really worried. When the doctor came to tell me there was no hope, I was desperate…

I wanted so much to have her living and growing up with us... At her burial I cried so much I fainted: I saw stars and I fell down. My heart was broken because she had given me so much joy, then so much pain...

I had wanted to give her a lovely cot to welcome her but I could not afford big expenses. Therefore I made some pretty lace decorations to put all around so that it looked pretty, like her pretty face...she was such an adorable little girl! My own mother had died too and I knew what it was like to lose someone one loves. This time I felt so lost not to have my little one any more... They had to bring me back home on a cart because the priest had not finished his speech. I did not want to hear all that gibberish, those empty words... My little one had gone, flown off elsewhere and I would not see her again. That's all I knew. My family helped me with the funeral arrangements, everyone lent a hand. I wanted something simple as the little one had not lived long, she was only a few months old if I recall, she was very young, she suffered nearly all her life in a way! *(This confirms people who have been a long time in Spirit recall more impressions and emotions, than labels such as names and numbers).*

I wanted a simple stone with a flower or two on it if possible - she looked like a little flower herself. With that, we wrote her name in pretty letters... My friends often helped me go to the cemetery to go and see her and tell her I loved her despite her short life with me. She was hardly...*(Hesitation)*... two months old? ... Or under two years old?... I cannot remember, she was very little but she had managed to make herself be loved... I am proud to have been her mother, even if only an adoptive one..." *(A brief silence then the pen starts again. I realise there is a change of communicator - Grandma Léonie comes back).*

As I told you, it took me some time to recover of 'her double loss'. My daughter had disappeared out of my life when

she was adopted, then she died soon after. You understand why I was so miserable for so long - my own daughter, my real daughter, disappearing twice! My parents did not know the funeral had taken place. They were not told therefore I was not either, which means none of us knew it in time- but we were not to know. We were not the parents any more, that's why.
(I struggle to concentrate, my eyes give up, close themselves and I fall fast asleep...)

22nd July 2000 - *The pen writes the first 4 words in French. It's my mum:*

We are all here. We've had a big family reunion recently! We had to talk to one another and help each other to manage to solve the problem of the age, name, dates etc. of the famous baby sister I had never known and which you so want to know! We ended up reaching a few conclusions: The difficulty was that it happened so long ago in your time and here it seems even further away, because we have to remember things some of us did not want to recall, or preferred to forget! The aim of the family reunion was to gather as many facts as possible so that we could have something to tell you.

- My mum's wedding took place after the birth of this little girl and even after her death.
- The date was fixed at the beginning of the previous century.
- The end of the previous century saw the birth of my own mum.
- The kind lady who looked after her has become more and more friendly here. We've seen her again recently and I think we'll be able to find out something when she knows how to remember those facts. She comes from 'far away in time', you know. It hurts to remember all those distressing things. <u>One needs a lot of courage to think of sad things here</u>, because one does not want to bring gloom to one's surroundings, as you know!

The common sense of your question is obvious: If we don't get the name and details of the little baby, you'll have nothing to prove what you are writing is true. We are doing our best here at the moment. Patience is needed as Mum's little daughter did not want to remain on Earth you see, she came here - so she 'died'.

We see her here as a young woman and even older, because since her birth <u>she has 'grown up' here by learning a lot of interesting things.</u> She did not live long - that's what causes problems since one must remember a rather narrow time span and there aren't many people recalling it. Only my mum, her parents if they want to make the effort, the old lady and the daughter herself. But everyone has 'grown' emotionally since, that's why they all have to make big efforts to try to 'get back' to that period, do you understand?

Personally I don't see why it is so difficult, but I am only a new arrival here, therefore I assume I would remember more easily than if it was one hundred years ago or something like that... It does seem weird, you know, to have to make efforts to recall something one has tried hard to forget, or not to bring back to the surface. I can see that I do <u>not want to forget you and cannot</u>, yet if one does not think about something, it seems to slip far away into one's memory, to only come out or emerge again when one calls it out with very strong mental efforts!..

(I suddenly wake up and realise my eyes had momentarily closed themselves and I'd dozed off because of the necessary intense concentration, at this rather late hour...I pick up my pen again in case Mum was still online but I do not ask any question, so I am surprised to hear what follows).

The birds in this, our world, do not sing 'in bird talk'! They sing in 'people talk' I'd say...<u>When we hear them, we have the impression their 'words' are human words! We feel we understand what they say, it's very strange</u>...

The little birds in our garden *(on Earth)* were nothing in comparison to the beauties I see here... There are so many I don't know, whose names I don't know. Names here are of no importance. What matters is to be able to appreciate what one sees or hears and to like it, without being concerned about little details like that!

I am quite happy about that, as I have no wish to rack my brains, you understand... I've never liked to have to be bothered by unimportant little details so here, when I am told 'it's not important' I leap at it and accept it as such! I don't ask anything else. I am only talking of small details. The main point, since our last conversation, is that the 'place' I accepted as my 'den' is not as important in my eyes as what I do here in general. An example of bliss here is to feel happy because we do not suffer any more. We remember we could no longer move or speak or drink well etc. that is over now and everything is possible, everything we want to do is possible! You have no idea how wonderful it seems! There were so many times when I could not do what I wanted, when I was suffering and now I feel so free!

Life here is the real Life, I do see that now. How can anyone imagine that life on Earth is real Life? I do not understand it, now I see what can be done here... Why waste so much time on Earth then resist the departure towards our world here, it is really silly, isn't it?!

My life on Earth has not been wasted or useless because I had you all, gave you birth and looked after you when you were young and even afterwards. But I see that if I had been able to have you here and bring you up here, it would have been so much better and more pleasant! Why bother giving birth on Earth? I do know there is a reason - to want to love over there, in order to learn to be a flesh and bone human, but in my opinion it's not worth it compared to what we have here, I assure you!

BR- What have you been doing recently?

I spend my 'time' between learning to manipulate things and facts with my thoughts, going to see people when I don't understand why something happens one way or the other and thinking of you all in a positive and useful way.

BR- For me an improvement is to find more work...

I've sent you my good thoughts of loving Mum, you see and I knew that according to what I was told it would help you get what you want to do or have. As for Touky and the others, I do the same of course! I don't always know what happens at the other end as I don't have as many communications with them as with you.

BR- Does Touky visit you at night?

Touky at night must be shattered in my opinion! I think his mind is too. He appears so tired, I reckon everything 'closes down' when he sleeps. He is here more rarely than you are, let's say. He too needs help, I send him some, as well as Mich and Pierre. I don't see any difference between you all, remember! I always wanted to love you equally, without any difference as you are all my darling children, whatever your age is now!

Besides that, there are, of course, details which make life even more fascinating. My dad comes to see me, my mum too. We have interesting discussions, they taught me a lot since I arrived. I am always afraid not to know enough, afraid not to be able to continue to communicate with you! But I don't appear to forget how to do it...

On top of that, there are other people who come too. They have all sorts of 'origins'. They may come because I need them to understand something: the very instant I do not grasp something and ask myself 'why?' and 'how?', someone arrives at once to tell me what it is about. Also the regularity of meetings here is amusing as one can meet at regular intervals or all the time if one wanted...to have the possibility of recapping what one knows and do or discuss new things.

BR- Whom do you have these meetings with? Are there some tutors?

It seems to me the choice of 'teachers' is enormous. When a subject is not very clear, there is a crowd of different people who can come and help you. <u>The difference between them is the light they project</u> when they are there. When a '<u>sublime Being</u>' appears to you, it is obvious he has within himself tons of 'super and sensational <u>knowledge</u>' so one is very happy to be near him (or her) to listen or learn more by trying what he explains. If that person has not come before, if it's the first time I meet him, what surprises me is that he knows straight away who I am, he seems to know exactly what I need and why when he talks to me!

BR- Has anybody introduced himself as your 'guide'?

I saw several people or rather 'luminous Beings' as I would call them, who came at the beginning, then from time to time, to speak to me and give me some advice. I did not really want to 'label' them in case I embarrassed them, but also because <u>what they were saying was more important to know than details of who they were</u> - nationality or identity is no interest here you know! <u>One has a thirst for knowledge, for a greater understanding</u>, so as long as one has a source providing the answers, the name of the source is not as important as the answer to the questions. Therefore I rarely dare ask: 'Who are you?' - I listen more than I talk, I reckon... Dad and I went together to some really valuable meetings.

BR- Which Dad?

My dad. He wanted to show me what can be achieved when one learns to do things at a 'higher level': it was most interesting as there is ever so much to discover, as I keep repeating!..

A tree with yellow leaves probably means to you a tree in autumn. A tree with yellow leaves here, is a tree whose life has passed from one colour to the other without stopping at any season. The leaves can change colour within the same 'day' let's say (but remember 'days' here don't feel like days). These trees have not finished growing in their life as a tree and feel like developing into shapes different from what is seen on Earth, so their appearance changes a lot more than when on Earth. Their colour comes from their 'state of mind', if you can understand that!..

BR- If you have understood it, please explain, as I am not sure I do!

I have not understood it very well because it seems so weird, doesn't it? But I see what is meant: An outer appearance does not mean one is like that all the time, it means that's how one thinks at that very moment. So, if the tree 'sees itself yellow' it's because it 'thinks itself yellow'… I really don't know why it should want to see itself yellow, but remember there are colours here that neither you nor me have ever seen on Earth; so why and how they exist becomes a much more complicated question!

Physics I guess… And physics and me, you know...it's not always been my 'forte'! Yet I do tackle it gradually, at least physics from here! I have made big progress you know, compared to what I could grasp when I was on Earth! I never wanted to bother with such things. But here, if I want to try to understand, first I must really want to, then I have to try to grasp what is explained. Sometimes it works, or it does not, but I suppose it's only temporary. I shall understand more later, I reckon.

Your dad and mine too seem to comprehend all that far better than I do, so I can always turn to them to ask them again. My dad has always wanted to teach me new stuff as you know, therefore when he says: "Come and have a look over here", I follow him. That's how I discover things gradually. He made me visit lots of places so that I know they exist and I keep in mind that I am aware they are there. I'll want to reach them

212

one day, though at the moment I am not too sure why I'll want to reach them!...

BR- Can you describe them?

It would be difficult to describe you know! I can only tell you what I told you. There are heaps of astonishing and incredible things - they have to do with <u>states of mind</u>.... And personally I have only just managed to get used to all that, you understand? So I'll have a lot to discover...but you will all know what it is one day, once I have understood it!

One state of mind or another does create a lot of difference, it's incredible! It changes your life, environment, point of view, the way you see things... So, since states of mind change all the time, there is a lot to do, see and try to understand! At least a lot for me. Perhaps it's easier for other people- I only want to learn more to pass it on to you and make you understand too, if I can. There will probably be lots I shan't be able to explain, because life here is different from yours on Earth, but if I describe using images and examples, I will perhaps manage to give you a general idea, I hope so anyway.

One day we shall all meet again here, the boys, you, me, the two dads etc. and we'll take great pleasure in discussing all this, you'll see!

(I give Mum the family's latest news, then check she's understood)

My ears are full of your news! Yes, I did hear everything. <u>It takes some time to grasp all the details, they appear a little entangled at times</u>... perhaps because<u> I must be receiving them in pictures rather than words</u>, I guess? I did <u>grasp the meaning</u> of each individual message.

So everyone seems to do better in their life to cope, apart for my poor Michou and his blasted headaches... Poor man, he must have inherited that from me, at least partly I guess. I am going to see whether we can help him from here. He has had so much bad luck, poor lad, I am so sad for him. He has not had much good fortune in life. Nothing seems to go well as far as his health is concerned, with those headaches, his sight, his tinnitus... I do want to check what we can do for him from here...

Yes, I did understand your Jim *(my son)* is going to join Touky for a cruise on the old boat, is that correct? It's great. I am sure he'll be pleased about it and the fresh air and sun will do him good! He can't be getting any often where he is. I see Anne-France *(my daughter)* knows how to do lots of things in painting, it makes her a real artist, doesn't it?! It's true her dad is very good too, and yours...and yourself too, you do quite well with drawing and painting. So we really have a family of artists, haven't we? Only I was not very good at it - but I was rather gifted with words, let's say, wasn't I? Writing, using words 'to paint pictures with words' rather than paint! Well, that's what life is about: To do what one can!

When it is your turn to come over, I'll be there you know. So never be afraid of dying, because if things go like they did for me, you won't have much trouble I assure you. You'll see me and you'll know your problems are over, all you'll have to do is enjoy here and we'll be so happy to be together!

But don't think what I am telling you now is to predict an early death! I am only saying this in general. I am not a fortune teller or medium. I don't see the future, not yet anyway! I would really like to be able to but shall I? I don't know.

One day we'll see each other again - that's a thought which warms up my heart, even though my heart is not made of flesh! Goodnight Sweetheart. Sleep well and get your 'beauty hours' whenever you can. I'll 'ring off' now! *(Oh 30).*

2nd August 2000 - *In French*:

Like little birds, your thoughts are flying off right and left! If you could keep them still on the same spot, it would help the communication a little... I'd like to say hello, my Darling, it's your mum here of course. We have all heard your call and explanations and would like to reassure you.

The little baby never knew her name you know, she was very small when she died... Now, here, a name is of no importance. We've done everything we could to try to solve the problem. You are going to have your work cut out and lots of it, if you start wanting to prove her existence.

BR- I really need her surname. She must have been registered somewhere?

We saw your despair and know it is not easy. There are so many difficulties in finding her, one would need a team of experts to trace her! My grandparents are not really reachable you know, we seem to have lost sight of them... *(A short silence. Then sudden change of communicator: Grandma Léonie comes online!).*

The name of my little daughter was a problem: I called her something in my heart, my mother forbade me to do it but I wanted to call her something and she has always been 'Odette' for me...but I know it is not the name the lady gave her. Since I was not allowed to keep her, I could not expect her to be christened what I wanted, but I know she was christened.

BR- Even in your 'situation'?

Oh yes, all babies were baptised at birth as it was feared it would cast a spell if they were not! So in my heart I baptised her, using the name I liked. My little Odette was my daughter, but the lady who looked after her must have given her another name. I want to try to make her remember but she finds it difficult, she says it was such a long time ago...

BR- Do you remember what happened when they took her away from you?

The day the lady got her was one of the darkest days in my life and I remember crying so much I became ill - but I can't remember the name of the woman who came...

My mother told me I had to forget 'all that stuff', as she used to say. All I recall was to have had a little one, practically for a few hours, then losing her as soon as she arrived! We had a meeting fixed at the house of my aunt I think or something like that…a house where the rest of the world would not try to find out what was going on… We had a 'deliberation', we could say, but I was not allowed to speak! All I had to do was listen and do as I was told. I had 'tarnished the family name' and this time I could only obey!

BR- Why couldn't you try to marry the young man?

My parents did try. He did not want to, he refused. He said he was not ready for marriage and responsibilities… He wanted more time to 'get used to the idea', but my parents said there was no time to waste - a baby was on the way and births cannot be delayed! One cannot wait longer than nine months! So he said: "Sorry but I cannot" and that broke my heart because I did want to be with him but obviously he didn't want me anymore! Why did I let myself be seduced?! I've never got over it. I've tortured myself and reproached myself all my life… It was such a stupid thing to do!

BR- Can you talk to me about the lady?

My daughter's lady came to help us and did it very kindly. I am not too sure what my parents decided with her. I think she adopted her officially, but I did not get any papers or documents as I "was not to think about it anymore" nor know anything! That's what was worse - not be able to know anything!

One day one of her friends told me in the street, that my daughter had been ill for some time. I didn't know it and it made me even more miserable. I wanted to see her and give her all my love, but my parents stopped me! I would have had to leave home for good to find her again… and that would have caused such a row! I could not really do it. I had already caused so much grief to my family! But the friend of the old lady knew where to find me and when to see me. She must have been watching out for me and all I could do was cry...

The time for tears is over now, I have difficulties living it again, yet I'll ask my lady to come if she can help us. You are right to want to know all that. I understand how it can help you prove all we tell you is true. But there is a real battle against time at the moment.

(Brief silence, then the pen starts again. Now my mother is online!)

My own mum had difficulties in her life. I can see that now, but I had not understood it when I was young, because I had not been told all her secrets! So how could I have known her sadness had a good reason?! I feel selfish to have reproached her for not having other children! 'My being alone', that's all I was thinking about! Not about her and her reasons...When we are young we don't know anything, do we?! On the other hand you, my children, have all been very kind and have never really reproached me with much... Perhaps to have told you off, but that's all, I think!

Last time we spoke I told you I did some 'research work' in physics, we could say! I mean, I was wondering why this 'light' exists here. I was made to understand that people and beings here (animals etc) create it from within their being, their soul - they have a lot of kindness within themselves and that is what creates that 'Light'! I only half understood the physics side of it, but as far as the result is concerned I could see they were right! So I asked myself what one could do with this light and this gift of creating light from within oneself...and my experiments ended up coming back to thought and objects and events around oneself!

You can have fun 'all day long' here creating or making things happen simply by thinking 'kindly' but also intensely of course! Intensity is essential for it to work and continue to exist. So that's how I keep myself busy. When I came here, I had fun making things, just for the pleasure of making things...

Now I take pleasure in seeing to what extent one can do it, how far one can go.

BR- What kind of events are you talking about?

My 'events' are more like a game of little scenes, I could call it, such as me saying to myself: "What would happen if So-and-So came here and I told him/her that and he replied such and such…etc." and I see it unfold as if it was a film!

BR- Could you apply this to your sister's adoptive mother… so that she recalls the good times, the adoption?

One day we'll succeed, don't worry! I can't imagine we shan't so don't fret. Think about it, we are thinking about it and I am sure it will happen. I don't know how at the moment but we'll have to find a way. You want so much to know it and I can see why it is so important.

BR- Good, because it would indeed be extraordinary to be able to find the proof of pieces of information which were unknown to us all and came from the Hereafter! Unfortunately it's over 100 years old, time passes, plus the war bombing, so I fear registers etc. may have disappeared…

Sweetheart, all of us here have heard your pleas. So don't worry, we'll have another go, even more vigorously and enthusiastically… Yes we've understood, so goodbye for now until next time. We all love you and hug and kiss you, the boys as well as your children.

"Let me get my spiritual tools!
Let me move forward bravely,
Towards Truth and the discovery,
Of what R- is seeking!
Off we go! Off we go, my darling!
Bang Bang!"

(I had the feeling Mum was singing this jolly 'march', proving she had not lost her sense of humour nor her impromptu creativity!)

12th August 2000 - *The pen starts in English. My guide covers many interesting points:*

We love to link up with you and you know it. We love to link up with the Earth because you are part of it and we want to help you. We are keen to link up because <u>we</u> *(guides and helpers)* <u>need to link up with the Earth to better our understanding of Human Beings and their situations and help them sort out their dilemmas</u> whenever we can. <u>We learn from helping you and you learn from being helped by us</u>. We have a lot to learn from you personally, because you have a wide range of emotions and you are never still - we need to learn how to cope with an ever changing Mind!

BR- Oh dear! I feel guilty... Sorry!

We are not telling you off, just describing the situation, as you often say. So we have a double-sided situation: You learn, so do we.

BR- When I had a sitting with the medium A.W, my mother talked to my daughter and me - was she giving the answers and advice herself?

Your question: You want to know whether your mother had given all these answers off her own back or whether someone was helping her give them. We are always here, always close to you. So when your mum wants to talk to you, we can help by showing her the type of answers she needs to give. She has not learnt to 'look into your future' yet you see. It is quite a complex thing to do and you should know that. Therefore what we do is <u>inspire her with the answers</u>, so that she has the satisfaction of talking to you and helping you, but without the risk of making mistakes.

As you see, she was able to help you and your daughter without having to go through the complex and at times heavy process of learning how to communicate so-called 'future' facts for you to grasp and prepare yourself for. You could not expect her to be so advanced as to being able to ***sift through***

219

all of the probabilities <u>to see what is most likely to happen and most helpful!</u> You know now what you wanted the answer to be - the Truth. We know you are always after the Truth and sincerity. We have always been true to you as far as we can see. Never have we tried to cheat or deceive you!

BR- I am concerned about proving the existence of the baby sister.

As we've told you in many different ways, you know perfectly your grandmother had not lied to you. You have indeed an aunt who had remained unknown to your own mother until now. So please do not doubt, as it does not help them!

Secondly, be patient as to her name, you will be told of course. We know you will be able to know it. We are sure of it, but we can't give it to you now because there are a few problems of memory and focusing, you see. The soul in charge of that little one has been here for quite a long time and <u>is in need of a lot of therapy to be helped to go back to those traumatic times</u> when she lost the baby. At least to when the baby died, or better said - came here. So we know it takes some time for <u>that soul to be able to focus</u> slowly but surely on that particular facet of her life, but when she does we shall do our utmost to magnify every little detail in her mind, so that words, names, dates stand out in her mind. And you'll be the first one to be told about it, believe us!

We know it can be done. It has to be done slowly, that's all, because of all the emotions involved. As the soul remembers, she has to go down, degree by degree, to <u>a sadder time which changes her environment here</u> and she does not really wish it changed to sadder times - so we must coax her gently, step by step. She knows why you want it so badly - she's understood and agrees to it. You have only spiritual aims in your heart as far as that is concerned, it's not ego or personal reasons. But we also know she needs the help this world can provide her with, to be gently 'lowered' to those sad times, to have a deeper, more thorough look. When all the information is retrieved, we'll lift her up quickly and will bring her back to her normal bright life here. We are all working on her now, so do not fret or worry. We are working on her state of mind and will bring her where she needs to be. But it has to be done at our pace and hers, not pushed or rushed or else the soul might panic or desist and refuse to bear the pain again.

Yes indeed, we are talking about the woman who looked after that little soul, that little child who was not born on Earth for long because the place was not right for her.

You have been guided so far, so do not think we shan't guide you anymore! You'll get there one day and you will know we have been with you all the way. We know you'll succeed but we are aware it will take some time. All this to wait for but what results in the end! It will be worth it, you'll see. You know we do not ever want to let you down, so never despair.

(Someone interrupts me, so I have to stop for a while. When I try to link up again, the pen starts hesitantly at first, then the flow comes quickly in French. Mum is online)

Just a moment Darling…states of mind are really complex things aren't they?! One gets used to them gradually, then another one arrives and everything changes! It's quite complicated.

I gather you want to talk to me and I am delighted as I wanted to speak to you too. It's been quite some time since we last had a chat, but it does not matter as it means there is even more to talk about! I wanted to tell you that I not only had the opportunity to speak to you via the medium, but also to have a word with Anne-France! That really gave me a lot of pleasure because she sounded worried and wanted some help. Personally I could not do everything, but I was helped by my friends here who showed me what to say or do. That way I had the great pleasure to be able to do something to help you on the Earth. I cannot see what is going to happen in the future, but I was able to give her a few pointers as to the way to turn...

BR- Is there a risk of making some mistakes?

No, no! I am sure the advice given will be good and we'll have some good results. As for you, I see you are going to move again! But this time will be much better, because the house you chose has much more space and pretty rooms where you'll be better able to do what you want, you'll see! We know it will be better for you, so don't worry.

The laws here are incredibly easy - in everything one does, one must aim at helping others and not think about oneself. So we don't need to worry about ourselves because others look after us in a way and we look after others!

BR- I thought one tried to improve oneself...

Yes, but to change and improve oneself always points eventually towards looking after the well-being of other creatures of the World (with a capital W), so it's really the same thing in the end. We made quite a lot of discoveries Dad and I...

BR- Which dad?

Mine. Or rather he makes me make them, as I am sure he had already done so before! Such as: Me who used to feel so confident and such an expert in the history of France and Europe...yet he showed me history has one meaning if you only look at it in one direction, but it has several aspects if you look at it from several sides.

BR- (Rather puzzled) Can you explain this please?

I used to see the French Revolution as a revolt of the working class masses against Royalty, but when I saw the other side of it, I saw there was more to see than that. For example, the feelings of people from all classes caused that revolution, not just the poor and the 'rabble'. The Revolution was a revolt of the souls of all those who knew, within themselves, that there were far too many injustices in that country, so the rising of emotions caused that great wave of anger which finally pushed people to attack the Bastille etc, but it began in people's hearts and Souls. When people's souls are shaken, everything is shaken, that's how it happens in the world. One must reach people's souls in order to have some definite results, results which achieve something.

My mother told me you are trying to know more about the baby sister whom I did not know. Personally I cannot do more as I don't know anything else. She said the kind lady has been asked to make great efforts with her memory (and her emotions too, I think) to manage to recall that period of time. According to what I am told, I think there is hope they'll succeed. Patience will no doubt be needed but you'll see that the day we give you details you'll be so glad, you'll no longer think of the long wait you had.

BR- I am sure! But there will still be the problem of finding proof of it on Earth, as it depends on whether those archives still exist...

We'll all be there, where you'll need to go. That way we'll guide you as best as we can. The end of your problems is going to come soon, the end of your worries. You have had a lot of worries lately. Well, you'll see now things will be better and you'll be more certain of what you are doing or going to do. They say they 'have got plans for you' apparently!

BR- Who are 'They'?

They? People who look after you, I can see it clearly. They are kind and 'advanced', one can feel it. For you to manage to receive what they want to tell you, you must have a clear mind - that's why you must rest, sleep and also take some time to be quiet and worry free...

Sweetheart, I think of you all to send you good wishes, all the time. I only wish you good things and success, I know you all need it! Therefore do not worry, there are always some good wishes coming in your direction, all of you!

BR- Thanks a lot! Do you want to talk about anything else?

No, I'll let you go and give you big kisses as always, with all my love. Dad does it too (He's just told me by thought transference...) See you soon! Ta ta!

22nd August 2000 - *23.55hrs - Late but I am not tired- French is spoken:*

We are going to tell you off for staying up and going to bed so late once more...but since we want to speak to you, we won't keep moaning so that you don't go away!

I'd like to tell you my family struggled a lot for you lately, in order to try to get all the information you are asking for. The hardest is for the kind lady to remember those details. We do know she exists, but you don't. So we must manage to prove her and the baby sister's existence.

I have indeed seen my sister but I must admit she appeared to me like a stranger since I never knew her! It's a pity in a way because I had so much wanted to have a brother or sister...and what happens? I discover I had and have one now, yet it's all the same to me!

But we want to tell you we are working at it. The kind lady is making great efforts - she makes 'trips' in her mind, in her memory. She has been doing so for some time since we asked her. She is afraid of suffering again the grief she endured when the baby died, but I think she is going to overcome it when she reaches that stage. We saw people looking after her, we don't know who they are. They seem kind and 'useful' as she seems to react to what they tell her. That kind of thing is always a mystery, you know! There are so many things going on here. When one ponders a little about them, one wonders where it's coming from and how it happens!

So there we are, unfortunately no 'great news' nor name or date, not yet anyway, but she is having a go and we all have hope she'll manage it.

The futility of daily life on Earth has been striking me since I came here! When I think of the hours one spends on Earth doing lots of things which are in a way useless and unimportant, whereas there are so many, many fascinating things to know, discover and understand, as I keep telling you! Why waste one's time with trifles and other trivia which will be of no use later on? Seen from here, everything appears petty and useless! How many hours have I spent in front of the TV, enraged and frustrated by the stupidity and uselessness of many programmes!

My own life has changed indeed since I arrived here and I can see there is so much to grasp and explore. I do keep very busy, I can assure you!

You must carry on listening to me and write it down, all right? I hope you are not going to stop, as there'll be much more to say! There are times when I don't have much to talk about but it doesn't mean nothing is happening here... It's just that I am experimenting with things they taught me earlier and I practise them, I do my exercises and my 'homework'!..

BR- Could a' Superior Being' explain why the adoptive lady has difficulties?

'Kind sources' have arrived from all directions to explain: "The 'old lady' had been making thought trips and expeditions in her mind which have taught her a lot of things to place her on a 'superior, more evolved' level. Because of that, she has moved away mentally from what she knew of her Earth life, especially sad times. Life here is not hard, life on Earth IS, compared to here, you know. So she has to grab moments of that life which is like a kaleidoscope in her mind: 'Which little lozenges represent those moments in that particular Earthly life?' Therefore we are all waiting for the kaleidoscope to become a picture of one era of her life and we shall all rush to go and see!" *(A long silence)* Goodnight...go to sleep. We all give you lots of kisses until next time.

225

6th September 2000 - *The pen forms the first three words in French:*

We are here. We came, Dad and I, to help you understand what is going on - my dad and yours too as he is very interested in all this, as you can guess! He would be the first one to go to Boulogne to try and find out the information you need!.. I tried to get mediums to tell you but I did not manage.

BR- Tell me what?

I wanted to tell you the search is ongoing. I don't have any results but we know where we are going. They told me: "There is a lot of work to do on our side for the 'old lady' to manage to find in the forest of her good and bad memories, the names, dates and places we need, as you asked".

I understand myself why it seems so complicated but it is very possible, as my own memories get muddled up when I look at them from here!

One does not feel like one did on Earth - one has access to so many other levels of thought that little details become fuzzy... That's why people here do not always remember who they were on Earth at a certain time.

For the time being I do know who I am. I say 'for the time being' because one never knows, it could happen! I don't see how I could forget names like my own children's and family's, my friends'…but one can assume that if one has made discoveries and trips in one's mind and soul etc. well, one perhaps discovers 'other aspects' and it must be confusing.

BR- Have your parents spoken to you about this or have they done it?

My parents haven't said anything on the subject but your dad told me he made excursions in his 'past', let's say, in what he was before coming on Earth the time we knew him, you and I: that's what so intriguing! What did he do before and in-between? I always wondered what kind of answers one would get to such a question…

He showed me a little of what he was talking about - they <u>are more impressions than facts. He saw them in his mind and projected them out for me to see</u> , but in my opinions they are only 'impressions'. I suppose they are aspects of his personality and his Spirit (as a Spirit being). That's what is so fascinating, if one starts trying to understand more! We have interesting conversations, from time to time, when he shares what he has discovered since he's been here. He has done more than I have of course, because he arrived before I did, but we are still in contact, on good terms and exchange ideas.

He helped me understand lots of things as soon as I arrived here. He wanted me to become acclimatised as soon as possible, so that I did not waste any time with the errors that lots of people make on their arrival. One does not need a bed, nor sleep or food! One can create it for oneself but what for really? The only truth is that we are alive! That is what must or should be the dominant factor. We do not need to worry about anything at all. <u>We are alive without a flesh body</u>! This is proof that the flesh is not the real 'us'! My own flesh gave me a lot of trouble during the last years of my earthly life. I had enough problems and operations to last me a whole lifetime! So I prefer this one, I assure you, I have suffered plenty enough but am all right now. As I was telling you, your dad and mine tell me really interesting things and I learn them as best as I can in order to better understand what goes on here.

BR- What happens when you and I speak? Do you see or 'sense' me? (Unfortunately I lose my concentration and the link with Mum! After a few moments English is spoken, so it must be my guide)

All is not lost. You have just lost contact for a moment that's all. Your mind has the rapidity of lightning and <u>it is hard to keep track of where your thoughts land! They land in different parts of our 'Thought world'</u>, but you won't understand this. They float all over like birds or butterflies flying around and we've got to catch them right, left, centre and above!.. <u>It's hard to find what is for us and what is for nobody in particular!</u>

That's why <u>we have come in to settle your mind, to make you focus</u> as you can talk to us more easily, I think. Let's hope you can link up to your mother again.

May I ask you to be patient with the search for the sister's names etc. There has been some progress but not in the sense you'd mean. We have moved forward in our own work towards getting those details, but it's not concrete yet in the way you would want it. The lady is very willing and happy to do it. All that needs to be worked on is her mind, her Spirit, her way of thinking, her memories, her emotions and all that's happened to her then and before and since...and all that is like a big 'now', if you see what I mean! So we are trying to help her sieve through that lot, to find what's relevant to your search.

You may think this is very strange, unreal and complicated, maybe even 'fake' or whatever you call it on Earth - but we can only tell you what is happening. Though to you it may feel slow and sadly unrewarding, we feel we have moved forward by a few steps. It has to take time for many 'technical' reasons, as you would say. We know you will get the answer eventually, but it will have to be worked for from our end. We have a large team of researchers helping her find out what she needs, it will be possible.

BR- Wouldn't it help her to see her little girl 'grown-up' and as a 'baby'?

We know what you are saying - her little girl has been to see her as a grown-up daughter as well as a 'little baby' as known then. It has helped her remember the lovely feeling of having a baby with her, but it has also brought the sadness of losing her.

BR- Surely it must be all right to see her alive?

It's not all right to see her alive if one remembers the sad times of pain and sorrow - that <u>stays in your mind even</u>

228

when one knows the end result! You have pain in your heart when you remember your mum's pains, traumas, bodily death and yet you know she is here, she is all right, without any pain!

BR- That's true!..

So why can't you see this lady has difficulties to reconcile the two? They are feelings that cannot be wiped off.

BR- Couldn't you ask the little girl?

The daughter of your mum's mother is very confused as far as that is concerned. She had not grown up enough to remember in detail, 'technical' information, those things you want to know. To her, as a baby, the need for love and food was all that mattered. Now she has gone beyond all that long ago and has certainly not paid attention to those points. So we are all wanting and waiting and trying to get things and thoughts on the right track so that all is recognised finally in its true 'human form'. That is facts you could find on paper, instead of emotions and feelings and souls recognising each other from the inner side of themselves rather than from the outer layers called 'names' and 'places'.

We have not forgotten so don't worry. We are working at it, all of us here who care for you and your goal. Our goal is to be with you in your endeavours, to help you succeed in getting your plan worked out, your searches successful, your love of life straightened up.

BR- What do you mean by this last sentence?

You love life or else you would not have chosen to be on Earth, but you have constant hiccups in what you want to have and what makes you happy. So we hope to help you find out finally what you need to have and to do in order to get to your goal. One's life plan, as you call it, has many facets... You can get to it from different directions.

BR- What is mine?

Your heart's inner desire, that is what you are on Earth for. To fulfil what fills you up and then you'll be fulfilled, your soul will sing as you often say, but you have not been singing lately. Only one thing to do: Try to listen within more often, to be sure to stay on the right track.

BR- Have I deviated a lot?

The right track is the one leading to the 'soul singing'. The soul singing comes from the 'Inner Real You', who knows where you want to be or what you want to achieve.The moment you feel unhappy it's because you've got off track. We shall talk to you about that another day. Please go and sleep and rest, you will feel better afterwards. We have the eternal good luck of not having to bother about our body! Do go and look after yours. We love you all.

16th September 2000 - *The pen starts the first six words in French:*

A hundred times have I told you not to go to bed so late! I only keep repeating myself, don't I? Why do you wait so late to speak to us?! You see you have difficulties in linking up because you are tired. I know you have things to do but it would be much better if you started earlier, you wouldn't have so long to wait!

BR- I know but unfortunately it's not always possible.

You want to find out whether we have succeeded in obtaining anything regarding my sister, don't you? Yes I know it's painful to wait but we can't do anything about that. All I can do is wait too as I cannot speed up the process. I don't understand why it takes so long, but apparently one cannot always manage to find such precise details without a lot of difficulties. The main question is to know who the lady was, her town and dates and the little girl's name. Why these don't appear clearly is not obvious to me, as I assume I would remember mine - but one never knows here as things are not like on Earth, therefore there must be some good reasons...

Now I have something else to tell you: I went to see

some friends whom I knew when I was very young and I had recognised when I arrived here. Since then we've met again from time to time. Last time they showed me their superb house, with staircases as you see them in films! Enough to dream about... but also to wonder why have marble here? The reason they surround themselves with beautiful things is because they could not have them when they were on Earth, as they were not wealthy enough... So they've made up for it here and created this villa for themselves, this sumptuous palace which costs them nothing since we don't deal with money here! It feels funny to find oneself in places like this in the 'World of the Dead' (Let's say it in a spooky and ghostly voice!).

In fact it is a world so full of life and so rich, it is a constant wonder I can't get over! Yet I have been here for some time, haven't I?

BR- Do you have any idea how long you have been there?

I no longer think in months and years now; it feels strange not to think that way as we don't feel days passing. We do not have time to see days pass by! We are too busy dealing with things which are so interesting and varied and learning such profound truths or doing such weird experiments... There isn't time to be bored or to wonder how long one has been doing it for! There is nothing more to fear now. I can assure you Death is nothing terrible - it is only a swift passage from one world to another. Life (on Earth) is far more terrible than Death and it can be a nightmare to live, so do not fear anything! I want to reassure you as you seem worried.

BR- I only wonder whether I risk getting cancer after the upsets in my life...

You have no need to worry about that. I am told you are going to live in good health for a long time still, so things are all right, do not be concerned. On the other hand it would be better if you went to bed now, as your mind is not very clear and you must be sleepy to have dozed off just like that in the middle of a conversation! I am going to let you sleep but I don't want you to be sad. We see each other and will do so often, so why cry now?

My darling daughter, you must go to sleep for the 'hours of beauty' which are indeed shortened each time you speak to me! We are not going to hold you back any longer! Ta ta! See you later...sleep soon and well! *(Further talks have been edited. This is said in case the reader thinks I have ignored my communicators for several months!)*

17th January 2001 - *15.00hrs. I send a thought in case someone wishes to communicate. The pen writes the first 3 words in French:*

We've wanted to talk to you for a long time, you know. I am sorry you had so much to do and I could not help you. Now you appear calmer, more serene. Things seem to be better and you are settled to your liking aren't you?

BR- Is this you, Mum?

Yes of course Darling, it's Mum. I came as soon as I heard you call. I was not doing anything special which could have prevented me from coming and chatting with you, at last! I don't know where to start!

BR- Tell me what you've been doing.

I did lots of little things which I found interesting. I am not sure whether I told you the luminosity here is so different from what it is on Earth, that it's a pleasure to look at light here and you don't get eye ache! I am not sure what I told you last time we spoke. My pleasure is to discover, learn and try those new things, but also rest now and then to assimilate all that. I think last time I told you I had seen birds sing and it was not like on Earth, didn't I? There are so many differences!

Here we don't need to think in words. One way or the

232

other we think in pictures and see and sense pictures coming from others. No doubt that's why the <u>birds' songs</u>, which mean something to birds, <u>are understandable to everyone</u>, because <u>their thoughts become visible</u>!

But there are other things too: Simply being here and realising it, knowing we 'died' one day on Earth, we no longer have a flesh body and yet we feel 'whole' in a way, is really extraordinary, you know!

You'll see when you come over, you'll think the same, but it's not for tomorrow, don't worry! We'll warn you, you'll see!

I know you have trouble staying online. I don't want to hold you back. I am very happy to talk to you if you want to. I saw many friends here, including those new friends who helped me a lot to understand all the new things I told you about. There are happenings which are impossible to explain because they are impressions, visions and levels of emotions which take... *(I must have been terribly tired for concentration to make me lose the communication in broad daylight! Poor Mum!)*

***

CHAPTER 5
Points in the universe: Centres of creation - Indestructible nature of thoughts - Choosing lives

18th February 2001 - *11am! The pen starts in French - It's Mum:*

Uplift your thoughts towards us and you'll see it's not as difficult as you think. We have been waiting for you for a long time, my poor busy Sweetheart. I am so glad to be able to speak with you. I have wanted, hundreds of times, to share with you things which happened or happen here, but I did not have a 'telephone link'!

You'll be pleased to learn that your mum's sister is close. She wants to try to talk to you! I'll put her through if she can make herself understood, otherwise you'll have to find another medium so that you understand each other. I am going to see whether she's been able to come...

(Change of communicator)...The hardest for us, in this world, is to 'look back' and not get mixed up with dates and places, because once we are here, we do not have any more points of reference. There are things we want to forget or not remember, so it's difficult to dig out what has been buried at the bottom of one's memory...

I asked my adoptive mother to make the effort for me as I did not have enough details myself. I learnt she had indeed adopted a baby girl - me and she had given me the name Angeline I think, but I did not remember that. She took the baby as the mother could not keep her, because of taboos and rules in the society of that time, which means the little one never knew her real mother.

When the baby was ill the real mother did not know it, but death has finally reunited them after many years. It seems the name of the family where she was adopted started with the sound B...?

My friends here say we still have to do more research to get more precise details.

It is harder to speak through someone's mind than directly, as your thoughts are like a kind of fog to cross. The adoptive mother does not want to talk for the time being, I think she will concentrate once and for all...on the day when we can talk directly via a medium or something like that. You have now the task to organise it as we'd like to help you prove we exist and you are quite right to want to do so. If we were able to give you all the details in black and white it would be wonderful, but one has to take them one by one, slowly. The very fact you are talking to me and me to you, is already an extraordinary event, don't you think so? I for one am very amazed as I had never known you and didn't really know you existed, as there was no link between us.

If you want to help my kind adoptive mother to remember, you can send her warm loving thoughts. That definitely helps, you know, even if you think it leads to nothing. I did try to say more the day you spoke to that medium but she had difficulties understanding what I was trying to say. A word like Marquise came to mind from somewhere...(*The pen tries to write something 'in Automatic' but I don't manage to decipher the word*). Being able to write is not my strong point, I have trouble doing it, you know, not having done it before.

I am told most people who died in France have their tomb very neat. It remains to be seen whether it will still be there and clear enough for you to read it easily. That is a problem we cannot solve from here but there could be possibilities.

My friends here say they hope you may manage to find the papers you are after. It will take time and patience but you can succeed because you are determined to find them, though it will not be as easy as we'd like. This will involve a lot of research but hopefully you should be able to do it. They reckon you should be able to prove my existence, though it was short-lived on Earth. Perhaps that is why I was born, in order to give you, 100 years later, the proof of Life after Death which, one day, you would research, for the good of Mankind, let's hope!

We are quite hopeful and we did what we could so far... The soul of the 'departed' is not something tangible but a web of thoughts it tries to transpose on your thoughts and it is not easy... I promise you we'll do our best to give you any detail we possibly get... *(My Mum suddenly comes back to talk!)*... The reason why she came is she wanted to have a 'direct line' but she knew she may not be able to give clear information...

As for me, as usual I have been busy discovering more and more. There is so much to do! I have made some progress with the control of my thoughts for them to be clear and reliable every time, so that I can direct them and get a result.

My ideas have not changed too much...and yet they have! By this I mean, I understand better the value and the overall aspect of things, their other sides, as one only sees one side when on Earth, one does not realise and grasp all the aspects of Truth.

I had always believed that what we saw on Earth, people's skin colour, their nastiness, their stupidity were what they were, their own aspect!.. Now I have been made to understand it was only <u>one</u> <u>aspect</u> of their personality. There was far more we did not see and that this little 'stain' was not <u>the real, whole person, who, of course, is not the Human on Earth but the Spirit who incarnated for that particular life</u>.

One must look more deeply to see the true 'colour' of a person, not his skin colour of course, but colours of his Spiritual Being. Those are wonderful, especially in someone who has spent a lot of time improving himself. The kind 'Beings' surrounding us look like 'people' in a way, but as soon as they start speaking to us, <u>we lose all notion of the shape they first appeared as and we only see the splendour of</u>

<u>the Spiritual Beings they are.</u> That's when someone's true light reveals itself, when it shines, because this person, this Being, is kind and superior to the average mentality of an 'Earthling', as I'd say. There are good and bad people everywhere but <u>the bad ones have not learnt to make their good side stand out</u>, that's what is sad.

You know, I do have difficulties always accepting everything here! I listen and I accept what I am told because I know they must be right. But between that and being able to assimilate the lot in order to change my views completely... Hum?! It will no doubt take some time, because on Earth I had to suffer from people's stupidity and nastiness for too long. Well, perhaps not suffer myself, but see them doing harm around me and in the world. I do hope one day I'll begin to understand, believe it myself and know it. One must improve oneself, it's the rule here, like on Earth, but it's easier here, I assume...

What matters is that you and I can get together from time to time. You have your own life to live and survive. You must do what you need to do, so I won't admonish you for not speaking to me more often! You have your own reasons I am sure, as I know how much you love and want to do it for your/our book, don't you! Let's say, I am a little bit sad because I wish we could do it all the time as I mentioned before, but it is not real sadness, you must not worry about it since I have all the time needed to wait! I can do what I want, I do not have time limits nor sleep hours etc, so do not worry Darling.

BR- Are you aware of what happened to Touky?

My little Touky was attacked, yes I know. I was told because we are aware of everything here you see. I was told not to worry and the best thing was to think strongly of him with love, so that these loving thoughts transform themselves into healing of his body. He was very lucky not to be more

237

injured. Unfortunately he suffered and no doubt still suffers, but I want to be able to send him healing thoughts, it will help him. We are thinking of him, don't worry, we are helping him.

BR- Who are 'we'?

Everyone around me and of course, your dad, me, my dad etc. We have your lives in front of us like cards to fill with love, so that the journey goes well. So do not think you are alone, you are surrounded and loved all the time. We do not forget you...

The visits of my Spiritual Friends, those who teach me so much, are the highlights of my stay here. When one meets them it feels so incredibly good, one does not want them to leave. They come from time to time to reinforce ideas or explain some things I am thinking about. For example, they appear in the middle of a 'discussion', a conversation, they get involved nicely and kindly, with so much knowledge one would like them to stay there all the time! They come...then suddenly one feels they are not here anymore! It does seem weird at times, instead of seeing them moving away gradually... But since I know one easily travels by thought here, all this does not amaze me any longer, you see (Ha Ha! Aren't I blasé?!). When we have received their teaching, we feel much more 'fed' and satisfied, as if we have discovered something we needed to find out a long time ago! The beauty of knowing more is an unimaginable pleasure you know. The beauty and the joy of learning, that's what gives <u>me</u> pleasure, do you understand?

My life (on Earth) has been filled with some good times; those when I learnt something new have been amongst the best! As you see, it carries on and I am very happy about it!

My personality is still the same, you know, I have not changed overnight. But I have learnt and I am learning more and that is what will allow me to 'progress', I suppose; to know more in order to help others and help you and the boys and people to whom you'll tell all this... It's like a chain with multiple links isn't it?! We help each other, we link up, we support each other, we teach each other and so on...

My darling daughter, you are going to delay your work if you talk to me all day, haven't you any urgent things you want or have to do? You've had the main points about my life here. It may not seem much but it is difficult to sum up things, events which are not really events but developments and conversations, practice and fun time, do you understand?

BR- Do you see your sister?

My sister does not turn up often because we do not think much about each other, as we did not know one another. But each time she came it was with kindness, warmth and friendship. She has always been kind and even funny, as she often jokes about the fact I thought I was an only child, whereas in fact I had a sister and did not know it!

BR- Poor you, that was sad!

Yes, sad in a way, but the funny thing was me imagining I never had a brother or a sister! When we met, she did not make any special efforts to show herself in a kind of physical way, because after all, I had never seen her in flesh and blood! So she didn't need that. She did it more by using emotions and contact through thought, the 'music she emanates' if you see what I mean, her warmth and the colours of its energy, I could say. That's how we feel people rather than by the shape of their body, because the body here is an imaginary body or reinvented, isn't it! So it does not mean anything any longer, except as a help to recognise someone for the first time and yet you need to have known them on Earth!

BR- I hesitate to 'call' you at times, in case you were busy...

There is no risk of 'disturbing' me if you call. I am always ready and willing to have a chat with you, like when we were together on Earth.

BR- I think I must have been tiring you sometimes!

You were not tiring me. The trouble was my body was worn out, so I unfortunately needed to sleep you see, but not nowadays fortunately! I give you a big kiss Darling *(I feel emotional)*. Please do not cry, I feel so well now I am here. I would not want to find myself in my flesh body which hurt me so much, so often! Be happy for me!

BR- Yes I know and I am. It's because I love you, Darling Mum...

I love you too Sweetheart. We'll talk again a lot and one day we'll meet again and will be happy together. Tell the boys I am not forgetting them!

21st April 2001 - *The pen starts in French. It's Mum:*

We have exciting things to do here and we'll try to explain them, as it is not always easy to put it into words. Since we last spoke, we've seen very interesting people who taught us lots of things. I guess it's probably going to be difficult to explain in words rather than as experiences. There is not always that difference is there? Sometimes I forget we have trouble explaining what we see and feel here!

Anyway, last time I spoke to you, I told you my mum's lady who looked after the baby was indeed willing to try and remember names etc *(I was not thinking about it and was taken by surprise)*. Well, I am told she saw, like 'in a dream', names and places she may be able to give now, so make sure to have a really good medium who could receive this information. *(Note: unfortunately the best I know have moved away! Usually, names are one of the hardest things to transmit between the two worlds. How frustrating!)* I don't know whether I'd be able to do it, because it looks as if it must be her explaining all that. She's let it be known she would come, but she is not here at the moment.

My mum tells me she is really pleased you are interested in her story! At the beginning she appeared not to want to have anything to do with it, because it brought back too many nasty memories and bad times! Now she looks very happy we accept it and want to know and honour her baby who, of course, is no longer a baby but is here with us as an 'adult', a woman.

The kind lady told us that after all that time, there will probably be some difficulties with finding graves and papers, but that she knows she existed... and would like to be able to prove it now! Isn't it weird, hey? All those people who are happy here, but whom you 'stirred up' in a way, have suddenly become interested in what they used to be. This is simply because what they want to do, in fact, is prove to people of your era now, that they too lived and are still alive, but in a world which is different in a way, yet far more real in another way!

The most touching thing in my opinion, is that everyone rallied round to your call for 'help' as far as looking back to the 'past', to prove or find or recall some names, places or events. I would not have thought one could have had such solidarity, yet we must remember we are in a world of kindness, compassion and mutual assistance. Nothing is too much for those here! Someone needs help? There will always be somebody coming to give you a hand or rescue you, even if it's simply to answer a question troubling you.

As for me, I don't have any more problems fortunately. All I have to do is have fun learning new things. Yet as soon as I ask myself "why?" and "how?" it's enough for a 'Superior Soul' to turn up at once, to 'meet me by chance' and provide me with the explanations I need. Isn't that smashing, hey?

My parents showed me lots while strolling with me somewhere or other. We go to buildings, or reunions, or meetings, where we may hear talks or do some kind of 'practice exercises' or both; that's what intrigues and interests me! Each time I pay great attention, because not only do I want to be able to remember it and understand properly, but also I want to tell you as much as possible about it.

There are hard things to grasp, such as light, sound and speed of light and things like that! That is physics and I really must make an effort to understand! Yet I think it will come gradually one day... I hope. Also there are some extraordinary happenings. If you found yourself in the middle of a crowd of people, all on the same wavelength of course, then you saw them disappear in front of you, what would you think?..

I assure you it gives a shock as one is not expecting it and one wonders how it happened! Though there is some complicated physics behind all this, I do see that in this world where I am now, there is nothing but 'Spirit stuff' everywhere, which is life, vitality and energy. There is nothing 'dead' or lifeless, in an energy context; everything reacts to everything else, everything vibrates, everything sings, everything is so alive that one cannot but feel it!

I see I can't find the right words to explain all this, me who could always explain everything before! I want to say the world here has no other aim than discovering itself, making itself known to others and elsewhere... Er... Blast! It's impossible to explain! There is only this desire to understand and make oneself understood. There is the wish to be able to solve and fix every-thing, but also the realisation that one can create more than one has or one is! That is what I find incredible! How can one make oneself different?! Yet yes, one can! One can improve oneself, that's the way to do it here. How? By working at it, by desiring it and by extending oneself, in the field of knowledge and under-standing, compassion, kindness and acceptance. There is a lot to do to succeed in improving oneself as it is not so easy, but the desire is present; when one tackles it, the problem decreases! My thoughts have become more visible to myself and to others!

BR- It must be inconvenient?

No it isn't really, because if you don't have bad or nasty thoughts, you don't risk being embarrassed, do you! Oh, I would not say I am on the way to becoming a 'saint'! But the joy to be here and the desire to learn and understand have no limits; the more one learns, the more one understands, the more immense the joy is and the more the desire to use it and to share it increases. When one starts grasping the enormity of the task in front of us and the need to improve oneself, in order to reach even higher levels of knowledge and possible activities, then one does not slow down, one pushes oneself to see what there is further ahead!

I can only tell you what I experience at the moment, but it's worth doing: <u>We see each other as lights, instead of flesh 'people'</u> as we were on the Earth! Already that is an extraordinary revelation because one has not got the skill to do it usually. But being able to do this allows us to <u>understand each other without having to speak.</u> Anyway, I had often noticed we did not always 'speak' to each other, in fact less and less and it surprised and amused me a lot... I could see that, indeed, it was something one could not do on Earth! The progress in knowing oneself and others is not limited nor judged. One discovers oneself gradually, <u>one must understand oneself, because one cannot go any further otherwise</u>. It's no use knowing we act or think in a certain way and that's all there is to know! We must understand <u>why</u> we feel that way, why we react like that. Afterwards it enables us to analyse more and grasp what has to be done to <u>change</u> the weaknesses and improve them!

Personally I have always tended to doubt things which were not clear and not to bother with complicated things! Unfortunately that does not help clarify difficult points does it?! But I do realise that if I let my soul, my mind open up like a big flower or a parasol or a large screen, if I let comprehension expand on its own, instead of forcing it or trying to force myself to comprehend, then it's much better. Soon after doing so, I notice I have understood and assimilated something which, previously, I found much more difficult!

I reckon you must think I am rambling on, don't you! But I know you too will try to understand (*Just then one of my cats disturbs me; I explain to Mum what happened*). We have cats here too you know. I look after them and still love them. Lots of cats of all colours and shapes, because they are happy to be with someone who loves them. There is no need to feed them because they don't have a flesh body: they know it in a way as they are not hungry. I look after them, I mean I go and see them, stroke and kiss them...

BR- (Teasingly) You used to forbid us to kiss our cats!..

Well, I can here, you see, because there are no germs! So there!.. I make them happy by loving them and they make me feel happy because they love me, they purr as 'spiritual cats' and tell me kind things because I know what they say when looking at me.

BR- How do you know?

I can sense what a cat thinks when he looks at me and cuddles me, because his thoughts are pure and filled with love. All he has to do is come near me and 'kiss me with a glance' for me to know what he feels and thinks! But I have the advantage of not being on Earth, that's why I can do that! You Darling, you'll have to wait until you come here to be able to do the same!

To return to our discussions on progress and knowledge, I have not told you that Dad has visited 'elsewhere', that is to say levels of Thoughts far superior and elevated...

BR- Can you give me more details?

It is difficult to explain what that means. I am going to try or I'll ask him to speak to you; he'll probably be able to do it better than me. I also really feel like taking you in my arms and kissing you, you know!

BR- I wish I could too!

I do miss you too and I wish you were here, so that we could make all these discoveries together, but I suppose, first, you have to do your 'homework' on Earth and I mine here.

BR- We still do meet at night, don't we? What happens?

Oh yes, we've met many a time, don't worry! But I think you don't realise because your body is fast asleep.

BR- Is my mind asleep too?

No, you are wide awake when you come here. You come and meet me at the place where we meet people in their sleep, because they <u>cannot come further than a certain level</u>. We certainly hug and kiss, but the joy of seeing each other again is always tarnished by the fact you must return to your body and wake up on Earth instead of here! Yet it is a pity you don't remember it, as you would have more happiness in your heart, less sadness, if you did know <u>we are often together</u>.

I realise you've managed to make me talk for a long time whereas you should be sleeping! I no longer need that sleep I used to love so much and was seeking at anytime! How things change!

I see my boys are still struggling with their Earthly problems. How I wish I had a magic wand to help them! I can only send you very strong loving thoughts as that will make you succeed and will protect you, I was told here.

So, I want to do my best, as always and I follow the advice of my 'superiors' as I call them to tease them (but here nobody gives themselves such titles, you see). There is no feeling of 'superiority' or 'inferiority'; it's 'all is one', everyone equal! Yet we do realise when some 'Superior Being' comes to join in our conversation to help us. In fact he is certainly far 'superior' to anyone in the group or the reunion, but there is no fuss or trumpets to announce it! They appear suddenly, or come in, or happen to be near you, as if they'd been there all along from the beginning! It really is Paradise here!

I am going to let you sleep so that you feel fresh tomorrow. Who knows, we may speak again then? So I kiss you goodnight my darling girl who helped me so much when I was ill. I love you forever, without forgetting we shall see and be together again one day. Don't forget that! I'll let you sleep now. Your Mum who loves you.

12th May 2001 - *01.00am (I had fallen asleep earlier so I feel wide awake now)*

There is no need to worry, Sweetheart. Everything will be ok... It's your mum. There is nothing to dread. The worries and concerns you have at the moment will be solved, you'll see.

BR- Which ones are you talking about?

To do with work and home and Anne-France and the rest... You seem to have clouds around you, but we can see from here there is nothing to fear as the clouds will soon disappear. I only see lovely sunshine for you all. The Law of Truth, I was told, is the one governing us here; I would not be allowed to say things which are untrue as it would have repercussions on my own and others' lives and you too would suffer from it, which I certainly don't want!

I only want good for you and am not here to do you any harm. So, you can rest in peace, everything will get better. The little problems you have at the moment are only passing showers as fine weather is on the horizon for good. The following facts were pointed out to me:

You should not be afraid of letting go of what gives you trouble, as it will allow you to do some good elsewhere, because you'll feel more relaxed. There'll be no harm letting a job go as others will come along, if you want them.

If life on Earth becomes too stressful, one won't achieve anything. Therefore the solution is to create for oneself a life where one can be useful and feel fulfilled. That's some advice for you. <u>Do what feels right for you</u> and leave the rest of the details to those who love you here. 'Help yourself and you will be helped!' Yes, it's really true as we can help from here, if you have your heart in the right place and intentions in the right direction. Darling, I think you had a lot of worries about your own children lately. There were some about Jim who had a lot of hard work, but you'll see that in the end there are always good results with him. You must not worry... He'll have even more work to do, but he'll manage it and will have at last a much happier life, more fulfilled. I am told all this, as you know I would not know how to see into the future like they can do here.

(Note: Mum was right. As I type this neatly later for publication, Jim suddenly decided to study for a degree in 'Music Production' at Leeds University College of Music. After 3 years of rather hard work, he gained his degree with high marks in summer 2004. Within a month, he found a job as a recording technician in a very large, modern and well-known studio in Wales, where at first they employed him on a temporary basis for a month: But in fact one week after he arrived, they were so impressed by his expertise he was offered a permanent job, with full board. He is very busy but likes his work which is varied and has access to a wide range of equipment for his own use. Great for him since music is his love and his life!)

As for Anne-France, there is nothing to worry about whatsoever. Everything is in good hands, we are going to see her much happier soon. She'll be successful, with good results and her life will be better from now on. There is indeed nothing to fear on any score.

(Later note: Anne-France decided in autumn 2001, to study 'Electro-Crystal Therapy' with Harry Oldfield, a well-known and internationally recognised therapy. She obtained her diploma and also started a degree in Nutrition Therapy at P.College (by correspondence as well as attending practicals

247

and lectures in London) to be even more knowledgeable, which will lead to giving private consultations, always superbly paid in the rich county of Kent. The owner of the health food shop where she'd been working part-time, impressed by Anne-France's efficiency and enthusiasm, offered her in winter 2002, a job as her manager, then later on as Health Consultant; therefore a secure and better paid job, which Anne-France loves doing as she feels she can help the public. Thus she can work full-time and take her time to study for her degree).

You are the only one seeing the bad sides of things, we see the good sides. So believe us, from here we can see further than you! The life you make for yourself is important because it prepares you for this one here; there is a lot to learn on Earth, but even more to find out here! If one gets used to learning when on Earth, one has no problem 'studying' here. In fact 'studying' is our life here, because we don't do anything which is not useful. We have so many opportunities to discover and learn, it's incredible! One would need centuries of Earth life to 'assimilate' what we see and discover in one moment of our life here.

There are indeed compensations on Earth; one can do different things without realising it. There are details on Earth which appear important, so one gets attached to them and for that particular moment it is a special experience and one enjoys it. But in the end, over all, it is not really important!

<u>What matters is that the life you lived was useful</u>, whichever way you lead it. So there you are, do your best, do what you can where you want, but <u>always do your best</u> and you'll see you'll get paid double when you come here.

BR- (Jokingly) Does one get 'good marks' and 'gold stars'?

No, not so much good marks but feelings of pleasure to have done one's best and also knowing one has helped others. It contributes to understanding and knowing oneself better and

248

adds to the 'sea of kindness' which we are constantly steeped in, here. It seems strange to say 'the sea of kindness' but it is nearly true in a way, except it's more air than water, as we are soaked in it, impregnated with it all the time. There isn't one moment we don't feel loved, surrounded with love and under-standing. I must admit it's an unbelievable feeling. I still cannot get over it, even after all the time spent here!

There are always things to learn and practise to improve oneself, so one is never bored! Not me anyway! There are 'days' (as we'd say on Earth) when there is so much to do and see, you'd think you won't manage it, yet it seems to 'get into your head' without you noticing! The vision one has of one's own life and of the one here is amazing!

BR- Do you mean the life on Earth?

Yes, life on Earth and the one here. <u>We see ourselves as we were on Earth, we analyse ourselves</u>, we understand our-selves, we can explain what we are and were. <u>We understand ourselves far better</u> than when we were there... It helps to progress in order to improve our weak points and expand the good sides. Indeed, we have plenty to do and 'enough on our plate' as you'd say! <u>If one sees one has done something wrong on Earth, one can rectify it using thoughts, to see it 'done right', how it should be</u>! But if one sees something done well, one can rejoice and enjoy it too, because it feels good to know one has acted properly and <u>one feels happy to have known what to do</u> in that situation.

There is also the advantage of being able to see how one could have done it even better; using thoughts, one activates it and it appears 'done even better', therefore it is pleasant to think one knows how to do it.

My friends here tried to explain to me (I was going to say 'explained' but I am not sure I grasped it all!), that <u>if one activates something from here, it can become real in your world! It's a weird and incredible *system of specific points in*</u>

the universe which are centres of creation, or something like that! <u>If one sends strong thoughts, it makes them appear on Earth!</u>

There are lots of complications for it to happen. I don't mean 'problems' but complicated things, as far as technique and physics are concerned, for it to transform itself into action on Earth. Yet that's what goes on, it happens and I find it unbelievable! Can you imagine: How can I rectify something I did some 80 years ago? I really cannot grasp how one can do such a journey backwards...but physics laws here are different from what is assumed on Earth, so facts and activities are different but hard to explain!

BR- Try to explain if you can, please…

I try all the time to 'patch up' what I may not have done well when I was over there, but it seems so weird to work on the past to make it become present! Does that appear normal to you? Not to me, I don't understand it at all to tell you the truth, but I do work at it as I am advised, I am a 'good pupil', you see! I don't want bad marks from my 'superiors', as I call them!

There are bizarre goings-on here at every corner; you think you understand something and can solve it, just then something else happens! It must be done on purpose to make my brain work, except here I no longer have a flesh brain fortunately! There is so much I would like to share with you, but it is ever so hard to put it into words, because over all it's to do with all kinds of thoughts and impressions rather than words, if you see what I mean. There are so many things which are strange but amusing and interesting, I am short of words to try to explain them. One needs to be here to understand…or try to comprehend them! Sometimes I manage to, at others I am lost, but kind people always turn up to explain and help me. That's the support one gets all the time.

BR- Do you feel obliged to do all that?

No! I am not obliged to do anything whatsoever! One feels free all the time! But when you have something interesting and intriguing in front of you, you can't help wanting to know more and dive into it, just to understand what it is about!

BR- All you wanted was peace and quiet. Have you got it?

Peace? Oh yes, I have it. It is not 'anti-peace' to do all that, but I understand that, while doing it, I am having fun in a way, as it is a discovery one makes of oneself or of new things.

Where I get confused is when it becomes too much like physics, the technical side, if you like, when they try to explain to me how some things work and it loses me... That's because there are terms and facts which are unbelievably beyond what any 'Earthling' could comprehend! I am still an Earthling in many ways, I don't always grasp explanations. Yet they tell me it does not matter, as it will sink in gradually and I'll understand one day. There are no limits, no deadline, I don't have any exam to take you see!

BR- Can you give me some examples?

One amazing thing is that 'Thought' is not at all what we think it is, when on Earth! I feel Thought has a voice, Thought has a power, Thought is a tool, Thought has its own ideas! It has absolutely nothing to do with what we imagine on Earth.

The voice of Thought is not just what we hear in our head, of course, as that is 'a thought', isn't it? But there is more than that; the very fact of thinking is a fact exterior to that 'voice', as I call it. The voice belongs to the thought; the thought has its own life, that's why one must learn to control it, in a way, to be able to use it. I mean the very fact of thinking demonstrates indeed we are a 'Thought Being'. The famous phrase: "I think therefore I am" is rather: I am 'Thought'. So I am a Thought, my Thought is me, I am a 'Being of Thought' and not of flesh; therefore I do not depend on the brain nor the

251

flesh but they depend on me! I only create what I want with my Thought, my Thought Being. The hardest concept to understand is that it is not a good idea to submit to one's Thought.

BR- What do you mean?

I mean if one does not control one's thoughts in the right direction, one is going to create things one does not want or must not create, because as soon as one thinks them, those thoughts go and get ready to transform themselves into action, on Earth or even in this world!

Where there is Thought, there is Life, Action, Creation... I repeat: Where there is Thought, there is Life, Action, Creation... It's unbelievable to see it happen! When they demonstrated it to me, it was just like a constant flow of facts and actions and thoughts transformed into Reality!

I did it myself, you know that, as I spoke to you about all the things I was thinking and which turned up or happened, but there is even more! So, on Earth, we don't really know anything, do we? There is so much to do and so few people take the trouble to do it. Action, everything is action; that's what Creation is.

One can see why 'the Great Creative Thought', in this immense and eternal world, has the power to create everything, because it cannot be stopped! We just live in a self-repeating circle: ***There is Life only if there is Thought and Creation, and the whole is One.***

Everything explained above is what I am told. Don't think I am inventing it or I have grasped everything! I pass those facts on to you as they were explained to me...and there are many more! Much more than that! One only needs to see the Earth world and think for a minute about what one sees: How could this exist on its own? Impossible! A Creative Intelligence was needed behind all that...and there is even more to see here! So you can imagine, trying to understand all this is enough to make you feel you are crackers! Yet it is interesting when one gets down to it: There is always a new door opening up, with something interesting behind. So there is no time to be bored here. I don't spread out my wings and play the harp! I don't have any wings to start with!

Another strange thing is the time things do not take! There is no 'time' in the sense that I have no idea how long I have been here for and I don't grasp why we have the feeling of always being in the present and not have any 'past'... Yet I know I was on Earth 'before'...but I see that it always feels strange here to think or speak of 'time'. We have meetings with friends when we discuss things like that, but it keeps amazing me. I don't feel it like 'past', I feel I went somewhere 'before', or I spoke to someone 'before' but when I think of it, it feels like 'now'!

That's all I can tell you; I don't understand it well myself to be honest, but there are things I have to accept, even if I don't grasp them yet, because there is nothing I can do about it, that's how they are! So I await the 'big revelation' one day! After all, it does not bother me, so why fret, hey? I no longer worry myself sick here, it's all over indeed. I have understood that there is no point whatsoever; one can do much more good by sending strong loving thoughts in the right direction, so that they arrive and act effectively! The only thing which bothers me, if I dare use that word, is that you have some bother! Therefore I try to send you 'anti-trouble' thoughts, so that you don't worry and live as happily as possible, until we all meet again here. What a wonderful reunion we'll have then!

You are right Sweetheart, one must do one's best to do some good and leave some good results behind oneself. Personally I thought I had done nothing useful in my life, but I was shown it had not been that useless. My 'path' had been to create the four of you, to guide you as well as I could, and I think I have not failed there! So, after all, perhaps I have not been too useless...

BR- Of course not! Do you remember the 'diploma-scroll' dedicated to 'The best Mum in the world' I wrote for you?

What a beautiful thing that was, that kind thought you gave me, the long letter with all those kind words! Yes, I do remember it when I think of it. It is here in my mind, like a beautiful gift made of gold, with your love all around it. I'll never forget it because it was so touching and straight from the bottom of your heart. I shall never be able to repay enough that kindness and that thought.

My little Darling, we do see each other often, you know, when your body sleeps. So don't think I forget you and don't imagine I think you forget me. We see each other often and we are happy to be together.

There will be times when I suppose you won't be able to speak to me 'via your paper', but that's because you have a life to lead on Earth and you must do it. After all, that's why you are there. So, do your best and help the world understand that no one dies. We do not die, the flesh dies, that's all! That is the best teaching you can pass on to Earth people, so that they do not feel miserable over there and lost when they arrive here.

You did help me a lot, when you talked to me about all this, before I came over. It has helped me greatly. I used to think I had not completely understood everything, yet in fact my mind had grasped it and as soon as I arrived I realised everything you'd said was correct; it gave me ever so much pleasure! I was so relieved to have made the 'trip' without too many problems...

My Darling, you have been my 'Guardian Angel', so I would like to be yours from here! Just be happy as much as you can, that way your thoughts will be clear like a blue summer sky and the love we send you will reach you even more easily, to help you make the correct decisions. Meanwhile I'll let you sleep.

BR- All my love and kisses Darling Mum...

All mine to you, Honey. Go and sleep quickly. I love you forever. Don't you forget it, and the boys too! Your Mum. *(2.45 am) I tried to tune in at the end of June and several times in July but unfortunately, because of a busy schedule, it was usually late in the evening and concentration made me doze off... So frustrating!*

4th August 2001 - *Grandma Léonie starts the communication in French, nearly immediately!:*

The first time I spoke about it, it was to tell you I made a mistake when I was young. I regretted it all my life; my daughter was given away to someone else and I never saw her again after that. Now I'd like to confirm my daughter has been with me ever since I arrived here and I am so happy about it!

My friends here told me you want to know her surname, her town etc and be able to trace everything and find official proof. You are quite right, my little lady, because we have a wonderful life here, without the 'Earthly' worries you have. The details I have are: The kind lady who looked after her, busied herself with lots of things, she was known for her kindness and honesty. She took charge of my little girl because she saw we had to hide her from the general public in order not to 'bring disgrace' upon my family, as my mother used to tell me. She had a husband but he died before her and she looked after little children when she could. That lady took mine because I could not keep her. It broke my heart but it saved her from being sent to some institution or other.

Her family name was typical of the North of France: I am going to ask her to come very close to you and to give it to you if she can... My own mother apologised for making me suffer so much after her decision to separate me from my first child. She had not understood it did not matter at all where a child came from, what matters is that it is loved and well

255

brought up. I had indeed understood it but my parents' view was it would 'dishonour' the family and one could not let it happen and that was that!

So I started looking for that kind lady here, to thank her for helping me at such a sad time in my life. She appeared to me like in a kind of dream because she had not really known me properly. I thanked her to have done her best for my baby. The rest you know. I don't know her name. I need her to give us her name on Earth because <u>here we have other 'names'</u> <u>according to our kindness</u> and other good feelings.

The first time I saw my daughter in this world, she did not really recognise me as she did not know who I was on Earth, but she knew the love I have always had for her was never extinguished. I had always loved her secretly, all through my life. My mother could not prevent me from doing that! At least for the rest of my life, I had a secret nobody could take away from me! But the sight of my little one grown up into a beautiful woman was an enormous surprise: It was for her too, as we had never met before. She started telling me what she had been doing during her long life here, but there were things I did not grasp at first. Fortunately I was helped to understand.

As you know, after she was taken away from me, I learnt she had died. My life as a deprived young mother stopped inside me. I could no longer dream of seeing her one day, as I had secretly hoped... So I did not resist any longer, I let my parents make me meet young men who might be potential husbands. Personally I was not interested but 'it had to be done' as one could not remain a spinster all one's life, it wasn't 'the done thing', if one could avoid it! Those rules are so stupid, aren't they?! As far as I was concerned I did not know any other. I was not given the freedom I wanted. I was punished more than once, because the error I made one day reverberated for a long time. Finally I married your grandfather and there we are. Your mum came as a charming little baby, she stole my heart in a way, as I had not wanted to love other babies after the death of my first little one. Then everything was fine, all in all, for the rest of my life. The lady had passed from our world to this one before I did, that's why I never got to know her until I came here. My mother never revealed her name or her address, can you imagine that?! It's indeed unbelievable cruelty, isn't it? The kind lady was courageous to take charge of someone else's baby, wasn't she? I suppose you may have different opinions nowadays? We were very restricted during my youth.

Even on her death bed, my old mother has always refused to reveal anything whatsoever! "Everything is over and buried', she used to say, "We are not to think about it!" If I insisted, she would become angry! It's incredible someone could be so hard!

BR- She was probably doing her best to 'protect the family's honour'.

Why did Baby die? She could possibly have had a good and happy life…

BR- Or perhaps she wouldn't have! Anyway she is happier in Spirit World!

The baby had been outside to get some fresh air, then fell asleep and never woke up. That's why the poor woman panicked, as she thought she had done something wrong and should have kept her indoors. Fortunately the doctor reassured her and made her understand nothing could have been done, because the illness had won the battle. I never had all those details before coming here, since as you know, I had been told nothing when on Earth! The worst day had been to learn she had died, because there was then no longer any hope to see her again.

Anyway, in the end I recovered from that, once I saw her here and we spoke and got to know each other. There was so much to catch up and explain! I hoped she would forgive me to have had to abandon her, because after all, that is what happened. I had 'abandoned' her even though it was against my will! In my opinion, one should never separate parents from their children. There is a bond far too strong to try to break it. They did it to me, it broke my heart and my body too I think. But the joy of seeing her again at last, was the reward for those awful days I endured... *(I lose my concentration for a brief moment... I hope Grandma is still there!)* My children have always loved me and I am happy about it.

BR- *(surprised) Who is speaking now?*

It's me, your Mum, now. I did not want you to leave without me speaking to you. I know you nodded off... I wanted to tell you I still and always love you, I am happy not to suffer any more and I do not forget you all. *(It might seem repetitive but it shows how important it is for Mum!)* I'd like you not to worry not to have any names for the time being. I was told it will come. We've had a lot to do here, they say, to manage to find answers in the kind lady's memory. There were lots of difficulties to do with 'Time' on Earth and the length of the baby's stay. I did some 'research' myself regarding the way they do theirs, because I guessed you must be getting worried to have had nothing yet. We saw amazing things, Dad and I. We went together. He helped me understand why it was so difficult to enter into someone's mind events here, to pick up events that are 'over and done with' on Earth, all the more complicated since the baby is no longer on the Earth!

I don't think I'll be able to explain with words why that is always more difficult, because there are levels of thoughts, emotions, visions, impressions, feelings, which are superimposed one on top of the other. That's what makes things difficult. We saw that thoughts from Earth life continue to 'live on' even after that Earth life! It's incredible, isn't it?! So it made things difficult because her thoughts developed and her hopes and pains carried on 'growing' like plants, even if the facts did not happen on Earth! This made searches even

BR- Have you got any news about your sister etc?

About my sister, the names etc, as I explained to you, there are problems to reach into the subconscious and memory of that lady, as they really have to delve very deeply to get to it, it's incredible.

I noticed my mum spoke to you first. I was amused to see she took the trouble and wanted to speak to you herself; it is not the kind of thing I'd expect from her, she must like to talk to you! She understood you nodded off. She knows it is hard to concentrate, people here explained that to her. You must not get discouraged, things will work out, you'll see, we'll manage it. Then it will be the 'great party' if you can find traces of all that on Earth, as it will help us prove to humanity that all of us exist and live on. Personally I can't do much in that field because I am still a 'newcomer' and of course would not know what to do, but I can think kindly and positively to help you succeed in this adventure between two worlds!

What I'd like to be able to explain to you about <u>life here</u> is so fascinating and yet so hard to explain, sometimes, as it <u>has to do with states of mind, feelings, waves of 'impressions', inner comprehension</u> one could say. <u>That is why it is not that easy to put into words</u>. Even though one might think: "Right, I'll explain it that way", words might then fail and disappear, because these are not things words can explain.

Here we think, we make ourselves understood via thought, we do not really need to put words to our thoughts. So <u>we understand each other, mind to mind</u>, not mouth to mouth!

I have nothing more to tell you for now, except I give you big kisses, in my mind, as if I was on Earth. I think of you and the boys. I really wish you were here, that way I'd know where you are, that is: a wonderful place without any worries or pain! We would have so much fun together! We would love each other without being apart because of distances like on Earth. You really are not lucky to be where you are, believe me! It's me and Dad who are lucky! You must not worry about us either, indeed! So millions of kisses forever, until we can say it to each other close up, one day (still far away for you!).

24th August 2001 - *The full flow is in French. It's Mum:*

It's been a long time since we last spoke, hasn't it! The problem is that we have to obtain the information from our side. The kind lady who looked after the baby says she is beginning to remember a little but she needs some help to do it. One has to make her 'go back' and look back, and that takes 'time' as we'd say on Earth... Here it's not so much a question of 'time' as of depth and intensity of thought.

BR- Have you discovered your sister's surname?

A name is really difficult to obtain, we can see that now; there are lots of obstacles we had not thought about. A lot of work is needed to be done here, that's what is causing a problem! Impressions and facts are different things! Anyway we'll do our best. The lady does indeed seem to remember more, but I don't know exactly how far they've got, as it is not me who deals with it. I had no idea she existed, so you understand I can't 'meddle' in it! The 'rules' here, of impressions, feelings and all that, are very strong. Therefore, even though I wish with all my heart to be able to help you, I cannot, personally, extract details out of the thoughts and Soul of the kind lady. So, believe they are doing all they can, let's hope they'll succeed in the end. They keep repeating: "There is a lot to do!" ... There are 'laws' here which are so different from those on Earth... I probably won't be able to make you understand them, even if you could understand the ones on the Earth...

BR- Do you mean physics laws?

Yes, I mean in physics. 'Earthly' physics are not physics in this world and that's what is so exciting and interesting, when you see results here, but it's so difficult to explain to you...and to explain it to myself sometimes!

BR- Please do try... And who exactly is speaking to me now?

Me? I am your old Dad, not so old now! You see, we become younger when we come here, it's good isn't it?! So I'd love to please you and grant your wish, but all I can tell you is this: On Earth there are <u>gravity</u> laws, here there are <u>none</u>. There are 'chemistry' laws on Earth, here none, because the basic units are vibrations of a kind we would not have understood on Earth, because we would never have seen or grasped them.

There are also other rules, in particular <u>thought being a tool for everything here</u>. We only do or make things with thought, we create with thought. We have nothing without ourselves, or someone else, having thought about it! The fundamental rule is to know how to control and use your thought power in order to get what you want and discover more, but even so there are limitations as it <u>depends on the intention behind the thought</u>!

Therefore you see how it makes things complicated when you compare that to 'science' on Earth! One needs to be here to grasp it and yet one can't manage to straight away, when one has not been long in this world. There is ever so much to discover... but the good side is that one can take one's time. There are no exams and one is not 'punished' if one makes a mistake; one simply does not get the result hoped for, that's all, so it's not terrible. Moreover there are always some kind people helping us in our research. Personally I do my best to know what I am doing with my thoughts, in order to control them properly and gain more knowledge about this incredible world here. There will be other things to acquaint you with, one day I hope. But for the time being I can only tell you I discover my thoughts and my 'inner intensity', what I am, what makes me and what I represent.

I <u>need to discover myself first</u> before trying to discover more outside. So even though I do try to understand the world which surrounds me, I must also go within myself to grasp what I am and have been, how I react, what it all means when one thinks one thing or the other... There is so much to find out about oneself!

All the discoveries being <u>within the self</u>, it's not something I could explain to you easily, you understand, because you would have to be inside me and be me! This, of course is impossible!

I hope I have not disappointed you too much. I assure you as soon as I have something worthwhile which can be explained better, I'll let you know very quickly!

BR- Many thanks, it's still very interesting! Has Mum anything else to say?

About your children, don't worry, you'll see everything will soon be well. Yes, that word 'soon' again, but that's all I can tell you in way of date! There are <u>lots of events which will change things</u>, you'll see. There is so much to look at to decipher the results... We only know that things will be fine and your children will 'soon' be happier than they have been recently. You'll see we have been informed correctly and you'll be able to check as soon as everything happens as we were told. So don't you worry, all of you! We are keeping an eye on you! You won't have any serious problems and we love you forever. Mum and Dad.

11th November 2001 - *I try to tune in, though it is very late once more, at 00.30hr, but I am a 'late bedder'! The pen writes the first words in English - it's my guide:*

Give yourself more time in the evening to tune in. You never have enough time and we have to struggle to get through. You'll have to have a better plan and be more organised so that we can arrange our visits to your pad too! There are many things we could talk to you about.

Number one will be our friends your mum and dad,

who have been waiting for you to 'tune in to them' as you say. It's very difficult for them to reach you if you have too much on your mind. It would be very advisable if you made it a time in your day when you organise yourself to be free to talk to them, as you seem very erratic about it.

You'll get nowhere at that rate in your search for more proof *(about the baby)*, as <u>we need</u> <u>your</u> intensity of wanting, your great desire and wishing for it to bring forward the desired results. As we've told you before, <u>the lost details are so far back in that lady's memory that they need to be brought forward</u> for a purpose. You cannot obtain it<u> unless she feels the want and the need</u> and that's what <u>you have to provide</u>. We need you to want it badly!

It will have <u>to be done more often to build the energy needed</u> to create the memory awakening which we cannot do on our own... We need <u>you</u> to want those details so badly that it will bring them back to her mind, which has moved on from these facts. You see <u>she has evolved from that 'time' and has let it go</u>! Now y<u>ou want her to go back into a 'different life time'</u> so to speak and that's so difficult! The love from your heart, the desire from your heart and soul, will help create <u>the wave of energy which is needed for the mind of the personality to revert to those times</u>, when those facts mattered, then she'll be able to think like in those days and hopefully will bring you the facts you need.

<u>All is needed is the desire to succeed and the patience to do it</u>. The sad loss has been resolved as she has met her baby again, so all that has been solved and resolved and gone, as far as the importance of it is concerned! Once more, we need the energy of your thoughts to make it happen...that was the main point: All you need is to find time for us over here and we'll do our best to link up to you from our side. The more suitable opportunity will be a quiet moment when your mind is at rest, if you can find such times!

Make your love of Spirit one of your goals, use it to help those around you and use it to help your progress. You'll have to fight the negativity you often have yourself, to make place for a quiet, peaceful mind, as you used to have at certain times. All is not lost, you only need to get back on an even keel, a mental equilibrium of peace and tranquillity. All the best in your endeavours - we'll back you up. All you require is your love for all that matters and you'll see all will be well. Love is what keeps things going. Love the world as you love your cats…

20th December 2001 - *The pen writes the first words in French:*

Communication has been very difficult lately because you were unable to do it and you lost the clarity of mind you needed. You can get it back if you practise more often. I want to tell you I am here Darling. I did not resent you for not being able to talk to me: I do know you are very busy trying to make a life for yourself. I am really pleased indeed we are at last able to speak together…

BR- Is it you Mum? I am ever so sorry… What must you think of me, you who put in so much effort in talking to me!..

It's me indeed, of course! I don't think ill of you, you should know that! I do know how you exert yourself with your work and all that! I'd like to reassure you: I am not angry and I still love you! You can speak to me without worrying, I love you Sweetheart.

My friends around me really helped me, as usual, to prepare myself better and better, to discover and understand more and not to cry too much for you … It's really a great pity I am to do it alone without showing it to you! If I gave myself free rein I'd start telling you everything we do here, but I know it will become difficult, as there are few words which cannot describe what really goes on, because we have experiences in

266

thoughts, emotions, feelings, impressions and it is very hard to put that into words... So do not expect very clear descriptions! I see I used to think we would be able to explain everything about here as one does in stories, but it does not work like that at all!

What I can tell you is that Dad and I have made <u>little trips within our thoughts to see what we wanted to learn out of our respective lives on Earth</u>. Personally <u>I wanted to be a 'Mum'</u> as I had not been that before. I wanted to know what it was like to bring up children, to love them, to see them happy etc and I do feel that is what I got to do in that life. Then we saw that the Earth as it is now is no longer exactly as the Earth used to be: there were terrible earthquakes and changes, people changed lifestyle...

BR- Really? Where?

In general, everywhere! Don't forget we do not <u>see</u> everything as physical earthy details but as <u>impressions</u>... So if people had to change their way of living it must have given them a shock in many ways and affected their way of thinking. We did not pay much attention to this as it was just in passing. What mattered more was to know why we, Dad and I, had come to Earth. My dad was there of course, but yours and I were wondering why we had come. Well, it was for you all in a way, <u>because we had to give you the life you had chosen to live</u>. So don't waste it and try to make it as useful as possible!

BR- Is that really you Mum, talking to me?

I always tell you the truth, don't worry, it's only me, your mum speaking, no one else. I wanted to tell you that, all things considered, <u>what gave me most pleasure was to have had you all, because that's why I had gone to Earth</u>, to learn to be a mother and I hope I did that work to the best of my ability... <u>Looking back at that time in my life</u>, it was indeed the best.

BR- How did you see that again?

I felt again all the impressions and joys I knew when you were little, then growing up. Of course there were times when there were problems, worries, but they did not appear as a blockage, they were just little clouds on the overall picture. So I understood my life had not been a waste, since I had come for this and the four of you are the result! My work as a teacher did not really matter that much in a way.

BR- But you helped so many children! It should count!

Yes, I did help a lot of pupils but that was my living. If I was able to help people, kids, well… so much the better, it's helped me as much as it did them in a way. My life was <u>for you</u> and you have been and still are my life. I have lived for you.

That is why it has been so awful to leave you so suddenly. I did not want to leave you alone: I did not want to be without any contact with you and be unable to help you. Now I see that I still can try to help you from here after all, by using my thoughts, by thinking about you intensely, in a positive way… *(I try to relax more …but doze off around 00.15h)*

***

Mum in her 20s.

My mum, Suzanne,
12 years old.

Mum and me.
(Brigitte aged 21 months)

Mum, 90 years old.

My maternal grandmother,
Léonie Leclercq Moleux, in 1918.

My maternal grandparents,
Léon and Léonie Leclercq.

My mum and dad, Nicolas and Suzanne
Bondaletoff in Algiers, 1959.

My dad, Nicolas,
in his 40s.

My husband, Dave Rix
on our wedding day.

Dave and me on our
wedding day in 1966.

The Rix family (left to right), my son Jim, me (Brigitte),
my daughter Anne-France and my husband Dave.

My eldest brother Pierre (passed away in 2009) and me in Nice.

My younger brothers (left to right), Michel 'Michou', myself
and Jean-Nicolas 'Touky'.

CHAPTER 6
Practical mind exercises - A touch of subtle physics - Life in dying cells - All linked up

11th January 2002 - *The pen writes the first words in French:*

Mum here. Listen, we need to speak to each other more often, it helps, you see. You have not been able to communicate for quite some time and now you seem to have problems. My mum told me you two had a chat, in a way you met between the two worlds. She was delighted to have made your acquaintance even though she was embarrassed by the circumstances... Yet I could see she was glad to have got to know you a little, though not a great amount as you have not spoken much about yourself, but she seems to know a lot about you, seen from here! It was amusing for me to have my own mother talking to me about my own daughter! After all, you and I did not talk much about her on Earth, but now we are all here, the four of you, my children, are the only ones missing in this reunion!...

My friends here are ever so kind. Their origins are very diverse and I only knew very few. Anyway, I didn't remember them, but they seem to remember me, to know me: "<u>We knew each other 'before'</u>" they said. 'Before' I came here, I suppose! We have a lot of friendship and affection and common aspirations, that's what makes it interesting and is the main link - to have the same desire to know and discover oneself, to learn new things in many areas. I do not get the impression of 'going to school' to learn all that. It's by getting together and talking, exchanging thoughts and impressions, that we discover more and more. That's what makes everything interesting here, because at each 'turn' of a conversation there is very often something worth delving into more. So we spend hours (I suppose they are hours!) of great pleasure enjoying and feeling we are making discoveries, progressing and yet at the beginning of a conversation we do not set ourselves a 'goal'. It's simply a conversation, sometimes trivial but at others deep exchanges of thought, but it always leads somewhere! I really cannot explain it any better, Sweetheart, I am sorry. It gives me so much pleasure to talk to you... and there I am without the kind of information I would have liked to pass on to you, because it becomes <u>so complicated to try to explain what one does with thoughts!</u>.. You must be able to understand, I hope, that it is difficult to find words to describe impressions and the knowledge the mind has, or emotions that cannot be described in a few words. It's a bit like trying to describe a moving painting or film, a picture of emotions altering and changing from one stage to another! Oh, it's so hard... I end up not finding words anymore when I want to send you my thoughts!

BR- What do you do? How do you communicate with me?

We speak to each other by exchanging thoughts Darling. I think of you very hard, I concentrate very hard, simply knowing you will be 'at the other end of my thoughts' since we don't really have a telephone. But I feel 'normal' here - I mean I do not go anywhere, I remain in the usual places here. Go to sleep Sweetheart... As usual this is what I want to tell you - you need some sleep and to rest, so do get your strength back! We'll be able to see each other while your body sleeps and we'll talk to each other even more easily.

BR- How often do we meet at night?

Initially there is no limit as to the frequency of your visits or our meetings. The only thing which makes <u>a difference is how tired or how preoccupied you are, as your mind seems to wander elsewhere!</u> So I do not wait for you all night, don't worry! I am warned whenever they know you are going to come.

BR- Who are 'they'?

'They' are the kind people around me. You and I see each other, we talk when your mind is calm enough and rested and you wish to come here. As you know, it can only be done at a 'special level', the one where we receive our visitors. It seems a bit strange to say that but that's what happens... Go to sleep quickly and perhaps we'll see each other again if you want to carry on with our conversation. Goodnight Darling, sleep well... I love you.

31st March 2002 - *10.30am*.

It's Mum. The day you were born I promised not to abandon you, to love you, to look after you. As you see, I have not abandoned you because although I left your physical world, I am still here, near you. I have not lost my strength, I am full of enthusiasm, I am younger and fresh as a rose! No, not really... but just to make you understand I am no longer the old woman you must be remembering, but much younger in the body (in a way, as I don't need to look after it) and the mind, which is exactly what I am! I feel I am a 'Spirit', in the sense of 'Spirit' and 'Mind', but I know I no longer have a flesh brain, fortunately, as this is what caused my death, I mean - to have become paralysed etc...

So, Darling, I would like to speak with you. I have not had the opportunity to do so for a while and I'd like to share with you what I have been doing since we last chatted when I had told you of my 'discovery work' here! I had not managed to explain things well, as it is becoming difficult when one must find words to depict things to do with the mind, mental things and facts, when one is used to describing physical facts! My life here is but one long discovery; on every corner and every turn, there are only new things which prompt me to examine them. I'd love you to be here to show you and explain them to you! Where to start?.. I spend a lot of time trying to understand everything I encounter, so you see I am kept busy! But it does not mean I do not think of you all, you know. I have not become selfish to the extent of only thinking of me and my intellectual pleasures here, while you are struggling with your material life over there! Darling, do you really understand?

BR- Of course! And we love you forever Mum! We are not forgetting you!

I do feel you love me, don't worry! I know how busy you are trying to work out your lives, whereas I have such an easy life here! But let us start from the beginning! I wanted to explain to you I am making some discoveries, so here they are:

I had asked them to explain to me the difference between the possibilities of thoughts. There are thoughts which are not as powerful as others and I wanted to see what the results would be. So when I was shown what can be done with one's thought if one really tries, I could not understand why we did not know that on Earth and did not use it! After all, I knew nothing of it then, now I have been taught it fairly easily.

So why couldn't I pass the tip to those who want to have a go? I only have to think of something for it to create itself! It worked well when I first arrived here and I had fun creating all sorts of things...but it was only a beginning! As I progressed along, I discovered it works for far more important things than playing with objects around oneself... That's why since then, I *have been able to travel in 'Time and space'* and to see places I had never been to, learn historical facts I knew nothing about and I had not heard of! I was flabbergasted and delighted and it still delights me!

Such feats as holding in my hand objects dating from 'prehistoric eras', seeing the Past as if it was the Present...and understanding all that is of no importance because 'past' events are not really 'past' - one does not see them any longer, but one can still go back to them since I was able to do so! I visited foreign countries all over the world, I made some progress in the Chinese, Hindu, American languages etc…because I was able to understand what people were saying in my 'travel dreams'!

BR- (surprised) Your…what?

Yes, because it feels as if one is dreaming. One journeys mentally towards a period and one finds oneself there as if one was dreaming, but it is much livelier because one is really there! I did have great fun doing that, as it was incredible to be able to leap backwards just like that!

I had wanted to see Versailles and the luxurious courtiers' life so I went there, because I had admired Louis XIV's lifestyle…but I also learnt to what extent ordinary people were suffering while the rich enjoyed a happy life in their castles… It was really unfair to have such a poor country, while the wealthy wasted so much money and gold 'crowns' as it was in those days!

I've had some very exciting 'holidays' making trips into Time like that! I had never imagined it was possible, or that one could do it once 'dead' as well! So long live trips in Time and space!

When I was on Earth I would have liked to see other countries but I had never travelled very far apart from a little in Europe. I would have liked to go round the world…in all directions, but I did not fancy dragging myself across airports and stations, then I did not have the money nor the time, then the health, to do it.

I have made up for it since, you see! <u>I have gone round the world several times since I have been here!</u> I went practically everywhere to see the most beautiful sights and with seasons changing in each country, I was able to see them at different times of the year. It would take an eternity if I tried to describe all that!

My favourite towns were the beautiful ancient Roman towns where marble buildings were so superb and so well sculpted! Those and the former Egyptians, (not the modern ones, of course) with their towers and their pyramids - they had all kinds of buildings with beautiful towers and palaces etc. Everything was so well made, so superbly sculpted and so interesting! I had never imagined I would ever find myself in person, one day, in Roman times with their superb villas and wonderful buildings. I had never liked the cruel side of the Roman arenas and circuses, but Roman architecture had always interested me. When you think that their theatres and roads still exist after all that time!.. Yet I do understand now that 'Time' is only a man-made idea on Earth, which has to do with the sun and the Earth, but which one no longer has once one is in this world over here.

My darling daughter, you see we don't get bored in this Afterlife world! I do not play the harp with angels either! Yet it would not bother me to learn to play the harp as well, because it must be much easier to do over here - all is needed probably is to think about it then one can do it!

As you know well, I used to love history and ancient stories, but I had never, ever imagined I would be able to do what I have just been doing recently. All those mind trips! I cannot believe it! <u>I had always wished I could do it, that's why it has been possible</u>. I had wanted to discover other countries and customs, especially historical times - because it interests me so much, it allowed me to delve into it easily, you see. <u>Interest, desire, wish and thought - all that turns the creation of a dream into a very real Reality</u>! It is really worth trying, that's what is lacking on Earth - understanding one can create things in one's life and that in fact one does create them without knowing one does!

BR- Did you learn something you did not know before?

Everything was amazing. All I could see filing past me were streams of facts, <u>emotions and impressions which were unknown</u> to me. I had never really understood before to what

278

extent the French king Louis XVI had indeed never wanted the crown... but the poor man had been obliged to be king, so he did what he could. Yet he had never been happy doing it and the guillotine got him out of that!.. It can't have been fun to be condemned but I suppose in a way, it was a fairly quick death, whereas some people's illnesses drag on for months and years before they die and meanwhile they suffer. All he wanted to do was to have fun with his friends, go hunting and do what the other young noblemen used to do - he did not have the interest of France and the Kingdom at heart.

BR- How did you get to know that?

He showed himself in front of me, in all his splendour at that time, but I <u>could see his feelings, thoughts and emotions</u>! His image as a king was only an exterior envelope, I actually saw 'inside' him and his thoughts in those days. It made me understand why people reckoned he was rather a 'drip'. He did not feel like being a king, that was all!

The way history is taught at school is not the way we should be learning it - one should be able to do what I did and still do, as I indeed still can! What should be taught is history based on the emotions of people of that period, not the number of battles, of dead, of treaties... There have been so many wars and carnage! It was and still is horrendous! We should <u>go within people's minds</u> to understand what was going on during that era. There are so many emotions, fears, desires; that's what makes the difference between peace and war. How people react at a certain period in history is far more fascinating than how many battles or treaties there were!

My favourite period used to be the times of beautiful crinoline dresses but the wigs would not have interested me, because I reckon one must feel really hot wearing them! Yet they were stylish, elegant and it meant you always looked smart with tidy hair... I would have liked that! On the other hand I would never have wanted to live in such times as those of Attila the Hun and all the horrors of invasions, pillages and massacres...awful! He was indeed a nightmare, 'God's Curse', as he was called! And there were others and worse too! I am really glad to have escaped all that as far as I know!

Personally I would have loved to be a Roman lady in her pretty seaside villa (with her 'slaves' in a way but I think I would have simply treated them as maids). I would have enjoyed having the time to do interesting things and to see all those superb buildings, temples, palaces, theatres etc. There have not been many buildings such as those, apart for the Greek ones. I think I would have loved it. Well Darling, that's a glimpse of what I have been doing for some time. It makes a change from lying on the sofa in the lounge in Nice, watching TV showing films which most of the time were idiotic!

BR- But you used to read some good books too.

Yes fortunately, I did read too. But since I have been here I reckon I have learnt far more than I must have grasped during my whole life on Earth! I only see fascinating things here. I am surrounded by interesting people whom I can ask questions and who have the answers, or who are able to help me find out or understand the answer. It makes one wish to die as soon as one is born to be able to understand all this! There are all sorts of things to suit everyone, you know. Heaps of activities to do in order to <u>open one's mind and tune in to ways of thinking so different from how one thinks on Earth in general</u>.

You see Sweetheart, I educate myself here, just like I used to advise you to do when you were with me. I remember saying "Do not waste your time! Learn something, read!"... Well, that's what I do too and it's real fun! So that's a little insight into my activities. I thought you may like to know all this.

BR- Indeed! Also please try to help Touky and Michou...

Yes we know everything you have just said. Don't worry Darling, we think of them and I do. I come and see you all in your sleep, I've learnt how to and I do it often.

Now I'll let you rest Sweetheart, as you need to catch up on your sleep. I selfishly wanted to make you share my adventures and fun here; but it's not just selfish, it is also useful for you and your own discoveries and your book! So I wish you goodnight and sweet dreams.

BR- May I come and see you tonight to carry on with this conversation?

Of course, I am more than happy for you to meet me! It all depends on whether you are too sleepy and your mind is tired and it falls asleep too! I'll wait for you. Now I give you big kisses and will do it again as soon as you arrive here. Goodnight Darling.

21st April 2002 - *23.45h - The pen starts in English - my guide gives me some advice. An interesting point is his reply to my question: "How can one manage not to be angry, when seeing so much evil or the wrong-doings of so many people all over the world?":*

The Law of the Universes is a Law of Peace: it brings Peace.

BR- Could you explain this in more detail please?

The Law of the Universes is: 'In order to bring peace outside, you need peace within'. To bring peace within, you have to work at it - to work at it with spiritual thoughts all the time, as material thoughts do not solve the problems. Make life around you a bed of spiritual thoughts: you can't go round resenting as you will be resented too. Make your soul understand that the way to inner peace is through understanding others. The way to make others do things right is through example.

BR- But what about someone who does not want to learn!

Learn yourself as you teach others. As the Light goes out towards others, it shines and lights everything in its way, thus transforming the outlook. He will learn eventually. You

281

need to shine and suggest over and over again. Love and you will be loved. Care and they will care about you. Look and you'll be looked at. Teach and they will learn. Heal and you will feel happy within, because you will have achieved something and made the difference. Look around you and count your blessings - you could have had a worse life.

BR- I know! I am not complaining about my life!

Try as I suggest - it will be the first steps towards more inner peace. As you wish to talk to your 'mother on Earth', we shall let you go and let her come near you. *(A short silence then the pen writes in French this time)*

We are meeting up again at last Honey. It feels so good! I too wanted to speak to you, as I always have lots to say if you want to hear it. Everything is fine here of course, since we cannot be unwell here!

I have carried on with my round the world tour lately and my studies of the states of minds of people of the periods I visited were very interesting! I wanted to know why some events of a certain period happened, if it was not because there was a war or some other cause. I was shown that what happens is because people have very fixed or powerful ideas and their desires or their fears cause those events. You see, as far as I used to be concerned, history appeared as a list of facts, dates, causes and consequences (but not so much to do with ideas and thoughts), wars causing massacres and /or annexations of countries etc. But I was not quite correct to believe that. In fact, when people in one country were beginning to rebel, it had not started on the day they went to shout in the street. It had begun long before, when their minds, their hearts and their spirits were outraged by what was going on around them. Therefore <u>it is the energy of their joined thoughts, their inner revolt, which triggered everything</u>. All right, it's obvious but here <u>I see it as waves of colours and intensity of emotions which I am made to feel</u> so that I can understand them.

282

I have seen so many countries and eras, it is hard to explain. <u>I see them as films, inner films, within me</u>. I wonder how a particular event happened and I am shown it as a film within myself... I have spoken to you about the French Revolution, and about the Tsar of Russia - they killed him and his family to have the satisfaction not to be governed by rich and selfish people. The wealthy could afford to buy themselves anything they wanted, while the poor starving peasants were dying of hunger and diseases. China did the same thing - there were tyrants, dictators and demanding emperors. The population suffered until everything gave way within; they could no longer put up with it. <u>The blending and linking of everyone's thoughts caused a kind of wave</u>, or even waves, which created their revolutions. The same thing will happen as long as there are people suffering because others crush them down.

We saw ever so much, my dad, yours and I, when we went to lots of countries and eras. I did not always ask to see a particular country. I <u>was shown it as an example, to make me understand that I must not judge facts from their material aspect, but by observing what was going on in the souls of the population in general</u>. Also to make me grasp the importance and the power of thoughts and emotions.

<u>A thought is a wave which can no longer stop</u>. It can only <u>spread and create others</u> by meeting other thoughts, whether its own or other people's. ***One can no more stop the power of thoughts than prevent the sea from existing!*** It exists and it will spread wherever it can reach. It will do some good or some harm according to its power but it will have some effect one way or the other. So be very careful and wary of 'nasty' thoughts you may have! <u>Thoughts are so powerful one must use them well and also be aware of them</u>...

The day you publish your book, I shall really be very happy as we will have been working together you and I. It will have brought me closer to you and helped me not feel abandoned nor feel I abandoned you by 'dying' as one calls it... But old age and my old battered body made me go away. I did not want to leave you, that is what was holding me back...

I could not get into my head it would help you if I was no longer there. Dad and the others came several times to show me that an old sick person was not going to improve your lives and jobs but would be a burden instead! I had not considered it like that. I was still seeing myself as fairly mobile after all... But Dad told me my body was half-paralysed and there was no hope whatsoever that it could be healed, as there was no way to recreate what had been destroyed because the cells were far too old and the mind too tired... Then I had to accept the time had come to leave you in peace, instead of giving you more worries!

I do see now I would have been a big problem if I had survived paralysed...and you know it, don't you? Therefore I was obliged to leave you behind in a way, but not in my heart and my mind. That's why I am always near you in thought - all you have to do is think of me, I feel it and 'tune in to you'.

Anyway, I do understand now that I can help you even better from here than from Nice, as I am able to constantly send you powerful thoughts to help things, to improve your lives, whereas from my bed in Nice where, without money and strength, I could not do much for you, except possibly give you more worries!

BR- What is there around you, your environment?

My life here is more and more a life of thought and exchanges of thoughts. I don't pay too much attention to what I see around me because if I think of something, it appears...so I have the impression of constantly cheating, since what one thinks about, turns up!

The best is to live in thought. That is fun because if you think of Nature, you find yourself in it... If you think of history, you live it! So you see what I mean?! What's the point of imagining you are in a bedroom or a house, since you know it does not really exist?!

I am waiting to see what is going to happen when I think of something, to see how it shapes itself, but to tell the truth it's not that extraordinary. We think of something and in the same way as when we dream on Earth, we see our dream change. Here it's the same, but the dream becomes at once extremely real; we feel totally part of it, we live it...and understand what other people do and think!

My friends here are people who know a lot about everything... As soon as I wonder about something out of sheer curiosity, the answer comes one way or the other, but not like on Earth. In general it appears like an inner film, an inner screen with such clear explanation and comprehension that one cannot forget it! That's why recently I had travelled to different countries and times... *(A short lull, so I give Mum news of my children and my brothers)*

Darling, don't worry, I did pick all your thoughts! You told me about your children's and your brothers' lives. I do see how much you love them all and worry about them. We can only love them from here and send them, with all our strength, loving thoughts to make things go well for them.

BR- Could you come and talk via the medium this evening, calling me by my nickname as an extra 'proof'? We have spoken quite a long time Darling, I am very happy to have had the opportunity to hear you and speak to you. You do know I am here, you hear me, you speak to me... Do you really need to have other 'proof'? I'll now give you a big kiss and I'll let you get on with your Earthly activities while I go and get on with my activities as a Spirit! Because I am a Spirit now! It feels weird to think of it that way!

BR- Ok. Don't forget I love you Darling Mum!

I love you too Sweetheart. I am very sorry to have caused you so much grief by leaving your Earthly life, but as I said, I am still there, not far. I do not leave you. So, once more big kisses with all my love.

15th June 2002 - *23.45hrs. Very ashamed to realise the last chat goes back to April, due to a busy life! I had the feeling we had spoken more recently than that… The pen starts in English:*

We keep telling you all the time to find some quiet moments to practise, but you do not do it! You can only blame yourself and don't forget it will delay your results! Each time you waste your so-called 'time', you have only yourself to blame for being unable or less able, to do things which require a peaceful mind or time to do.

As we said before, we come to help bridge the gap between you and your mum since she needs the reception point to be a peaceful mind for her to reach you. She cannot manage if yours is in turmoil - it's like landing on a heavy sea with big waves, when you have no control over the waves. Not that you don't want to reach her, it's simply that you have difficulties calming your mind… *(The pen starts again in French)*

It is such a great pleasure to talk to you my Sweetheart. I can't tell you enough how happy I am to be able to let you know what I do and think from here! It feels as if I had not left you when I can make you share my activities, how I live here and the very fact that I still exist! I can think of you and let's hope I can help you from here, though the fact it's possible is hard to grasp …

I want to reassure you. You seem to be so sad to have not had time to communicate with me for a long time. It is not your fault. It is not a crime to have been unable to do so! Don't worry so much! All we have to do is catch up now! My friends have invited me to go with them to 'do some experiments' as they call it. These are experiments, 'practical mind work', if I can describe it that way. They have so much experience of life here, that they can show me or make me do things I have not done before - so I am always ready to go with them! What we have to achieve doesn't always look easy, when one comes from the Earth like I do, because one tends to think: "It won't work" or "There is no reason or goal for such and such"... But once one has done them, one gets fantastic results!

These are cases of 'delving into depth' - I mean I have to go deep into myself as they call it. I need to look within to see what I can discover which is new, which I was not aware of...that can truly be a revelation, believe me, because obviously one does not know oneself that well! There were times when I thought I was looking <u>into</u> another person because I was not recognising myself! <u>I saw sides of my personality</u> which I was not pleased about...and other sides which were 'too good to be true' one could say!

It's like having a mirror within oneself and asking questions on what one sees... So I saw facets of my life and personality which worried me and others which, let's say, pleased me a bit more. But it's useful after all, because if <u>we don't know ourselves how can we judge others</u>? One needs and must be able to judge oneself before being able to decide anything about other people! Once one does that, one sees things very differently!

So I saw but I did not exactly conquer, at least I understood certain things better... It still does you some good to achieve this, even if it gives you a shock! *(Unfortunately, I feel sleepy and relaxing more makes me doze off.)*

31st July 2002 - *The pen starts in French:*
Mum is waiting for you. I'd love to have a little chat with you as we have not met 'on paper' for quite some time. You've been on a trip I think and all went well, didn't it? You saw new things and new places without any problem, I am pleased for you. You were concerned things might go wrong,

weren't you, but you see all was fine, as what matters is to keep thinking positively - things always go well if one has a positive mind and one is not afraid. *(Suddenly, out of the blue)* You have met somebody new recently and I am told I have to tell you that you will be helping her *(A young lady to whom I give French tuition at the Ministry of Agriculture & Fishery, yet I had not spoken to Mum about it!).* You must talk to people about what you know, so make her understand life does not stop, one does not truly die - one changes body, that's all! So good luck and happy explaining! *(So made Afterlife next topic and learnt she'd lost her grandma!)*

After making trips in the physical world of the Earth and imaginary ones too, because one sees things in thoughts, once more I analysed my life with you. I had seen some aspects but there were others to inspect. So I did it and realised what truly matters is how one thinks and feels within oneself and how one behaves towards others. As I go along my journey of self-discovery, I see I did not really harm anybody, in fact in general I helped them. I was, unfortunately, not perfect but I did not kill or injure anyone. On the other hand, I had some nasty thoughts towards certain people and I don't regret them... I reckon those people deserved it at the time...but since my 'bad' thoughts did not really affect their life, it does not count in my opinion! It's only the real evil deeds committed wilfully that I would regret if I had done any...but I am really glad not to have done anything like that!

Poor Darling, you imagine your mum is perfect, don't you? Of course not, you know no one is, but at least my conscience is clear - I have not caused any catastrophes as far as I am aware...

Last time we spoke I think I talked of trips using one's thought power, but they are not over - I still go on journeys. It's rather weird, they are a bit like strange dreams - one sees oneself elsewhere, one discovers new and different ways of thinking: It's constantly very intriguing!

During those trips, I went to Polynesia because I had always wondered why people there plonked flower garlands around visitors' necks and it irritated me! Now I saw in my 'travel dreams' that the reason behind this is the importance and value flowers have in the eyes of Polynesians. They are proud of them, they love their flowers, they find them beautiful and want to honour you and offer you the best. It <u>has also to do with the 'energy' emanating from flowers</u>, energy in the sense of electrical or electro-magnetic field, an 'aura' as you would say? That's what they sense, and they wish to share this 'energy' with their visitors. I used to find that so stupid! But since it makes them happy and after all, it appears to have a 'raison d'être' ('reason for being so') then I'll say 'amen'! Let them carry on if they wish to! Anyway it does not bother me anymore as I am no longer there, in a way...

So now the matter is solved, I shall no doubt go and see other things which annoyed and bothered me... I guess it will be proved to me there was no reason to let them make me wild with anger! Everything is like that here, <u>one learns gradually to accept what one rejected or did not understand before.</u> I suppose it's part of what is called 'progressing'! Personally I don't give a toss - I am quite happy to get rid of prejudices and other irritations! What's the point in worrying about trivial and insignificant things, when one has so many wonderful ones to discover?

Therefore Sweetheart, make sure you <u>don't get bothered by little things</u>, ok? Save yourself some time in this (Spirit) World, so that you won't have to do all those little trips to 'weed out' wrong ideas! I quickly get rid of incorrect ideas: I say: "All right, all right, I agree!" as soon as I am shown the error I made. What's the point of hanging on to useless points of view, hey? The main thing is to have peace within, that is vital! But to have it, one must get rid of little idiocies which spoil it all. One must quickly have a big spring clean in order to make 'space' within oneself to enjoy the new discoveries one makes when one is here.

My mum has not been to see me recently as she knew I was doing all these 'exercises' - I call them my 'homework'! I think she'll come back when she learns I have time to concentrate on her. It does not really take any 'time', it is more a question of concentration and focus, of being engrossed in an activity.

BR- What about your dad or mine?

My dad is often there, practically at all the 'experiments'. Yours not as often. It depends on what we are doing. But he has appeared many a time, by that I mean he turns up suddenly, unexpectedly. It gave me a bit of a shock, at first anyway, but I got used to it... He always has good ideas and good news to give me. He talks to me about what he does or learns, and we try to understand what it's all about. He understands better than me, as I am only a 'beginner' here and I don't have the experience the 'old ones' have who have been here far longer! Yet he tries to explain, because it is always useful to know what we may have to do one day. I gradually understand a little better, as I realise to what extent everything is in one's mind and takes place within ourselves. That is why there are things difficult to explain to you in words, it would be better to make a film of it, as they are visions, impressions, internal creations - not events to see with our eyes. But one gets used to it over time. One senses what one must do, one understands what one should have done, one feels what other people feel or felt or sensed and that takes place within oneself!

Being able to find words to explain impressions will make this book turn into a piece of work with literary merit, if we manage it!.. I would need subtle descriptions, nuances in impressions and feelings, inner waves of emotions and all that in a flash! So I wonder where I am going to find the right words for that!

290

BR- Don't worry about it Mum!

I am all right, I feel good you know. Not that I do not regret to have gone so quickly and suddenly! I know I must not look back but look ahead to the 'future' as you would say, yet it is sad to think you cannot be here with us to experience all those fascinating and even amusing things! While we have fun, you have to struggle with your daily life in order to survive and face all your problems, like that poor Touky (*because of the nasty Mr T. who played dishonest tricks regarding the boat*).

I feel guilty to have gone so quickly, I would have so much wanted to be able to help him solve his financial problems! But I know it couldn't be so, therefore I must resign myself to it, say "Amen" and look ahead instead of behind. I have learnt to send positive thoughts towards you all and I do it constantly. I hope it makes a difference to your lives…

Darling I have never forgotten you and do not forget you, so do not worry, I am not far. I am ready to speak with you whenever you wish.

BR- (surprised) Who is there?!

Me? It's Dad speaking. I came to talk to you when I felt your thoughts.

BR- What a good surprise Dad! I give you a big kiss…

Me too, I kiss my little girl who has grown up ever so much! I too have made some trips and had experiences like Mum. We've often met, we exchange tales of our adventures and talk about them… I have seen extraordinary things which we'll have difficulties to explain; it is a question of physics, electricity, thought, non-existent 'Time'… It is Reality seen as it IS, instead of being hypotheses and assumptions made by Earthly 'scientists'.

BR- Please, give me some examples, do try to explain…

There would be so much to say! My life here is a matter of discovery, of questions from me, of efforts to understand, but also of wonderment at the realisation of what could be

291

known on Earth if only they had the knowledge available here! Most (Earthly) scientists have no inkling about what they should know and even if they had, they would have difficulties in explaining or proving it. Some have 'inner visions', sudden comprehension and inner knowing, but which cannot be explained or calculated rationally, so they do not use them and sometimes even doubt them! It's a great pity because it means a lot of lost knowledge from here, I mean lost for the Earth world...until someone else is inspired and does something with it...

I can only look at and discover things I didn't know or did not understand before. Yet it saddens me to think there is so much to be aware of and so little of it is understood, or some things are supposedly 'known' but erroneously. In other words: Mankind imagine they know certain things but those are wrong and false! For example, the Earth is round or nearly, yet there are people who fancy that it is flat, can you imagine! Well, that's the same impression we get, thinking: "How can they believe that, they are mad! It's so obvious it is round!"

I see beautiful atoms, wonderful molecules. I understand the radiation between molecules and other objects which are invisible to the eye. I realise there are electronic and magnetic radiations, all of a much greater importance than people on Earth may imagine, if only they would make the effort!

Cells in a body have a very precise function - to make it live by being a battery and communication centre for it. If the cells die, everything stops in the body. Well, in a cell, there are far smaller areas which are absolutely invisible to the human eye and even to the microscope. These areas have very important functions: When the living part of a cell 'dies', there are reserves of life in infinitesimally small areas of it. If one knew how to wake up or revive those areas, one could help to keep the functions going of the 'dying' or dead cell. This description is not very clear, I know, but it is things like that we see and wonder: "Why don't they know it on Earth?!"

292

Seen from here, looking into the innermost aspect of things or events is an incredibly fascinating journey. There are discoveries at every step, we would all need to be Einsteins to really understand it ... Still, I am very interested therefore I can understand fairly easily, at least the main points, but that's because it's explained to me as I go along; there are always teams of very knowledgeable people available to guide and inform.

The human race is nothing but a series of molecules, animals too of course, as well as plants and minerals - nothing new there! But <u>when you look into the inside of those molecules, the heap you see is no longer a 'man'</u>. <u>It is a mass of whirls and electrical connections</u> which are not limited to the interior of the body in which they are, but which escape and <u>spread</u> far beyond it and <u>have an extremely enormous influence around</u> themselves! That is something which of course I had never seen when on Earth!

When one looks at those electrical, electronic, magnetic etc., connections and exchanges, one realises that <u>everything is linked up!</u> So the moment a horse sneezes or scratches itself or snorts, it has an influence on people, on other animals, rocks, blades of grass...can you imagine! How can we go and tell 'scientists': "Careful! Do not think in such or such a way, do not say this, you are wrong!" ? We need to manage to prove it first. Personally, at the moment I am just discovering. They are very <u>simple</u> things, you know, nothing extraordinary like different civilisations or worlds, but what is going on inside and even on the exterior of what we know on Earth... To me, it is <u>seen from a different angle. The explanations are not words but visions, images, sensations and reactions that I feel</u>. All that leads to comprehension.

<u>Life on Earth is meaningless unless one understands life in the 'Other World'</u>, where I am, which is the <u>real</u> world. It is here that one truly lives because we have all our faculties,

293

we cannot lose them. They can only be improved upon, whereas on Earth they degenerate!

My Earthly life has been interesting but was nothing like the one I live now, when each moment I spend examining something, teaches me new and constant things which are pure truth, not erroneous suppositions! All one has to do is look around to understand that what is taught on Earth is 'baby stuff' compared to the truth we have here! For example, one thinks of a hole as being round and empty. Have you ever seen a hole 'full' when it is supposed to be 'empty'? No. But I have! I have seen holes filling up with electrons, all sorts of nameless particles as we don't need names here since we think with visions. Those particles were forming rings circling around within the 'hole' and filling it up... To me, that 'hole' was full to bursting point! But to human eyes it would appear empty because people cannot see what's going on... There might nowadays be microscopes which could detect this, I don't know to what extent science has moved on; but this is to say that what one sees on Earth is not the truth, it is an illusion. Even if a giant microscope could see them, it probably would not understand the rapport and link between each one of those particles, themselves saturated with rays, radiations and other forces which attract and repel, because the relationship between them is a totally different definition and resolution... I reckon it's probably impossible to explain with words; they are inner sensations that I feel and which make me understand what is going on when I observe such things, do you understand?

(Suddenly, without a pause, I hear the following commentary given in English by my guide) A version of the Earth seen from our world would be unrecognisable to Humans - that's a way to sum it all up! Your father has tried to convey facts which cannot easily be put across by a person new to the subject, using human words to translate a 'language' that has

no words! So the best thing to do is understand that <u>he is discovering inner, subtle physics</u> and <u>still has a long way to go to reach 'substantial discoveries'</u> as you may call them, but to him they are wonders, like a child discovering what an adult may already know. We are all proud of his efforts and excitement and he has done well to try to make you understand what he is doing.

You can rest now as you seem to be getting tired. Your loved ones are still close to you but won't mind you stopping if you so wish. You have done well to concentrate and capture the gist of their thoughts.

1st November 2002 - *The pen starts in French:*

My thoughts are going towards you. They take time to transform themselves into words and in writing, but we end up managing it. I'd like to try to talk to you straight away without having to wait for someone else to 'open the way'.

BR- Who is speaking to me? Mum or Dad?

Mum of course, not Dad, he is it not here at the moment, he is dealing with his own activities and hasn't got time to come. Sweetheart, I wanted to speak to you because I was unable to wish you 'Happy Birthday' on your day... I hope you still had a bit of fun to celebrate it. I do love you my darling daughter and wanted to tell you again.

We have all been very busy lately as we made some trips into our <u>past lives</u>! I saw one of mine <u>when I was not your mother</u>, but a woman I did not know until I made her acquaintance...to discover she had been 'me' in a previous life! I wanted to tell you this as I know you are interested in reincarnation, whereas I used not to believe in it much when I was on Earth! You see, once more you were right and I was wrong! You were correct to think one lived more than one life, because it would be unfair and illogical to make only one journey in one type of body and not in another one.

I saw myself as an older woman because the beginning of that life was not interesting, I reckon. I had not realised that I had thought other lives occurred one after the other, whereas I seem to understand now that in fact they all take place 'at the same time', which I find really difficult to grasp because I still have the idea of Time in my head. But my helpers here constantly do their utmost to explain to me that 'Time' as is known on Earth does not exist in reality, since it depends on clocks and the sun...and we have not got any of those here!

The old lady I met told me she was me 'before', elsewhere. I did not appear to be 'French', I think. I was old but also with a different skin, with rather more colour to it, I reckon. I saw loads of unknown people who looked familiar even though I don't know them really! They said hello etc as if they knew me well!

BR- Who were those people?

Those I met made me feel we knew each other well, but I had forgotten them. They introduced themselves, one after the other, to try to make me remember... Although I did not actually recognise them properly, there were some who felt familiar...

My visit to the 'previous' or 'other me' had no other aim than to show me I had existed before, that other lives do exist and that we all knew each other, you, me and the others! You had other goals in your own life then and me in mine; we did not have family links but we were close and did like each other indeed. Then you wanted to come to Earth to learn what you are learning now and I wanted to be your mother to give you my support, my love and help you in your 'adventure' and there you are!

I think I did not have anything particular to do except be a mother to you all. But it helped me learn more about the Earth and the Earthly world and to be useful to those who needed me. I saw one does not need to be a saint to do some good and help others. Also among the people I knew 'before', some went back to Earth too, at the same time as I did, apparently.

BR- Do you mean a life before the one you have just left?

Yes, those I had known before 'your lifetime' had come back with me, when I decided to become your mum. We had all decided together to come back for one reason or another. That's the main point.

BR- Do you know for example where and who you were?

Details were not important (where I had lived etc.), it was not interesting. What was worrying me was to know whether one did return to Earth. I was shown that, of course, one could, since <u>one life would not be enough to learn everything</u> one wanted to!

The children of those other people who had followed me are still on Earth too! But they are unknown to us as we <u>did not need</u> to be recognised. There are people who were my friends when I was younger *(during her 'latest' life as my mother)* who are here now *(in Spirit)*. During this trip into the 'past' they revealed to me that we used to be friends 'before', we used to have things in common and that's why we had decided to go back *(to Earth)*.

You are probably thinking all this is rather vague, but I have not had the opportunity to delve into what I was, because it did not seem important to me. What I needed to know was that yes indeed, <u>people do meet each other again on Earth after having left it 'before'</u>. This system of coming back and setting off again can go on for quite some 'time', because it depends on the length of your lives and the quantity of information and knowledge <u>one wants to accumulate</u>.

BR- Can you give me more details?

You know, the details of each individual life did not seem clear. It was more who knew whom and where, rather than why. We felt close or not and we saw ourselves wanting to meet again after that 'death' (in the life before).

BR- (Feeling embarrassed) - It is fascinating but I have an appointment to go to, very sorry! I'll have to leave you but I'll link up again later on today.

Darling, I sense you have to stop. You can go, don't worry. I only wanted to tell you this to make you understand what I do here. All that is very interesting new stuff for me, though I assume you will find it quite normal since you believed in it before! You can talk to me later if you want. Come here and we'll meet again. I love you Sweetheart, take care of yourself in your life so that nothing goes wrong and all will be well, you'll see. I love you and kiss you and let you go without your feeling guilty!

Of course I am not annoyed! You have your life to live. I am really glad to have told you all these things! Talk to you later.

(I link up again in the evening as promised. Yet, instead of Mum as I hoped for, my guide comes to speak to me!)

Lonesome makes the best link. If you are lonesome you will be in the best position mentally and physically to link up with us, you see. You need peace and quiet, you need to get rid of the world of physical activities for <u>your mind to slow down to a pace we can cope with from our end</u>.

You have a very active mind which you need for your own life in your world, but you do need to be able to switch it to a quieter mode or nearly off, if it is possible, for us to be able to reach you easily. We have a wall of sounds and thoughts and pictures in front of us, whereas we need a quiet place, <u>a blank space if it is possible, for us to send our pictures and sounds</u>, you see. You have a big job ahead to bring peace to that effervescent brain of yours, we know! It is not easy but we can help you from our end, if you try more and more often to give us some time and quietness and peaceful relaxation.

You have that job to do, we'll have another one on our side and both of us together will produce some acceptable

298

media to work from. You can be assured we are not leaving it all to you, we do our best to help you, as soon as you try to sit down quietly, but you need some time to settle down even before you can attempt to go to a deeper, quieter rhythm. We suggest you have that sort of time every day, as often as you can, wherever you are, <u>even for just a few minutes,</u> so that <u>your brain learns to put a brake on</u> now and then...

BR- Is it true we only have one 'guide'?

One and only one personality is in charge of your welfare, my dear Earthly child. You have always had the same person looking after you ever since you were born to this Earth. You have been protected many a time by me, because my job has always been to make sure you are all right, as we have all got plans to work with you if you so wish. You have always been my child at heart, as <u>you have been my beloved child before in a previous life</u>, if you really wish to know! You asked so I am answering. You and I knew each other before, because you and I were linked to be <u>parent and child in one of your lives and one of mine</u>. Now I am here and you have gone back to continue your training on Earth and we have the same loving link.

BR- Which race were we? What is your name?

All names mean nothing, you are aware of that. We understand you like labels to categorise things and people. You know me as 'Silver Arrow'... Yes, we are talking about us, you and I, aren't we? So, I am the one who has helped you ever since you were born and you have found me when you started writing with your pen and I inspired your words.

BR- And in that previous life?

You know it does not matter where and when. All you need to understand now is that I am your teacher, protector and guiding light and shall always be by your side, even if you don't know it. So, there'll never be any reasons for worrying about anything. You cannot expect everything to be perfect in your life. You still have your free will of course, but you will be inspired as to what to do in case of emergencies or important situations. Beyond that, there is no need to fret about anything...

3rd December 2002 - *During one of the weekly mediumship practice sessions at home with a small group, I hoped to get some 'messages' for one of the members. But Mum came instead, unexpectedly, to speak to me through my writing!:*

The best for me, really, is to speak to you now, while I have got you within reach...or rather within earshot!

BR- Who is speaking to me?

Mum of course. Give me some time a bit more often, if you can? I would love to speak with you more regularly if you can manage it, as there are things I have discovered. I have had some wonderfully happy times. I have seen people I loved when I was very young and people I would have liked to know and also I was able to travel. The most pleasurable aspect is to do what one enjoys! In my opinion, travelling 'through Time' is the best! I saw many a historical period which had always interested me. If I had been able to bring you back some films or photos they would have fascinated you! You know what I mean? There were so many different aspects to each event. When one travels 'through Time', one does not actually pay attention to the events themselves, but more to the impressions, ideas, feelings people had.

If I could have gone back to the prehistoric era, it would have really been great to see how Man was really created...and whether there was an evolution as Darwin assumed... I mean it would have been amazing to go and see the beginning of the world, even seeing dinosaurs would have been incredible! I did not go 'back in Time' that far, but I did go back to various periods in many different countries, I think, as I was shown people I did not know. I believe this was to help me understand how people reacted to the emergence of new ideas. Waves of emotions and fits of anger appear in colours, sounds, lines, circles, in all sorts of shapes! I only see what I feel, as people's impressions are what one experiences...

8th December 2002 - *The pen forms the first word. Because it's incomprehensible, I ask for it to be repeated again. This time it is clear then the rest flows well, in French:*

Slowly...your mum is here. Yes it's me indeed, why doubt it? Nobody else but me, I wanted to come and talk to you a little as time is precious for both of us and we don't chat that often.

BR- Darling Mum, I am so sorry and ashamed of those long silent gaps!

No, don't worry; it's not a reproach, it's only to say it feels so good to speak to you from time to time!

BR- What discoveries have you made since last time?

My 'discoveries' as you call them are little steps right and left, in my spiritual life as they say here. That is to say it is only by understanding oneself and grasping facts one did not comprehend before, that one can move forward towards a more complete understanding of what's going on here and in the Earth world too.

There is so much to take in! For me who was not used to it, as I did not delve into it like you did, it was and is new. I know I had read and even 'studied' the famous bible of the Jehovah Witnesses but now I realise that lots of their 'facts' were, in my humble opinion, in fact rather nebulous and unfounded compared to what I am experiencing here! Also their promises and 'threats' let's say, were only to force people to behave well or join them. They mean well but I've discovered that, indeed, one does not 'await the Last Judgement', one finds oneself here, hey! You did tell me so but I did not have any proof of what you were telling me, at least not before arriving here myself...and that was an incredible shock and a good surprise to find myself here when my dad and yours stood in front of me unexpectedly!..

Poor Darling, do you remember me in Nice with my awful old face? It upset me so much!! Whereas now I don't have it any more, you know. I made myself look younger so as not to see myself again like I was when I'd aged so much... I can reassure you that you will no longer see me old when you come over yourself, one day.

BR- It does not bother me at all if you look old!

It does me! It upsets me to have you see me old I used to like to look youthful when I was younger! I wanted to tell you that the day I arrived here was one of the biggest surprises in my life or my lives (here and over there!). I cannot think of anything more flabbergasting than to know I was in a room one moment and the next to find myself completely elsewhere, with my deceased husband and father standing in front of me in all their splendour declaring I too was so called 'deceased'! Moreover they were laughing about it and enjoyed my being surprised! You should have seen them splitting their sides because I couldn't get over it! I was nearly offended because, after all, no one had warned me, had they?! So, how could have I known I was going to make the big leap from one world to the other? It probably happened in the blink of an eye, whereas you were with me on Earth a few seconds earlier! You can guess it churned me in every way. First, the pleasure of realising I had not suffered *(during the actual leaving of the flesh body)* and will no longer suffer because I had been in great pain (but let's not think about it anymore, hey!) Then after that, there was the shock of realising I had not said some kind of farewell to you all, or kissed you one last time, and the shock of never seeing you again at all...

That was horrid, it was as if it was <u>you</u> who had died, not me! Because I was feeling very much alive here, you understand. So the mixture of emotions was atrocious in a way, a huge joy mixed with a huge despair and sorrow. I no longer knew how and what to feel. But I was sternly 'told off' here, I can tell you! Well, not quite sternly... but they had to be fairly firm to make me listen to them, at least at the beginning, in order to make me stop crying out of despair. They wanted to make me grasp that you were not 'dead', you were still alive and that I too was not 'dead' since I was here with them! Therefore "Why cry since nobody is dead?!" they kept saying! Then gradually I understood the pain caused by the parting would be reduced if I could learn to communicate with all of you and yourself in particular. If I knew how to use my thoughts and my love for you, it would become useful to you and help you during your poor Earthly life which appeared sad, dark and full of worries when I compared it with mine which looked so beautiful and felt so good at any moment!...

However I had to teach myself to do that, you see, it was not that easy! I know I was telling you what I was seeing and doing and what amused me. But I did not tell you of the hours (if one can use that word here!) I spent crying for you, because I wanted to be able to speak to you and kiss you. I managed to calm down gradually, but it was a battle against my sorrow and a constant reasoning: "They are not dead, why cry? They too are alive since I am still alive, so I shall see them again, therefore why cry?" That's what I kept telling myself throughout those long sad days, to help me grasp the fact you were all going to join me one day, it was not going to be an eternal parting. It was more like your being on far away journeys, which I was used to since, after all, you all lived in different countries. So, all I had to do was get accustomed to it, accept my new life, obey the new instructions I was kindly given to help me and understand that any help offered here was for the best and for my good... After all, all those here were right, since they'd been living in this world for much longer than me! This is what I ended up doing after nearly wanting to

303

'commit suicide' out of despair... But one cannot commit suicide here so there was no point trying! Anyway, you know the rest because we have been talking to each other ever since. Yet it did take me some time to 'straighten myself within', you know! It was not as easy as you could think, because I did not want to make you even more unhappy by telling you I was crying for you! As you were talking to me, I could see that indeed we were able to communicate, that all of you carried on living and all was apparently well. So why ruin my life here, if all was eventually going to end well 'one day'?!

Also I wanted to discover where I had landed, since you wanted to know about it in great detail... Then my mum and the matter of a little sister for me gave me another shock and difficulties to solve to make her reveal the details to you... Therefore all that kept me busy and proved to me there was indeed a good life to discover here, so it was worth finding out more to understand it and tell you about it.

Yet nothing will be like the pleasure to have you all here again one day, you know! Because all my life I have been first and foremost your mum, well...since I had you. It occupied all that life and was my only concern... Therefore I don't want any of you to think I could forget you all just like that, hey!

Now things are a little different here, that is to say I do not worry as much and I learn much more - that way it will be me who will teach you everything when you arrive! You must not be concerned. I certainly don't mean you'll be coming over soon! It's only to explain what I do and think. I've finally understood that if I kept worrying myself sick instead of investigating what there is to comprehend here, it would be of no use to you, or to me either! So that's the way things are - you are over there, I am here. We talk to each other when we can. I hope you will pass all this info to your brothers one day, then when we meet again, we'll be able to update everything.

Before that day, I hope to have learnt even more, if

there is more to find out. That way you'll become even more knowledgeable than me, once I've explained it to you! It will save you lots of time...

My children, I am speaking to the four of you, even though at the moment I am only communicating with R-(*my pet-name*), because it's for you all that I talk to her. She believes in it, she understands it, but some of you may not... I do hope by the time you read these words, if ever you do, you will accept and understand that your mum has never really left you - only visibly but never in thought. She's always been near you, sending you good 'protective thoughts', wishing you every possible happiness and peace of mind. Being problem-free means one feels so much better...But it is difficult to prevent problems. From my point of view here, I can only send you positive thoughts to help you reduce or solve your troubles.

That's what I want to make you understand: My life has been for you, whether when on Earth or here, I shall prove it to you even more when you come here! Now I'll close this subject and tell R- to go and sleep as she still goes to bed as late as ever and does not listen to me, as usual!

BR- You tell me you have discussions with 'people around you': Who are they and what do you see around you?

My 'entourage'? They are my friends from here, my friends in this new world, that means people whose task it is to explain what I wish or need to know. So it's a small group of the 'same people' I could say, although if I need to know something somebody else can explain better, then that person comes...

BR- Are you aware of who they were on Earth?

No, we know one another's 'attitude' rather than job. What those people did on Earth is not what matters most - what is essential is what they know and can teach. There are 'males' and 'females', but this too is not really important since we all know that what we see is only a representation of what each

305

one wants to project, or how they want to show themselves. Therefore, since I too did it (showing myself younger because I had lived a long time and aged a lot...) well, ages or other people's appearances are of no interest to me, do you understand? Even if I was told what my 'décor' (as you call it) consists of, I would find it difficult to see it like that... because I have the feeling each person sees what they want to see! That's why I was not replying to your questions about what my surroundings look like.

There are times when we meet in a 'room' if you want to call it that, but it's more for the sake of form, it's more an impression of a room, so that it appears more familiar to those who are used to one, I reckon. It seems to me the 'walls' are ideas projected out of light, as if the walls are not really solid, if you see what I mean. I vaguely recall something like that existed on Earth, something which appeared real but was not - some light or laser special effects or tricks, or something like that?

So this system is good as far as giving a general impression for everyone. However, if we want to visualise ourselves to be outside, in Nature, while the others imagine they are in a room, it has no importance whatsoever. What matters is the knowledge we gain, the ideas and concepts offered and shared. Exchanging ideas, that's what is smashing!

We cannot go wrong, because if one does, a kind person comes and explains where there is an error. We are constantly guided, I find that great...at least for me anyway! There are perhaps some people who like making mistakes, I don't know!

What I find the most difficult now is to follow your thoughts!.. I see you are sending me several questions. I am getting mixed up - I do not receive the question clearly and I need somebody to help me unravel the fog which this causes!

BR- The fog?

I have the feeling of being surrounded by fog if I don't grasp your question or questions - that must be like a bad telephone

306

line. I must ask for help to clarify things. Therefore the best is one word or fact at a time - it's something I need to learn to do better. But if you wish to stop now you can, don't feel obliged to continue!

BR- No, up to you to decide!

Well, I decide you should sleep because I know it is late where you are. Here it's never late but you do need to sleep to have the strength to do your work, to live your life... So go to sleep now, to please me if not to do yourself some good!

BR- Millions of thanks darling Mum for all these fascinating details.

18th December 2002 -

I tune in just in case. The pen starts in English, so it's my guide:

We cannot be certain who will come and talk to you until they learn to make the link. It has to come from them; they've got to want to, then to learn to do it. Make sure you have a 'line' available, that is a regular sitting session, so that whoever wants to come to talk to you can be sure to be received. The main thing is to be willing on both ends and then you'll see that the flow of conversation will start, slowly at first perhaps, but eventually it will become clearer and steadier! *(Alas, I doze off!)*

21st December 2002 - *23.00hrs - I had a snooze earlier in the evening so I feel more refreshed. The pen writes the first three words in French:*

Hello, Mum speaking. Nothing very new recently, you learnt the main points the other 'day'. I have seen again some people I had not seen for a long time. It's always a pleasure to feel I am linked up to people I liked or knew. Once more, the main thing is not so much whom I speak to, but what we talk about - that's what is interesting to me, as you can guess...

BR- Can you tell me more about those conversations with others?

The friends I was with a moment ago were very dear to me when I knew them on Earth, then I did not see them for a long time. I wanted to talk to them to find out what differences they have discovered here.

They seem to know quite a lot. They've seen things I have not seen, but I suppose everything depends on the state of mind one is in at that time. I suppose if I felt sadder I would go to 'darker looking places'… I don't think I'd actually 'go to a place', but my surroundings and those around me would seem much duller and gloomier to me… I notice that I have to make an effort to send you my words, perhaps you should stop and go to bed to rest Darling?

BR- I am all right, please carry on if you can.

My friends would not recognise me if I had shown myself as I was when I was old, because they knew me when I was very young and 'pretty' compared to my decrepit body… How ugly I was before dying!

BR- You were not ugly Mum! Only aged and your body was in a bad state!

Yes I was, I hated myself. I looked at myself in the mirror and would wonder how and why I could have become so awful! But that's over fortunately. You must try to think of me as younger please, because I am no longer that old horror…

Having said this, I must tell you that you have not slept enough lately, that's why you are tired. From here we can see your 'aura' as you used to call it, your luminous glow which is not as bright as it should be; that's because you have been working too late in the evening and have not slept properly, so you are burning yourself up instead of re-energising yourself!.. You must rest more…

To finish off I'll tell you this: I have seen your dad recently, he has made even more 'discoveries' for his own benefit

- he will perhaps tell you about it one day. He came to see me to discuss it and try to make me understand what he's been doing. It's all to do with mind and thoughts, that's why it is difficult to follow because everyone has his own way of thinking and understanding things. Yet I still grasped that he has made some interesting discoveries. No doubt he'll talk to you about it; he has lots to explain. I don't know whether I could do it, it would be better if it was him talking.

BR- Can you give me an idea of what it's about?

The value of the power of thought or something like that... He has delved into the topic of sending one's thoughts towards other people and things. He studied the <u>effect we have on everything which surrounds us</u>. So I did see he was right indeed, as he gave me a few examples and did a couple of demonstrations. He knows how to do it much better than me, because I am not used to it as much as he is - he has had more practice and experience!

BR- Of course, he's been 'Upstairs' for 18 years!

The importance of what we think is incredible - we have an enormous influence on what we see around us... That's what was used to create all the things I marvelled about when I arrived here! I know I still do it now but it is less of a shock, because there is less desire for objects or things like I had on Earth. Now I am more interested in deeper subjects, in ideas rather than objects, therefore it does not show itself in the same way - they are impressions, symbols, rather than 'solid' objects as I thought I was seeing them.

I now know <u>if I see something looking like it was on Earth, it is probably more a projection from my thoughts than a reality</u> and it's pleasant to realise it...because I feel more 'knowledgeable' in a way! It is comfortable to see things one is used to, it's more reassuring, but when we know they are invented by the mind to console or reassure ourselves, we give them less importance than if they were real. The main thing is to know we are doing it and how to do it! After all, it is what our environment is made of - we find ourselves in the decor we invent, if we want to have one. If not, we can simply concentrate on what we are thinking and the rest is of no importance.

The best is to stop chatting now because you are struggling to stay awake, you have difficulties reaching me and I finding you... So I kiss you goodnight my Sweetheart and I'll let you sleep.

***

CHAPTER 7
Past lives extracts - Earth life as film - Brain is not mind - Mum tours my Earthly home!

2nd January 2003 - *The pen starts to write three words in French:*

I wish you all an excellent New Year, my darling children! As I told you before, I wish for everything to go well and for all of you to be in good health. Me who always wanted to help you all, yet I cannot do much materially now! Anyway, I am told things will get better for you, so I hope they are right!

You are perhaps going to reproach me with not having a magic wand to create a perfect life for you? Unfortunately I was told it's not possible as there is no magic wand, only warm loving thoughts sent to you all from the bottom of my heart and that should help you apparently. So I send them hoping they will manage to reach you and help you.

BR- Have you got any details so that I can prove your sister's existence?

I'll do everything I can. We have already discussed all that, haven't we? Personally I am not too bothered about not knowing who that lady was, because all this is 'ancient history'... but you think it will help you with your books and the boys, so of course, we have to manage it! My own memories are getting rather vague, but I suppose when one is here it can become clearer: some people here specialise in 'memories'!

BR- What do you mean?

Some tell very detailed stories of what happened in their lives! On the other hand, personally I have understood it is not really important, because they were only passing events on Earth! Yet when we live there, we think it's worth paying attention to them, don't we? The problem here is to remind oneself that what happened on Earth was only a passage from one life to the other and what matters in the end is the good one has done. If someone has done nothing with his life, it must be very unpleasant not to have anything to congratulate himself about, when he arrives here!

To finish off, I'll tell you quickly a few little things. For example, the day you asked me to meet up with my mum and to convince her to tell you what had happened, I succeeded, didn't I? Even though at the beginning she didn't want to talk about it nor to you!.. Therefore there is some hope I may manage to obtain those names you need so much, to successfully convince the world I am still alive here. No doubt we'll need a lot of patience as I don't know where I'll find all that!

BR- I guess your own mum should be the first one to trigger the search?

You are right. Mum should be able to start off the line of information and communication. So I'll begin there. The other thing to tell you is that since we began to speak this 'evening', you changed colours several times!

BR- (Astounded) What? You see me in colours?

There are times when I have the impression of seeing you in colours, with different hues. It is you in my thoughts, but you have different colours! If I think hard about you, I see you better, more neatly, more clearly, but if I become sad not to have you any longer near me, the picture becomes blurred and greyer. I thought you probably would like to know that.

There are times when I do not see you at all, I only understand you are there and I feel your 'sound', your thoughts, but it's not always the same thing. When I see you or feel you in colours, I have the impression you are near me. When I see you greyish, it's as if you are further away and I have difficulties in communicating. I send you my thoughts but it is not always clear whether you have received them or not. When it is very clear, it's visible at once.

BR- Does it have to do with the way I communicate?

I do appreciate your problem. It cannot be easy to

understand me and hear me, because I too have to concentrate really hard to ensure you receive the thoughts I send you. Well I'll stop talking soon so that you don't get too tired, especially since it is late where you are no doubt, because you always go to bed late!

I would like so much to be able to kiss you Sweetheart and to say goodnight...

BR- Me too Darling Mum! I love you. Talk soon again... (During the rest of January and February I tried to tune in but, unfortunately, always late at night so I kept dozing off...)

8th March 2003 - *Mum comes to talk straight way:*

I wanted to tell you that you must not worry because you have not been able to talk to me for quite some time lately. I do guess you have so much to do. I have Eternity in front of me, I reckon...

There have been lots of explanations given to me about things I used not to understand. For example, when we saw a beautiful sunset here, I could not help wondering why we saw it since we are 'dead', therefore there is no sun in our life and landscape. They explained that <u>images from Earth days continue to exist in our Mind, therefore we would see them like a kind of dream becoming reality</u>...If we were thinking there would be a sunset at this time, then we would see it!

There were also weird goings on such as my being in the middle of a meeting with interesting and clever people and I suddenly found myself elsewhere doing something else! As I was concerned to have left the reunion so unexpectedly and rudely, they reassured me it was what happens to lots of people when their mind takes them somewhere else and people in the meeting are not bothered about it. I thought it happened because I had been 'transported' by their thoughts but it was more by my own thoughts! Someone probably said something which made me think of something else… so it sent me on a trip in thought elsewhere. This happens often here, I should get used to it!

I always enjoy myself when I am in a reunion, which is what happens most of the time. Of course there are times when I do something else as I am not 'obliged' to attend the meetings. It's me who calls them meetings, but really I reckon they are simply people chatting together for fun and to exchange ideas. I know there have been times I was asked, or it was suggested to me, to go to a particular place to listen to someone otherwise I go where and when I want.

If I am not amongst other people, I take pleasure in getting to know myself, would you believe! Me doing some introspection, it doesn't sound true, does it? Yet I was taught to 'look within myself', to discover the real personality which is underneath the 'Me' I thought I knew.

I still think of me and see myself as your mum, of course, don't worry, but there are other sides one does not know before coming here. There are layers of personalities, previous lives, all to be understood to get to know oneself perfectly apparently. It does look a complicated muddle to me, believe me! Yet I was told that by doing it, we manage to unravel, little by little, small clues or a glimmer here or there. It is important to understand oneself better in order to 'progress'. Progress to where? I am not too sure yet, but it means to *leave behind ideas of the 'Earthly Self' to understand better the 'whole Self'*. This 'philosophy' must seem very profound, don't you think? But I am only repeating what I am told, taught and made to understand.

What seems to interest you is what I am actually doing at the moment, is that right?

BR- Yes indeed.

Well, I see myself in the open, in a large garden full of trees with shiny green leaves and flowers all around their roots.

314

I sat down on the grass, which is dry and green, by this I mean it is not damp. It feels so good to be in the cool fresh air and I think of you very strongly. When I think of you I see you in my mind as I know you, or knew you, you'd say. I feel you near me as if you were there but I don't see you. I see you in thought not in reality, you know what I mean? If you think of me at the same time, then we feel united and that's when I can talk with you. When you speak to me or send me a thought, I see it as a kind of brighter light in my head, I sense it within me, I sense the meaning. What you want to say to me is in my head, as if you were saying it into my thoughts and I answer you in thought too.

There are lots of people around but they are not noisy and do not disturb me. I simply concentrate on my thoughts and yours and that way we can communicate. If I think of something other than what you are asking me at the same time, we get a bit muddled up, or rather I get muddled up. That's because I have to 'dissect' and sort out in my head what I wanted to tell you and what is coming from your thoughts. But if you let me speak, we have a good steady flow, it is much easier, you see. At the moment I see you as a calm, receptive and clear light; you seem to listen or receive, so it is much easier for me to send what I am thinking.

The easiest is to know in advance what I want to talk to you about. That way I can prepare it in my head and send it to you more easily in one go, instead of stopping to ponder about what I'll tell you next. So today I wanted to tell you I had made some experiments, trials and exercises like those I have mentioned a moment ago. I am only a 'baby' here as far as knowledge is concerned... I realise one must spend much time at it and delve into it deeper, in order to understand more.

BR- Could you give me some examples?

I find the most difficult thing is to get to know oneself. You think you know yourself, you tell yourself you know who

315

you are...then it all changes when you go deeply into it! I used to see myself as rather thick and not very intelligent, thinking I could not do difficult and skilful things and here I am able to do stuff I would not have envisaged I could do!

Also it is by analysing one's life on Earth that one sees the kind of person one was, has become, what one would have liked to be yet has not been able or wanted to be. It is very useful to take a look at oneself and see one's life 'like a film'. You say to yourself: "That stranger is me, she should be unfamiliar and yet I feel I recognise her!" You feel timid, embarrassed and moved to see the poor person you were, struggling with Earthly life problems and somehow managing to cope one way or the other. It is embarrassing in a way, certainly at the beginning, then I suppose you get used to it! *No one is judging you*, definitely not! It is yourself who looks at 'you', *judging yourself*, saying to yourself:

"My goodness, how could I do such a thing? I should have realised it was stupid, or useless etc!" But over all, if one has not committed any crime, it's not awful. I would not want to be a Hitler or Attila the Hun or any other 'scourge of Mankind'!

Yet it does help to tackle this. We have certain ideas of what we think we are, then we discover we are something else, someone else...not completely different but with facets we didn't know we had, or had not noticed... *(I began to lose my concentration for a brief moment)* As soon as I felt you were disappearing, I stopped sending you thoughts so as not to 'waste' them and get myself confused! I saw your light disappear, switch itself off and I no longer felt your presence near me, so I knew something had happened. You probably fell asleep or were distracted.

I have one or two other things to tell you, if you have time for it? The friends I speak of have only been friends here since I arrived. There are indeed a few people I knew from

316

before - they <u>have known me for far longer than during my life with you this time round</u>. Moreover there are also some who seem to be there just to help and answer questions we may have. It looks as though it's all 'pre-arranged'. They turn up if we wonder about something and no one has got a proper answer, or if we have not really understood it.

There are also other activities, such as looking within oneself, or even just discovering the beauty of this 'country' I could say. It is not a country of course, rather a world, isn't it? It is really worth wandering there, in thought and in reality, to see what others have created around themselves and to share their pleasure in having those things near them. I realise 'my trees' are not really mine nor for me, but for everyone here, so that all can enjoy them, I mean those who love trees. I think that, should anyone not like trees, they would not be able to see them - this is what it looks like to me anyway.

Personally I only see things I find pleasant. Therefore it must be true that we only see what we are interested in and we ignore or don't see what we dislike or are not interested in.

I have animals left and right, cats especially, a beautiful dog now and then, a little fox who comes to see me too, lots of little birds flying all over the place, swarms of butterflies, lots of lovely flowers I don't know the name of but which seem to 'smile' at me! They are all around me because I see them and find them pretty. I bet I would not see them if I was not interested in them.

Also there are the kind people I know who pass by now and then, or give me a smile, or more exactly I suppose, send me their 'smiling thoughts', since we do not need to talk with a mouth here, I have understood that. I told you that long ago, didn't I? You see all this is ever so delightful! How could one complain about being here when there are only pleasant things to do?! I am certainly never bored as I've got heaps of things to discover!

I also have books as I've already told you, but they have gradually changed - I see different things in them when I look at them. It has more to do with how we behave and react towards others, how we understand ourselves, rather than details of my environment.

I've seen your dad now and then. He comes to talk to me about what he is doing or to see how I cope. He has 'learnt his lessons' well, I reckon, because he can talk of much more difficult things!

<u>Your dad has seen a lot about his previous lives</u> and fully understands that the idea one lives 'only one life on Earth and that's it' is totally false and incorrect. What a stupid idea indeed when you think about it more deeply! It seems normal to believe it when one is not informed of what there is after the death of the body. Once you are here it is so much more sensible and intelligent to grasp there must be some times when one returns or returned to Earth, or elsewhere perhaps! There is far too much to do, understand and learn, to be able to 'assimilate' it all in one go, in one life.

So you see, I who had difficulties believing in reincarnation when you used to tell me about it...well now I do talk about it 'with authority and great knowledge' (ha ha!)... No, just joking! Though I do say I have understood and understand we do need to come back or go back depending on which direction of travel you look at it!

So much for my sermon on reincarnation! You see, I am learning indeed...You should be proud of your pupil whom you probably did not think much about when you used to wear yourself out trying to explain all that to me and I was answering with what the Jehovah Witnesses were telling me!... Poor Darling you!

BR- Can you talk to me about one of your past lives?

My friends tell me it is very difficult to see again a whole life from A to Z, because it's not the way we see it here.

318

There are important moments in one's life - whichever it is - and that is what one remembers...whether it is because one did some good or not, whether one suffered or was happy, etc. <u>One sees those moments more like 'extracts'</u> than as a whole film showing. That is why, if I am to believe my friends, I probably would not be able to tell you what I saw or did throughout a whole life, or what I was in great details. I think it will be, above all, the personality and temperament rather than the fact one was rich or poor or had a specific job.

BR- Please tell me about the 'extracts' you saw?

I saw one or two little pieces here and there. I was told that at one time, in 'another experience' as they call it, I wanted to know what men did in some circumstances. So <u>I was a man</u> apparently. It's <u>his personality at that time which appeared, rather than the Earthly details</u>, but he seemed to be kind. To me he felt like a stranger, yet in a way I recognised him: a very weird impression! It was as if he appeared in a dream, but I have not been sleeping anymore since I arrived here, so I did not dream it.

As for his personality, his reactions became like 'printed' in my mind when I saw him. He appeared to be a brave fellow, I think he had to fight in his life, not just in a war but in his family life. Yet he always tried to do his best and be fair and honest it seems to me. So I hope I kept this attitude in the other lives. I would not want to discover I had horrid facets like having been a murderer or an executioner!

I saw separate little incidents, like small images not linked together - that's how I could understand it meant he was kind and carried on being kind... because my friends say all <u>these people are **not** dead!</u> Hang on to your seat! They did not really explain this in details, but I suppose if I am not dead, or rather *<u>since</u> I am not dead, so why would they be?!* How one can make head or tail out of all this, I don't know yet! But I am sure there will be a good explanation, very neat and logical and one day I shall understand! For the time being I see myself in various little cameos - a little bit of 'me' as a man, a little as another woman, a little as you have known me which is what I remember and what I think of as 'me' at the moment.

So I suppose one day all these little pieces of 'me' in various shapes and types, these colours of different personalities, will stick themselves back together into one big and single 'Me' whom I shall recognise more, probably or perhaps in fact, whom I will recognise! After all, since that is the goal, I should therefore manage it one of these days, shouldn't I?

It is going to be summer where you are I was told.

BR- (Surprised) Oh! You do know that?

Yes, I am kept up to date about what goes on generally in your lives and I know you love summer, so I think you are going to be happy to be warmer and be in the sun...if you have one in your country! I assume the boys are probably still struggling with their lives. I do not spend my time just thinking of me you know, I love you all too much for that! I always find times to think about you by sending you very loving and positive thoughts, to help make things happen for the best for all of you in your world where everything is so slow and negative.

I would not have ever believed that one day I would find myself here, talking about the Earth as another world and a 'negative world'! But one realises it is, even at my level as a beginner and 'new arrival'. The Earth is so beautiful without people on it, in my opinion, seen from here. Of course I meant without other people, not without you my children!

There is always something to say but you must get tired of concentrating so much... Shouldn't you be going to sleep?

BR- I am all right for the time being, it is so interesting! Do you see your guide or 'guardian angel'?

Most people I know here give me the impression of having been some kind of 'guides' for me. I see them often, they are very kindly interested in me and help me without

320

being annoying. I could say they are discreet, that's so pleasant - nice but unobtrusive people!

I am very fond of them, much more than of the few people I used to know on Earth whom I called friends! Here they are so kind, always ready to help you without seeming to impose their ideas on you. It's difficult to explain but that's what it looks like to me. So you see, I don't know whether my 'guide' or 'guardian angel' disguises himself as one of these people, but they all appear as kind as each other!

Let us end this conversation for today Sweetheart, because you look tired and we are losing the thread with the interruptions. You can come back whenever you wish; it never disturbs me, as you can guess! I love you and give you a big kiss Darling. Bye!

6th April 2003 - *The pen starts in French:*
Mum would like to speak to you now. We have not met up for such a long time. All <u>my thoughts are a parcel I prepared in advance to be able to send it to you</u> well 'wrapped up', so there it is!

You know, before too long there will be lots of changes in your lives *(Sadly true: Dave fell terminally ill in November)*. You will not need to worry as much about money, because things will get much better, you'll see. I have the feeling I have already told you something like that not so long ago. I have no idea of the gap between your 'now' and that time to come. I only know it won't seem as long as you may think. The only thing <u>I was told is to let you know things will get better for you all</u> so I wanted to tell you as soon as possible. The only way to move forward in life is to have securities, that is, solid things you can rely on. So make sure to have securities, make sure not to have to regret any action, do not regret an offer (not taken) simply because I told you things will go better for you. That's all I wanted to tell you - just to reassure you if you were concerned…

17th April 2003 - *Mum is online:*

I've come to chat with you, if you don't mind Darling. We don't often have the opportunity so I make the most of it! I saw you try to work with some mediums to learn to communicate better with the 'Other Side'. It is a good idea as I never had that type of course, so I was only able to do it the other way round by coming here and I had to learn how they do it from here! It is fairly easy if you think about it, because what matters is to have a clear mind and concentrate on what you want to say. If we get muddled up once, it confuses the whole lot, therefore it's essential to know exactly what we want to say and prepare ourselves. I had to use my 'black telephone' as I used to call it, because it was a way to concentrate, but now I see what I need is simply a clear and precise mind with ideas neatly lined up so as not to forget one or mix them up.

If you want to try to talk to me, all you have to do is remain calm and I shall know what to do to reach you. There is always someone who warns me when you are ready for a chat with me if I don't notice it myself. I suppose they are aware of it because they know what you are doing or want to do? There are so many people here who seem to know so much about everything, it is incredible and wonderful! The pleasure of a good conversation with intelligent people never runs dry you see!

If I had known I was going to land here so quickly, I suppose I would have prepared myself better... I have no idea what I would have done but mentally I think I would have prepared myself more than I was regarding abandoning you out of the blue! Me, leave you behind, all alone! Can you imagine that? I had never done it during my lifetime and just when you need me to console you I was not there as it was me who caused you that grief by leaving you! It is a very painful paradox.

On the other hand, perhaps I would never have had the courage to forsake you that way, because no matter how ready one feels, I am sure one never is since it is such a big step to

322

make from one world to the other! One cannot imagine what it is going to be like, how it will be for oneself, who will want to be there to receive you or why they come... It is as incredible an event as a birth I suppose but in the other direction...

As far as I am concerned, I do not have any desire to be reborn because I would not be with you anyway and if I was, I would only be a baby... who could only give you problems or inconveniences for quite some time! So I'd better stay here and wait for you while having fun learning what I am learning and discuss it with those around me.

If I was asked: "What is your favourite topic of conversation?" I think I'd say: "People of all origins and different centuries when they were on Earth". There are some who talk of their memories of those times. This is also interesting because as we discuss it, there is always a more serious and deeper aspect emerging, underlined by another one and that way we learn what we should have seen or known in History, what we do not see when we live an event and which remains hidden even to historians.

People who say a war is useful do not really realise the harm it does to all the populations, not only the ones we go and kill, but the one in the country where war starts. Because to start a war is to say we <u>want</u> to go and kill for one reason or another - but <u>to go and kill is to destroy other people like ourselves</u>, that is certain!

The worst side of wars in my opinion is the physical and mental suffering for all the people involved; they kill or they are killed. If they are killed, their families cry at their death and grieve for years and years. <u>If we go and kill, we harm ourselves because we harden ourselves, we accept we can go and destroy another life</u>, other lives and 'that's ok, it's good' because we have 'a good reason for doing so'.

But if we do it 'for a good reason', there must have been something triggering that 'good reason'. That's what we needed to go and attack, that situation or event which is <u>at the origin</u> of the wrong doing we want to rectify. If we do not <u>attack the wrong doing at its roots and kill people instead</u> (because the situation has become unbearable, at least for one section of the population of another country), those for whom it has become unbearable have not learnt much about the true reason for the creation of this 'wrong doing'. If they delved into it deeper, they would realise that very deep down <u>there are sources which should be dried up, not by killing but by teaching about 'doing good', by helping those suffering, by bringing help and better education, etc</u>. This is where we need to find the strength to help the 'enemy' to rectify his 'bad ideas', instead of attacking him with guns and canons...

I am told you have at the moment a war in your world and Arabs are the cause of it. They are a terrible race indeed! At least that's always been my opinion... But I am told <u>I need to rectify my way of thinking</u> because <u>if I see them as individuals different from us, I create a barrier which does not exist in reality</u>, since any person is a Spirit who is part of all people and Spirits and also part of the rest of the world; because nothing is separate, as they keep telling me.

<u>Everything is linked up, everything has the same origin,</u> whether a plant, an animal, a person or even a rock! So I tell myself if I have to respect a rock like an animal or a person, I shall have my work cut out for years and centuries here! That is really an enormous mouthful to swallow! To put oneself in the place of a person, well, one can do that, even of an animal, but to feel sorry for a rock, that's is a different kettle of fish and will no doubt take me more time! Surely it does not suffer like, let's say, a plant... It just stays there, plonked on its soil or mountain and has no feelings, at least that's what it looks like to me. There are always surprises round every bend in what they are constantly teaching me...so I do not dare to argue too much because, in the end, they will be absolutely right, I can see that!

For the time being, this is what they advise me to do: "Think of them as if you thought of a single and same person, then you'll see it becomes much easier!"

The amazing thing is that even if it's something about which I would never have been in agreement when I was on Earth, here gradually I realise they are always, and I mean a-l-w-a-y-s, right! So it shows to what extent we can be wrong when on Earth, doesn't it! I tell myself: "If I want to feel at peace, the best is not to argue too much and disapprove, instead, better listen, learn, ask and manage to understand". That way I can learn what will in the end, turn out to be the Truth...so why delay it by hanging on to what we thought to be right on Earth, hey? I may as well jump in the water and learn to swim with the flow of the river!

What I wish for is peace of Mind, so I am not looking for a fight. I am willing to say 'Amen' when they demonstrate they are correct. That means we can pass to another subject, or enjoy what there is around us, or do experiments with what we know or can do.

That's how I spend my new life here, apart from the moments I think of you to send you loving, warm, positive thoughts, full of good results and excellent health so that everything goes well for you. Boredom and idleness are two states absolutely unknown in my new world and I never knew them myself on Earth either as I never wasted my time as far as I know!

To have a mind (I shall no longer say 'brain' now as I can see it is not the brain which thinks, because mine is dead and probably rotten...and I can still think) and not use it is really a pathetic crime, because the mind is what directs you and allows you to live here.

'Beings of Mind', 'Spirits', this is what we all are, so no arms or legs etc. are needed since those only belong to the flesh body. Each one of us is a Spirit who lives his new life in a

325

very original and different way from the life lived on Earth. All we have to do is develop our gifts and know what our mind can do if only we use it correctly, instead of blocking ourselves with erroneous or preconceived ideas. That's what I wanted to tell you Sweetheart.

Thank you for listening so well and for such a long time. You did help me a lot by not interrupting me, that way I was able to concentrate on what I wanted to tell you. It worked well didn't it, don't you think so?

BR- Yes, very interesting, well done and thanks!

Thank you. I am glad, I see you have understood well and it appears to have interested you. So let us hope one day you'll be able to convince 'the lads' I taught you something new! I feel really very happy to have managed to speak to you as we don't do it often. Therefore, if I have the opportunity, I try to make the most of it, to share with you what I know or discover... so that you are not deprived of that at least, even if you no longer have your mum near you...

BR- Many thanks darling Mum, I give you a big kiss and kiss Dad for me so that he does not get jealous! (I am joking!)

We are not jealous of our family here, you know, we only want the best for them!

8th May 2003 - The *pen writes the first sentence then I hear the fast flow. It's in French:*

People's names are difficult to find when one has not seen them for a long time. It is very difficult to remember one's own name here, because we concentrate on matters which are totally different--we nearly bash our head against a wall of probabilities!

About the sister I found here, I am sorry not to be able to do much in that direction Darling. There seems to be a lot of complications. My sister is here, I saw her, she exists, she spoke to me, but she does not appear to know who she was on

Earth exactly, because <u>she had lived for only a very short time and did not have the time to create a personality for herself and to know herself as a Human Being</u>. On the other hand, the others, her helpers, said they will try again with the lady and her memories of events…I am more than willing to help Darling. It's the others who have problems with the reconstitution of events. All we can do is trust and hope they'll manage to bring you something…

1st June 2003 - *Earlier in the day I had a 'sitting' with the medium Ann.W.(via whom Mum and Dad spoke to me). During the session Mum excitedly confirmed she does communicate with me when the pen produces 'Automatic Writing' and when I write down what I hear her tell me. She reiterated that the information provided is genuine and correct - she <u>is</u> dictating a book to me. Once this is published, she was told "something else will come"… Now the pen starts the first six words (in French) on its own:*

This 'morning' I had a good surprise - being able to talk to you without having to make mental efforts, because it was really easy with that medium. All I had to do was think what I wanted to say and she seemed to understand and grasp everything I said and thought. So we had great fun Dad and I, to see you were near us and we could talk to you without any problem… *(Unfortunately I dozed off by concentrating more at this late hour… It is indeed ridiculous - my getting tired spoils everything!)*

7th June 2003 - *I hum songs from my childhood Mum sang to us.*

We can hear what you are singing! Yes, I know you were singing those songs I used to sing to you when you were little.

BR- I can't believe it! You can actually hear me sing to myself?

Of course, it's easy to listen. All I need to do is tune in to you and I see/ sense/ hear what you say and sing - it's great, isn't it?

Now Darling, I would like to thank you for coming and joining me. So what's new since last time? Well, I have seen strange things which I did not believe in. To start with, such things as fairies and goblins and all that... It was explained to me these are things which some people believe in ardently, therefore they will see them! Those who don't believe in them will probably not see them. That is certain, we must be careful what we think of here and you too on Earth, though you don't realise it.

So I said "Surely fairies and all that are...fairy tales!"(HaHa). No, I was told, not for certain people. There are people who can create a character out of a light or energy. So they possibly see the energy from a tree or a Being living on Earth, such as a plant, a flower etc, they know they have heard of a fairy therefore they imagine that's what it is. If their books show a fairy with a pointed red hat, that's how they'll see her. If she is shown with golden wings, they will see her with some. I was thinking, personally I wouldn't mind seeing some, but as I did not really believe in them I am not likely to do so! It does not mean there aren't any Beings in Nature - there are energies emanating from everything which grows, that's what people do not understand. Anything you want to see, you can see, but it does not mean it really exists, as it can be an invention created by yourself! In my own books during my childhood, fairies always had shiny wings and leapt from one flower to the other etc. But I could not get round to believing they did exist really so I never invented 'real' fairies for myself!..

The other thing I wanted to talk to you about is the matter of the piece of land at St Y- which seems to be discussed at the

328

moment. I think we had told you some time ago it would eventually be sold? Yes indeed, we were not wrong. All we saw was the result 'in the distance' but it was not easy for us to know when it would happen. We have nothing to measure Time here, especially when we try to compare with the Earth. We know it will be sold, there will be doubts and questions, but there'll be offers and 'interested' buyers. You'll have to do what you think to be the best at that time.

BR- Don't worry, we'll be careful.

Yes, I know you will be sensible and even will help the boys with their problems! I count on you all to get on with one another and never fight for such petty things as money, which is only useful to live in fact. After all, what does one do with it once one is dead, hey? *(We don't fight we help each other.)*

Now I'd like to take the opportunity to tell you something else in passing. While I was strolling here with some friends in this wonderful world, they were talking to me about the Creation of things in general, so I thought it might interest you. They told me that at the 'origin' of everything there was only ONE 'Thought', but that 'Thought' is eternal in itself, therefore it is 'at the origin' but in fact there is not really 'an origin' since that thought itself has always been in existence…if you see what I mean!

The 'Thought' created 'the Energy' so that everything exists. It did not take place like it says in the Bible, definitely not! Those were 'fairy stories' too! It happened in a much more subtle way - there were ideas which gave themselves creative Energy and doing that, they created other ideas... Those ideas not only created other worlds (which I know nothing about for the time being), but also many a starting point in different directions. That's how one of the ideas was (or is!) to create 'the Matter' which we are all made of, that is to say atoms of the world of physics.

It certainly is not as simple as I am saying…but overall

329

it's a bit like that, rather than a man called Adam etc! So, since I do not understand much in physics, I am not likely to write a technical masterpiece, but if I manage to transmit to you little details like this, I'll do it from time to time. I am sure there is much more than what I have just told you, but there is food for thought isn't there!

BR- It is fascinating, please don't forget to tell me if you are told more!

Yes, I'll tell you. As far as the rest of my activities are concerned, there isn't a minute (What is a 'minute' here? There is no watch if you do not look for one!), not a moment when I am not discovering or practising something. Just the fact of being able to walk without any pain is a miracle for me, after so many years of suffering or discomfort! But I am not complaining as there are so many people who suffer from torture compared to the little problems I had. So I go for a stroll here, whereas I could not have done that often when on Earth, simply because walking had never been a pleasure for me. I could not understand why people liked walking just for the pleasure of doing it! Probably because I would get out of breath or find it painful, I don't know, also I used to think it's a waste of time when one has so many things one should or could do!

Therefore now life has changed for me, I walk alone or with people for my own pleasure - I would never have believed I'd be doing that one day! When I go on those walks I look at my surroundings to understand why it is like that or how it happened. There is so much to grasp because each gesture may have a hidden reason or source. If people want to make things, to create them for their own pleasure, they do it, but others do it for other people's pleasure.

Therefore we are constantly surrounded by people doing or receiving kind gestures and who in turn want to show their gratitude... It is a merry-go-round, a circuit of kindness and pleasant pleasures here! Especially intellectual ones for

330

me, when I realise I did not know much about this, I mean the subject of Life after Earth life. Now I am here, there is so much to understand and absorb that we could certainly spend an eternity doing it! My own life has changed so tremendously, at times I don't recognise myself in a way. I mean I've realised I have facets within myself which I simply did not know, a 'me' who existed and yet I am totally unaware of!

The 'little girl' in me, as they tell me, is the one who liked to paint when she was young but who was not very good at it. I disliked sewing but just because I was not very good at it. All that can be rectified now by simply wishing it and doing it! That way those desires are fulfilled and do not remain unfinished and 'hooked' inside me. If I had not satisfied them, I would have them throughout my new life here - it's like a thirst one has to quench! Therefore I also have fun painting and drawing and taking photos and looking out of the window and admiring what I see outside.

I can only do what I see at the moment, but there are people here who can make pictures of their 'inner landscape', that is to say, of what they feel within as they study, analyse and discover themselves. It will have taken them quite a long time to manage that, I reckon, but we have all the 'time' in the world here, there is no rush! We can only do some good, whatever we do.

Therefore my thirst for drawing and painting is nearly quenched! I would really have liked to play the piano much better than I used to, but there was never any time to practise. I can do it here so I have got down to it 'now and then', but it's less urgent. I did like music but not as much as writing and learning. So there I am. I now write what I discover and do and you will also get it in bits and pieces. There will no doubt be some things difficult to describe and explain, because when they make me do some exercises to 'delve deeper' as I call it, to make me understand some problems or some rather philosophical and specific points, I think there will not be any words for it. It's more impressions and feelings and 'beautiful moments' of revelation we could call them! How can one explain that with words? I wonder. Well, that's it for the time being.

BR- Have you got anything else to tell me?

There isn't much to tell you now.

BR- Tell me what went on during your communication via the medium A.W?

My experience with your medium was very interesting as I had not had such an opportunity to speak for so long, I think. I wanted to make her say everything I was thinking and she grasped everything I was telling her. Here is what happened: When I knew you were going to see her, you can guess I wanted to be there and your dad too! We arranged for our friends to be around us so that we were well settled in the best possible conditions - we have to feel peaceful as we sit and concentrate on you. You have to do the same if you want to speak to me, haven't you! So do I here. When your lady <u>arrived in our thoughts field</u>, she grasped what I was thinking.

BR- How did she do that?

When she concentrated on what I or Dad was thinking, <u>she opened the door to our thoughts so that they could reach her</u>. I think she needed to listen and I or Dad needed to send one thought at a time very clearly, so that she could receive them.

If there was a doubt, she would 'meditate' a little and tell us: "Please clarify" and I for example, would show myself more in detail, doing something she could recognise. The friends explained to me that the solution for communication is clarity and simplicity of thoughts. If a simple, precise thought is sent, it will be received much better than a flow of turbulent waves! So Dad and I learnt to 'simplify ourselves': We are still learning of course, but <u>we practised sending very clear thoughts</u> which allow someone else to receive them precisely and understand them.

BR- Do you practise doing that?

Yes, we practise here. We gather in small groups and we have fun sending each other thoughts or messages or reflections or images in order to learn to clarify all that. If the other party does not grasp at once, we then must gather our thoughts and start again in a different or better way. There are a few things I know really well - all the rest is still new and it fascinates me. I reckon your dad has done his 'homework' superbly over the years he's been here. He appears to know a large amount of stuff which I don't know, but I hope to manage it one day.

BR- Could you allow him to come and share, or tell you things so that you can pass them on to me?

Yes of course! You can guess I will not prevent him from doing so! But there are strange happenings, to do with physics. I don't know how he or I would be able to explain them.

BR- Can you give me an example?

At the end of a discussion on a particular subject, do you know what happens? We have the impression that all the explanations or even the questions and answers given during the conversation are suspended in the air in front of us! As we look at them, they seem to enter our head gradually as if by osmosis, you could say!

They are like images rather than words as such. There are movements, waves of words or impressions, I suppose, images of what we spoke of. All that 'floats' above us as if we created those 'clouds', those flakes of thoughts and ideas and they do not disappear. They remain there, floating in the air, then they approach each one of us as we watch or think about them. They infiltrate our minds and get assimilated into our own thoughts. That way we remember, or we learn if it is something new!

The best is that even if you don't notice, they can get into your head, so you do not risk forgetting what has been discussed since they slip into you without you knowing! Amusing I suppose, nearly worrying, except there is <u>no reason to be concerned</u>, as no one would do you any harm! We are only surrounded by good people and personalities who would never wish to harm us, therefore we have no problem here!

You see this is truly Paradise, isn't it?! Perfect for everything! Yes we are lucky Darling. I look forward, impatiently in a way, to the pleasure of showing it to you one day.

BR- Good but I cannot come yet, I have this book to finish and publish!

Don't worry, I did not mean to insinuate you were going to come... I simply wanted to say it will be smashing when you arrive as we'll have the joy to be together - and it will be my turn to show you how to cope here.

BR- If there is another group further away from you, can you see their thoughts in the air? Do they risk entering your head?

When I am not far from others discussing something, yes I can hear well, not really hear since we don't have real ears or brains, but my Mind hears and I grasp what they are saying. But if I do not want it I shall not receive it, because it does not interest me - there is a kind of invisible barrier separating me from them, that way I am as if 'protected' by it. Therefore we are fortunately not bombarded by everything other people think, I reckon it would be unbearable! Luckily we are in Paradise so we don't have such problems you see! Everything is fine, everything is always perfectly organised so that all is well. There is no need to worry about the slightest thing, because order, kindness, simplicity and honesty settle everything. It is amazing how easy life is here in a way, even though it is an incredible world with 'systems', let's say and laws of physics among other things which are absolutely staggering! I cannot but marvel at every step and every corner. Everything is set so that all goes well, that's all I can say to describe it…

BR- Let's go back to the session with the medium. What was the role of your friends meanwhile?

The usefulness of having other people near me during the conversation with your medium is that if I don't know how to transmit a thought or an idea, they will help me do it easily. They always explain to me how to do things so that I learn faster. Very helpful, isn't it?

BR- Doesn't Dad know how to do it?

Yes, Dad knows better how to do it but he wanted to let me speak, because after all it is you and I, mainly, who are creating this book, so he wants me to learn to communicate well, so as not to fail in the despatch of my thoughts. The more I do it, the better it gets. Dad is not refusing to come and talk to you too, if he has something useful to tell you, believe me! I am not preventing him either! We both have things to tell you. But personally I would like to do it nearly all the time because it gives me so much pleasure to help you learn what goes on here! It used to be you wanting to teach me what you knew... I could see you looked disappointed if I did not grasp everything you were trying to explain. It was a bit hard for me sometimes I suppose. Yet you see, I did not ignore it since I am here on form. I have been so ever since I arrived, thanks to you in a way, because you had put correct ideas in my head! Otherwise I would have probably gone to sleep for eternity in the Jehovah Witnesses' big 'black hole' and God knows whether I would have ever woken up from it! *(Hence vital to promote this book!)*

So both of us are here for the same cause: You want to explain it to others and I am dying (Ha ha, am dying! How could one say that here, hey? No more Death!), dying to pass on to you all the details I can.

BR- Do you move the pen? If so, how do you do it, when it writes in 'Automatic Writing'? Perhaps you don't know exactly?

On the contrary, I can answer you: If I start speaking to

you by writing the first words, I think it is because you prefer it that way. You like to feel the pen move without your brain knowing what will be written. So this is why I do it. All I have to do is think very, very hard about what I want to tell you and see it writing itself alone - it is easy now. Before, I used to have to write it down myself with a pen, but I have progressed by learning that if I sent those same thoughts as a picture, written or writing itself, I could obtain the same result.

BR- Do you influence my muscles?

No, not at all. I do not touch your muscles. I don't think I would know how to do it anyway! But if I wanted to I suppose I could learn, couldn't I, everything can be learnt here it seems! So I don't touch your muscles. I send the thought of those words in my head, as if I saw the words writing themselves on some paper near me. They then appear in front of me as well and obviously in front of you too! But afterwards if you have grasped them, then I don't need to think so hard or to imagine them written for them to reach you.

BR- That is magic!

Yes, simply magic, wonderful, so incredible it does not seem possible. After all this 'time' here, it still feels as if it is the first time I am doing it and I marvel at the simplicity and the extraordinary feat of what you and I are doing: We are speaking to each other from both sides of the 'Death' everyone dreads so much! It is absolutely incredible to be able to do it so easily and it is a disgrace people are discouraged to do it, in France at least! Yet me who knew so little about this topic did believe in it!

BR- Could you appear in my 'dreams' so that I remember it?

The trick is not to show myself to you, because we do it often, it is that you remember it! If your mind is too tired you will forget everything. Therefore you must go to sleep quickly to help you recall our meetings and I'll prepare myself to see you in a short while, I hope. Goodnight Darling.

13th June 2003 - *The pen starts 'in automatic' in French. It's Mum:*

There are beautiful things around you - <u>I saw your house when I came to see where you lived</u>!.. I saw your trees and plants, the cats and your little terrace on the side, the pretty trees all around and the décor in your home. I was told if I wanted to see where you were they would show me, so I said yes...and there we were! *(What amazing and unexpected news!)*

I did not know what would happen as I never had to do such a thing, but since it wasn't me doing it but my 'friendly helpers' all I had to do was enjoy the trip! They told me to <u>concentrate very hard on you</u> then while doing so, to <u>wish to see your décor, your surroundings, your house</u> and all that...so I did it!

You have no idea how much pleasure it gave me to feel you live in a pretty place with lovely trees and flowers around you ...and your little house simply but smartly set up. It's not fussy but elegant, neat and really cute. Your garden is very pleasant because it surrounds the house. You can have friends coming round and feel at ease. Your home is so sweet indeed! Everything is there without being cluttered, you did very well. I had rather too many things and pieces of furniture around me - it was a nuisance when I moved about. You did very well, bravo!

My friends made me go round your home in thought just for me to feel the atmosphere, the ambience, the feeling of living there. You have a quiet street like I had, but yours is more interesting as you have cars driving by not far and shops, so it is a little more lively than it was for me. I did like my home, you know, don't think I was unhappy, but when seeing where you live I notice the difference, that's all.

BR- Oh dear! My study is not tidy at the moment! I did not expect a visitor!

We did not inspect the details, don't worry! We only

337

saw the décor in general, the overall impression and it gave me great pleasure to be aware of where you live. That way I can visualise it when I think of you.

We do realise you try to please me and I know you would like me to be there 'in the flesh', but at least now you know I came, I saw... therefore I conquered too (like Caesar said)... I conquered Death because from the 'Hereafter' I came to see where you were and from the Hereafter I discovered where you live, whereas you had never been to that house when I was on Earth. Therefore I did not make it up, since neither of us knew it!

BR- It's amazing and wonderful!

It is wonderful for you, but it's even more incredible for me as I had never imagined being able to do such a thing! You have no idea how excited and enchanted and amused and astounded I am to have been able to! I, the 'Dead woman', came to Earth to see my living child! You know, it is as exciting for me as for you!

We do not realise, when we are on Earth, that life is continuous on both sides. That 'Death barrier' is a nuisance indeed, because it prevents people from communicating easily, whereas <u>you and I are both still alive</u>!!

Why complicate one's life by dying! Or rather, why complicate our life by being born? Indeed why bother to live years of misery or hardship according to the cases, when we could all always live in the 'Great Beyond' and have fun and learn without getting landed with those Earthly years! I think we should go and tell 'God' he made a mistake and would do better to start the whole lot all over again! Life here is so marvellous, my poor Sweetheart - why couldn't you be here to enjoy it as soon as possible!

BR- (jokingly) You sound as if you want me to die!

No! I don't want you to die, certainly not when your children are still young, nor before you have done what you wish to do on Earth. But as soon as you think living is no longer worth it and you feel life has reached its end, do not hesitate to come and join us. I certainly do not mean 'Kill yourself!' Of course not! I mean if your Mind and Spirit within incite you to leave your body, do not be afraid of what is awaiting you on the 'Other Side': It will be me and Dad so you will not be lost.

BR- I do know that, but it won't be yet unfortunately, as I have lots to do including your book and of course help Jim and Anne-France.

My friends tell me you have understood the importance of our 'reunions' and chats. I had tried to make you grasp this via your medium, because I did not want you to lose heart, to be fed up and start doing something else!

I want you to know I am thrilled to bits at the thought of getting published 'post mortem' that's to say 'after my 'death''! I had not managed to get my famous 'French history Résumé' published, but we shall do this together and we will get it published, just you see! They told me there was no reason why it won't be, so our path is clear and we will do it, won't we! Unfortunately you'll have to see to it yourself, to find a publisher etc. but I reckon they'll inspire and help you from here, when the time is right.

My own pastime here is to learn, not only for me but also to be able to tell you about it so that people you speak to realise we never die! We are still alive but we live more happily after the departure from Earth, if we had lived a good life without causing any harm - that's the secret!

BR- Please talk again about your visit to my home? How did you do it? Give me some details, did you see any particular objects?

Coming to your home has been the biggest journey I have ever made, apart from the one between my hospital room to here in the Hereafter! But not with the same pleasure...

because the pleasure to go and see where you live was so exciting for me! Do you realise that?

BR- Who had the idea of doing that, your friends or yourself? What did you have to do and what happened?

Well... The idea came to us because I was wondering where you lived now and whether you were happy where you were, as I wanted to find out how you felt in your life... So my friends said to me: "It's possible to go and see her if you want to. All you have to do is learn to think correctly, in the right direction, a little like when you talk to her, but you'll have to concentrate very hard to manage to project yourself to where she is. We know where she is, all you'll have to do is follow our instructions. So if you wish to try..." I did not believe them at first... because it seemed weird to be able to go and look at something on Earth, but you now see it is possible, therefore I absolutely do not doubt anymore what they tell me!

So we went to a calm place here, one of my favourite spots with a lake, rivers, meadows, trees, it is very pretty. Then I asked where I had to settle down. They replied: "Stay there, sit down, look ahead and think of your daughter. She will possibly feel a presence, a thought of you at the same time, but we shall not be able to start a conversation because your attention will have to be focused on what we'll be doing, won't it?!" I said: "All right, that's fine. I don't want to fail, it's too wonderful a feat to make a mess of it!" We settled in this field with river water near us and I started thinking of you, very strongly. I thought of how happily we chatted as 'good friends' when you used to come and see me in Nice and how much you did for me when I was ill or unwell and how much I love you...

Then my friend said: "Now look ahead and tell yourself you really, really want badly to see her and her house. You MUST want very strongly to see her house!" So I obeyed and suddenly I saw a big shadow in front of me, like a screen, and a large house I think, a large 'block' blocking my view of the river and the field. Then I realised I was looking at a film of your home: I could see your big tree and afterwards we moved backwards and saw your house!..There were cats in the garden and a bird very close... I felt the pleasure you have when you are in it and I understood you were more of a gardener than I am, as I did not really bother with our plants and the garden.

I then tried and wished hard to see more. So they showed me round your home. We crossed the little terrace and saw your green plants there, then your rubbish bin I think or a big box? Then there was a darker area, it seemed, before going back to the sunlit front of your house. There are some pretty plants, going up or down, pots, trees close by, a tree very near your house... You tried to make this little garden pleasant, that's the impression I got. You wanted it to look comfortable, welcoming, not forbidding or ill-cared for, nor too starchy, didn't you? That's what one feels - you want to welcome and have plants around you. The overall impression is really charming.

On the other hand I did not know what to do about indoors, so I was told: "Think of the house you saw and glance through the window." I had not noticed the window at first(!) because I was concentrating on the pleasant impression given by the garden. But when I was told 'window' I suddenly saw I had one in front of me! So I looked, wondering what I was going to see and it did not take long as your 'indoors home' appeared at once! It seemed sober but neat, with lovely colours; the red and light yellow go well together I think. But I did not know you still had the piano. Therefore I had a surprise to see it there. I believed you had sold it or given it away! I wanted to look more closely but they said: "Careful! One thing at a time or else you'll lose your concentration!" So I wished to see another room and entered the next one effortlessly. I think it is your dining room. There is a table in the middle but it is easy to walk around it, not like mine hey! Also you don't have as many chairs either. I looked at it with pleasure as it seemed comfortable and bright, a beautiful room with windows and light. *(Piano: Mum recalls my vague suggestion years ago!)*

BR- I am in it at the moment!

Yes, I did like it. I thought I would have indeed enjoyed living in your house. I would have loved it, for a while anyway...since, after all, nothing is as good as living where I am now in the Great Beyond, because there is no housework to do nor meals or problems!.. I am free!

BR- What else did you see?

My impressions were provided by the kind of 'film' I was watching, but I felt as if I was there. It was strange because at the beginning I was on my grass looking at an imaginary 'screen' in front of me, but the next moment I felt as if I was at your house!

BR- Was I there? Or anyone else?

No I did not see you. I don't know where you were, I saw some cats but not you, in fact no one. I think the house was empty yet the visit has still been worth it, it gave me so much pleasure!

BR- Did you go anywhere else apart from the dining-room?

I was told I could carry on if I wanted, so I said I wished to see the rest overall. I was shown upstairs, the bedrooms with carpets everywhere, windows with curtains, some cupboards. But the room I preferred was the one downstairs with the table in the middle because it looked so comfortable and pleasant. I too love a well-lit room and this one has plenty of light. It is so beautiful, bravo for succeeding in creating a good ambience in your home, Mrs the English lady! You managed it. I too used to love having my own cosy area. You seem to have your garden and your dining room, haven't you?

BR- Did you see more details, like paintings on walls for example?

The friend told me that what mattered was to get a

'general impression' so I went round quickly to get this overall impression in case I lost the link and could not see the rest! I am a novice and am afraid to get it wrong or make mistakes…

So I obeyed, looked around quickly and '<u>felt' how you feel when you are at home</u>. I had the impression that what matters to you is to be left in peace. You don't seem to have much time to have some peace and quiet, but there are moments when you feel comfy in your cosy corner, your home. For you to be home is to have some quiet, if you are not hassled with work for your teaching etc. You have so much to do elsewhere that your house is your den, isn't it?

BR- Absolutely correct!

Yes, I thought so. I sensed it and understand it well as I too enjoyed being at home. But here it is still thousand…millions times better! You are going to get some other surprises, I gather…

BR- What kind?

My friends want to do some things which may surprise you, so we'll see… I am not saying anything in case it does not work… But if it works you'll know I foretold you, won't you!

BR- How did your visit end?

My visit was fairly rapid, you know. It is hard to concentrate a lot, for a long time.

BR- Yet you do it when you speak at length, like now!

Yes, but it is more difficult when thinking without speaking. Therefore I tried to see more very quickly, or to see again what I had already looked at so as not to forget it and remember it well. Then <u>it gradually faded away as if in a fog and the screen became clear and blank</u>. The river and the meadow reappeared in front of me and I had nothing else to see!

But it had been enough for it to be a fantastic visit for me, as you can guess! Not only have I (yes ME!), learnt to communicate with you, but now I've been to see your house, your animals, your garden with its little birds, all of this is so cute! One cannot criticise it at all, it is ideal for you. I felt and feel it now as I can remember and visualise it. I am with you, on the Earth, nearly as if I had landed from the Hereafter, but it is even better because <u>I can sense as well as see</u>, it's much better than being in the flesh... Well, no, not really, because if I was there I could kiss you and speak to you easily etc.

But let's not think of this as I risk saddening you again and me too, I'll start crying because I can't kiss you...

BR- You'll have to go and see Touky and Michou!

I would have liked to go and see them after you, but I was told I should wait a little as one exercise at a time is better than several, one after the other - if we repeated it at once I would lose my concentration.

So it's for another time. They'll guide me, I am sure of it. I hope they will show me where Touky is and I hope it can be proof for him if I can describe him or his surroundings, but it will be worth having a go. Of course I'll go and see Michou too! I'll have to see everybody including Pierre, but I do have to learn to do it properly and not too fast. So it's better if I am helped while I am concentrating. They probably bring a pinch of magic powder or something like that to make sure I don't fail!

My life's ambition had always been to write one way or the other... But to imagine I would write a book by dictating it from the Great Beyond would have been beyond (Ha ha!) the greatest imagination!

Not only I did not know I would be able to survive 'Death' so easily, but I could not imagine you and I would manage to speak to each other with such facility and without any problem, without big problems let's say. What is needed is for you and I to concentrate from our respective sides.

The Bible says people must not meddle with 'talking to the dead'! Well, Gentlemen of Jehovah Witnesses (and anyone else!) let me tell you that you are very wrong! Not only is it possible to speak with 'dead people' (because no one dies), but also the 'dead' are not out of reach and do it of their own will - it is them who approach you not you approaching them! So be sensible and understand that their Bible is wrong and leave people alone instead of knocking from door to door! There, you see! I have at last realised (since I have been here evidently) they misunderstood everything and are making big mistakes. Why wait all those years and centuries to 'wake up' as they say! What a waste of time!

The 'Jehovah Witnesses' children must have nightmares at the thought of finding themselves in the dark for centuries before 'waking up' after their death... Such a weird thing to teach them, hey! Anyway I escaped from that, I feel good here and thank you for having obviously opened my eyes, otherwise I would not know I am here, I would be in my 'inner black hole'!

What one must aim for is to have one's Soul at peace, you know - to have nothing to reproach oneself with, so as not to have to regret it later and the rest of one's life on both sides of 'Death'. Therefore to do one's best in order not to feel guilty one day.

If you do your best you cannot and must not have any regrets, you understand? It is the key to having a Soul at peace. Always do one's best, without being selfish, by thinking of others before oneself.

My mum tells me you are often surrounded with your cats, like we are here. We do have cats too, you know! Cats who adopted us because we adore them. They are just happy to be loved and cuddled, that's all. They do not need to be fed fortunately, so it feels good to have them near us just like on Earth.

BR- How does your mum know I have my cats near me?

My friends will probably have taught her how to concentrate on you, I assume! I haven't really asked her. She is very interested in you, you know? You must be like her in some ways. I do know all that stuff about the little sister shook her a lot when she had to tell you about it. It made her live again some horrid times and she remembered it for a long time in a way. She was going back to it in her mind, which was not a good idea considering my sister, her daughter, was already here! Anyway she is better now.

I must tell you that <u>emotions and impressions that you have whilst alive stay with you forever</u>. It is not just select thoughts which stay with you. When you try to relive them it is like suddenly finding yourself in the film of your life! You yet again have to feel and experience the same emotions, so I'm sure you can understand it is upsetting if it is a sad situation you are reliving.

BR- I do feel guilty to have pushed her to talk about it...but I had to! (Unfortunately I was disturbed, so feeling tired I kissed Mum goodnight).

***

CHAPTER 8
Soul knows of imminent death - Casting off Earthly fears: exercises - Everything is 'present'

19th June 2003 - *The pen starts to write 'in Automatic', in English:*

A visit has made your mum so happy! She does not stop talking about this 'special trip' (for her) to all those she meets! She was so delighted to be able to go back to Earth to see you! It is one of the happiest and most wonderful things she's done... Apart from coming back here to discover she was not really 'dead' and had her good health back again of course!

Watch out for ideas coming from our side to help you convince the people around you. We shall inspire you from time to time, so always be ready to link up with us, as you call it, to 'be there' when the ideas arrive in your head. One minute you are here, the next you have disappeared, that's often the problem. Try to learn the art of having a calm mind and to listen to the 'inner voice'. The more you practise, the easier you'll find it - you'll get all the proof, messages and conversations you want!

BR- I am listening to you at the moment! To what extent is it different?

You are indeed listening but the concentration is on the writing. Now you need to make sure that you hear better, for that you'll need to have some quiet times. These past days have been very hectic, we know. It had to be so in order to help you with the financial side of your life, <u>that's the way we helped you</u>...*(A sudden offer of big translation work!)*

BR- Thanks very much!

There will be some quiet moments you can use by spending a few minutes now and then simply listening to silence. We shall always be there so do not worry about when or where to do it...

BR- But surely you have your own occupations too?

The whole world is in your head. You have mountains of thoughts, seas of emotions, streams of joy and lots of sadness deep within - you are an Earth on your own! You have to turn to the Earth to unload your baggage of sadness, anger and upset... Play with the sun and the sea and see life in plants and birds and trees...Feel the wind or the sunlight and enjoy the feel of the Earth. As you become a quieter Earth by listening and feeling, you'll unload what you have too much of and you'll load into you all the positive sides of this Earth that you love. You'll make a swap for the better. *(Suddenly, French is spoken! It's Mum)* Keep going my children, I shall never leave you alone- I shall always and forever be with you. My life here has only one goal: To help you survive on Earth without too many problems and not to disappoint you when you arrive here one day.

BR- Why are you saying 'disappoint'?

I mean not to have 'disappeared' when you arrive - I shall be there. I hope you will have learnt a lot since my 'death', as I shall have spoken to you all and explained what happens here thanks to R- who jots down on the notepad all the words I send her to make her understand what I do and learn.

I learnt something new since we last spoke! During a conversation with my friends, one of them (who had been a lady on Earth a long time ago apparently) revealed to me that the first time she was on Earth she did not believe in reincarnation. Then she 'died' in that particular life and after settling down here for a while, she decided to go back to see what she could do better 'second time round'. However when she went back, she saw life had changed ever so much from what she had known before, as there had been quite a lot of centuries in between! So, because she'd made that leap between the two lives and two eras, she decided to become a writer to tell what she remembered about her first life and compare it with her new one. That is when she realised that the more 'ancient facts' she recalled about her previous life, the more conscious she became of similarities between that one and her new life! Each time she had an event or a big emotion in her new life, it seemed to awaken a memory of a similar moment in the 'old' life. Therefore she began to understand that <u>when we do reincarnate</u>, <u>it is for a reason which we have chosen ourselves, to improve ourselves</u> or learn again a lesson, a feeling or correct some previous misconceptions etc. She made the parallel and constantly saw that what she thought at the very depths of herself, had <u>repercussions in her present life</u>. To such an extent that every time she wanted to make an important decision, she learnt to <u>only do it if</u> she had listened deeply within herself to see whether it seemed correct, whether it felt right. The others here agreed with what she was saying as they seemed to know all about that or to have experienced it too. As I am only a newcomer, I have learnt to listen carefully and not to talk too much when I am not well informed on a topic as most of the time one learns much more by listening than talking! So the lady explained all that.

Afterwards, the friend who had helped me travel to your house took me aside and said: "If you want to try again the experiment of the 'other day', we can do it again if you wish. But if you want to see what your daughter is doing more closely it might be better to warn her, so that she will be alert and feel your presence when she has quiet around her." So you can guess I replied at once: "Of course! I am more than willing to do that now I know where I am going and how to do it!" But my friend said: "We'll have to explain to her she must practise to be much calmer, more often, that way she'll be more used to doing it and you will sense each other better. It will have to be more sensations than actual conversations since you might lose your concentration whilst talking." I was very surprised. I did not expect that as you can guess! I thought he was going to tell me I had to reincarnate! (*This reaction is natural, humorous and typical of Mum. It made me laugh!*) You can be sure I would have refused if they had suggested that, because I don't want to miss all of your arrivals and I have a job to do - to help you from here as much as possible.

We weren't able to do more the other day because I was afraid of losing my concentration, but now I have felt what happens and having already done it once, there are more chances I'll know better and will not risk doing anything silly which would spoil the lot. Darling, we do not have the opportunity to see each other that often, so I wouldn't want to ruin all that!

BR- It would probably be me who would risk messing it up!

We are all there close to you, understand that. Dad and I want to always be able to help you if you have problems. My house (on Earth) has got problems too; it's not in good condition is it? It has aged a lot since we moved in, such a long time ago! Well, perhaps you should try to repair it a little, renovate it more, to be able to either live in it or let it; that way you will all have more money. To let it would be ideal, you know, because all you'd have to do is put it in the hands of an estate agent. He'd do everything for you including checking that the lodgers behave and don't damage anything.

BR- We'd have to renovate it first... That will be costly...

It always comes back to having more money doesn't it? We are trying to send you what's needed so that all goes well... All we have to do is think of you and want the very best for all of you. After that we await the result... Since I am still with you for a few extra moments, I want to kiss you with all my heart to assure you I shall never forget throughout my life... and even my lives...what you did for me when I was unwell!

BR- No! Come on! It was nothing! It was absolutely normal!

Oh no! It was not 'nothing'! You tried <u>so hard</u> to help me by sending me all those parcels and other helpful aids to give me relief or improve my health, I'll never be able to thank you enough, do you hear me?

BR- It's embarrassing, thanks, but really...

Come on, don't be modest or timid!

BR- Please don't mention it any more. It was absolutely normal, end of story!

Now I'll let you sleep. You seem to be very tired, I'll try to meet you during your sleep.

BR- What can be done to help me remember those encounters?

The matter of your remembering is quite complicated and has nothing to do with us... It has to do with you, your mind and your brain. So do not think I shall be able to influence your mind for it to recall what your brain has not seen... But if there is just you and I, we'll be able to meet all the same, to have hugs and kisses and feel happy together. That in itself counts for a lot, don't you think so? I am ready to receive you. Therefore go to sleep, so that your mind is free to come here with me and Dad of course, as he'll be called as usual every time you come, to let him know you are visiting for a while. It makes us so happy! Good night Darling, see you soon!

25th June 2003 - *Tomorrow will be the 4th anniversary of Mum's passing.*

My memories of my last days on Earth are quite clear but also rather vague... because what I remember now is the suffering and the atrocious craving for a drink of water, but also the pleasure of knowing you had come for me - that really touched me in a way as I knew you must have had to drop everything to come! You did so much for me Sweetheart! But I

351

do remember your little talk before I 'left'. *(Nurses said at the time that, though she was drugged up against pain, Mum could hear me!)* You thought I could not hear you, yes I could! I was able to listen but unable to speak to you, I felt like I was paralysed, I had no strength to talk to you or wave, but <u>when I saw the two lights approach, I assumed they must be some sort of new-fangled treatment</u> for my health problem and I was wondering what on Earth it could be!

<u>After actually following those lights</u>, although I thought I was only looking at them closely, <u>I found myself here with your dad and mine</u>! It was one of the biggest shocks of my life, as you can guess! In fact 'death' is a big shock when you don't expect it! I suppose it is for everyone. Therefore it was fun for me to realise I had found a way of making 'the leap' without even noticing it... Yet there was also the harrowing grief when I realised I had left you 'over there', without me, alone forever, without any help, left to struggle without being able to turn to me and without having had time to say goodbye one way or the other, at least a little...

I suppose it would have been terribly hard for all of us if we had known I had to leave you... I don't know whether it would have been a good idea after all! It is awful to have to abandon those we love! That's why I want so much to let you know I am really here indeed, I do not suffer at all any longer and I am having some great times learning lots of fascinating things and trying to apply what I am taught! All those around me are friends either from long ago or new ones, who seem to have given themselves the task to look after me in a way by chatting so often with me and my other friends, to answer our questions and teach me new things I did not know. Most of the time we talk, passing from one subject to another it seems, but I am sure there must be a theme or a line of thought, because in the end it leads to something very useful or very interesting!

BR- An example?

There is so much to say, it is difficult to find an example! The day I arrived everything was so incredible I thought I was becoming 'mad', just seeing my thoughts taking shape, happening, like I told you and described before. The action of thoughts is amazingly powerful! They are so alive, so real, it is incredible! We hardly have time to think something when it takes shape in front of us, so much so that we live in a world constantly on the move here! But we get used to it and think of something else. We create for ourselves a cosy little life by concentrating on what we are thinking, but we also learn to watch what we think of, otherwise it would take shape…and it makes a shambles to have too many things in mind!

That is why one must always pay attention to what one says or thinks, even on Earth, you see! I always used to say: " You must never say something you don't really mean, as you risk regretting it one day and it would be difficult to 'un-say' it, undo it, swallow it back!" But I suppose people who don't think about anything don't have that problem…

BR- Do you see what other people think and therefore create?

We see others' thoughts indeed, but we do not see them as 'trains of thoughts'- long series of things- it is more the emotions behind the thoughts that we see in colours around each person. There are people who think of those they left behind on Earth and they are so sad at first, it's normal. But they are taught, as I was, to try not to cry too much, because it does not help those they want to help. When we look at them here, we see clouds of sadness around them: It is similar to, say, bad weather on a mountain, very cloudy and greyish… Then when they are happier, their 'beautiful inner sun' shines and they are surrounded with a lovely light, an inner radiance we all have shining constantly - this is what seems to light up this place here. There are all kinds of thoughts creating all sorts of colours, but we notice mainly colours rather than objects.

BR- You had created a vase at the beginning. Did the others see it?

My friends have just spoken to me to reply to your question. It stands to reason we don't need to look at what others are thinking, but if we wanted to we could, I suppose. The solution is this: Here, someone thinking of something has either a great desire for that thing or a need not satisfied, so they think of it.

It is their own emotion that creates the object (If there were no emotions behind those creations, there would not be any problems).So this person may find himself in something like a strange dream, where the slightest thing appears in front of him without him being able to stop it... People see what they wish and things they think about strongly. If they don't feel an intense desire within, they are not creative enough. That is the key. Desire is what creates. Desire is like an engine and an accelerator creating the matter necessary for the object or result to become visible. That is why at the beginning I did not know where I was because I had strong thoughts about all sorts of things. However, by controlling them, one can reduce those 'apparitions' and only have what one really wants.

As you know, personally what I wanted most was peace - no more worries, no more pain and a soul at peace. But it was a bit hard to get because I knew you probably did not have it! All the more since I must have given you a lot of grief by disappearing so quickly and suddenly. My life had changed for the better, yours did not seem able to do that so easily and it made me despair. But I was soon taught not to cause you problems. On the contrary, I have to try to do some good in your life, by sending you my loving and positive thoughts as I always have for you all, including your own children... and the cats! Goodnight Darling, I'll let you sleep.

27th June 2003 - *4 years since the first day Mum started speaking to me from the Hereafter! I try to tune in as I listen for the first time to a new CD I bought from two young Peruvian musicians travelling through York. Unfortunately the CD has rather noisy tunes unknown to me, which at first hearing are not particularly pretty! Yet I don't worry, thinking I may get used to them. The pen begins to write vigorously in 'Automatic' but I can't decipher the words. I ask for it to be repeated then I hear French spoken:*

There <u>are</u> tunes which are not pleasant and this is what we are telling you! Bring some nice music if you want to have some sounds, but this music does not help meditation. The noise you have here gets on my nerves!.. *(I switch off the CD at once! Several minutes of silence, then suddenly it starts again clearly)* One cannot concentrate if sounds are disagreeable. We feel them here as out of reach vibrations*(!)*. We all find this unpleasant.

BR- I apologise, it was just a trial...

No! Not to gather your thoughts! It hindered the gathering of one's thoughts and prevented concentration!

My life has slightly changed here. I have made more efforts to progress by learning more difficult things. I need to know as much as possible, so I must be a 'good pupil' and learn new stuff.

Well, after popping round to your home I pondered about what was needed to make such a trip. I thought about it a lot to remember it well, so as to be able to do it again as easily as possible. It does make your mind work, believe me! I have to concentrate so hard and not lose the thread of my thoughts, while at the same time examine what I am looking at to be able to recall it. But when one has done it once, one can remember what needs doing, then one concentrates even more next time. Therefore this is what I did: I recalled what I saw in your home, thought about it and saw again your pretty plants, trees

355

and other things like your dining room and other rooms. I said to myself to make it worth it, I had to go and see the others, my boys, as you were my prototype'! So I popped over to see my 'little boy' who likes houses in a forest!

(*My eldest brother Pierre, living in a South American rain forest*) It was not difficult! I saw him in his 'hut of a savage'! But in fact it is not a hut. It is very well set up. He's built some kind of 'construction' around it to protect himself from possible invasions? He has topped it with a sort of parasol or I don't know what, I suppose it is to protect it from violent rains?.. Anyway it looks very solid and protected. He has several little houses nearby, not far from him. It's simple but really nice and there are so many trees and plants around, it does give the feeling of being in the jungle. Between you and him, you are both surrounded with trees, aren't you! Yet his 'wife' did not seem to be there. I did not see anyone, I didn't see him though I had hoped to, but I wasn't able to manage it. So I had a good look around and saw a little animal like a cat or a dog, some little things about, but it was simply his books, his table, his tools, his kitchen, his lumber room or cupboard, all that seem to be in the shade. I think if the sun got inside he would get too hot where he lives! (*Indeed! It's near the Equator*) My visit was fairly rapid as I was not very used to doing it. I only wanted to try and see whether I knew how to manage it again, so that I can do better each time.

BR- Did you notice anything you did not know about before?

The house was very well-built, it is clearly evident, but it is quite different from our home. One could live there all the year round and not notice time go by because there are so many trees around, it seems to me like one is lost and cut off from the rest of the world. Life feels peaceful there, so calm... I should have gone myself, I would have liked that! But nowhere is better than where I am now! So your houses on

Earth will not make me miss dwellings, now that I have learnt one can very well do without them and not have to cope and bother with houses!

BR- Can you describe other things you saw?

No, I popped over to his place but I could not see much, it looked rather dark I reckon. For me light in a home is important, you know. I think one needs a lot of it, real daylight I mean. So many are so gloomy and dark! The impressions I got from his place were good. He appears to be happy there, busy but glad to be there and to do what he likes doing and not bother with what he dislikes. You see, he has done what he wanted to do throughout his life nearly. He never wanted to be locked in a city, it made him panic or he found it unpleasant. He always wanted the freedom of open spaces, so once more he's got it, for good it seems!

Following this visit I travelled towards France in a flash, as all was needed was to think of it. I had hoped to see my Touky at work no doubt. He's had setbacks as usual, poor lad. Just seeing what he needs to do on this boat drives me crazy with worries if I allow myself to have worries…but 'they' teach me and keep repeating I must not let fears come over me; on the contrary I must be filled with hope and positive wishes for you all…So I tried to do that for his work and his wretched boat, though he does love it! Personally I really wanted to like it but it caused us such a lot of nightmarish problems ,I used to wish I could set it on fire!! I would have done it myself had I been able to get to it, but it would have been of no use… so all I could do was champ at the bit! However nowadays I don't set fire to it, I send it good, 'friendly' thoughts so that it becomes a 'well-mannered' boat! I mean hoping it behaves well and does not cause any problems for Touky, so that his life becomes more normal and no longer constant hell as he has been having for years. A good lad, a brave lad! It's bad luck when you see how kind-hearted he is! But having a kind heart in business does not make things better…

BR- What did you see?

My visit was not long for a first time as I had just been to Pierre's, so it meant a lot of effort to concentrate since 'Time' is not really felt here. The town has not changed much, I saw the town again roughly, but I found Touky in the harbour I think, in a harbour anyway! He had what I took to be a big sea jacket; he must have gone to sea, he looked wet. He was busy with some cables I assume, I could not see the details. I was trying to <u>sense</u> his presence rather than focusing on the details around. He looked worried or concentrating deeply, perhaps simply bustling over something. If I felt him so clearly, it's <u>because I came close to him and kissed him to give him a surprise, but I am not sure he sensed</u> it. I would have loved him to turn round and see me there near him.

After that the vision seemed to get clouded over and he disappeared in a kind of fog. I did want to stay there but I was unable to keep the picture going… It saddened me as I had not really seen him on Earth since I departed. He had helped me to get to the hospital, then after that everything was blurred unfortunately…

I do want to be able to do it again, I want to go back to see him to make sure he is well and to try to give him some proof I am indeed alive and not 'dead' as he thinks. I know he must have a vague notion I still exist somehow, but he does not really know how or where. I would love so much to make him understand I have never forgotten what he did to help me, all his kind gestures in spite of his moments of bad mood and grousing! He is indeed very kind-hearted my 'son number two' and I want him to know I love him and have not forgotten him.

I'll have to teach myself to travel further to go and see my Mich too, because in a way he has done even more with his huge monetary sacrifice, which I was never able to give him back because I 'died' too soon to reimburse it! Also I had misunderstood what happened in New Caledonia between him and Touk and I am so sorry if I distressed him! I wanted to be able to tell him I love him before 'leaving' to come here! I do regret it, it is very sad indeed. So I'd like to try to go and see him one day. Next time we talk about this I hope I will have done it; you'll be able to write it down. I do need to practise that intense concentration, it's ever so hard not to think of something else! <u>One has to isolate oneself mentally and intensely focus on one single thing, otherwise the mind wanders right and left like in day dreaming and it ruins everything</u>... My ideas about what the Hereafter was or could be have changed a lot I can assure you! I had never imagined it would be as it is here! It's incredible! It makes you wonder who could ever visualise it, what with stuff we are told on Earth - all that talk of angels with harps and the good Lord sitting in the middle is in fact all childish nonsense... As for me, I am delighted to have discovered the 'real' truth and there must be lots of things which I have not found out yet and will have to seek out! They are probably waiting for me to do so!

Better go to sleep Darling, because you must have a big sleep debt as usual!

5 July 2003 - *07. 45 - Early morning for a change! In French:*
Failing to sit quietly every day definitely delays your book. You must absolutely get down to it regularly to be able to finish it, but if you can't, we understand, it's Earthly life which causes this delay.

My friends asked me to pass on this message Sweetheart. I think it's rather harsh because you have so much to do, but they insist you must get on with it more regularly so that we finish it.

BR- But surely you'll no doubt have more to say later on too?
There will always be more to say but it could be a second

book, you know... So we must do as they advise us, because they are always right in the end! I did a lot of 'research' recently on apparitions appearing on Earth. Since I was able to go and see you, or at least see your house and garden, I asked how you would have seen me if you had, because I was not sure whether I was really there or whether your garden just appeared on my screen...

So they explained that for you to be able <u>to see me, you'd have to be really well relaxed and calm</u>, which is rare for you, let's admit it! Also you would need to be the type of person who can see Spirits rather than just hear them. Then I asked: "How could I make myself be seen, since I now know how to make myself be heard (by talking to you)?" They replied: "You must know how <u>to project yourself</u>. You need to <u>accelerate your thoughts by thinking about yourself</u> first. You must <u>remember what you looked like</u> or how this person *(me in this case)* would remember you. Then keep this vision in mind to be able to project it into space, in the 'air' and maintain it there - remember it until the other person (on Earth) realises you are there." It is not easy as I tried to practise with my friends. It's hard to recall what I looked like in detail and to keep the thought in mind! *(A short silence then Mum carries on)* My friends remind me it's hard for <u>you</u> to concentrate for a long time, therefore I should give you details in 'paragraphs', in little parcels, that way you can rest your mind and eyes (and your hand!) for a moment in between.

BR - That's very kind, thanks!

So is it all right if I continue? We have therefore to concentrate on ourselves until the person on Earth notices. Of course there will be people who will not notice or will ignore it. But if we do it for someone whom we know, we are more likely to succeed if we can warn them in advance. Therefore I would really like to try to appear to you, if you want me to.

BR- That would be wonderful...but very sad when you

disappear again! Do show yourself as you imagine yourself now, that is, looking younger...

I am told that when we appear to Humans, we must first put ourselves in their place and understand it will probably be a huge shock. So I'll make sure someone will help me not to give you a shock! I don't want it to be unpleasant for you, do I? I would like you to be happy to see me, not frightened or sad!

BR- I'll certainly be happy, but yes, it will be sad when you leave again...

You must not be sad because I feel so well here! You will surely be glad I do not suffer any longer - but I do understand you being sad that I cannot remain amongst you, visibly and in flesh and blood. So we could try that couldn't we? I need to learn to do it properly, it will probably not be as easy as it sounds, but if I seem to manage it here, we'll try it, no doubt several times before you realise I am there! Yet it will be a nice surprise for you when I arrive, I hope.

BR- Of course! Yet so far I have been more clairaudient than clairvoyant...

My friends advised me to talk to you first, to warn you so that you don't get a shock and also to encourage you to sit in peace and quiet and relax, thus becoming more receptive. You have to be, otherwise my efforts will be in vain... I don't think the lads would see me if I went towards them. I could try but I don't know whether I'll manage to show myself. My friends recommend not to tire you out each time, I mean if I appeared...

BR- Tire me?! What do you mean?

That's what they said. I'll have to see what they are talking about...

BR- It's more likely to be you, rather than me, getting tired by the effort!

My friends know everything, so I say 'Amen' to whatever they advise! It saves time and avoids useless mental efforts in pointless discussions, when I shall have to accept that, in the end, they are right after all! This happens all the time! As I told you, I give in to their great knowledge! Anyway, why argue when one is a beginner still learning? I may as well absorb their knowledge and use it!

BR-I am very proud of you and your progress! (I give Mum my latest news and plans)

We've understood everything, all you said, it's super!

BR- (surprised) 'We'? Not just you?

'We', because my friends help me grasp the flow of your thoughts, I don't always manage it sometimes. I see your thoughts as pictures, you know, that's why. So they slow down the pictures for me.

BR- (Even more surprised) How do they do that?!

I have no idea how they do it! It's far too clever for me! But they manage to project them more slowly for me.

BR- I am really sorry if I am too fast!

I understood you'll be going away and you'll have someone in your home to look after your cats, so I understand it's always a chore to have to prepare your home for a stranger... 'An English woman's home is her castle', isn't it?

BR- Do you see my thoughts and your friends' like a film?

(Short silence) Just a moment... I am coming back now. My friends were explaining something to me: If one concentrates very hard on someone, one can see their thoughts as a kind of film filled with colours and emotions, like little waves. It is hard to explain because we don't analyse it when we see it - we just understand it!

So if I see thoughts as a film and they arrive too fast, I need them to be slowed down: my friends do that for me at the moment. I did learn to do it when I speak to them but it is harder to do with you. Therefore if you think more slowly, it will be easier for me, all right? That's how we communicate amongst ourselves here. At the beginning I thought we had to speak to each other like on Earth, but I soon realised we use telepathy and understand what others are thinking.

BR- What happens if several people send their thoughts at the same time?

I don't think this occurs because usually one concentrates on one person at a time, or else one person at a time expresses his thoughts. We are polite here, we don't interrupt each other it seems! I have still got lots of things to tell you...

BR- Go on! I've got time.

I went to see my grandparents to speak to them about the baby and the kind lady. They took some time to accept to make the effort to remember, because they disliked having to, since it had been a horrendous time in their life... But they told me the lady was known for her kindness and skill in looking after newborn little ones, that she adopted them or looked after them. They had contacted her to get rid of their problem, but they did know their daughter was terribly unhappy! They were obliged to be harsh on her because it was necessary to save the family honour etc...but they do not really remember the lady's name as it was something they no longer wanted to discuss after she left. They kept repeating "It had to be done. We were forced to do it so that our own daughter could rebuild an impeccable and spotless life. Yet it did not help us personally, because we saw her being so very miserable and obviously she must have hated us for having broken her heart. But what could we do?!"

BR- Can we get a name? The village? First letters? A year?

Darling I am doing my utmost to ask them to give you something. All they could say is she lived towards the country not far but not near Boulogne. It had to be outside the town so that my mum did not risk meeting her with her baby. The people who recommended her lived fairly near them and they must

363

have obtained some information without appearing to enquire…as they did not want people to guess, you see!..

My mum is still sad when she talks about it, or rather if she has to talk about it because she does not want to, all the more since the little girl is here and is not little anyway! But it awakens all those bad memories and she does not wish to suffer for nothing.

BR- The lady must at least know her first name?

Not much else. Nothing at the moment, sorry…

BR- (Insisting desperately) What is needed is a meeting with your grandparents, the 'old' lady, the little girl and your mum! Names would prove this book is genuine and the information is correct. So the tragedy will have been useful, one century later, to help prove Life in the Hereafter... I beg you all... Did you hear me Mum?

Your thoughts reach me clearly, yes. We know what you were thinking. All right, we'll try again. It is evidently important Darling. Have a good day! I hope you won't have too many chores. Your mum who still loves you, even from the Great Beyond…

7th July 2003 - *In English, so it's my guide:*

Make a neat break from your daily activities to be able to speak to us. It's difficult for both you and us to catch each other's thoughts when there are distractions all around. You should try to be totally free from distractions. The quieter you are the better it is for you, so do appreciate what we tell you. As an example we'll tell you this: The bigger the tree, the more shade there is. The more shade there is, the less plants can grow happily. But if you want sunlight to come through, shine on your flowers and make them bloom, you need to discard the leaves or make sure there are no leaves in the way.

If you let your thoughts and other flimsy passing distractions come across your mind, we have difficulty sending our rays of light, our sunshine, you understand? The better the link, the more information you'll get and then you won't complain you are not getting any details. While you are on the go we'll just say this quickly: If you want more details about your mum's sister, we know it can be done but it will be quite difficult. We are trying, believe us we have been trying, there have been many problems. <u>Our world works on vibrations. Everything which lives here, exists here, is made of vibrations and emits vibrations.</u> So, if a thought is sent towards the lady to ask for more details, it will help them come, you understand? She'll receive your thoughts, believe me, she'll pick the positive vibration of your requesting thought and this <u>will help her reconstruct in her mind what has been missing </u>for quite some time now. *(So I send such thoughts to the lady as requested)*

BR- Since Spirits teach there is no past so to speak, and everything is present, why are there difficulties in remembering names etc?

<u>All is 'present' in as much as nothing disappears.</u> Yes, all is 'now' on a certain level of thought but since things 'have happened' and 'are happening' now, it is important to <u>pick the correct moment among all those happenings!</u> The lady has lived those moments, but she has also <u>seen lots of other moments relating to it.</u> She has wondered what would have happened if the child had not died, how it would have grown, what her reaction would have been; she saw the good sides and the bad sides.

She is not on the same level of thought as your parents and grandparents. She has moved on further. Because she has known so much pain in her life, it has taught her a lot and she has evolved to such an extent that 'coming down' to these past experiences is a shock and rather confusing.

BR- Really?

You may not quite believe it my friend, but we know we are telling the truth. As you think about her and the child,

365

the dates, names and all you want to know you are re-building the situation for her and it will come back more alive for her to remember as you call it. So be kind, do so.

BR- Yet as my grandmother, the child's mother, met her on Earth, she would be better placed to explain to her, all the more since they are both in your world now!

The mother of the child knows. She'll be trying too. You have all joined in this endeavour because it is a mighty leap 'back in the past' and you have to help her recall all this. Be prepared for some delay in your 'Time' but you pull all the strings as you go along. Keep at it and you'll find things will get easier to be remembered.

11th July 2003 - *06.50hrs - Morning for a change! The pen starts in English, so it's my guide:*

All that is needed is a peaceful mind… May we remind you we are always willing to come through to talk to you; it is not us blocking it, it's your busy mind stopping the flow from our side.

BR- I don't mean to! I feel guilty now…

A steady flow of thoughts would not be so bad, it's a barrage of random sudden ones which affects the continuity. Let's start again then, now you've reached us, hopefully your mum will be able to latch on now and stay linked up. Look out for a busy mind interfering! Please concentrate on listening rather than thinking…

(A brief silence then French is spoken) Hello Darling, I am here at last! I had tried earlier but it was difficult to make myself understood. Right, I think I am well 'anchored' now! So I wanted to thank you for coming to talk to me, it gives me so much pleasure when we meet. I have been doing my usual 'work' of conversations and experiments with my friends. I've done lots of stuff, like going to the shore of a pretty beach and experimenting travelling on water... without getting wet!

I learnt to walk on water but by 'hovering above it' rather than touching it! We use this to develop ourselves mentally, to learn to use our mind in order to guide the 'body' we have here. All there is to do is think what we want to do, as usual. Thought is such a magic tool, it's wonderful!

So, I practised this stroll above water, or just skimming the surface, to make me feel the difference - it really gives you the feeling of flying. We can do it over the Earth too, though ours is not really the Earth you know. It's all in our imagination and mind. I could have just as well imagined I was on Mount Blanc or Everest...it's the same. But the practice is very useful because we get used to seeing that we can do things which seem impossible. As we do them, we no longer fear to get it wrong or make mistakes about the details. There is so much to do, you see, we have far too much to choose from. We'd need centuries to learn everything, yet have fun while doing it!

My fears are pointless because we cannot get injured here since obviously we haven't got a flesh body, so there would not be any injury... unless we imagine them! As for me, I've had enough accidents and injuries to last me a very long time... I am not going to give myself some imaginary ones! So, I went for a stroll not on water but above it! I did enjoy it a lot once I learnt how to do it properly. It is great fun to feel like a bird or a dragonfly hovering above water.

For the time being that's all I've been doing lately. I had to learn to 'think correctly'. I must think: "I want to float, I can float in the air, I can remain 'suspended' without falling. I don't risk anything." You see we have to change the way we have been forced to think, because all those years of life on Earth teach us to learn not to touch, to be careful and to be afraid of hurting ourselves. Now, here, I must tell myself all that does not matter! I can do what I want and am not in danger!

The surroundings here are far more interesting than on Earth because we can imagine them and visualise ourselves.

One must think: "This is what I want to see" and it appears! So, my sea has no rocks, it has beautiful fine sand and no high waves, just pleasant little undulations without any depth. The water is clear, I can see the bottom of the sea and since it's not deep it is very nice as it's another reason for me to know I am quite safe, you see! I have fun hovering above imaginary water while you, poor Darlings, are struggling with your Earthly lives and all the worries, problems and chores which no doubt surround you. That's not fair is it?

BR- *You deserve it! You've had your share of problems!*

People from here don't seem to have anything else to do than help me and my other 'student' friends.

BR- *Who are they?*

It seems to me they are people I did not know before.

BR- *Whom are you talking about - the students or the 'teachers'?*

The students like me. We chat as if we've always known each other, but I don't recall having known them on Earth. They are like me, learning to do new and weird things, but fun. There are about a dozen of them. The 'tutors' are our friends too but they know so much they are obviously also teachers from here. They are there to help us and appear to have nothing else to do but guide us, showing us how to do all those things. That business of <u>using one's thought as a tool is constantly the key to everything we have to do here</u>. It began when I arrived and I wanted to talk to you for the first time to tell you I had arrived safely without any problem. They showed me how to concentrate so hard that I could join you mentally. Now that is much easier and other such things too. We must think hard 'unilaterally', they say, think of nothing else but what we want to do and not let the thought go.

BR- *Is it harder to do where you are or on Earth?*

I think it is hard everywhere, whether you are on Earth or here, since <u>the mind is the same, we take it with us</u> or perhaps

368

it would be better to say - <u>we are our mind</u>, as we do everything with it here! We don't have the impression of having a body because we don't really pay attention to it. On the other hand we do realise we are constantly thinking!

Ideas are like grasses growing at full speed, aren't they? When they invade us, we have trouble getting rid of them... Climbing, smothering thoughts are a nuisance at times. I do understand that, I too have this problem here! It's indeed harder than it looks, isn't it? So to get back to what I was telling you, I managed my strolls on water, no sorry, above water. In the end I did not get my feet wet! But if it happened it would not be disastrous of course. Then I was told there were other things we could try, like sitting on nails or such like... because what matters is to realise it does not matter, <u>we do not risk anything since we don't have a body</u> which can be injured.

Those are my pastimes at the moment. Yet in a way there is not one moment when I don't think of you, because you are 'in my heart', even if my flesh heart is dead. I think of you there because I love you all so much! But I also do all those things with great care and attention to be able to teach them to you when you come here one day... as well as to tell you so that you can put them in this, our book, which you and I are creating together.

So you see I am very busy as ever and at last I am at peace, in a way... but I am not so sure I am totally at peace because I often wonder how things are going for you on Earth. When I start thinking about that, I realise I start worrying for you which is not good I am told here! Therefore I need to 'reverse' and instead of worrying, I have to send you good positive thoughts. Darling you are very kind to have spent all this time with me.

BR- The pleasure is mine, Darling Mum!

Do go on and finish your jobs. All I have to do is have fun, it's not fair!

BR- No, it is very fair and I am really happy for you!

I give you lots of kisses Sweetheart. Work well and have a good holiday if you go away. I love you ever so much my darling daughter.

15th July 2003 - *In the afternoon- In French straight away:*

You seem calmer and I am very pleased.

BR- Is that you Mum?

Hello Sweetheart, yes I am here. So we'll have a little chat if you wish... I've had a visit from my mum recently.

BR- A 'visit'? That sounds rather formal...

Yes, visit, as we are not together all the time. We see each other now and then. Well, she told me she tried to help you by sending her thoughts towards the 'old lady' and she tried to recall everything she could in order to help you (in your search) to make her remember what she could.

There were some rather painful times for her as this reminded her of so much grief and unhappiness, but she did it to please us both and to help us too. She told me she didn't know to what extent it will have helped, but she did it because we'd asked her to. By doing this, it brought back to her mind what she was thinking at the time when she had been obliged to abandon her little baby and she'd sworn to herself not to ever have other children so as not to betray that little girl. But I arrived later and she felt a bit guilty to have betrayed her promise, made on the spur of the moment and without anyone else knowing about it. That's how it is; one never knows what will happen later in life, hey!

So now I make the wish for us both to succeed with this book, so that you are happy to prove to the world that I still exist and therefore that anyone who supposedly 'dies' still carries on living. That way we both will have fulfilled our promises: You want to be able to prove it and I had promised you I would tell you what it's all about here, as soon as I get there! We are both working at it you see.

The hour of my departure must be registered somewhere, I reckon? It may be good to have it in your personal papers so that your children can confirm it later. I mean, if ever they get 'messages from Beyond' mentioning day and hour, they would have the information at hand proving to them it is correct.

My own mum has told me again her own story as we were chatting, because at the beginning we had not spoken much about it, since she did not want to discuss it - it embarrassed her and upset her. She told me that sorrow never left her throughout her life. Even when I was there I could see she was suffering somehow, but I had never understood what it was actually from. She always looked unwell but I thought it was 'fatigue', whereas she suffered from a broken heart and terrible remorse to have been forced to abandon her first child! She was saying to herself her first child should be special, yet she no longer had it!

It was really a very cruel and hopeless situation for her, I guess. But we spoke about it and I reminded her we are all here now, so there is no need to torture herself about it anymore, as it seems to me she still had it on her conscience... The sadness she suffered all her life must have been reflected in her attitude towards me, as she was very strict with me or so it seemed to me anyway! She wanted me to do everything correctly, very well, without any mistake. I could not understand why I had to be so good and so perfect...

It took me years to get rid of, or try to get rid of, this complex in a way! I always had to be so well-behaved, so polite, so kind, so good at school and so perfect a little girl, it was a nightmare in a way, I think! Yet I knew very well she loved me, but I did not see it clearly, whereas my dad was doing his utmost to be incredibly gentle, so kind and so patient.

371

No reproach towards me ever passed his lips; he spoilt me and helped with everything. Then he had to go to war and it distressed me because he had to be away for a long time, so I missed him a lot. Mum must have been sad too since she loved him very much and had lost him just like I did. We missed him and wanted him home as before, but that's what war does to people, isn't it? So that's it. Just to tell you that my mum and I had at last spoken more openly, more honestly. I think she had always avoided the topic, but it brought us closer in a way, as we told each other how we felt, what we'd thought. All this is really a bit silly, isn't it? Since we are both 'dead', therefore alive in the Hereafter…and there we are, still with regrets and remorse! I find this stupid indeed to keep them within ourselves without realising!

My parents met again with great joy, she said. They saw each other and picked up from when death had parted them. I mean they carried on as if death had never parted them. I have not left you, my own daughter, have I? That is fantastic! I have kept you, we have always talked to each other. Even after my 'departure to the great void' which is not a void but a beautiful world, I managed to stay in contact with you. That is a very, very big success in my opinion!

My little pet, I am going to let you go as I feel you should stop to be free. We'll talk again. Your mum who always loves you.

19th July 2003 - *To my great surprise, without me thinking about or asking for that topic, Mum arrives at once to continue our conversation from 4 days ago:*

I had always been told I had no brother or sister and I used to be ever so sad about it. I could not understand why I was not able to have one or even buy one, as I used to think when I was young it looked so easy to go in a shop and buy whatever we wanted!.. But that's the problem - I did not know that business with Mum and her heart-breaking misadventures and sorrows. It saddens me to think I used to reproach her for not giving me a brother or sister, but she did not resent it. All she kept saying was: "I cannot have another child, that's all." I never understood why. Now I know!

Therefore this is the conclusion of this long story, but of course you would like to know more, since you would like to prove it and I wish I could tell you that. I can do no more than ask them to help you. Apparently there are quite a lot of complications. I don't see why but they seem to know...Even if we could remember, I wonder whether the papers still exist after all this time - all that must be ages ago, mustn't it?

BR- Probably 103 to 110 years ago...

A very long time indeed! In my opinion it would not be worth the trouble to rack your brains so much, but you seem so keen to want to know...

BR- It's not for me! I know and believe firmly that your sister exists! But it would help prove this book does come indeed from you, dictated from the Afterlife and it's not me who invented all that!

Yes I see, but all the same I am concerned you fret so much because of it! It's going to give you worries and efforts to try to prove it... Anyway, it's up to you to decide of course, I can only be delighted about my tranquillity and lack of chores here! But it does look selfish to say that! So I'll just say I agree with everything you do. If I can help you, I'll do it.

One point though: There are a lot of people in this world where I am. If I could find you someone who has lost his loved ones like that and would like to prove he still exists, perhaps we could do some research more easily if it was not so old?

My little Darling you have tried so hard to give me the freedom to tell you what I wanted to say, you are so kind. When I was on Earth I used to wonder what indeed one could have to do when one was in 'Heaven', apart from sitting down to play the harp if one was an angel! I am joking of course. Well, now I do realise we do not have a moment to waste and we don't waste a moment either.

I am indeed 'over the moon' even though I don't see any planet (nor do I see angels, since I don't notice any as described by the Church, with wings and all that), because I can constantly enjoy pleasant discussions, explanations and meetings with people who are intelligent, kind and really lovely. I do wish you were here so that you could join in the conversations - you would have so much fun!

BR- Well, tell me as much as possible now...

The year of my 'death' must have been very hard for you as it probably was such a shock, as well as the chores you must have had...and wondering whether it was really me talking to you... You must have been so shaken my poor Darling. I feel guilty it was so easy for me in a way, except for the terrible longing to see you again and the despair to think I could not do so for a long time!..

BR- Don't think about it Darling Mum! Tell me what you've been doing?

Now I am on a kind of comfortable bench near the water of a river. I am looking at myself in the water, I don't see myself really, I stare <u>at the water as a concentration point</u> and I tell myself I want to speak to you and listen to you.

BR- Are you alone?

Yes, just me here. I feel comfy. I knew you wanted to speak with me. I sensed your thoughts when you sent me a message, I assume, saying you'd like me to chat with you. Is that right?

BR- Yes indeed, absolutely correct!

So I am thinking of you, speaking to you in my head and it seems to work, doesn't it?

BR- I am doing the same! It's so easy after all...incredible isn't it? Have you done anything interesting lately?

An amusing incident recently: I was with my friends and they were talking of the future, the present and all that... I could not grasp how one can talk of the future and the present as being near each other. They laughed and said: "If you had known you were going to come over here, you would not have come, therefore we did not show it to you! But in a way you knew it unknowingly. Your soul knew it, but not your brain, we hid that from it! On the other hand we had warned your daughter in a slightly disguised way that it was going to happen soon and she sensed it, she did what had to be done, she went where she had to."

"But," I said, "how would she have known it was now and not in ten months time?" They replied: "She knew it within herself without her brain knowing it either. You see we hide from your brains what we don't want them to know, because they would want to get involved and spoil it all!"

The more we switch off the brain and switch on the Inner Spirit, the more we are on the right path when we are on Earth. So if we do that more often, we end up paying more attention to our Inner Spirit than to that brain, which is really only a machine after all.

We then end up learning to live 'ahead of ourselves', to listen to a level superior to the Earthly life and also to learn to see the future in the present - what is due to happen has in fact nearly happened already, so to speak! It is difficult to explain but it's something like that... That's what I think I understood. Therefore if you knew I was going to die and leave you, you were well ahead of me because **I** did not know it, you see! And it is me it was all about! What cheek! My friends always try to explain something or other to me, but often it is too hard for me to grasp well - there are points beyond my comprehension. I suppose it's because I still think a little like on Earth, but I hope it will come. The longer one is here, the more one senses and assimilates what people explain to you. There are constantly new things but my friends don't seem in a hurry, therefore I don't worry if I don't grasp everything at once. Those people are very kind indeed. It's not 'lessons', only interesting conversations which 'enlighten' me more each time. So I don't mind being enlightened. As long as it does not confuse me, it's all right! Thanks for talking to me. Our being together gave me a lot of pleasure. I wanted to share with you what I learnt as I thought it may interest you.

BR- You were right! Many thanks. Lots of kisses for you, Mum.

From me too, my darling daughter. Be very careful on the road. I love you.

25th July 2003 -

I am here again Sweetheart. Thanks for calling. I heard or sensed your thoughts and here I am! I see you must have had a good holiday as you appear to be more rested.

BR- What makes you say that?

I feel it, you are calmer than before. I am like that all the time here, you see, that's the difference. I've made some progress with my trips on water or rather above it! I learnt to do it with great ease without worrying any more, which is a good sign as one can't help being concerned at first, when one is not used to it... It's just a question of habit, that's all...From ideas we had on Earth, we need to pass to new ideas. We do not have a solid body and that's that! Even if we feel as if we have one...Personally I don't care really, because if I don't have to look after my body, I am asking for nothing more! It gave me enough trouble when I had one! Now I am concentrating more on my mind in a way. Ideas, thoughts...

So this is my main focus I could say. But if I want to understand correctly what goes on, I must have experienced it to be able to explain it to you. My friends let me know what we have to learn when we come from the Earth, so as to get rid of old human, Earthly ideas and get used to the way of life here.

It's a strange idea to tell oneself one needs to learn to fly over water, but it's a good one too basically for those who are so preoccupied with their body that they cannot manage <u>to get rid of the idea of a solid body</u> which has reflexes, a weight and problems! I don't really have problems, I have not bothered with my 'possible' body since I have been here, but <u>I had to do those 'experiments' to let you know what newcomers are taught</u>. Therefore those are my latest experiences...

BR- I 'dreamt' about you last night...

We do meet now and then you know. It's difficult to explain because it is in a different way now. When I see you and your body is asleep, you look a bit sleepy and we talk from mind to mind... It's not like what we are doing at this present moment, when I know your brain is involved.

During your sleep your body is asleep and sometimes your mind also if you are tired, but if you are not you look a bit different. <u>I feel you as a kind of shadow here</u>, I don't know why. I feel you near me but I do not see you as being really 'solid'. I could say it's more like a kind of 'ghost'... There are people who see their loved ones or friends seemingly 'whole', I do not always see you like that...

BR- So sometimes you see me looking 'more solid'?

The shape you take appears to me less solid than if you were alive on Earth, I suppose it's obvious since you don't have your flesh body (here)... So that must be the reason.

BR- Can we talk to each other?

We talk, yes no problem. We hug and kiss even in a way, but it is more a warm and affectionate embrace. Last time you came appearing 'more solid' was when I saw you for the first time when I left your Earth and came here... We met and I explained to you I shall never abandon you. You 'cried' in a way because you did not want to return to your Earth. I had not told you before because I didn't want to sadden you more. But it did appear to me much more 'solid' than what we are getting now, I am not too sure why.

BR- Why don't you ask your friends so that they explain it to you?

The desire to see each other again must have been so strong I suppose, we could not help doing so. Since I was 'freshly arrived' from my Earthly stay I reckon it's what triggered it... I don't quite know at the moment...

The ease with which you hear me astonishes me you know, as I guess it can't be that simple after all! So bravo on succeeding in doing so, because hearing a 'dead person' and writing down what one hears is not a mundane daily occurrence is it? Anyway once more 'well done'!

BR- Bravo to you for speaking to me! I had had more practice than you!

My friends here helped me start off as you know; there are always people ready to help if I have a problem, even for when we communicate...

BR- What do they do exactly?

They are there, they concentrate with me I think. I reckon they send thoughts in your direction and help our thoughts link up! They keep telling me: "It's a question of vibrations and energy". It sounds so skilful I find it always a bit frightening! Yet it's so easy after all once we get going, isn't it? As you know, personally I don't like complicated things. As long as it works once they've shown me what to do, it's the main thing.

BR- I am very interested and I would like more details... You could ask your friends to explain more and all you'll have to do is repeat what they'll say!

I didn't grasp clearly what you said, sorry...*(So I repeated more slowly)* A friend has just come close to tell me that each time you and I communicate, there is a line of energy between us. That line is a very strong power which has its own intensity, resonance and frequency. To maintain it, one has to stay on that frequency. It's like when you listen to a radio; you have to remain on the chosen waves not to lose them. So if you remain on the correct wavelength and frequency, I can receive you and vice-versa. But if one of us loses her footing, or gets mixed up or if the brain gets in the way, then it causes a muddle and it's hard to get out of it! That's when the kind friends intervene to help us both. They come very close mentally and know how to link up to you and me, then in a way they're-tie' the link, like one does a knot... But it's more like joining up two electric wires, if you understand what I mean. Apparently there are so many wavelengths and frequencies that we shall always have trouble to remain perfectly on line at any given time. <u>If there is some 'crackling' or loss of concentration, we need help to link up again.</u> This is what the friends do when they are there, always ready to help. It's incredible, I have the impression they spend their life here just helping others!

BR- They are perhaps 'guides' or 'guardian angels'?

They do not look like guardian angels, at least not like churches show them, with wings and all that! Come to think of it they don't even seem to be from one era or another! I only see them in thought, nearly.

BR- (Intrigued) What do you mean? Can you explain?

When I think of them... *(Unfortunately sudden interruption, someone comes in then the phone rings etc. At last I can try to tune in again and mentally send my apologies...)*

We are being helped... The friends here told me to reassure you. We are certainly not angry because of the interruption, things like that are inevitable. Don't worry Darling.

So I was telling you that when I meet them they seem to be in thoughts rather than real, it's really difficult to explain! There is a difference between sensing people near you and seeing them in details, nearly physically, if you get my meaning? I do see them, yes. I do sense them - I sense their thoughts or I hear them, I am not too sure. I think I 'sense' them, let's say, like in telepathy, because I don't really pay attention to whether there is a 'sound' of words or not, do you understand?

BR- I thought you told me you saw them and chatted...

Yes, I see them...in my head in a way...oh, it's so difficult to explain! I believe I see them in front of me as if we were sitting together, ok? But if I ponder about it, I don't really see them as if they were in 'flesh and blood', it's more like I 'sense' them. I <u>know</u> they are there, I hear them in my head, I hear their thoughts and we have conversations like that! (*This is similar to how a medium can perceive Spirits*). It's rather weird to have to explain this with words because, in fact, if I think about it, it's more sensations than real 'visions'.

One must be here to understand it, but I know saying this is no use to you! Yet you do grasp the problem? There are such strange things here which we accept without thinking about it, until you ask such a question... Then, because of that, <u>I start trying to analyse what is going on and it appears 'weird' instead of staying 'natural' as it seemed to me...until now</u>! I got used to it, you see, I understand it must look bizarre to you.

BR- Ask your friends to explain more? Then repeat it to me unless they wish to speak to me directly?

I am told the level of frequency is of great importance. <u>If we do not tune in to the correct frequency, we cannot communicate with one another</u>. Everyone here <u>is on the same frequency</u> so much so that they can hear, sense and see one another in a way. If we had different frequencies we would not see each other, in the same way as people on Earth do not really see 'Spirits' and vice versa. It's a question of adjusting and tuning oneself to the correct frequency, but once it's done there is no longer a problem. Of course we must stay on it! Here we don't have a problem, they say, because we are all on the same frequency where I am. But there are other frequency levels that are superior or inferior to mine, therefore we do not see nor 'sense' each other easily and we have to make special efforts to meet up. When I have to join my dad, he must certainly make a special effort for me, as I imagine he is at a level far superior to mine since I have just arrived in a way, whereas he has been here for much longer.

The problem is not there. It is easy to see and sense each other and also read one another's thoughts when we 'live' on the same frequency! But if we wanted to go and see or sense the thoughts of someone at a superior level, he would have to lower his, because here we would not have the ability to elevate ourselves to his level. Our frequency would not be able to reach him. On the other hand he could lower his, 'reduce' them, he could bring himself down to our level. I am sure that a lot of those kind people who come and chat with me and us from here are Superior Beings making the effort to bring themselves down, lower themselves to our level, my level... because their knowledge is such that I do feel they don't come from 'here' but rather from an even higher 'Great Beyond'!

All this is well balanced. It's really clever, complicated and incredible in my opinion! Whereas on Earth we can talk to anybody, here we only really have access to those who are at the same level, or else to those who are kind enough to lower their frequency level in order to be reached and make themselves understood. That is real dedication in my opinion!

Earthly pleasures are indeed only such ephemeral and superficial things, when one compares them with pleasures here which last far longer since we feel them constantly! Actually, to have a good, extraordinary experience, or profound and interesting intellectual experiences, is worth far more than a little physical pleasure lasting a few minutes or even a few hours, which will disappear in the end.

Here, once you've discovered something new, it's so exciting, moving and encouraging, you never lose it and you never lose that feeling of joy to have learnt or discovered it. It is indeed very special, do you understand? Whereas I remember that on Earth, once we've eaten something good the taste does not last, once we've done something physically pleasant, the pleasure does not last long either...so what a waste of time, isn't it! Here nothing is lost, everything is valuable, everything is worth it and everything is exciting or interesting - it is truly 'Paradise'! I can see why it is called that!

My kind friends here are 'angels' in a way, I mean they are darlings to willingly spend so much time to help me and explain all sorts of things to me, yet I do not give them anything in exchange. When I think of it, I find it embarrassing and frustrating to be unable to do anything for them!

BR- Have you told them? If so, what did they reply?

Telling them is useless; they don't want to hear a word about it, do not want thanks or praises! They simply say: "We get a lot of pleasure teaching you all this and there is nothing to thank us for. Everything is normal for us. We love doing it, we love sharing what we know. Perhaps you'll do the same when you know as much as we do. So why be upset for 'not giving us anything in exchange'? Yes, you do give - you give us your attention, your efforts, your interest and most of all your enthusiasm when wanting to share it with your family and daughter. So don't you think it is worth it?"

You see, we can never 'argue' with them and certainly not risk to have a quarrel (which never happens anyway), because they have the right answer or a good logical answer or an attitude showing they know the Truth and that, sooner or later, we shall reach the same conclusion ourselves! So I say 'Amen' to all they say, as it saves time. We can then pass on to something else!

I hope your children are well? You haven't talked about them for quite a while. I hope Anne-France is happier than she had been? And my big Jim? Has he understood how bad smoking is?

BR- He smokes when he is stressed; he really needs to find a good flat. Also he wants to gain a top grade for his

Music Production degree. Please send him your good thoughts!

Your big Jim has done a lot of things in his life indeed! He tried so hard to be successful with his music, didn't he?! It's sad … Anyway I do hope he'll be helped by that degree you say he is studying for. I don't really know how, but it proves he can work hard and study and learn well, so employers should appreciate all his good points, shouldn't they? Let's hope our good positive thoughts will reach him quickly and keep reaching him so that he succeeds and is happy in his life.

Personally I do regret not to have seen him much. He came for a while but it was not often and I would have liked to see you all more often… (*We lived in the UK- Mum was some 2000 miles away*). But that's life on Earth, isn't it? We cannot do everything we like when we want and that's it! So one may as well not think about it anymore and do what one can each step of the way, day after day, that way one has no regrets, at least one can try to do that. You've spent a lot of time with me, thank you! So I'll let you go back to your Earthly life after your little visit to my 'home' here. Thanks again.

29th July 2003 - *08.20am for a change! The pen writes the first words in French:*

What is needed to succeed: Put in the time and the work, also the effort and keep your heart in the task, as famous writers used to say. Where there is desire there will be success, because <u>desire is the inner fire of a success</u> and <u>to succeed one must always want with all one's heart</u>. It's no good 'wanting a little', one must want with all one's being to make things happen. This is what they constantly repeat here you know!

BR- Who is speaking to me?

Me Darling, your Mum. I am always ready to tune in you know! But I wanted to remind you what I am told so often here: "Be filled with an inner burning desire, so that what you desire arrives as soon as possible".

You must really want it for it to happen and yet there may still be some problems but the desire which created it will allow your goal to flourish. You must want, want with hope and certainty within you and have no doubt, otherwise it spoils everything! Then, when you've succeeded, you can say to yourself: "It's worked this time, it will therefore work another time!"

The amazing thing is that it is true, at least here. There will perhaps be a few more difficulties on Earth, I don't know. I suppose being surrounded with people doing the opposite of what they should do, it risks either failing or at least being hindered... But on the whole this is what I am told to remind you of, so I remind you! I would love you to have an easier life and the lads and your own children too, but you must make the effort to 'want' very strongly and not lose courage... Once one has succeeded a couple of times, one no longer doubts and one knows that is a safe method for success...children don't know how to use this.

BR- Mine? Or are you talking of children in general?

It is essential to teach them this as well as possible. Your children already do it often - I am talking of the rest of the population. They should be taught these facts because the more they try it, the more they will believe in it. Then they will become adults and will be used to applying them, do you understand? That way the population will learn to use the power of Thought and will really believe in it when they have obtained some success several times.

My friends are very persistent. They believe in it so strongly they don't stop talking about and repeating it to get it into our minds... I was going to say 'into our head' but do I really have a head here? It's rather an imaginary head I reckon, since my brain is dead, poor old thing! I am young again whereas my poor old brain was far too worn out to carry on I think. It had started to deteriorate gradually and I hated to suffer from memory loss...it was not terrible nor serious, yet it was exasperating to be unable to recall details Touky remembered and with which he reproached me! Well, now I am younger than him, so there!

But to come back to the subject of seeing in your thoughts what you want and desiring it with all your strength, you really must try to practise it Darling...

BR- I do try to do it...

You must have a go as much as possible to succeed more often - it is the only solution. After that you'll believe in it even more! My poor children, when I think I've left you to cope on your own...it's so sad to have been obliged to do it, indeed without wanting it nor knowing I was doing it!.. *(A short silence then it starts again...in English to my great surprise. My guide has popped in!)* Make the most of your day my dear. The more you can cram in, the more you'll be able you progress, achieve, move forward and have time for. Waste of time is no help at all, only concentrate on what matters and you will feel satisfied instead of frustrated and dissatisfied. Be happy with your life, you have been 'lucky' in many respects. Be happy and fulfil your destiny by trying harder each day. Make up for lost time, have a future of good happenings ahead of you by making them happen by wanting, willing them... Look ahead and see the results, they are awaiting you. Then walk towards them by doing what's needed to obtain them, you understand? The hardest part is to believe you can do it. Once you believe and know you can do it, you'll have no problems...

4th August 2003 - *I send a thought saying I am free to link up. I hear French spoken:*

One day you will understand more when you are here; it is always so difficult to explain all this. We do our best but there are not always the right words...

BR- Who is speaking?

Mum of course! I am always ready to speak with you Darling. I have just come because I heard you call and it's always a pleasure to know you want to talk to me and think of me... I do think of you all so often, you have no idea! Anyway now you are here, I'll tell you what I have done recently. Nothing complicated just a few exercises and conversations with my intelligent and interesting friends. So I'll tell you my latest adventures, well...not really adventures, just 'exercises'.

We went to a very peaceful place, in fact everywhere is peaceful here I'd say, but this is a pretty place I often go to just by thinking of it and I find myself there immediately! That way it saves me having 'to walk for no reason', since I used to dislike 'walking for nothing' like you do!.. We did a bit of 'relaxation', with soothing thoughts which calmed my...brain I was going to say but of course not since mine is dead; therefore calmed my mind. I did learn to be very relaxed, even more than when I think of you to converse with you and we made a few little mind trips...

The places I went to had nothing to do with the Earth, it was 'places of wishes'. If I wished everything to be pink, let's say, well, I would see the whole place, the décor pink! If I wished everything to be made of gold, I'd see it in gold, do you understand?

This is to practise wishes and their actualization. It was great fun to find oneself in places one invents and which have nothing to do with what one had seen before, whether during an Earthly life or even here. We only need to think of it and we see it and live it because we feel as if we are there. It's really enjoyable to do this - in fact I had a lot of fun. My friends are amusing you see, as such exercises are very interesting, different and I am certain it teaches me to do things I would never have thought of doing! *(Unfortunately, a sudden and very long interruption cut us off. Two hours later I tried to link up again. The pen starts in English this time)*

386

Moments of disturbance are not dreadful happenings here, but do realize it means a lot of adjustment for your mother to reconnect! The simplest way is always to listen until she finishes her piece if she has something to say. We'll always help her to practise and improve but you could do with some of that practice too... The lessons learnt before are still valid...look, listen within, do not hesitate, feel the whole spectrum, the whole picture, look at what is offered to you when you look within...

(Suddenly the phone rings, I must have been deeply tuned in and in a slightly altered state of consciousness because I felt a shock as if I was falling from a storey above, I even heard a kind of 'ping' ringing in my head!..)

6th August 2003 - *As I tune in, I feel a tingling sensation on my face. The pen writes in English - it must be my friendly guide:*

Confirming what you feel. You say you feel something on the side of your face somehow. We are sending close energy towards your face, so you must be feeling it.

BR- What do you mean by 'close energy'?

My friends and I are close to you. To show we are close to your mind, we send a certain type of energy signalling our closeness, you understand?

BR- What do you mean by 'a certain type'?

All energies have various degrees of strength and vibrations. We choose one which you can feel quite easily and recognise, because there are rays you may not feel, not identify.

BR- I feel it less now...

Once you have linked up with us, you know we are talking to you, so we don't need to send anything at all, or at least not as strongly, do we?

Making the most of the fact you are here, may we say we are very pleased you are obviously trying to sit quietly

387

more often. We thank you, you have been making progress lately and it's all thanks to your own efforts to open yourself up to our vibrations! We cannot receive you if you don't try! You cannot receive us if you don't try. So it's all to do with your trying. As you see, results soon show themselves to be worth the effort!

BR- Please explain how 'messages' are passed on via a medium, from someone in your world, to their loved one on Earth?

Part of the work is done by myself but make sure you understand the work has to be done by several people in my world. The person who is on Earth has usually many people in my world. We all link together. Their family, say, and myself as a go-between and you as the 'mouthpiece'. We ask the family member to come close to their loved one on Earth if they have something to say to them or if they simply wish to let them know they are all right and alive in our world.

BR- How do they come 'close'?

They need to think strongly about their loved one, say a daughter, so that they come within her auric field. We know where she is, you know where she is. So then the work is much easier - we can convey to you what the person here wants to say to the girl on Earth! It's a type of relaying of words. If you are careful enough and listen well, you'll pick up most of or everything we say to you. You have to be very careful, to be listening all the time and not try to think in the middle of the conversation... otherwise your mind will indulge in great interferences! This is what a mind likes to do to get a hold on what is going on. All in all it is quite easy enough, but it is a question of fine tuning all around.

If the family member does not think hard enough, or does not remember things well perhaps, or is not really interested, the conversation will soon stop, as the flow is broken, the interest is waning, the intentions are not there and most of all the love vibration is not carrying far enough.

But if the person here is so keen to communicate he would do anything for it, then the flow will be smooth and if you, on your part, are doing your best to listen and let things come at you without thinking or analysing, you'll find you'll have no problem relaying what you are presented with or told. You can always think later, can't you! The principal is to let us put over what we need to put across to you in your world. Make that little effort and all communication will be great, to the satisfaction of all.

Always look within, listen within and look for what you want within. That is the only place to be, you see. You cannot find in the outside world what your soul wants.

You *(talking to me, BR)* made the trip to Earth to learn enough to be able to teach others about all this. You took a long road but you got there eventually or nearly there. You need more and more practice, that's all. The more you practise, the easier it will become for you, so do not despair, you have found what you want to do; you know what you have to do. All is left is to do it, agreed?

BR- It would be easier if I didn't have earthly worries...

The road is clear ahead of you, you have free access to your 'Inner Self' and you can do these things now. All you have to do is have the discipline to allow that work as much importance as the other things you need to do, to make sure you have the time for it by not wasting time with other pursuits.

BR- I hardly have any other pursuits!

Long ago you and I were pals, in another life. You said you wanted to come back to help people on Earth understand what they were missing. You have not done too badly up to now. We decided we'd be together in that venture. You've gone to Earth - I stayed here to look after you. You've been quite a good friend and a good person. So all is well set for the venture to succeed. You do your bit as much as you can, I'll keep doing mine. You have not always listened to me- but that was your prerogative! You have fallen back on your feet now, you are on the right track, you understand?

So do not worry, do not waste time, just constantly do your best to achieve your goal. You and I will make it, be assured! You cannot be alone when we are all behind you. My friends are your friends, we are here for that. Do your bit, learn and practise so that all flows easily <u>from one world to the other</u>, as <u>there isn't really a gap between the two. It is only a feeling of difference but not a reality. You are within ours and we are within yours. We both need to simply adjust the knobs of vibration to find each other</u> and that has been done for a long time now, hasn't it? You've found us so there is no problem. The hardest has been done …

BR- Would you be kind enough to tell me who or what we were in that life as mates?

(As I relax even more I sink into a very receptive inner calm, a kind of semi-trance. It helps me hear him speak very fast, but in fact the sound is rather weak and his thoughts arrive unfortunately much too fast for me to manage to write them down as I receive them - that would have slowed down and therefore spoilt the flow. I listen with great attention without thinking anything, in order to grasp as much as possible… As soon as he finished and I 'surfaced' again, I jotted down the main points I vaguely recalled:

- It was one of the lives, long ago. I've had other lives between that one and my current one.

- We were both male, kind of roaming adventurers. I forget the details but there is an impression of being rather hard up. Later on I wanted to be re-born a female and have children, to learn to love. I thought having children would help me do so, as well as myself having a loving mother who would teach me that too.

***

CHAPTER 9
Baby's name revealed - Synaesthesia (Sounds in colours) - No languages needed in Hereafter

10th August 2003 - *07.15hr - In the morning for a change! The pen doodles, loops and scribbles but at last the first words become legible - it's in French:*

We've got there at last! It did take some time, didn't it! Anyway you've made it. So, good morning Sweetheart since it is your morning. I saw my family once more in order to try to get more information regarding what you keep asking, the sister, the lady etc. Well, I think there might be some development if they can get something out of the lady. She has been contacted and is making some tremendous efforts to remember and help us. She made some trips 'backwards in Time', which for her does not really exist. Apparently she's made visions…

BR- What do you mean by 'made visions'?

She has projected in front of her what she saw within. She thought of those times and tried to remember names, places and about herself… Initials will perhaps come first - she says she 'feels some letters coming'. So she needs more time to manage it but we are beginning to have some hope.

You do realise there will still be a lot to do, don't you? One does not trace things just like that, but if you have the courage to tackle it my friends say we'll do what we can to help you from here. There'll be so much to deal with you'll need to have time for it, but obtaining the name of the town and of the lady and the date will already be something substantial. We should be able to do more as soon as she can recall more details. Apparently it is a very complicated process when someone has been here for a long time and memories fade away. They need a lot of courage and must make great efforts to gather the pieces, but once done it will have been worth it.

Mum's acquaintance, who told her the little girl had

died, was someone her parents knew. She must have guessed what had happened but was kind and discreet enough not to say anything nor talk about it. But when she heard of the death, it seems she tried very hard to reach my mum yet, one way or the other did not manage it. She did not want to tell Mum's parents of course, as they would have been furious because she knew the truth. So she kept trying to contact Mum. She was very brave because in those days one did not meddle with other people's private business and one left them alone! Yet that lady had understood my mum was in despair after losing her baby, so she felt very sympathetic and wanted to help a little. Evidently it was not a success. The amazing thing is she was able to contact Mum, even twice! *(Unfortunately I am disturbed, then no longer feel relaxed enough to link up again. I hope to have another go later on).*

13th August 2003 - *As I tune in the pen writes in 'Automatic' in English - "Open your mind". Then a short while later, French is written and spoken:*

We've made it Darling, we can meet up at last. The pleasure of being here is to be able to speak to you and tell you what is happening. Recently I've seen scores of people who spoke to me about all sorts.

The first ones were about people asleep or awake. Apparently when people are asleep, they don't need to worry about their destination because they all come here! It is not the same level as, for example, the one I am at, but there is little difference. It's a level where newcomers go and it's where we can find people who are not 'dead' but are <u>asleep on Earth</u>. They <u>come out of their body and come here</u> <u>to meet up with their friends</u> etc. They rarely remember their visit because their body is not involved, therefore neither is their brain - it is <u>their mind and their 'invisible body'</u> which come to us. One is lucky here as there is no problem coming and leaving again when one

392

is asleep on Earth, though in my opinion, who would want to leave again?! It feels so good to be here, except of course we don't have the joy of seeing our children and family in the flesh.

This is one of the things they showed me by pointing out other people, but I knew it was possible because you do come over here from time to time and this gives Dad and I so much pleasure to see you again and to feel you near us!

I see the boys again sometimes, but I think they are so exhausted they don't appear very awake; they always look rather sleepy. I reckon their brains must be so tired that their minds are too! On the other hand, you have travelled over many a time and you don't always look sleepy mentally.

BR- What do we do?

We talk, we hug and we feel happy to be together, we meet up for the sheer joy of being together as that means a lot! Most of the time we tell each other what we've been doing, I show you things I did which I cannot explain in words - there are sensations, visible thoughts which are difficult to explain, aren't they! So you saw them, felt them and understood what I meant. Yet you were not able to come exactly where I am usually, because I am told it is a level higher than the 'arrival level' and the reasons why you can't have access to it are technically more complicated. But it will change one day, when it is your turn to be here and I shall be the one receiving you!

BR- I have first to publish this and prove the existence of your sister if I can!

I 'discovered' a simple way of sitting down without moving - one thinks of the sitting position and one is sitting! Yes, I know, I had told you before that when we think of anything it happens, but at times there are little details I don't notice, or forget to do or note down. My friends have fun when I do something which is 'new for me' yet which I should have known before… They have a laugh but they do it kindly, they

393

do not mock me, they only tease me nicely. It's always a pleasure to be with them.

Getting used to doing things using one's thought power arrives gradually, you know. One cannot be converted to doing everything that way overnight, without automatically trying to act as we did on Earth. Getting used to it does take time.

The time, or perhaps one of the times, when I spoke to you about delving into history, it was very interesting to find myself in ancient eras, to see famous people from an angle I had not thought of, or under which they had not been 'painted'. I now understand many an historical figure whom I was interested in when on Earth, but who weren't as well known as it was thought!

All those French kings, what a shambles! There were so many of them! Well, a lot of them did not want to be kings at all, there were all forced to be! That's why they often were bad rulers unable to govern the country, or else were weak and let the control of government go to ministers or to some favourites... while themselves, they preferred to go hunting or have fun with ladies!..

The worst was that atrocious Revolution which killed so many poor innocent people; it was triggered by so much suffering beforehand and by human stupidity afterwards! It's incredible! I sensed the feelings of the population and saw the stupid things done by some people wanting a change, but who didn't always know how to achieve it. It led to so many errors and crimes being committed! It was indeed one evil replacing another evil! It was not worth murdering so many poor souls, some of them very intelligent and intellectual, who would have been useful to their country if they had been allowed to live... But that's what the human race is like, isn't it?

Now I don't really bother about history as such anymore, because I have got an insight of the main points 'seen from within' so to speak, therefore it changed my mind and gave me a new perspective, a new angle. Yet I don't spend my time looking at those 'historical films' as I call them because that's what it feels like when I discuss them with my friends; those impressions appear like films in front of me, so it's a bit like watching TV!

As I said, I don't spend my time doing this. I often think of you too. Having the hope to see you again one day cheers me up you know! I trust my positive thoughts reach you and help you in your life. There is so much to do on that Earth for things to succeed and go well! It's incredible compared to how easy it is here!

Have you done something to your foot?

BR- Yes, I broke the metatarsal of my left small toe!

Good Gracious! Poor darling! You who exert yourself so much, it's going to delay you!

BR- The worst is over now, it is in plaster, don't worry!

My friends think our conversation has turned into chatter! I reckon they want to get back to their 'teaching'! So I'll tell you that the first time I was shown a 'living person' here (who was in fact asleep), I actually thought he was 'dead'! I was on the point of telling him how great it was here, but I was told to keep quiet so as not to throw him in a panic, otherwise <u>he would think he was dead and the mental shock would perhaps cause him to have a cardiac arrest</u>! I was indeed going to put my foot in it, wasn't I? Fortunately, my 'entourage' is kindly and keeps a good watch!

So that was one of my blunders, if you want to know what happens here!..

BR- (Teasing) I'll tell people about your 'faux pas'! They'll have a good laugh!

Hey! I do not often make any! Don't make me look like a 'clot', even in the Great Beyond!

BR- Don't worry! I admire you, everybody knows!

Any news about your sister? (Short silence...The pen starts again in English: it's my guide)

Help will come one day, with a name, don't fret... We have a lot of work to do but we'll manage eventually... You'll have to back us up by sending loving and willing thoughts to propel the memories forward, but you <u>can</u> help indeed from your side. We would request more help, more often, if you could please, because it does make a difference. You'll be satisfied with the results so do not despair. We are not ignoring your request, believe me. The lady in question has been approached on many occasions and is well aware of the dilemma and the situation.

BR- Are you sure?

Making yourself a go-between with plenty of loving, helpful thoughts will help us in our task. You will not fail doing so. We have to do a lot of work in helping the lady remember a very small portion of a certain period she has lived, among many periods on Earth! So it is not as easy as it may seem to you, seen from your world. But when we do succeed, you'll be overjoyed and you'll then have a lot of work yourself to do and sort out! We reckon we can safely say you will be pleased to have what you are looking for. It will be in an undetermined time. I can't say exactly, as it has to be sorted out here, our world not having any time period nor clock, as you know. But the thing is to understand that while we try here, you need to try too! When all is revealed, at least as much as can be, the clock in your world can start ticking towards revealing it to the outside world.

So please make sure you have advanced the preparation of the book, not to waste time with that when you could and should be researching for your mum's sister on the terrain, all over the area given hopefully...

14th August 2003 - *It took me a while to relax and tune in. French is spoken:*

Once we meet up it's fine, but it's blooming hard to 'make ends meet'! It's not so difficult for me but it looks like hard work for you, doesn't it!

BR- Sometimes...

Thanks for calling me. I always love having you 'on the phone'. So I'll sum up what I did and what we spoke about recently, since 'last time' if we can say that here. It does feel like everything is at the same time in a way, yet not quite...difficult to explain that! I did a few experiments, with my dear friends of course, they are always there for that. We visited several places where I had not been before. For that, one must make a certain mental effort in order to concentrate in a certain way.

BR- What do you mean?

There are different ways of concentrating apparently. Well, this one is the method to get transported more quickly from one place to another, but those places are not so much 'Earthly' let's say, than 'mental spaces'... I mean states of mind rather than physical places, though evidently physical things do not really exist here, since it's not the same as on Earth.

Where they took me was a very interesting area in fact, as we do not realise the way we think when we are thinking. One thinks within oneself and it comes out of one's head in a way, or rather one's mind I should say, since we imagine having a head yet it does not really exist! Therefore we are transported by our thoughts towards where they are going, that is what my friends wanted to demonstrate to me.

I who did not really want to believe in this famous 'power of thought' when I was on Earth...well, I was shown here that the power of thought does exist! (They are right once more!)

If one has an unpleasant thought, it comes out of you as

black or dark waves and goes towards the person or object you thought of. If that person does not receive it consciously, they receive it anyway, it seems to get into them! It's weird to see that wave of thoughts enter someone else, believe me! It looks as if it's going to attack or strangle them, because the thoughts are not good, they appear rather frightening...

Yet you have not sent or thrown anything physically, just thoughts. When thoughts are good and kind, they completely envelop the other person, they stroke them in a way. It feels so gentle and good, it makes you want to do it all the time! That is what they demonstrated to me. The journey of thoughts.

If one thinks 'in general', the process is almost the same, except it does not reach anyone in particular, but reverberates all around and creates either a thick, heavy atmosphere or a light and pleasant one. It's fascinating to see the thoughts trail around and create in a way 'layers' in front of you, as if they were some kind of cloth. They wander right, left and centre yet seem to know where they are going! I don't know whether they actually do know, but they appear to!

To witness this, I had to sit down quietly and calmly, to relax and rest my mind, tell myself all was fine and I wanted to feel light and not tense (something I rarely am, except if I think of the loss I imposed on you and the sadness of not being together). Once I felt comfortable and relaxed, I was able to make my thoughts travel. First I was told to go mentally to a river bank and imagine I was swimming, to make me understand and remember we can make ourselves do anything we want. But once I did it, I saw that my ideas and thoughts of a 'river' carried on existing - even when I decided to stop, the river kept flowing, the colours kept existing, did not disappear. They kind of 'floated' in front of me and 'flew off'!

I asked why it did not stop existing when I changed my mind. I was told everything which is created cannot cease to exist, because it was created. The more one creates, the more

398

things exist! It seems logical and weird at the same time, but I realised I had not paid attention to this before - when I wanted something it would appear and that's all that mattered to me. Now I am told: "Watch, everything you think creates an atmosphere, an ambience, as you know, but it does continue to exist and it affects other people, animals etc. too!" So if you could do that on Earth it would change a lot of things, wouldn't it? Why don't we manage to do it as easily over there, I do wonder? It is so handy to be able to use one's thought as an everyday tool!

This is another advantage of being here! But the best is that it seems to me this state of thought is not just a separate tool, it is part of everything which exists here. Everything seems to think, everything appears to send pleasant waves all around. So I tell myself it must be because the kindness from all those around and the beauty of what exists emit those lovely, pleasant waves which surround us constantly.

The pleasant thing is we don't risk receiving nasty thoughts from other people, since all those here are good, kind, welcoming and ready to help you - we cannot do better! So you can guess there is no chance of us being 'attacked' by nasty thoughts!

I am told the habit of positive thinking comes by doing it often. The more one thinks in a positive and loving way, the easier one finds it, so it becomes natural and is no longer a problem. At the beginning one doubts, one wonders whether it can work, but since here we are constantly surrounded with proof that it does, there is no reason, not only for being attacked by negative thoughts, but also for it not being successful to achieve a positive mindset if and when you tried it on Earth.

That is my friends' message: "Tell them well" they kept repeating, "Tell them clearly". So I hope I have been clear enough for you to understand what I was talking about and to explain it to other people.

22nd August 2003 - *16.50 - The pen starts in 'Automatic':*

Mum is here to speak with you. I'll tell you in one go, ok? Right, the first thing is amusing: I've made some progress in swimming 'over water' rather than in water!

I did not really need to do that, but I had fun trying to become better at this method of floating above water without getting wet! The aim being to prove to oneself there is <u>no need to fear</u> falling into it and drowning! It's just to demonstrate that the body we have here does not really exist, we only have one to feel 'whole' but it is indeed not necessary! The <u>feel of a body is a relic from the times on Earth,</u> but we have to get used to understanding we do not need to look after it. As far as I am concerned, it suits me, as you can guess! I had enough being concerned about my Earthly body, now I no longer want to hear about it! But I did have great fun playing at being a dragonfly by floating or rather hovering above the water!

The other thing to tell you is different. I made a few <u>trips within myself</u> as they say. I had to inspect my motives and desires, my wishes, what saddens me and what makes me happy, my ideas on what happiness and unhappiness are. I had to do things like that before, from time to time, but each time they make me do something a little different. It's not that easy for me to describe to you using words, as it happens within oneself, you understand? We have to look at ourselves like into a mirror turned towards the inside. We analyse ourselves...me who used to hate that! I used to laugh at people who analysed themselves too much and pampered themselves!

Apparently one must do it here in order to manage to grasp who one really is. When one realises one was someone else before, and even several persons before that, it is after all important to come to understand at least a little! Especially since other <u>people see you in their thoughts and sense you as you really are!</u>

BR- Can you 'read' people too?

Yes, I realise that I too sense the personality of the people I meet! <u>I see them like waves of colours, sounds and impressions</u> within me. We don't pay much attention to it as it seems normal for these impressions to come to mind. But since others see you, we've got to at least know what they see! Therefore I must analyse and inspect myself! I used to think we went to Paradise to have a rest, yet here we are having to do some psychoanalysis and the like! But I am not really complaining you know...

All that is much better than being in pain all the time and having an awful, wrinkled old body like I had towards the end... *(Sudden silence. I do not hear anything for about ten minutes)*...

The pleasure to talk to each other was interrupted suddenly! I don't know what happened. We were cut off, like on the telephone! Anyway, I was saying I've been doing the work of a psychologist and a psychiatrist, trying to understand myself as they say here. We must know ourselves and grasp what makes us react in such and such a way, in order to understand 'the other layers of our psyche', can you believe! It sounds clever and complicated... I am happy to do what they suggest, that way as they make me do things, I learn, I get better here and I teach it to you! So it's all right, isn't it?

The most amusing in all this is to realise one has several layers in one's personality. When they tell you: "Look at that woman over there - <u>it was you in another life</u>. She has the same ideas as you but she wanted to learn something else, so she went back to Earth to have the time to learn more", it does feel bizarre, believe me! You feel you are acquainted with 'that other woman', you know her without really remembering... It feels so weird! A little like in a kind of dream, you recognise her yet can't manage to give her a name or recall where and when you met her...

401

My friends always have the time to explain things so I am not afraid to ask them. I asked who she was. They replied: "It's <u>you in another era</u>, when you were not mother of four children, because you were doing something else in your life which was more important to you than looking after children. In those days you did not want a child, you only wanted to travel, know the world, do some research, study botany, geography etc. and you didn't want to be stuck at home with a family. But later on, you regretted not to have known the joys of having one, so you decided to return to Earth to experience having children and loving them. You did not lose your inquisitiveness and your avidity to discover and learn, but you concentrated mainly on the family side and their education, which was easy enough for you as you like to share your knowledge.

So that's who you are now, at least who you were on Earth in that recent life and that's who that 'other woman' is, as you call her".

Now Darling, I understand better why I did not do anything extraordinary in my life with you. It is obvious I had a planned and organised job - having you and looking after you all as much as possible! This is why it tore me apart so much to have left you so suddenly, to have abandoned you. I love you too much to play that dirty trick on you but...we are here together, you and I, so we are carrying out the rest of our project - to give you proof and information and I hope my boys will at last believe it is me indeed who speaks to you!

I see you have finally understood it, for quite some time fortunately, but at the beginning I was despairing when you did not seem to believe it was me talking to you!..

BR- I forced myself to be careful and 'be wary' so that my brothers, or other people, could not accuse me of letting myself be deceived by my so-called subconscious or some other idiocy, in this case! (Unfortunately the telephone rang and I had to answer it)

402

27th August 2003 - *The pen starts in 'Automatic' - 17 words linked up (no crossed T nor dotted I). I struggle to decipher them, then I realise it's in English - it's my guide:*

An adventure on a big scale is coming. One can only guess at it. All we say is true so please don't doubt. Many a time have you asked for proof and help. We've got it. Allow your mind to be very relaxed.

As we talk, there is a beautiful light as a link between you and us. We had waited for years to see that light, you know. This desire to have our link started long ago but we could not get it going until you were ready for it! Now you've got it, we want to keep it shining and the shine will increase no doubt when you hear what we have to say:

The name of the famous baby you long to trace has been given to you before. The baby was indeed Angélique as the lady loved her so much and thought she looked angelic, but the surname of the lady had nothing to do with that. It was a northern name and started with a B... and another letter after.... A - L - D - U - C - K. Make sure you've got it right. Make sure you are relaxed, names are always hard to spell out and then you can try it.

(Amazed, I relax even more deeply and ask they use the pen in Automatic Writing to make sure! Twice the pen wrote on its own, while I did my utmost to 'blank my mind' and let it happen; after all I had no idea what the name was really, so this one or a correction would make no difference to me!)

Balduck Balduck. We know there is a problem with finding names in your world, so be careful not to get it mixed up.

We asked our lady to make a tremendous effort and she's been very helpful because she's understood the importance of it from your point of view. She'd been trying for quite some time but we did not want to disappoint you earlier, so we waited for more positive results. We knew we'd get there eventually so she tried hard and lived the moments again. She went through the whole sequence of events and felt the emotions and sadness and joy she had felt then. The moment the baby died was the worse for her as she loved her very much, but the shock of having to bury her made her faint as she said before. So we worked together and went deep into the whole process - she's felt all there was to feel and remembered bits of importance. Now what matters to you is where, how, names of places - all is here...

(I feel a bit panicky, hoping my mind would not interfere, unknown to me)

Often enough have we told you not to doubt us, we are not here to invent stories and you have nothing to fear of your subconscious and all that! We are here for real so if we say she said it, we mean - she said it!

(I let the pen do what it wants, and stare at a blank wall, thinking: 'blank wall, blank wall'- It writes the following pages in one very flowing sweep)

Armentières, 1898, south of Lille, a little town to be visited to understand the layout of the place then. Then look at the records of the cemetery for that year, 1898 and then ask for the name of the lady Balduck and then look at the baby adopted under this name: Angeline or Angélique; maybe we got the ending slightly wrong. Angeline or Angélique, meaning 'little angel', then you'll know we've told you the truth. Maybe the records will tell you more exactly but the lady, the new mother, said the baby was given her family name so that there was no problem for your mum's mum, then all was over for her. But what you need to do is go to records in Armentières and make sure the lady's name is correct: B a l d u c k - that's what we believe she was called and that's what the baby became called, even though her real mother was not of that name, since she was your mum's mum.

The baby was born in 1898 in December - a cold month which added to the depression of the real mother and the lady came soon after that to pick her up. It had to be done soon so that your mum's mum did not get attached to her and change her mind, not that she would have done so of course, as the parents were there to rule the nest... All my friends say is the lady Balduck is sure that is what it was and the lovely little baby was blondish, with lovely dark eyes and a pretty face; she was a sweetie, she wanted to live but fought in vain against the disease that hit her. Your Mum's mum was horribly distressed when she was told and had never really recovered from the shock of it all. All we have is, the mother adopting the baby - madame Balduck - first name not too sure, maybe ... L ... ? Lived in a small town of Armentières, near heaps of coal - maybe that's what killed the baby, she said. Loved outside, the country, but could not go far with her. That baby coughed a lot, from an early age. The little one died and was buried in the cemetery- not too far from the coal heap, she remembers - the coal took her, the coal kept her, she felt.

Then she herself felt unwell for a long time then died. The shock of it all affected her health. Baby died about 1899-1900 she thinks. No more really. All this is from the bottom of one Soul, in true love for you and your great efforts to teach the world what you have learnt from us. We are grateful and we would like to thank you for all your efforts. Look them up, search, we hope you can find what you wanted to prove and we'll be with you all along.

BR- Do you know by any chance whether the papers still exist?

Maintaining the link is hard now, try again.

(Note: Later on I looked up the name Balduck on the internet as it did not sound or look French to me! Yet I discovered to my very great surprise it seems to be quite common in the North of France! So my 'mind' certainly had not 'made it up'!)

The baby was one year old when she died, says Madame Balduck. The lady was so upset... So the year was

405

1899 when she died, about Christmas time too - so bad when one is unhappy! All we know is this, the things you asked for were, town or village:

- Armentières. Years: 1898-1899.
- Baby Angeline or Angélique. Name of lady: Balduck

She made her, her own baby so that there would be no problem. Lots of love given to her, lots and lots of love as much as if she was her own, because she had her from the day of her birth practically. All that was needed was to look after her and she did. That's all we know, my friend.

Now you can start your research and we wish you good luck. We'll go along with you to see how it happens. We hope you'll find her. We cannot guarantee of course since it depends on Earth life details and events, but we know we did our best to help you and we gave you what the lady you mentioned told us, having herself made extremely great efforts to be able to remember such little details!

BR- Could you explain how she did it and why it was so hard?

Over the years of your time in this world, we all progress one way or the other. It makes sense not to stay at the same level, doesn't it? So, as people progress in their development and evolution of their Self, they need to get away from what they have known before. That means the lives they've known as individuals on Earth. The more you can cast and shed from those details, the better and the lighter the load a Soul carries with itself.

So the lady had to learn to 'go back in time' as you would say, but for her it was not so much 'going back' in time as in an inner space of seas of knowledge and also emotions. She had been through a lot of emotions in that particular life and she first had to relive all that, in order to fit her Soul into that particular personality, just like a glove, a garment or a disguise, if you understand what I mean. She stepped back mentally, you see? <u>She had to relive all that as well as the rest of her whole life 'then'</u>! That was the problem - she had to fit all the pieces of the puzzle together again, so that the seas of emotions and happenings fitted together to make a whole. When the whole was made, she was able to look at it more closely for 'technical details' as we could call them, such as names or dates. Because when it comes to lives, <u>what matters is the emotions, the feelings, the elevations and depressions within</u>, which create such strong emotions and that's what you come back here with - what you have felt, joys and sorrows, why you have felt them. <u>Not so much what name or what year you felt them</u>!!

<u>This is why it is so difficult at times to 'remember'</u> as you call it, because we do not see things your way from here. You only have a narrow viewpoint of your life, you do not see the whole spectrum of emotions and upheavals which don't stop at a date but may last a whole lifetime. If you have suffered many upheavals of emotions, they'll overlap each other and spread over each other, or drag one longer than the other. All that is intermingled, you understand?

Our lady did her homework very well indeed. I must say she took your problem to heart and said she would do her best to help, because she is a very kind Soul. She understands the necessity to try to prove to your Earth world that nothing and nobody dies and all can be proved if only they listened. As you hope people will see it as a 'proof' we wish you courage and 'luck' in your endeavours and research... We are proud of your efforts and thank you again. All will be great when we can hear that you've found her on records and that she existed. Then our work will have been worthwhile. But <u>she has to be allowed to rest emotionally now because all this stirring of old emotions has disturbed her inner peace</u>. It is a little difficult to explain but imagine a lake or pool with peaceful, quiet waters and then someone goes down deeply to stir the mud and silt

407

and soil and plants at the bottom. You cannot expect the still pure waters to remain so - they'll be disturbed for a while until all the stirring has died down. That's what is needed now. So we hope you are satisfied with what you've got. It should be sufficient to get you going and help you reach your goal. You've got all the work on your shoulders now.

BR- *If I am on the right track, I don't mind. I am giving big hugs to Madame Balduck! I am also sending her healing to get her 'still waters' back.*

The ball is in your court now, my little friend. Best of luck from all of us... *(Short silence then the pen starts again ... in French)*

Mum is here Darling. You see, I told you we had a surprise on its way to you, but I did not dare say anything in case it failed! I had been asked to say nothing until they were certain to have some good results, because apparently it's really difficult to obtain details going back so far when someone has 'progressed', as they call it. I wanted so much to tell you not to fret about it, but I wanted to obey my 'superiors' since they always know the very best way to do things - I did not want to botch their efforts! We'll join forces here to send you good thoughts so that you can find them. It will no doubt take some time and give you a lot of work and even journeys, I assume. But it will be worth it for you to have waited such a long time. We have a cushy time here; it's you who'll have the work!

My friends are all excited to have succeeded, you know! You should see them! They are delighted, excited, they talk a lot... They had to make that poor lady do lots of great mental exercises (I think that's what we'd call them). She had to dive into her subconscious, her memory and all that in order to extract the details sought for. Apparently it's not easy at all, as I suspect too!

Of course it was not something I would have been able to see 'unfold' as everything was done inwardly. Moreover the lady is not really part of my 'surroundings'. Personally I've hardly seen her, perhaps once or twice at the beginning. She had her own 'level' or environment. She is involved with things which are very different from what I do here myself of course, since she has been living here for much longer, therefore we do not really meet. Yet she has obviously been extremely kind to sacrifice herself that way, to force herself to live again such painful moments in order to bring up to the surface the information we wanted.

We do hope you'll be able to find them on paper for yourself. Then the whole world will know I had a little sister, yet I never knew it! It seems incredible doesn't it? I had to 'die' to learn that, after all, I never was an only child!

But what a shock when I arrived here (after the shock to see my dad and dad Nic) to learn I was 'dead', at least from your view point, but on top of that to discover that this pretty young woman telling me: "I am your sister" was absolutely right! It's enough to send anyone round the bend if it was not for the fact that here one does not go mad, fortunately!

So there you are my Darling. I guess you must be excited and must be 'dying' to go and check all this, so perhaps I should let you get on with it? I do not have much else to tell you for the time being, except that my mum helped, she encouraged those researches on our side by sending good positive thoughts towards the lady who, after all (she's understood it now), had done nothing wrong. In a way she'd saved her life since her kind acts allowed Mum to get back to a supposedly normal life, at least on the surface; that way she could get married and the family honour was safe, like my grandparents wanted. They did not really wish to help, I gather. I suppose it had torn them apart enough in the past! Anyway, my team of capable people has succeeded, so let us applaud them!

BR- What do they look like?

I told you I no longer pay attention to their outer

409

appearances, as what interests me is their thoughts and opinion, therefore this is what I 'see' in a way, if I think about it...

It's hard to explain! When I talk to them, <u>I sense and 'see' their thoughts in colours, in actions and waves of emotions etc. so it provides me with a beautiful 'painting' to understand</u>, rather than my seeing someone with two arms and two legs, which he would have imagined anyway! Because the way he shows himself can only be an invention on his part, therefore why indeed persist in wanting to look at a 'made-up ghostly body'?! As far as I am concerned, I prefer the intelligence and knowledge they display at all times, that is what helps me here. Their constant support is fascinating as they seem to be inexhaustible - the more we ask them, the more they know! They never run out of answers and explanations!

Of course I guess they must be some kind of 'angels' disguised as some kind of humans. I say 'kind' because, as I told you, they have a body like people but I know what matters is what they tell us, therefore that is what I concentrate upon. These are my impressions as seen from here. You might see them differently if seen from where you are. As I've never had to do it from that direction, I don't know what they would look like to you.

BR- Have you seen my 'guide'?

I was told it is your 'friend' who helps you. He was not in front of me when he spoke to you of course, since one does not stand in front of others in order to communicate elsewhere... It would seem strange I reckon! But I know this person is your friend, your 'guardian angel' as I call them, although no one has any feathery wings of course! I saw a very likeable chap. He looked rather 'ancient' as a person, something like Roman or Greek or similar, because I saw 'clothes' of a kind which gave me that impression. He was not very tall, appeared rather young and cheerful and looked very kind. Really nice and friendly. I only saw him once or twice or so. We don't spend our time together, you understand, but I was told you have someone who looks after you very kindly and who knows what he is talking about, who has made a lot of efforts for you, so be glad you have him! They told me he has studied here at a very advanced level, therefore he is very knowledgeable so don't be afraid to believe him! He has also learnt to teach others what he has learnt, therefore he can explain things well. He seemed to me to be really nice, I am glad he is looking after you. Don't forget outer appearances have nothing to do with the real person within: we can give ourselves any outer appearance if we want to have fun and show ourselves in a 'bodily disguise' (without flesh of course!). So that is my reply.

As far as mine are concerned, I have lots of people around me when I discuss various topics, but there is one in particular who looks after me and who comes round when I need his help. We have done loads of things together, he's taught me a lot since I arrived and he is smashing! One feels good in his presence (At least I feel good in his presence!) and it is incredible how much he made me discover! He seems to be a brave man who is intelligent, kind, interesting and very profound.

He is also an excellent teacher as he explains everything very simply and easily, or at least as simply as he can. Therefore his appearance doesn't really matter, as I told you, as his knowledge and kindness are what stand out most in his personality. That is what I see in lights and impressions, apart from the words or images he shows me to explain something. I have never seen wings grow on his back, up to now anyway! I'll have to ask him whether he left them in his 'wings garage'! I am teasing you and joking of course!

BR- I don't really believe in that stuff about wings either!

He's done everything he could to help me become acclimatised to this new world and way of life, so I realise he

411

must have had a lot of work, poor fellow! But that's it, he has succeeded, I am here, I learnt to speak with you, we are writing a book together…and you have just received the information you wanted so much and which you despaired of ever hearing a word about! So my mission is accomplished, Mrs my Darling Daughter! You'll be able to get your teeth into it now, I hope. We'll let you sleep now if you can, because I wonder whether you won't be too excited for that!

BR- You are quite right!

Goodnight Sweetheart, I give you a kiss as usual. Don't cry, I am here you know, I have not really gone away and we shall meet up again one day. So don't worry about that. Do your work, have as much fun as you can, love your children and the rest will be fine.

I often think of you, you see - the result is on your paper… Go and sleep soon and rest your mind… Tomorrow you'll be able to start your work as Sherlock Holmes. You wanted to be a detective when you were young, do you remember? Well, there you are, you can do it now! Goodnight Darling.

6th September 2003 - The pen starts the first line in 'Automatic':

Dad and I are here with you Darling, if you wish to have a chat. My friends came to spend some time with me. I wanted to know what I could do to manage to see you more easily, because it's not that easy to concentrate, you know! They told me all I needed was to do the same things hundreds of times over: think of you, project myself mentally to your home even if I did not know where it was, just tell myself I was there, and that would work!

It appears simple to say but is not so easy to do. I know I did it once to go to your home and I tried Pierre's, but I don't know whether I did as well with Touky and I would have liked to do it alone without being helped. So I suppose I'll have to practise more and more to be able to go and see you without having to make too much effort! It looks hard to me when I think of it but I did manage it, didn't I, so why worry? It's because I want so much to be able to do it more easily, and if you could see me at the same time it would be wonderful!

BR- Yes, it is difficult for me too - we both need to be clairvoyant!

My friends here seem to think it is easy; personally I find it exciting to have a go. It is a big project. It's true I did it once, with my friends guiding me, but I do have trouble doing it alone. I suppose I am not used to concentrating enough that way. So I warn you all, you will probably have a 'visitor' one of these days, coming from much further than the planets of the Solar System!

Something else to tell you: The lady (of my little sister) apparently made big efforts to let you know the name of her daughter. I am told she now has to rest mentally and emotionally. It rather shocked me and made me think, as I realise that because everything here is in our Mind, it is essential to rest the Mind if it works too hard - if emotions are stirred then one must heal them. She was very shaken to have to experience that particular life again, as she had forgotten that nightmare in a way and we made her experience it all over again! It makes me feel guilty to have asked her to do it! But I am sure she will be looked after and helped to recover. Yet it is strange to think people forget their previous life and feel unsettled when they have to live it again and to dive into it like in too hot a bath. She had obviously closed that door in a way and gone else-where mentally. I wonder whether it will happen to me one day! I don't want to risk 'forgetting' you, at least not as long as you are on Earth and are waiting to come here one day. I doubt very much that will happen to me!

She has been here far longer than I have, that must be why she has 'evolved' towards a totally different level of

Mind. Moreover she knew her 'little one' was here with us. Therefore it must have been weird and unpleasant to be forced to 'go backwards' towards an era when she was not as happy as she is now. This in order to have to see and live again times which were especially sad, since the little girl was ill and died!

All that intrigues and saddens me at the same time: I wonder what takes place, you see. I am told not to be concerned about that as it will not happen to me for a very long time! I would have to want to evolve towards ideas far from my old Earthly life. But I said: "I am staying near my loved ones as long as they need me: They'll need me to protect them from here and welcome them when they have the joy to come over to this wonderful world, without worries, problems or pain!". Indeed one must be mad to want to go and live on Earth when one is aware of the difference!

There are so many pleasant things to do here, as I told you, why go and lumber oneself with a life on Earth?!

BR- Have you asked them?

Of course! My friends here tease me all the time because I often say that... All they do is repeat the following: "One chooses one's life my dear, chooses it to go and learn something, you do know this! We showed you what you had wanted to learn on Earth so why ask? It comes from deep within oneself. Suddenly one has the intense desire to go and develop more, to meet people one had known before or make the acquaintance of others one did not know. All this opens a range of unusual experiences which enrich the Soul".

It does have an effect to think or say this, doesn't it? When on Earth, we usually think of ourselves as Beings struggling with problems most of the time... Few will be saying to themselves: "Oh! I am enriching my life and my soul through this suffering!"

Sweetheart, I must tell you that I do realise I have been learning a lot of strange and unusual things since I have been

414

here; that allows me to teach a little of what goes on in this fantastic world, yet an invisible one to most humans.

Well, I hope everything I have told you until now will have interested you and helped you discover something new, as well as let others know about it and be intrigued too. That way it creates a chain of intrigued people, doesn't it? I am certain it's not over; I shall have plenty of other interesting facts to tell you!

As for me, I shall have to practise to come and see you as much as possible and also doing it for the boys, but it will be difficult to know whether they are going to 'sense' or see me. Where you are concerned, at least I'll be able to tell you and ask you!

BR- I suggest you show yourself to my Tuesday group of trainee mediums. Dad could also come to the Friday group, during Spirit scientists 'physics experiments', it would interest him! Did you understand?

We both did hear perfectly what you said. Your dad is near me too, he understood you are going to have a group of people to practise 'scientific' experiments. I was told it's going to take place soon, so if he wants to participate or witness what will be done this end, he has the opportunity. Our group of friends is always ready to inform us, it's great! So we've understood: You and your 'Tuesday' group would help me show myself and communicate, then on 'Friday' it would be more complex and Dad would love the 'physics' and scientific side of it, correct?

BR- That's right.

Well, we'll have to get down to it!

BR- Does Dad want to speak to me now? (A short silence. The pen starts the first words, then the flow comes back)

Mum says you would like to talk to me too, my daughter. I am still your 'old dad' you know, even if I no longer feel old!

You are going to have a lot of work with all the information Mum has been giving you since she's been here, aren't you? It gives her so much pleasure to tell you what's been happening since she arrived, it made her transition so much easier. It is painful to feel cut off from one's loved ones, you know.

BR- I had not realised this at the time of your departure... I am really ever so sorry poor Dad and feel guilty not to have tried to speak to you then. Do you want to tell me what you are doing?

We did love you very much, you know. Mum and I have always loved you. We were obliged to tell you off or punish or forbid you to do things when you were young. It was because we were afraid you'd get into trouble, or to protect you. Do not think I do not love you! I am annoyed with myself, you know, I reproach myself now, but at the time I used to think it was what one had to do to bring you up properly...

BR- Don't worry Dad, it's all in the past! I too have had children to bring up, so I know what it's like...

I wanted to tell you again so that you do understand I did not hate you, as you may have thought!

BR- I know. I love you! Now tell me about what you do nowadays!

There are lots of interesting people around me, a bit like with Mum. But I want to know how things happen and are made, so I am shown gradually. For example I have made a few experiments with the 'Light' we have here. This 'Light' is not like sunlight on Earth, you know, it's totally different. Here, Light has vibrations of emotions rather than photons and other particles. Here we create it by thinking hard! The more one thinks well (meaning 'kindly'), the more one creates good and beautiful Light! It's a very weird feeling to see oneself surrounded with Light one has created oneself, without using machines or one's hands! So there you are: I was taught how to analyse that Light, to see how it creates itself, why it exists etc.

416

You see, it is different from what Mum talks to you about, because physics does interest me. The other people here are scholars, most of them scientists. Lots have lived on Earth at one time or the other and were interested in this kind of thing, so they work at it in a different way now because they are here. There are other things one can do with that Light, you know. Not only does it light up around us but we can send it with our thought, without any difficulty. We think of something, we send it 'with Thought'.

BR- Can you please explain that last sentence?

If we want to use this Light towards something...

BR- To do what?!

For example to increase or shorten something, we can use the 'Light' from our thoughts. We think of an object, let's say, and by projecting <u>our Thought (which automatically means a beam of inner Light</u>), we send it towards that object and it will make it do, or will make it become, what we are thinking of. It makes things much easier not to have to use one's hands, you know! There are other people who do different experiments. Light is my interest at the moment but some others play with sounds.

There are so many <u>sounds one can create too, just by thinking!</u> One thinks of it and the sound comes, the 'noise' arrives as if in our head but in fact <u>it is external,</u> it is not within ourselves. It is bizarre to <u>see a sound in colours</u> because that is what happens - <u>not only do we hear it but each vibration is a colour</u>, so melodious sounds create lots of colours which blend and float about in the air in front of us... <u>It looks like 'visual music'</u>! It's great fun, you know! I am sure you would love to see this. I had fun with it for a while, then I passed to the work with Light. In fact there is a link, you know: Since everything is vibrations here, it's only a question of different types or levels of vibrations which create light, colours, sounds. Then when we stop playing with that, we have the impressions of having a sea of colours which makes music and which is music! Very weird but admirable! Those are a few of my pastimes. We often have discussions with other learned and scientific people.

One must also analyse oneself, you know, because it is important to delve within to really know oneself, in order to get rid of problems and regrets which are like weeds inside you and gnawing away. That helps you 'to rise mentally' towards a freer and happier way of thinking. If one has some regrets and is sad, it is very difficult to think 'lightly', do you understand? Lightness in one's thoughts enables you to reach superior and different levels of ideas. That way one can begin to grasp things one could not manage to comprehend before. The freer one is within oneself, the more one discovers outside oneself. Can you understand this?

BR- Yes, perfectly.

That's good, because this is what I had to do and still have to do now and then. I had to free myself inwardly in order to be able to think more lightly.

BR- But you were no criminal! And Mum forgave and forgot what upset her.

It is the inner sadness I had which was holding me back. The sadness for leaving you all behind, for being severe at times, for everything I may not have done well, for what I could have done better... Just one 'big sadness', that's it.

BR- In fact this is how I feel too, actually!

Well, we are both in a jam then! I hope you'll get yourself out of it quickly and before coming here, not to spoil your life here which is indeed superb and marvellous!

BR- Do you still carry out 'Soul Rescues'?

My rescuing the Souls of newcomers? No, not really. It may happen there are some now and then, when I am needed, but in fact I don't do many now. It has indeed taught me to listen to others, to pay attention to how they feel and to deal with their problems and not mine.

Now I do what Mum does: I try to find out as much as possible about what I can learn here and see things from an angle different from the Earthly way. As far as I am concerned, it's the 'why' and 'how' which interest me, that way I understand better and get interested. In fact you told me, via Mum, you'll be having a group at which some scientists from here are going to try some experiments in physics?

BR- Yes indeed, that's correct.

Good, that sounds intriguing. I am going to ask whether they can let me see what they'll be doing and how they'll do it. It will be something new for me, I had not heard about it before.

BR- It will no doubt take quite a long 'Earthly time'!

We don't really think about Time here as we are not concerned with it - no sun, no clocks, if we don't create any. Therefore I await to see what is going to happen with your 'inventions' there! As for you, what will you have to do?

BR- The same as the others: We need to be in a good mood and most of all in harmony with the other group members. Our energy fields must be on the same wavelength so as to create a harmonious blend of energy which the Spirit scientists use to create physical phenomena, that is to say, which Humans' five senses can grasp. They use not only energies from your world, but also from the Earth and the occupants and objects in the room.

Well, we are going to have fun with that, I reckon! Yes, I would indeed like to attend! Let me know when it happens.

BR- We'll start in a fortnight. Ask around you and Mum to know about it.

Now I'll let Mum come back to talk to you because she waited very patiently. I give you a big kiss my 'little girl'. Have fun with your experiments, I hope to be there too!

BR- I too hope you'll be there!

Me again Sweetheart... It has given him a lot of pleasure

to speak with you, you know. The thought of knowing what is going to happen when you have your experiments made him happy and excited! He has nearly become younger... Not that he is old here, but it has invigorated his spirits and made him look more joyful and 'luminous', he is so pleased!

BR- I am too! Thank you for letting him talk to me!

We'll let you go Darling, you must have things to do, as usual... We give you a big hug for struggling so much and trying to do your best.

BR- It's worse for Touky at the moment!

Give him a kiss from us when you can. We do think of you all. Your Mum.

18ᵗʰ September 2003 - *Slow at linking up. The pen starts in English - it's my guide:*

Better late than never! We've been trying to get through but it has been difficult today: You've been very tired I think, we could not reach the part of your mind which we need to speak through.

BR- How do you do it?

We need a quiet mind to be able to put in what we want to say. You need to be very still and attentive as we have to pour into it all our thoughts and feelings.

BR- Why do I receive it in English?

I send my thoughts to you, my dear. Your brain translates them into words of your understanding. If my mind links up with your mind perfectly, we have a good communication. If you are upset or distracted, the link gets broken and it's less smooth. We need perfect stillness to be successful.

BR- Do you send words?

We send thoughts. Thoughts are not necessarily words, are they? They can be a picture or a feeling. If my mind thought 'sadness', you could write the word sadness, but you could be translating it into another word more meaningful to

420

you, even into your own French language if that made it more precise, you see? <u>We just send thoughts</u>. There is no doubt that <u>we</u> give you the material, you just receive it 'with one hand' or two hands or even two feet (symbolically speaking of course!), but <u>you receive it and you put it down as felt.</u> That is the difference. If we use the pen for the words to be written, we have to imprint your brain with the correct words so that the pen writes them. But once you get going, the easiest for us is to send thoughts and you can do the rest faster.

Make yourself available more often, as often as you can. We have so much to tell you!

BR- Well, I am here now, so please go on!

The <u>lives</u> you lived on Earth have been hectic. You have always rushed from one thing to another, been busy and involved! You had to learn to let the mind rest and the Spirit come through. You have not exactly chosen a quiet life now but you have chosen to be a teacher, an imparter of words, a giver of words to instruct and enlighten others. So, now that you have learnt how to reach people, you have to go to the other side of your 'pact' to be quiet within, so that the knowledge you want to impart flows in then flows out to others. We need you to feel at ease within yourself. You are still churned.

BR- I don't know how…

You need quiet. Let there be peace in you.

BR- Can you heal me etc?

Make yourself as much a tool for Spirit as you can. Make yourself a spokesperson as often as you can.

BR- Am doing it, you know that!

Make life a challenge, not a battle. Life is a battle at the moment. You need to turn it into a challenge.

BR- What's the difference?

One rises to a challenge, one does one's best for the sake of doing what is needed. You don't have to feel you need to beat someone or something.

421

BR-I always avoid having to 'beat', I don't like that! To change the subject: Could you tell me about yourself?

On the whole you know what you need to know. You and I were mates at one time. We had a lot in common. We loved travelling; we were great adventurers in a way, always all over the place with our horses and walking. Then you wanted to learn more about the depth of the soul and <u>chose to come back</u> (to the physical world) as a student not knowing it all at once, but discovering it gradually. You went back to Earth, I stayed here in my world to look after you from here. We do have constant contact but you don't always seem to realise it.

BR- Could you give me a sign?

You have my voice in your head, you often think it is your thoughts but it is my voice... I do not need to have a separate, distinctive voice, you know what is said is right. I send the feeling of 'It is right/correct'. When we don't agree I send you a feeling of negativity, you know it too, so why worry? We have our code!

BR- Can you recall which country, or names or years?

Most of our time together was spent travelling across Europe. We did not really stop for long in one place. We had 'homes' where we slept - inns or outside, depending on our mood or the weather! You had lots of friends everywhere. We met them, stayed with them. We spoke the universal language of friendship. We knew a bit of each language, enough to cope everywhere.

BR- What about our origins?

You were rather Eastern, more like Polish or something like that. I had similar roots but came from a neighbouring country. We had so many friends, it was wonderful! We sold trinkets and bits of buyable stuff. You were good at making things with your hands. We sold them easily and we lived to travel. You were not married and neither was I. We wanted freedom and fun.

422

BR- Were we male or female?

We were both males of course. You could not travel across Europe with a female without any problem in those days! We had a little dog with us for quite a long time, he followed us everywhere! You had a special link with animals, you could talk to them in a way. You always found one somewhere to feed or to see to! But we could not get attached to one place as the spirit of adventure was calling... We just travelled and saw many, many countries, places of interest, people of interest; all that mattered was freedom and discovery.

BR- How did we die?

Probably sheer exhaustion and ill health! We were so tired of galloping around...

(I was interrupted and could not get a link afterwards.)

28th September 2003 - *8am! The pen starts in French.*
It's Mum:

I know you want to talk to me so I am here Darling.

(I am disturbed for a brief moment by a spider...) Your little beastie made me lose my thread (...spider's thread! Ha ha!). Little animals can be as disturbing as big ones, hey! So now we are 'tied up together' again, here is my latest news: Most of the time as you know, I make efforts to concentrate on what I learn here and to practise as much as possible. There are always some amusing moments because I often do something 'daft' by making a mistake or forgetting to do something.

The other 'day' I took an object in my right hand and wanted to make it pass, on its own, into my left hand, just to prove to myself I had a 'great' power of thought...but I had forgotten to have the essential intense desire and I was waiting for it to happen without putting my heart into it! I wanted it to do it on its own but it does not work like that. They keep reminding me one really must want with all one's heart, from deep within oneself, for it to be successful!..

423

Other times, I take one of the good books I have here to guide me and I have fun looking at them, since, as I told you, there are no actual words but moving pictures and I find that very interesting. There is always something to discover, revise or practise: because it's for a 'good cause' since it is to learn to do things here and get acclimatised, it's always useful.

The people who are with me are either people I knew formerly if I had been fond of them, or 'strangers' at the beginning, but they turned out to be kind and intelligent people with so much knowledge that they can explain very clearly. Since I always have questions, it suits me to have them at hand!

As for animals, there are some all over the place! My cats from before and cats from here, I have plenty of them everywhere! It's fun as they seem to know they don't have to eat or drink, yet I would have thought only people would have understood this! I suppose since an animal only reacts to hunger when his physical stomach asks him to eat, therefore here they are not hungry, are they? So we have them around, they are affectionate and love us. I stroke and cuddle them and they do the same to me.

My mum always loved cats and dogs, that's why she has some around her too. She had to recover from her emotions about the little sister and her 'stirred' memories, but it had not been as hard on her as on the old lady who apparently had to live them again throughout... It's weird, isn't it, because we would think that since she is here, she knows her daughter is fine. But the fact of having to delve into it and relive every minute must have been like a very long and real nightmare in a way. Anyway I think both may have recovered from it. It feels strange to hear of people suffering from something which took place here! It is indeed the World of Spirits but also of Minds. Therefore if the Mind suffers in our world, it does hurt as much as if it was in physical pain!

My parents are often together. I think they look after

young children who arrive not quite knowing where they are. Mum has always been kind to little ones. She receives them, cares for them, reassures and cuddles them so that they don't feel lost. My dad is still a good teacher as he was for me - he teaches them how to cope, explains what to do to get used to life here, shows them games to amuse them etc. My parents have 'large families' all in all, because there are so many kids coming over and once those are settled, there'll be others taking their place to get help!

Mum cried so much when her first born died (on top of 'losing' her with the adoption), that she is catching up now. I know she looked after me very well too and she is very maternal and kind with these little newcomers who have lost their family in a way, haven't they, since in most cases the family stayed on Earth. So those are the activities here.

Your dad comes here now and then, or he goes and enjoys himself with his scientific friends. They show him things I don't always understand and about which he tries to talk to me when he comes here. We are really lucky to have no more worries about houses, repairs, money, health... We spend our time doing pleasant or useful things just for the fun of it. It does make me feel selfish when I think of you all, knowing you must have problems and worries. It's as if I was on eternal holidays and I had abandoned you to your fates, to cope and struggle on your own and I was washing my hands of it like Pontius Pilate. Yet I am not doing this as I am applying what I was taught concerning you. I try not to cry anymore because I miss you terribly. Instead I send you all my love and my good, positive thoughts to encourage you to have a pleasant life and to learn what you have to and solve your problems.

My darling children, you have no idea how much I do love you!

BR- Oh yes, we do know it Mum!

The hours spent on Earth to look after you were not

nightmarish years, you understand? I know that it was tiring and difficult sometimes or often, but I have never regretted to have to do it. I wanted to look after you and do it as best as I could. Therefore do not think it was a living hell to have you and see to you all! You were my life.

BR- Yes Mum, we do know, stop worrying!

Good. I wanted to remind you. I would not want you to think I was unhappy and regretted to have had you all. My life was to have you. All of you going away used to break my heart, but you had to live your own life! My leaving the Earth feels as if it is you who have moved away from me...but we have discussed all that before, haven't we?

My growing 'passion' here at the moment is to amass knowledge and assimilate it so well that I can use it without any problem and teach you when I can. Sometimes it is difficult to explain what is going on because they are impressions in my mind; so it's hard to put into, or find, words to describe what I want to express, but it's really interesting, you know! You'll have to do all this one of these days! But not before finishing your work on Earth and publishing our book!

The pinnacle of my life here will be when you have all come back with us, we'll be reunited like before and Dad and I can show you all there is to discover. I'll have then the impression my life is complete and well balanced. Afterwards, as we shall never really be separated, I'll be able to busy myself by discovering even more things! Dad too no doubt, but we shall no longer have any difficulty in sharing them with you... We shall have then proved to your brothers that life does continue after 'death', we never really died. We only left you temporarily, just as if we had gone on a long trip round the world or even to another planet, but we have not actually disappeared, have we? This is what we would like the boys to understand soon and you to be able to make people you meet grasp: Life is eternal, much better, more joyful and interesting than on Earth! No matter how many good times there may be on Earth, the flesh or Earthly pleasure only last but a moment, whereas the joys and pleasure here are very long-term!

Do not ever feel abandoned Sweetheart. We are near you, invisibly but in thought, we send you tons of good thoughts and courage, good health and our very best wishes.

3rd October 2003 - *00.45hr. Late because it's after our experiments with our '3 Energies' Group...but it's worth trying to tune in just in case, as I went back to the room we used. There is always a lot of energy left over after an 'encounter of the two worlds', therefore I hope it will facilitate the communication. The pen writes the first five words in 'Automatic':*

Mum is here Darling. My friends tell me you are trying to talk to us so I've come quickly to answer you and not miss the opportunity! What a lot of years we must be spending here without knowing... It's incredible as we do not really have a sense of time or years! It's a little exasperating in a way because it does not make sense if we try to compare with the Earth! As we do not have a proper comparison point, we are usually fine most of the time. It's only when we think of the Earth and those we left behind, we start wondering how far they've got to, how old they are etc. and we say to ourselves: "Er... I've lost track..."

If we could count the days, we may see time pass by? I don't know what would happen exactly... There is no sun, no clock in a way - we can make some up of course but it is not real, it's a kind of 'disguise', a fancy dress or masked ball when we do that, because we know perfectly well it is not 'true', we invent it for our own pleasure! So I wonder sometimes how old you are now, how old I would be now if I had grown (even) older on Earth?

We would like you to begin typing this book for good now.

427

There will be so much to do to get yourself published, it would be right to be able to start it. You'll have a lot of work unfortunately, you'll have to find a publisher, but although it will take time, apparently we know you'll manage it and it will be published one day. So perhaps you should get going as soon as you can... Meanwhile there will still be plenty to tell you and even afterwards I am sure, but the editor will probably limit how much you can put in, so it may be two or more books? It does not matter as I know there will be lots to tell you, not half!..

My Darling daughter, you wanted to get it done, you managed to link up with me and we are doing it together. No doubt there'll be times when it possibly feels like a nightmare to have all that work to do, as you'll have to type all the stuff! But believe me, it will be worth it! I am told it will happen, you'll cope, so do not despair!

BR- I have started writing to archives to try to trace your sister, but it's hard to find out because of the war and the bombings!..

We'll help you Sweetie. You get down to it and we inspire you, encourage you, invigorate you...they promised me they won't let you struggle alone. You'll have all their and our support from here, so it shouldn't go too badly! We shall let you sleep now, I know you are tired and you'll have things to do tomorrow! So I give you lots of kisses. Sleep well. Sweet dreams! Hopefully we'll be in them! Your Mum who always loves you from the other side of this invisible wall.

18th October 2003 - *08.00hrs. In the morning for a change! I am hoping to speak to Mum, but the communication starts in English. My guide lectures me as to the remorse I feel because I wish to have done better during my life. He insists that, not having done anything wrong willingly, I must from now on forget any past error and concentrate on the future and my spiritual work.*

When I ask, once more, whether by any chance he could be a 'facet' of my personality (I always try to think what misinformed readers could imagine or con themselves into thinking they 'know'!), I find the information provided in his reply very interesting:

I am the voice who tells you what you need to be aware of and learn. You know who I am. We have met years ago here and before, you have grasped that! I am your guiding, counselling helper. My existence is not to be doubted, I do exist here in this world where I now live, to be of service to you, to be of help to you. You cannot think I am your own mind or even 'part' of your own soul because I have and am my own soul too. Yet on the greater scale, from plants to Spirits and Souls, we all are part of the same Spiritual Force that creates us and lives in us all, or 'is our driving Force' would be more correct.

But you cannot doubt my words, <u>they come from my own thoughts and wisdom</u> at times, to try to help and guide you when I feel you have problems with your own path and dither or stumble. If I can be of help I am delighted for you, because that's why I am close to you. You cannot wonder, every time we talk, whether it is me or your own 'subconscious' and all that stuff! You have no subconscious able to write; it only lies dormant. You have a link to me which we built over the years and we can easily talk to each other, or more exactly communicate with each other. That way hopefully, some guidance may, if you allow it, help make your path smoother.

<u>Life on Earth is not the best place to be happy but the best place to learn</u> to do <u>what you have decided to follow and experience</u>. Let me encourage you when you need to be encouraged or uplifted and if possible, guide you in the right direction, but as always you have the liberty of choice, the freedom of choice, your will is free to refuse my offers of help.

BR- Who is 'Golden Sparrow' who spoke briefly when I first communicated?

All around you are personalities ready to help. There is one indeed who jokingly said "Call me Golden Sparrow". That was his little pun and joke. He was here to help as well and is still available. We all melt our thoughts into one guiding block, guidance from all to one - <u>you</u>. It is wiser to have many wisdoms rather than one. All of us know what the 'Law of Love and Understanding' is and all of us chose to help those in need of guidance. You may thus get another voice popping in to help you. But in the end, they all come through me to say their piece, that's all! Be of cheer, you are cared for, looked after and loved. Why worry! We are all here, close to you to help you.

BR- How come you speak to me in English?

Our communications are always in English because <u>you</u> started the pattern when we first met 'on paper' so to speak. You had that language in mind. We can speak in any language you want, it will be all right.

BR- Why? How?

If you knew German or Russian or anything else, we could communicate. I would make sure you had the words in your head that express what I was trying to say. We may not know a language but <u>we can transmute from one into another</u>.

BR- Really? How do you do that?!

Our thoughts are <u>vital Energies which don't have a set language</u>. They live on their own level but they can be translated into another set of pattern of words, according to the recipient. If you thought in Chinese, I am sure we could do so too.

BR- My dad said he communicates in French as he doesn't know English!

<u>Your dad has not learnt to elevate his thoughts to the right vibrational rate where they can transcend languages</u>. When they become pure vibration, they can be changed into

various words in the head of the person receiving them. Make your thoughts clear and precise and they can be channelled to the recipient into his or her main language, that's all it is.

BR- What was your own language?

My own language in <u>which</u> life on Earth? Languages are Earth tools, not Spirit World tools! You have to understand we spend 'time' (as you call it) to <u>learn to undo the ties of Earthly life, to get out of the harness of languages and Earthly thoughts</u>. We do know how to <u>uplift our thoughts to such high vibrations that they become self sufficient</u> and their vibrations can be brought into any language for them <u>to be adapted and moulded and shaped into words and sentences</u> so that you can understand them.

Mine to yours have been and are shaped to fit in with the English language you know and like. If you wanted to switch to French, let me know and we'll change them to that. <u>All that matters is the content, the heart of the thought, not the words themselves</u>. Make yourself more available and more open every time we meet and you'll feel the difference in heightened thoughts. When we are discussing profound subjects, you may feel the vibrations are different. Help yourself to our knowledge and thus enrich your own.

BR- Fine, thank you very much.

Let our thoughts blend, yours and mine/ours and you'll feel you are not detached, not cut off from our world, but belong to it as well as being in yours. That way you'll be better able to cope with what you need to do on Earth, until you come back here with us.

BR- Thank you! It has been very interesting, enlightening and unexpected!

You can always come to me to refresh your Soul. We are here for that and you can keep on track better if you have a 'check up' now and then...

27th October 2003 - *French is spoken at once:*

We are here Darling, Dad and I. We'll tell you about the interesting things we did if you wish to know. My dad <u>helped me translate words into thoughts. There are words which are difficult to express as a thought, one needs to think about them in a different way</u>. For example, if we wanted to express the word 'misadventure', we'd need to find a way to put across the problem by showing adventures of travellers in trouble. That is a difficult word but there are others like that.

The more one thinks about it, the more one finds ways to bypass the problem and to try to explain with pictures. The only solution is to have a good think beforehand in order to <u>build for oneself a vocabulary of images</u> into which one can dig to be understood. Here we have the advantage to be able to exchange thoughts by using pictures; we can thus communicate rapidly. But there are times when one has to put across a feeling. That is not always easy if one is not used to symbols. In my opinion, one has to start early to have time to create for oneself a long inner film of vocabulary in order to know in advance how one will express all that! But my dad knows so much that he passes his knowledge to me, so it's all sewn up and saves me time and effort!

(Sadly I doze off trying to keep my concentration and my inner calm!)

***

CHAPTER 10
Ectoplasmic transfiguration - Thoughts' resonance - Time of death: Soul's choice

1st November 2003 - *Trying to link up after a demonstration of 'transfiguration' earlier in the evening when the medium's face is veiled by Spirit Scientists with an ectoplasmic film, a kind of thin mask, which they can then shape to make it to look like someone else! Spirit Teachers call ectoplasm, 'Living Energy'. It is extremely sensitive to light (in the same way as one could not develop a photographic film in full light but needed red light), so the medium was lit up by a gentle red light placed right in front of her. Because the Spirit loved ones have to use a lot of concentration and energy to help 'project' their own face, they often do not have the energy to project a voice through the transfiguration medium. So on that day another medium on the stage assisted the proceedings by 'tuning in' to them, in order to hopefully convey aloud what the loved ones might want to say.*

Throughout the evening various faces of 'departed' communicators appeared that way, superimposed on to the first medium's face. During this séance the hall was full, as it was the first time this renowned medium was visiting us, but I was at the back and could not see as well as I would have liked.

This is when, unexpectedly, Mum seemed to have tried to show herself, as the older lady she used to be in her later years! She pointed out my pendant and the ring I wore and our joint love for cats was conveyed too. When on purpose I asked the question: 'Have you tried to communicate with me?' Mum lifted 'her' hand forward and seemed to shake it, which I understood as her 'writing'. Unfortunately, the woman assisting the medium supposedly 'interpreted' what Mum wanted to convey and said to me: "She is pointing to the red light, so she must mean she flicks the lights in your house". That threw me as I had not had any light flickering! I wish I had not listened to her, as doubts started filling me about the whole episode, which I deeply regret now, after hearing what Mum told me subsequently, here below:

Dad saw what happened, he'll be able to explain better than me. All I know is I tried to speak to you but could not; I could only make gestures. I wanted so much to speak to you but the words did not come out as if I did not have the strength. I saw that woman in front of me and I saw a 'corridor of dust'. It looked very dusty on both sides and I entered it. I had to force myself to recall what I looked like when you knew me, then I saw your hand wearing my wedding ring, and my pendant and I felt so happy!.. I wished so much to be able to kiss you but I had been told I would not be able to move, I could not walk. I made the lady sense what I wanted to say by thinking about it very strongly. I thought of you and your love for cats and that I had one with me. I wanted to say yes, I had communicated with you (as you asked) but I could not say it in words. I made a gesture and I think you all misunderstood but I did not have the strength to stay any longer to explain better.

My friends tell me you are doubting what I am telling you. It is indeed very difficult to make you understand or believe anything, isn't it? I did my best tonight and I was hoping you had recognised me. I wanted so much to be able to say to you: 'I am here at last Darling!' I did manage to show myself but I don't think I did it well.

BR- It's not your fault Darling Mum, it's mine…You did very well!

My friends had done such experiments before so they knew what it was all about…

(Unfortunately, once more, concentration and fatigue, plus the emotion and the great sadness not to have enjoyed more that very special experience, made me doze off! It is ever so frustrating…)

2nd November 2003 - *The pen starts in English. It's my Guide:*

The session you went to 'yesterday' or so you call it, has been very informative and revealing, as you saw what could be done when someone tries to come through in that manner. The fact that your mum managed so much was to her great credit. She did try to come through, she did show her ring and she did say you had the pendant - you had understood this correctly. The fact that the other woman interfered made it hard for you, we know. You could be getting the 'flickering lights' *(The other woman told me wrongly Mum was flickering my lights!)* but it is not what your poor mum was trying to convey! You had understood the right message and then they upset the apple cart by saying otherwise! Your Mum could not deny it enough because she did not have the strength to communicate as well as show herself. She had appeared in front of you but you could not see her well, that's obvious. I am sorry for you and for her because she wanted to give you a surprise and it did not quite work out as it should have done.

Many times we say trust us and this is one more time when we need to say it; that is how it happened. The interference of the woman was not planned; she took it on herself to say so. You could ask them but what's the point! So we can only say your Mum had made the effort to learn to concentrate her thoughts on you and on her task, which was to feel herself as she did in the days you knew her, because you may not have recognised her if she showed herself as she sees herself now. If you had been able to come close you would have realised that she had a very good resemblance to those days and it could have confirmed for you and the others that indeed the face at least was correct if not the words given by the other woman.

You may feel upset by this because you think you missed out on a great opportunity, but we'll find some other time when she could learn to do it again. You must not cry, she

435

says, you must not be sad, she did not want you to be upset either way. You have to know the truth - that's what happened.

My main concern is that you trust what we give you instead of doubting - that lady having said something about lights threw doubts in your mind. So we need you to trust us and be reassured. You will be able to see your mum again, we'll do our best about that and you will be able to tell your brothers about it. It will have to wait till the opportunity arises of course. A useful exercise will be to try yourself to speak to your mum and ask her what she has to say about it. Do you want to try now?

BR- Of course! Not half! (A short silence then the conversation starts again, in French this time)

My poor Darling, I am sorry you were disappointed! I had tried indeed, they had shown me what to do and I had worked at it to be a 'good pupil' and do my homework correctly.

My tutors had made me practise elsewhere, with people who did not know who I was. It was not important, as it was only to train in showing myself simply by thinking of what I used to look like.

I was old when you knew me during the last years, so it was better for me to present myself as 'old' even though I would have been so much happier to show you how I see and feel myself to be now, you know! But we must do what seems to be more logical and sensible!..

BR- Bravo and many thanks for coming! What exactly did you have to do?

My friends had prepared me for what was to happen. One feels surrounded by some sticky stuff in a way, it's greasy, gummy and rather crumby; it looks dusty but it is sticky when one gets into it. I put my face in a weird whatsit, which is this sticky and dusty thingamajig, then concentrated just like when I used to 'phone' you at the beginning when I arrived.

As soon as I got into it, I focused on you and on me as

the 'old woman' of long ago. That makes happen what is supposed to happen apparently! But I did not see much as I was too busy thinking of all those things. You were there but rather far away in the hall, I would really have liked you to be nearer. So I saw you and your pendant, it made me happy. I wanted to say it to you but it was not understood. The light, red to you, was not that red for me, it was quite bright in fact, yet I could see people- but it was giving me too much to do and think at the same time - I was not able to stay any longer.

BR- Did you make any gestures?

My hand showed that I was writing and you received and receive what I send you in thought while writing. But my vision blurred, I lost my sense of direction and found myself back at my starting point whereas I had hoped to stay longer! It felt strange to have been able to catch a glimpse of you and believe I had indeed succeeded. It's a shock which seems unreal, doesn't it? We'll have to try again and this time we'll make ourselves understood, we'll talk to each other without other people disturbing us or meddling in!

BR- Yes! I am so sorry about that! How was all this organised?

The organising of all these things is always done by my friends and companions here. As for me, all I do is obey 'the orders'! I am only joking when I say this you know, they are very kind here! So I was told: "You'll be able to have an opportunity to show yourself to your daughter in a fairly easy way, why not have a go? She will certainly be surprised and delighted, but she has not been warned about it. Do you want to try?"

When they told me that, I thought 'of course', as you can guess! One does not get this kind of offer everyday here! So I learnt what to do: To think of oneself, remember one's face and hands etc. and project it forward by thinking 'as if one was making a mask with one's thoughts'. That's what they said to me.

437

They took me to a calm spot where I could concentrate without any distraction. I managed to do it I reckon, but we had the problems mentioned earlier! Afterwards, my reaction was "Oh! It was so short! I would have liked to stay longer!" One catches oneself thinking: "What if I had done or said this, would it have been better?.."

So the regret not to have managed it longer began to grow! But I know I must not go down the road of regrets, as it will cause shadows in my life and yours. Apparently that never fails - sad thoughts reach their goal and create a sad environment elsewhere. Therefore you can guess I did not want that!

BR- Did Dad see what was going on?

My friends say that you want to know exactly what Dad saw. My dad was present. He checked I was doing correctly what I had been taught. I had always obeyed my dad, so you can be sure I was not going to risk making mistakes, all the more since I wanted to see you! You looked very pleased to be there. You looked nice but I could not see very clearly, you know. I caught sight of your pendant, just when I was beginning to lose my footing with my concentration. I wanted to tell you I knew you had it on you and thank you.

BR- What about the sticky stuff? How much was needed? Was it in a container?

The material I was shown was like in a large basin and someone lifted it up like a kind of curtain. That is how I had practised this exercise. I had to get used to thinking of myself as 'old', think of you as you are now, put my face in that sticky but also dusty slime and concentrate all the time, they told me! If I lost my concentration I'd go backwards and would find myself where I was in actual fact! So that's what happened.

BR- Even yesterday, with the basin etc?

The lady has a guide, as you call him. He was there, next to me - a big man, who seemed quite pleasant. He said to me: "Here is the material into which you must concentrate. Be careful not to forget who you are and whom you wish to speak to. This will help you communicate, to make yourself be recognised, but...do not lose your concentration!" This stuff about concentration is terrible; we have to think of it constantly, it's incredible. In fact at times one feels like saying: "I've had enough of concentrating, leave me alone!". Anyway, we've done it. There you are. It is not so difficult if one knows how to do it... It's like everything, isn't it - Christopher Columbus' egg, once more!

Mum is always near you know. All you have to do is think of me and you'll be able to feel or hear me, I hope. Everything I tell you is true, don't worry, I would not tell you any lies.

8th November 2003 - *21st anniversary of my dad's departure.*

Dad here. We watch you and love you for making all these efforts! You'll have an enormous job to type all this neatly, then probably translate it into English!.. But we hope it will be worth it... The year of my death was not a very joyful one when it happened, but after a while I got used to it and I succeeded in getting rid of my worries and regrets, yet it took some time.

BR- I am really very sorry not to have been able to help you, because in those days I didn't know as much about the Hereafter as I know now!

The present time and here and now, that's what matters and must not be wasted. Therefore do your best so that everything you want to do is done and everything you want repaired is. It will save you time when you are here.

My friends told me you had started our famous book - you doing that pleases everyone. So we wish you good work and courage for this Herculean task! The love of your parents will never diminish, remember that!

439

21st December 2003 - *Mum speaks:*

Oh, how happy I am that you are here at last Darling! Yes I know you have been very busy with 'your/my/our' book, haven't you?! It's so good to know you've done it and even sent it to Touk...

BR- At least the first 50 pages...

Yes that's fine, at last it's started to go and reach him, I am so pleased. I hope he will finally understand we are not parted. We are still together all of you, me and Dad. All we have to do is talk to each other after concentrating on one another. It would be like a large family conversation if we could all do it together! Anyway you are here now, that's what matters at the moment.

BR- Talk to me about you, but in one 'block' so that I don't lose my focus...

My news about here is not particularly extraordinary you know, but it is good to meet up and chat, as I was wondering when you'd have time to do it again. I see you have a bit of a break, according to what I am told, so you may have a little more time for us here.

BR- Yes, I am using it to type your manuscript...

The most important thing is that you are happy to be with me and Dad too of course, you are glad to be able to communicate. I know Touk has not yet received your parcel *(of the first part of the typed manuscript)*, but to me, just knowing he's going to receive it feels as if he has already got it!

So I am touched, happy and wait impatiently to know how he is going to react. I do wish I could say all this to him and all of you personally and aloud! He probably talks to me in his head and I sense he is thinking of me, but I am not sure whether he receives my good thoughts towards him. As I always send him positive thoughts and 'inspiration', I hope there will therefore be times when he feels inspired and encouraged as this is what I try to have him receive!

440

My mum tries to teach me what she does here, because she has fun communicating with animals, you know! I must say she is doing well. She has been doing it for a long time, so she is better than me. Mum has always loved animals, like all of us, hey! All there is to do is think of them with love and send them one's thoughts - they receive them, not as words but as impressions. We can see they understand what we tell them. I shall try more often from now on.

The system of Thought as a 'conversation tool' works so well, we have enough to have fun with it all day long without tiring ourselves with speaking.

My little she-cat from Algiers is here you know: It's the one I regretted so much to have had to abandon to her sad fate after we left Algeria. I thought of her so often, feeling so guilty! She'd had her kittens and they must have all suffered, poor darlings, but finally they 'died' or as we say here: "They've come back home". They thought of me, or at least she came towards me and kissed me with one tender look in her eyes when she rubbed herself against me. She had a beautiful grey and brown fur if I recall, that's how she is here. She suffered so much, poor pet, she must have died fairly quickly I reckon, with all those Arabs around her who did not know how to be kind towards her and her little ones. Anyway, she's just visited me to say hello like she often does, then she strolls around with her other cat friends as if they have been doing that all their life, here or elsewhere!

I also wanted to tell you one of my 'books' talks about that and the affinity some people have with animals. It has to do with the link of affection which an animal can give you, if you manage to understand it. One must put oneself on the same wavelength, one must love it like one would love somebody. The book explains this love resounds like a vibration or a musical note. It allows their musical note of love and affection to resound or vibrate in such a way that our note of love and affection responds to it at once - one literally feels on the same wavelength!

It is true, that's what happens: <u>Any thought or emotion does this, it emits a kind of sound, has a resonance which has a particular characteristic</u>. This is what allows it to be placed on a kind of scale, like to play the piano. So we 'play music to each other' by sending those notes of affection, or of course hatred if one had those feelings...but this one does not exist here! Friendship, love, affection, understanding, interest and amusement, yes. But the bad side, no. We no longer feel it, at least not where I am! Any negative idea or of hating someone is promptly explained, analysed, dissected by the friends, whose job is to make us understand all this.

Therefore we 'play music to each other' by exchanging thoughts, that's how we could describe what's happening. True friendship, sincere and profound friendship, that is what matters and it is wonderful, you know. When you think of all the people on Earth who pretend or imagine they are your friends...they just imagine it or pretend, that's all! There is nothing neither sincere nor profound, it's nauseating when 'seen from here'. Only genuine friendship counts, the one you can rely on - when you do like someone a lot and he or she shares this feeling. This is why I marvel so often about the beautiful friendship offered by the friends here. They came when I arrived and they stayed by my side. I am talking about those who were some kind of 'strangers' in a way when I came here. I think I must have known them in one or some previous lives which I do not recall, but they say it is so!..

What is superb and great is the friendship offered has no boundaries! I can only appreciate and enjoy it and do what they suggest when they advise me, in order to teach me things here- because they give those pieces of advice out of sheer kindness. After all, they could go and enjoy doing something else, elsewhere, couldn't they? It's probably not fun to have to convince new arrivals that they are 'dead' and need to learn to do all those strange things! But the friends do it willingly, with a big smile every time we meet. You really feel that what they do or say is indeed done to help you and support you in your efforts.

There are not many people on Earth who would take the trouble to spend their free time looking after you that way, don't you think so? I do love them dearly, admire them and am grateful to them for all they have done for me up to now! So there, I am thanking them via our book, officially! But they also know how much I appreciate them, I tell them often.

BR- Good! I am pleased for you.

Perhaps we could say goodbye for now Sweetheart? I feel you are sleepy and you keep disappearing like a little cloud floating off and coming back then off again... So we'll leave each other on paper, it will be better, but you can come and talk with me during a visit here if you wish, while your body sleeps. Do you fancy coming around?

BR- And how! You can guess I do!

So I'll go to the 'guests' reception' to receive my darling daughter. Sleep well, human body of R-...but you Darling come, so that we can hug and love each other closely while your body sleeps Sweetheart. It does need it, I am certain! Goodnight. See you soon!

28th **December 2003** - *Early morning: I find my cat Timmy dead in the garden.*

4th **January 2004** - *The conversation starts in French. Mum is online!:*

I have been experiencing lately the new way I think at the moment, the mental attitude, do you understand?

BR- What do you mean?

I have noticed I need to think in a slightly different way.

443

There are times I feel ever so ethereal, my thoughts are so light I have the impression of being a floating cloud, or something like that... I am nearly 'evaporated'... I suppose it's <u>because I do not pay attention to my body, since my physical body is dead</u> and buried I suppose. The 'real me' is here, so that suits me!

The sensations I have at the moment are very interesting to analyse. I must pay attention to my thoughts as they 'fly off' so easily and I have to try to follow them...they take off like a bird or a butterfly. I feel as if I have to follow them by 'swimming' behind, without always being able to catch up with them! It's really bizarre! There are times when I feel a bit lost, as I wonder why I feel like that. The reply they give me is that the <u>thought energy, of any thought, is a very light and infinitely rapid energy</u>. So I have this new task of <u>following my thoughts to know where they are going and how they transform themselves into physical Reality</u> for me!

It's rather a cranky story I reckon, but I always obey what is suggested to me here. If it pleases them to teach me this new way of thinking, let us do it quickly so that I manage it and understand why and how to do it! You see, I am very willing to do anything here, as it teaches both you and me! Since there is absolutely no danger, as there is no body to injure, why not do as I am told like a good pupil? But you must be wondering what I do exactly?

BR- Yes indeed!

So here is an example: If I imagine myself sitting on a river bank, let's say, a little higher than the level of the water, I make up little stories like: I am going to row a boat on it, or I swim in it, or have fun walking on the water without falling into it ... and such things. But while doing so, I must think 'higher and higher' as they say. I must tell myself these actions are very useful and will help me understand more complicated stuff. So I do it. I imagine I am on the water and do follow the flow of my thoughts (That's a good pun, hey? The 'flow' of thoughts on the water!). By doing this, <u>I see myself creating those thoughts - I see it in duplicate</u> in a way! I am there, on the water, imagining those things, yet I <u>see myself, from elsewhere, doing it</u>! In a way, I am 'floating' in the air and the more I think "I am on the water", the more the picture of me on the water shows itself clearly - it's fine and light! I have the impression of being my own double, <u>I see myself as if I was my twin</u>! It is very bizarre!

I don't really understand what the use of all this will be, at the moment anyway, but I am certain that 'one day' I'll know. There are no details to give, it's mainly impressions to gather, I reckon. I have to feel light when having these thoughts I need to follow. So I work out a 'plan of action'. I decide: "I'll go there/I'll do that". While doing it, I wait for 'the strange things' to happen. Since I know something is due to take place, I expect it and must observe how I feel and what goes on. Therefore I must pay attention to my thoughts; they have to be 'light', not negative and accept anything happening, if something happens... So that's what I do.

I hope to be able to tell you more, later on, but for the moment I have made up those little exercises, as I have the right to create my own exercises, would you believe! So I make those 'action plans', then I have fun following what takes place in my 'head' or more correctly in my Mind - <u>I see myself think</u>.

BR- How do you do that?

<u>I see my thoughts take shape in front of me and I see myself doing those exercises</u>. For example, I see myself sitting by the water edge or floating on the water in a rowing boat, but I see myself 'from above', I get a bird's eye view, seen from the sky as you may say, but we don't pay attention to a sky here.

There are interesting moments, like when I have such joyful and light thoughts, that I feel like a little cloud floating in the 'sky' but I know I am not a cloud! I feel free and light, I look down and I see that woman sitting in a boat or on the riverbank and that woman is me... who is no longer there! It's a bit like dying twice, isn't it?

I got out of my body, my real flesh body, when I left you all. Now, I suppose they <u>are teaching me to no longer feel my imaginary body</u>, as I am out of it and <u>enjoy being just a Thought</u>, drifting with the wind. But there is no real wind, you know. So that's it. I do strange things here, don't I? Creating this kind of work, but obviously it is or is going to be useful. All is needed is to apply it.

BR- Do you do this alone?

My friends help me by explaining what I'll have to do, but after that they leave me in peace, so that I do it when I feel like it. This, Darling, is the main core of my present activities here! Now I'll let you sleep, you look very tired! With all my love and kisses.

31st January 2004 - *Early January my husband Dave who had been feeling unwell throughout the festive season was diagnosed with acute jaundice. Thanks to an intensive week of private treatment from a naturopath, his body was cleansed enough in time for an operation to place a stent to drain the gall bladder.*

The scans revealed the cause was a large malignant tumour on his pancreas!.. Now I am at his bedside in hospital, the day before his stent operation. As he is asleep, I tune in hoping to get some guidance from my Friends from Beyond. The answer comes in English.

I include it here <u>to help any reader</u> in a similar situation understand the <u>complex intricacies involving the reason for anyone leaving their flesh body</u>. <u>One needs to learn to think</u>

446

beyond the boundaries of the Earthly personality and remember every one is a Spirit with a' life plan' chosen for their particular 'experiment on Earth'. Of course this can be very hard to grasp when one is emotionally involved with the patient. Nevertheless it is the Truth, as taught by evolved Beings, a fact which we will all eventually have to accept, whether we are in this world or the next!..

Also, if you went to a genuine medium to find out whether a loved one is due to 'die' you are unlikely to be told they will, or a date! Not only would it be illegal and unethical, but as the text below explains, no date is set in concrete! Even in private conversation with our own spiritual helpers, they rarely give us automatically such answers. But in my case, my Spiritual helpers understand me very well. They know I always prefer, ask for and need to have some warning, to prepare myself mentally, emotionally and physically:

My dear, make sure you understand our position is one of elevation above and beyond what you call 'Time'. So be prepared to understand the difficulties we have in pinpointing things, facts, events and happenings. Life on Earth is such a flimsy suite of events which are all interconnected, yet you see them in 'files and lines' of before and after! We can tell you this though, if we have not misread our information which comes from Higher Sources: **Life is not a web of straight lines! It is a complex *superimposition* of facts, which can change at any moment, according to many factors, depending on the wishes and will of those involved, or related to those events. So everything can change at any time!**

But where there is a line of conduct right through, it is because the Will of the one involved has demanded this to happen - and that Will is embedded in his Soul and Spirit...so he can conduct his own band of events around him, like a conductor conducts an orchestra.

If he wishes in the depth of his Soul for something to happen, that is what will happen because he will make it happen, by willing all around to act accordingly. If you think we are 'talking rubbish', as you call it, do say so.

BR- No, I don't. I am aware of the importance of the Higher Self and Spirit person's long term plans…

Because we would understand if you thought that too hard to comprehend. Make sure you understand that the life of a loved one is very dear to those in that particular life, but also to others who have known him before or have gone beyond the Earth before he does!.. So will you accept the fact that someone cannot remain on Earth forever? They have to go at some time or other... It is their Will from the bottom of their heart and Soul which will determine exactly when… You'll have to explain this to others, including your own family, because it is very hard for one person to go when all those around he loves are hankering for him to stay on Earth, whereas the Soul yearns to go… Love those around you as if you are never going to see them again before long. That way you will never regret anything. Being annoyed is not a 'sin' or a catastrophe, being nasty brings a lot of guilt and regret later!

My dear friend, the love you have for those with you will help you, and them, survive what they have to go through. You have a noticeably big heart but you have too much passion and fire in you and you lose your temper too easily… That's what you need to control to reduce the amount of guilt you may feel later, you see?

Prayers are always answered one way or the other. You will have sent enough prayers to help an army, don't worry! He'll get through this operation, he'll make it. You need not fear the operation. He will need time to recover and will be quite a while in hospital, because life on Earth demands you follow the pattern of physical life. He will come out; you will have him back home. He will be ok and happy enough to get on with his 'pottering about' life. He will be happy for a while and you'll be able to help him without burning yourself out. But you need to recognise that we cannot promise he'll live forever... Make the children realise they may not have him forever, so they need to keep in touch more often so that there are no regrets...

BR- What span of 'time' could we be talking about?

Unless you understand our difficulties in pinpointing events you'll never grasp the problem we have in being exact and precise. We see a man resting at home, a man recovering and a man happy to be back in his own environment. He will be ill from the operation because it will be a shock, but that will be while he is in hospital. When he is out, he will be ok and will enjoy his life for quite a while. But one day, later on, to do with something else, it will be the time you have to get ready for the parting... That will be announced to you in advance, so don't worry about it now, that's all. He'll be fit for a while but then he'll have to go. You'll be told. You cannot be hoodwinked, so we tell you the truth as usual. You can prepare yourself and others for the eventuality. Your man in hospital now will be ok for quite a while, so do not fret. But we gave you the overall picture so that you can organise your life accordingly.

BR- Thanks, this is what I always want, to reduce regrets ...

Life is weird and unpredictable for those on Earth. Yet very clear for us seen from here, because <u>we know that what goes on inside a person's mind and Soul has a great effect on what happens</u>... Make sure you don't regret anything anymore. You have been given the chance to wipe off an old slate.

BR- Am not sure of that...

Yes, you have. You cannot blame yourself for what he has now because that was old history, he has lived a long time in between so do not think that. Many have asked to be told in

449

advance and many regret it once told... That is why we wish people did not ask, but if it helps you run your life in a smoother way and make up for past mistakes, we are prepared to let you know to help you. Over the years your man has had so many knocks it will have shaken his body and Spirit. All knocks reflect in every body. You'll need to be there for him, you'll need to be strong for him, you'll need to love him but you must not feel guilty about it.

Peace of mind is not something you can get overnight... Make time for the ones you have on Earth, so that you do not regret not to have had time for them. You'll have to reorganise yourself somehow to spend enough time for them and with them, so that when you lose them, you'll have no extra regrets and remorse. It will be bad enough to be alone. We suggest you go to sleep now to recuperate from your exhaustion. You'll be better off in bed than on a chair...

February 2004 - *Whenever I was able to tune in, my guide was on line, concentrating mainly on Dave's state of mind and giving some advice.*

10th February 2004 - *During our practice circle, my guide gives us food for thought:*

Make everyone understand that the life you lead on Earth is only a speck in the overall lot you will have experienced or will experience. It is not possible to live only one life, because you could not learn all you'd want to know and experience in that particular span of so-called 'time'. You'd miss out on a lot of possibilities if you'd only had one single Earth life experience!

If you wish to argue with us, that's fine, but you will not win because in the end we would show you, once you are here, that you can go back if you wish and that we had the truth. So not only were you mistaken, but you had blinded

450

yourselves to the teaching of more experienced Beings from our world!

Having said that, you could argue that one life may be enough for some who do not wish to stay on Earth longer than needed, since the 'Spirit (or other) World' is so wonderful. The answer will then be yes, you could have only one there, but you would learn less by going elsewhere. The Earth is a good school for you, as you have chosen the field of Matter to make your experiments.

So, to come back to our first comment, the life you live here and now is only a speck out of many. You will need to get used to the fact that people do leave it to go elsewhere, carrying on their experiment, as their Soul decides to choose various activities to enhance its knowledge.

All of you *(in the practice circle)* have been chosen for the work which needs doing on Earth, that is for the 'spreading of the word' which is 'Eternity never dies!' No one ever dies, one passes from one realm to the other. All that remains is aches and pains for those left behind of course. But the Soul who has moved on will find solace within, when it has opened up to the possibilities now within its reach. It gathers the new knowledge acquired on Earth and adds it to the facts and experiments achieved and gathered within other lives.

That should help you be happier when someone you love leaves your Earth, because he has gone on to learn more or to congratulate himself for what he has done beforehand... It is not an eternal parting as you will see each other again at some point, but in the long run if someone leaves, do not mourn for ever. Just think he has done what he came for, he has earned good marks! Now he is allowed to be freed from the hassle of the Earth and has attained the freedom of our world!

So, rejoice and be glad, do not cry, be glad for him and wait for the moment when you will meet again. That means others no doubt will cry for your departure...but you, in turn, will be happy to have been freed from the Earth's shackles and hassles and you too have obtained that ineffable freedom which all here love so much! You cannot understand the relief, the joy and happiness felt by those who arrive, even though their joy is tainted by the sadness to have left you crying and lonely, as you have been bereaved of your loved one.

An eternal circle of leaving and arriving, of tears one side and joy too! But the results will be worth it in the long run, as you will all understand one day! Have faith in those who have been where you are now and who will be here for you when you arrive, to welcome you and make leaving the Earth easier, so that the pain of departure subsides in front of the joy of arriving in Freedom Land, Loving Land.

My friend, you have understood what I said. I thank you for passing it on to your friends to try to ease their pain when they lose someone. Remind them that no one loved is ever far away from you. He or she will still be near you when needed, will still be sending loving, helpful thoughts to you on the Earth where you all struggle one way or the other! But they will also have the opportunity to blossom, as they discover new facets of their personality and blend with the other facets they have known before but have forgotten. That way the flower of their Soul will obtain more 'petals', the colours of their Soul will be brighter and richer. <u>Their Soul and Spirit is what counts</u>, you see. Remember that.

One more thing: The little insect on a branch does not know where it is going exactly. It only sees that little twig or piece of blade. The big man standing in the field can see much further and can guide the little insect if he wishes or if needed. So do not fear for your life and your loved ones. You will always be guided back onto the middle of the twig - you will not be left to fall off and injure yourself. You are looked after my friends, you must know that. Not just assume, know it! We are all here to help you, you see, because we love you for what

452

you are - kind Souls who care about each other and would not want to hurt anyone. So be brave and face your Earth life full of hope and trust, as you will not be let down. The happenings which hurt you are part of the lessons and the learning. One day you may look back and think: "Thank goodness, it's over but it was worth it!" And we shall be by your side to witness this and congratulate you on your successes. You will all have 'graduated' at the University of Earth Life. What a title, friends, what a title!

30th March 2004 - *During a practice 'circle', the pen unexpectedly starts the first three words in French then I hear the rest:*

The first person whom you should be talking to is your poor Mum, who has been waiting for you for such a long time...

BR- Oh! I am so sorry...

No, I am only joking Sweetheart! I know how busy and overworked you have been, you must be worn out... My life here has not changed much so you have not missed anything, but there've been some interesting little incidents and events, such as when I learnt to 'change myself into a bird', in a way! I mean to feel like a bird, to know how they feel when they fly...it does not appear very useful or impressive, does it? Yet it was to experience how one feels to be so high and so free, without an old body holding you back like I had towards the end of my Earthly life... My flight was rapid and interesting. I saw from above what I usually see at ground level here, but the most beautiful part was the feeling of freedom and the joy of wandering about like a bird does!

BR- Did you have a body with feathers on?

I did not really make a whole bird body for myself, but I told myself I was a bird, therefore I was free to float and fly high without any danger of falling. I managed it successfully!

This is because here, when we tell ourselves something, we make it happen or appear. So I created for myself this flight, this feeling of flying, floating and looking down.

BR- Did you perch on a tree?

Seen from above where I was, trees looked small. I had fun flying and fluttering about from one to the other, just for the pleasure of feeling so light and free! One of the reasons for doing it was the sheer fun of it. The other reason being to know how to control one's thoughts and to tell oneself something…which then happens once one has thought it! We create our own environment! We make ourselves do things we used to think we would be unable to do!

My friends here are very pleased with 'my progress', as they say! I am delighted too as I am learning more and more and it's great fun. There is so much to do, yet we are simply enjoying ourselves. This 'work' in fact is amusement. Why bother with real work when there is constantly enjoyment around us, that is if you wish to do it and if you enjoy it! I reckon there are some people who may not want to do what I do and who carry on crying and longing to be on Earth! It would be silly to want that, because there is indeed <u>nothing in the Earthly, material world of equal merit to what there is here</u>; though of course on the subject of affection and love, there are those we love and have left behind…but we know we shall see them again.

So, as I was told, it is of no use crying here, as all we then do is get ourselves depressed and envelop our surroundings with a gloomy cloud. Moreover it does not help those you want to help and whom you are crying for! That's why I understood perfectly there was only one solution - to stop weeping, think of you all with love and send it to you constantly in order to assist you. Also I want to learn as much as possible in order to be able to tell you about it as often as feasible…

April 2004 - Guide advises us to think positively about Dave's condition, to help him by surrounding him with positive energy.

21st April 2004 - *Poor Dave has his third endoscopy and metallic stent put in. My guide comes first to help the link, then says Mum is waiting to speak to me. He advises me to listen and not interrupt her:*

Mum here Sweetheart. I'll talk to you without stopping as I was told, so as not to make you lose the thread of the conversation. Quite some time ago, I think I was able to speak to you during your meeting, but I didn't have time to say much so I'll say more now. There are 'days' when I no longer know how long I have been in this 'new country', as it feels to me I have been here for ages in a way. I thought you might like to know what happened recently to me, Dad etc. My friends took me towards areas where one can see what others do, without us disturbing them. There are '<u>places' where people learn to do more complicated things</u>, but we cannot interrupt them, we can only watch or listen to what they are doing.

BR- Give me an example please?

There are all sorts of things. When they want to do stuff with their hands, they do it and it feels a little like on Earth - they use objects to create something. But when they use their Mind, it's even more extraordinary. We <u>see them concentrate and we see the object appear</u>, gradually stronger and more 'solidified' let's say! They have fun making things come just for the pleasure of it and it feels strange to see this 'from the outside' in a way, since it is not us making it appear, it's them. So it looks like magic tricks! There is so much to do here if one wants to have fun or even learn, because this is to have fun as well as learning to do something new. The people around me are so likeable, one can't grow tired of them, you know! There never are any boring moments with them; they dedicate themselves to help me and a few others too who are learning like me... But we do not have the impression of being at school. We are more like in good company, listening to some discussions or taking part in learned and very interesting conversations! I have often told you this. So, I have fun.

Yet I have to say we all must understand how to use the power of thought. It's incredible how effective it is and how it always works. There is no reason why it would not work on Earth, since we come here with the same Mind and ideas we had on Earth! All that is needed is to apply it with even more fervour and desire, then it really should be a success. The study of this 'power of thought' is getting fascinating indeed, I intend to try to delve more into it ... There is so much to do, yet the very fact of thinking and making things happen is ever so easy! I don't see why we do not use it better when we are on Earth!

My dad told me that when he first arrived here (long ago, I suppose), there were moments when he had difficulties doing it and coping, because at times he doubted he would succeed. But his mother and his friends showed him he had nothing to fear, as one can only succeed if one wants to succeed. All one has to do is tell oneself one is going to do it, create it, see it (what one wants to do, create, see etc.)...and indeed it happens! He doubted because, like anyone using reasoning at first, one thinks: "It's impossible for me to manage it; there'll be some obstacles, some problems..." *(I must have lost my concentration as there is a short silence. Then I hear the following)*

We should have been able to carry on more easily, it's quite difficult if we are interrupted, isn't it?! Most of my friends have the same goal: Making us understand that business, that project rather, of the use of Thought, so that all goes well when one wants something. All we have to do is think of it positively and assuredly.

They keep saying: "You simply need to tell yourself:

I want this to happen/ to come/ to leave/ to disappear." The fact is, everything you wish will take place. You mustn't have any doubt, as it <u>will</u> happen! Haven't you had many a proof? So why doubt?

What matters is that you should do it often, so that you do not get out of the habit of doing it automatically. This world here is <u>a world of Thought, where Thought reigns- you must use it in the same way as you use the air around yourself to breathe on Earth without thinking about it.</u> The 'air' here is 'Thought' in a way! One must get used to not thinking of it as something separate, one must understand it is an integral part of ourselves, one must not doubt it but use it as much as possible, to do one's best to improve results by thinking in a more precise and well-defined way.

It is intriguing and interesting, that's why I wanted to talk to you about it my Darling. I reckoned it may intrigue and fascinate you too. Dad (mine but yours does too!) often says to me: "Do not doubt! Just do what is suggested to you to save yourself time. If you doubt what those with experience tell you, all you do is delay yourself, don't you? Do what they say, then reserve for yourself the right to argue <u>afterwards</u>, if it does not work... But fortunately it is not possible to make mistakes if we do as we are told! The only thing which holds us back is the thought 'I can't, it's impossible', as that does block! But if one understands one cannot fail when one applies the rule 'Be positive!', then it works..."

(I was struggling to keep my eyes open and was beginning to doze off, so I apologised to Mum and switched off the light to go to sleep. Throughout May I tried to tune in 3 times but kept losing my concentration).

8th June 2004 - *During home circle. The pen starts in French unexpectedly:*

Your Friends' Spirits are beautiful to watch. They are

457

all relaxed and their individual 'Lights' shine. My mum used to keep telling me one must try to see people's mind through and beyond their body, in order to know them inside rather than externally. That's true, it is what matters.

BR- Who is talking to me?

Mum of course Darling, yes, it's me. What I am studying at the moment is to see people's Mind through their outer envelope. They try to show themselves from a certain angle, but their true Self is in their thoughts - their <u>thoughts are reflected in and by their shining Spirit</u>. If one did not see this, one could be caught out and believe what they try to project! Therefore I am learning to see them in a different way. Their thoughts are visible when they express them, yet they sometimes try to hide the truth by saying something but thinking something else...

BR- Do you mean in Spirit World?

Yes, here of course. I cannot see Earth people as easily. But I do see your friends gathered as a group *(in my room)* - they have a brilliant light which bathes you and them too so it creates a pretty effect. Their light is radiant and varies from blue to a kind of gold, it's golden. It's so beautiful to look at! I only see what is pointed out to me. Perhaps I might not have seen your friends properly if I had not been shown them more clearly.

BR- How was it done?

My friends here have ways of explaining things which then always seem easier when they are there too. Since I last spoke to you my life has carried on being more and more interesting. I have seen lots of people whom I knew before and analysed them, then I started doing those 'spirit light' experiments. It's a bit different from what I had done before. Now we are concentrating on the difference between what is said and what is really thought, in order to learn to see that difference indeed...

The effect a thought can have is incredible! If we realised the scope and impact of thoughts, we would never dare think in public and as importantly in private, because *thoughts move, travel, spread, multiply and mix with others' thoughts.* They have therefore much bigger an influence than one has ever realised or imagined! As for me, I used to think thoughts were personal things which remained within the very depths of oneself...well I was entirely mistaken, wasn't I? In the end it's always the same thing - one must be aware of one's slightest thoughts, so as not to risk doing some harm, to reveal oneself without realising and not to influence others in an unexpected way! Apart from that, one can do what one wants, ha ha!.. My problem is not to hide what I think, since I do not really think anything unpleasant; it's more constantly asking myself whether all this stuff is true, all those extraordinary things I am constantly shown at every turn!

During a meeting with friends 'the other day' I noticed I was thinking 'aloud' so to speak, because the others knew what I was thinking and kept answering and commenting on facts I was secretly thinking! At first I was surprised they were so 'psychic'. Then I laughed at myself when I realised I was thinking and saying daft things. Of course, here we do see people's thoughts, therefore they can see mine; of course they are psychic, they live in the 'Spirit World'! So, those are my little adventures. I indeed never grow weary of discovering or delving deeper into the little details they have fun making me pay attention to.

BR- Good. How is my dad? Please give him a hug and kisses from me. (But unexpectedly, it's my guide who replies straight away!)

All is well with your father, my friend. You have to be patient with him as he has reached quite a high level of understanding now, he is deeply involved in grasping the workings and mechanics of what makes atoms visible on Earth.

459

He knows one can see them, but he wants to learn and know how they can become visible from having first been some kind of vibration. Therefore he is learning all this at a higher level of understanding, which cannot be explained in words of everyday language for you or your mother to understand. It has nothing to do with either of you not being intelligent enough of course! It is because the knowledge acquired means it is felt and experienced, rather than worked out in words and symbols and formulas, you see? So the work your father does now has some more significance and depth, which will be difficult to analyse and explain at times…but that should be sufficient for you to know that he has progressed and is progressing. He is doing some things he is really very interested in and may talk of to you one day. But it will be less clear to you than it is to him, you understand?

Lots of love and affection emanate from both your parents; you must realise this and understand they'll never stop loving or caring for you ever! But they will have to go on and learn more for their own sake and progress; that may mean that at times they won't always be able to talk about it or even have 'time' to talk to you if they are in the middle of something deep and intricate. All the time they'll still send good, positive, loving thoughts towards you all, but perhaps there will be no words, whereas the love will still reach you. Do you understand?

BR- Yes, of course, perfectly.

You can rejoin your friends now, we'll talk to you later again.

15th June 2004 - *During home circle:*

Mum is here. I have the impression that the only time I can talk to you is when you are with your small group! It's not a problem but it's a nuisance if we are interrupted… I've made good progress I reckon, as when I do something I often get

460

congratulated now! So I must be managing things which are perhaps a bit more difficult than what I used to do before?.. During one of our previous conversations I described experiences I had when talking to people who had not understood what I think I have grasped.

Around you there are scores of people who wish to help you, you know. The beauty of the loving kindness of those people here, who look after you, is wonderful to observe. My own friends told me your friends (in my world) are very special. They have lots of knowledge to pass on to you, to share with you and they wait for you to be able to give them more time alone, them and you.

The beauty of Spiritual knowledge is even more beautiful and exciting than knowledge of Earthly things such as geography, biology, even history. (Me who loved history so much!) To be by the side of those who are more knowledgeable than you is a pleasure hard to outdo!

Whereas I used to believe that one would know everything on any subject simply by reading a book, I did not think or realise there was so much to know, discover and accumulate and assimilate if one wished to... The knowledge of my and your friends would fill thousands, millions of Earthly books! You would forever have to type them if you were writing them down after receiving them from here! So perhaps you'd need to find a bit more time for us from time to time?..

Freedom of choice is what they teach me most here recently, on top of other details. This is what Earth people do not understand - they have the freedom to do what they want. They chose to do what they want. When they arrive on Earth, they are shown the type of life they could have if they want to achieve a particular goal, but they are not obliged to follow it. They have the choice to have other ideas and try other experiences and even to get weary of some... They can even come back here without having finished what they intended to learn

461

in the first place! But it's rather a waste of time, in my opinion, if they have to go back to being a child and start again growing up in order to learn a particular type of experience! Instead of reincarnating at once, I reckon one should first learn more what one must do or can do here, then, when one has understood it properly, one could go to Earth to explain it to Earthlings to help them improve themselves? Perhaps I am wrong, as this is just me saying I think it might be a good idea...

The main reason for being on Earth is to learn; learn and practise what one should know how to do naturally. My recent life on Earth does not appear very interesting seen from here, but I suppose I learnt lots of things I needed to grasp. Here it is different. It seems to me I learn far more, nearly in a flash! That's because it is pleasurable rather than a job or an exercise one must to do.

It took me some time to acclimatise myself and get used to this strange new environment and those 'weird ideas' which, in my opinion, they seemed to have when I arrived. Now I do understand them better and it is much more interesting to have made 'the first discoveries' in order to be able to grasp the rest. I'll talk to you again later about the good times in my life here.

19th June 2004 -

Mum here Darling. At last I find you at home and not in a group! We had not finished our conversation last time. I wanted to tell you about my little adventures. When I had tried to explain to 'my new arrivals' that I had been here for some time but not as long as my other friends, they wondered and asked me why it made a difference. I wished to make them understand I did not have as much knowledge, as I didn't want them to imagine I knew everything there probably is to know! My aim was just to help them to become acclimatised and to make them comprehend one can become happy here, once one has understood what there is to do and not to do.

My friends congratulated me for coping so well with the newcomers, so I assume I must have helped them well. This is my new role of 'pupil becoming a teacher', as I told you. My 'adventures' are not extraordinary in themselves, it's simply the fact that I have fun seeing myself helping people, whereas not so long ago it was me who was helped...and who is still being helped! But I now do more 'internal' stuff, let's say. I no longer need to deal with making things, but rather making myself understand how one feels at different levels of thinking.

When we think of joyful or sad things, it makes a difference in the 'vibrations', I was told. Because of this, the sensations are really different, a fact we know on Earth, I am aware of that, but the very fact of feeling happy creates emanations round oneself. Similarly, if one is sad or unhappy it changes the surroundings, that is what I learnt to grasp...if I change the environment for myself, I change it for others here too! So it's not fair if people around me are made sad or unhappy just because I am! On the other hand, if I make them happy by being happy myself, it does them good so that's fine!

Personally, I knew it when I was told not to cry for having left you, as I was surrounding myself with sadness and fog and it was really true indeed! Now we are going a bit more deeply on the effect of my thoughts on these other people, and that's what I do at the moment. Life around me is still the same as before, but the moment I feel happy (as we often are here anyway), joy shows itself as rays of joy, of light which come out of me towards others!

BR- How come you had not realised this before?

Joy is the best thing to notice, because the light is brilliant but also 'lively' I could say. Joy makes me think of multi-coloured rays of sunshine. We do not see them in one colour here; it's in lots of colours of all kinds. Sometimes colours I had never seen before! In fact being aware of other people's

463

joy around oneself is like seeing lots of 'suns' shining without being dazzling, but suns made of gems, gorgeous reflections of all colours, superb radiations! The beauty of all this appears normal when one is used to it because we do not hide anything from one another. Sorrow and sadness which could be felt are displayed in grey, in thick clouds or mists. That is why no one wants to feel this here, because it is really unpleasant to have that around and we would be embarrassed to impose it on others...

The last time I saw sad people was when I welcomed newcomers. Their <u>sadness was oozing and spreading out of them; we had to gather together to create a wall of cheerful and pleasant thoughts to try to help them</u>! Our happy thoughts enveloped them and supported them but we had to talk to them too, because their grief was, unfortunately, very real, as I understand very well since I too am still very miserable to have left and abandoned you, but there was nothing else I could do. So now I try to help you from here by loving you with strong, positive thoughts... The friends here did everything they could to help me. Therefore I would like to do the same for poor people coming from Earth, deeply unhappy to have gone away as they left behind loads of family, friends but also animals.

My sadness softened a little when I saw all my animals from before; my cats and even the dogs we used to have at my mum's - she also loved small dogs. I've always had animals at home, that's why they came to me when I arrived; it felt so good to see them again here.

The strangest thing was when I saw again my big bear from Algiers, as I told you. That indeed was a great surprise which caught me unawares; I really did not expect it! He's been so good and loving. It was amusing to watch him ambling around, not bothered about anything, yet no one appeared amazed or afraid to see him wandering! He had come to me to say 'hello and welcome' no doubt, and I suppose also 'thank you' for his sardines during the war. He must have suffered ever so much, poor boy, in his horrid cage of wood and metal without anything to eat for probably a very long time. He must have blessed me, in his own way, each time he saw me. So there we are: My good old bear recognised me, remembered and waited for me here! That was one of the most beautiful moments here, apart from seeing your dad, my dad and Mum and knowing them to be fine, alive, pain free...and me too, brand new!

It was worth the trouble of making the 'Great Extraordinary Trip'!.. But the grief and pain to have lost you cannot be calculated; it is immense, atrocious, that's all I can say... Darling you really should sleep now, you look worn out. I'll leave you in peace so that you can rest. I love you, my Sweetheart and shall talk again soon, I hope.

26th June 2004 - *5 years today since Mum's departure. I wonder whether she is really aware of the length of her absence from us. The pen starts slowly in 'Automatic'. I hope it is Mum but it writes in English, so it's my guide:*

Make the most of it, we know you are in a hurry today. We'll reply to your question then. Your mother is well and happy, actually learning ever so much for her level: she does well indeed. She has 'absorbed' whole books of knowledge to speed up her advancement here. We told you before that she'd be leaving now and then for higher realms, to acquaint herself with more elaborate techniques of progression and we would be sorry if you felt she'd left you or abandoned you. She has not and is terribly fond of you all. Only <u>she's got to progress for her own good</u>, you understand.

So we'll answer your question: The 'Time' subject is quite tricky and complex here since we don't need time. You'll have to say to yourself that when you are happy somewhere, you don't watch the clock, all the more when you don't want

465

your pleasurable activities to stop. So, we don't watch either time or clocks. Yet the feeling of 'Time' can be construed as a feeling of passing events, so if we know an event took place before another one, then we know that it is a 'past' event...

To help you understand how she feels about her passing over 'so many years ago', you'd have to take into account the fact that she's learnt and learnt as much as she could all the time and that makes 'time' feel different, because when you are active and busy and your Mind is occupied, it feels as if no 'time' has passed at all or hardly. So this is our opinion: She won't feel as if it's been so many years exactly. It will only feel like a huge mountain of information has been built within her, to help her grasp all there is to grasp for the time being. Entering a <u>new level of understanding</u> implies knowing a lot of new facts and <u>learning to feel differently within yourself</u>. You have to look at facts and new knowledge in a different light, because others are presenting them to you in such a way you feel it is true and yet you could not have grasped that on your own...

Let's take for example a fact that you knew out of a book: When you read it, it looks ok, acceptable, familiar maybe. But when you see it acted, lived, felt with feelings, it may feel totally different. An event is never really an event unless and until it is felt as an emotional aspect of Life.

BR- (Rather puzzled) Did I hear this correctly? Could you repeat it please?

Yes. <u>An event is only a true event once you've felt it as an emotional act and action.</u> You need to feel the emotion side of it to <u>understand why it is taking place</u>, because <u>it is the emotions and the thoughts behind it which have given it life and power</u>.

So, no event is completely understood until the emotional side and aspects of its creation is grasped and understood. Then it will be seen under its own true light. Then but only then, can it be understood. Having said that, we need to let your mum have a few words before you go away. We know you have business to attend to...

...Mum here. Poor Sweetheart, I am told you are very busy and will have to leave soon.

BR- Are you aware of Time? Do you know how long ago you left?

Just a moment... My darling daughter, you have aged a lot and I have become younger! We may not recognise each other! No, I am joking, you are right, we don't need a calendar to think of each other, but I must admit I don't really know how long I have been here. I know it must be quite a while but am not sure how many years, unless I asked someone who knows how to do 'conversions' of Time.

BR (Amazed) What! How do they do that?

There are people who seem to know how many years they've spent here. Personally I have never paid attention to it...because I do not think it is of any importance...

BR- You have no idea at all?

No, not really.

BR- Do you want me to tell you?

Yes, if you wish.

BR- 5 years today. It was in 1999. I am told you've learnt a tremendous amount since!..

Well, I would never have guessed! 5 years, that's a long time, yet short too... I do have the impression to have been here much longer in one way, perhaps in another way not as long...difficult to say!

(I explained to Mum I have to go and fetch a hire van, to drive it to Leeds to help Jim with his house move, which is why I have to hurry now. The pen starts again after a short silence, in English!)

She is saying: "Make sure all is well on the road. Don't take any risks". We are helping with the link; she has trouble getting on line again.

467

BR- Did she understand what I told her?

Yes, she got the message about you and your son, so all is well, she knows what you said. "He's passed his degree and she is proud of him and of you for being his mum", she says. She is "proud of all of you in fact" she added. You have to go so we'll let you leave. "Make sure he knows of her love for him", she says. "We love you all, she adds. We love you all, don't forget, never ever forget it!"

6th July 2004 - *The pen started the first words, in French:*

We don't chat often Sweetheart... You may come as often as you like, you know

BR- Am sorry... Whenever I tuned in, one of my Spirit Teachers calling himself 'River Man' came to pass on his knowledge and dictate a 'Wisdom' book!..

Yes I know, you've been receiving information from someone highly evolved here who is teaching you very interesting facts apparently. I'll have to ask them what it is, for it to prevent you from talking to me!

BR- I am very sorry, but I have so much to do, as well as having Dave ill!

Don't worry Darling. I know how difficult it is for you to find some free time, but do try whenever you can, you are always welcome!

BR- You are too!

My life here has not changed much but I have had more and more interesting experiences. If you like I can tell you a little about it. My friends here managed to make me see things I had not seen before - periods in history I did not know. Since history has always interested me I really enjoyed being able to do this.

The first journey they made me do was during the era of the 'Rois Fainéants', the later Merovingian kings. I had never understood why they were labelled 'idle' or why they wanted to be kings! But it seems to me they were obliged, rather than wanted, to rule! That is what pushed them not to do any good for their country. All they were thinking about was their own pleasure and they did not deal with governing France.

On the other hand, when I saw the times of the Revolution when everyone wanted to be right to the extent of assassinating each other, I did realise how wrong they all were - because murders do not lead to anything in the end! You get rid of the person, but you do not get better results because the sinister thoughts you have and are surrounded with, keep circulating around yourself and sending you even more sinister or negative thoughts! It's a bad bath into which one dives more deeply without being able to get out!

Much better to have a good 'religious revolution', meaning 'thinking more spiritually'. That is to say - not wanting to kill, wanting to explain instead. To discuss things and explain oneself would be a better solution than murdering each other... The efforts my friends here make to explain all that to me is incredible! They do their utmost to show me all kinds of things and events, they explain patiently.

They realise that politics and history used to interest me, because I used to think if one knows one's country well, one would behave better... Obviously it has not always led to that... They tell me here that what matters is to grasp the other person's point of view before wanting to kill him. It is not easy when one is on Earth, I do realise that. I myself did or thought things 'in the wrong direction', in their opinion.

But if one realises that the other person (whatever their origins) whom one is fighting or one hates, has chosen this Earthly life to learn something, then one must think I too have done the same thing, therefore we are both in the process of learning something. Why are we fighting?!

469

As for me, I used to 'hate' some Arabs because they made us lose Algiers and our belongings etc., but if I'd had my friends from here show me the right path, I would have perhaps seen that those Arabs had their own ideas too. Of course it was not all the Arabs - there were some kind ones like Messaouda. But those who made war had ideas which should have been discussed more in depth and earlier, instead of fighting straight away?..

BR- I say! You talking like that is astonishing!

My point of view has not changed much, as I do think they did us some harm personally...and those criminals murdered a lot of poor innocent people who were kind and had not done any harm! Yet I do grasp the 'ideal and spiritual principle' which would be a good thing if one could impose it on Earth! But when will that be? I do wonder!

9th July 2004 - *08.30 hrs! The pen starts with loops then writes the first words in French:*

You are calm, we hear each other better. It's Mum, Darling. Now that you are here for me, I'll make the most of it! I wanted to tell you I am ever so pleased you found someone from 'my side' who can explain to you complex things which I could not do, because I know how much you love learning new stuff.

My life here is less 'exciting' than before, as I simply go further into what I learnt or am learning, but it does not mean it is not a good life... It is always great not to suffer any more. In my opinion it is the main thing, after being in pain for so long! Now I realise the physical body is only a tool, a vehicle to move about, we should be able to get rid of it and replace it, like we do with a car!

My life is as before, I spend most of my time with the friends. I am not always with them because they have other things to do, I guess, and me too. I do enjoy strolling in the garden here or do the exercises they suggest or 'read' their books, but as you know, they are not really books like I had before, on Earth.

It is a way to concentrate in order to see things one did not know. It appears like a kind of film within oneself! It's very strange yet always very interesting...

Most of the time I 'look within' as they say. These are exercises one must do regularly apparently, to know who we really are, because <u>the mother I am to you and the boys is not the only personality I have been or will be</u>, so I am told! Therefore the 'Real Me' exists inside all that! To find it, I must sit quietly and <u>look for it</u> within the shambles of my thoughts.

I reckon everybody should do this, since, whether one is here or on the Earth, this 'Real Me' is always hidden within oneself... When one loses one's flesh body, it must be easier to calm down a little as there are no distractions from the physical world, no bodily pain or discomfort. But the very fact of listening within to find my 'Whole Self' is very intriguing indeed! Last time I was made to do this together with some friends, *I realised that the woman I thought I was, is only one facet of several personalities whom I am or was.* There were so many aspects, it was weird to think all those were me! I saw it as if it was a kaleidoscope and they told me: "All that is you, but you only recognise one side at the moment, because you've come from it very recently. Once you have done more exercises and tried to know yourself better, you will see that *the basic, fundamental personality which is the 'Real You' will look like a multifaceted diamond".*

So one has to 'find oneself again' to understand properly who one is, because it is frustrating to imagine oneself as only one person when in fact one is more than that, isn't it!

I saw, once or twice, another person I was. I saw that 'woman' whom I did not know at all...yet who seemed very familiar! It was someone else but it was also me! Very weird to observe! The fact I do these exercises does not mean I shall no longer see myself as your own mum, you know! I shall carry on loving you all and not forget you, I am certain. But I am told to do them, so it must be useful to advance and understand more.

Perhaps you should try to do it too, if you have time? It may teach you more things which you don't know about yourself? Also it will save you a lot of time when you come here... We'll then have more time together if you have already done your 'homework' on Earth!

The way they teach us here is wonderful. They do not appear to give you a lecture, yet just by chatting, we realise we are learning more and more and always discover something new, or else they explain a point I was not grasping well earlier.

It's marvellous to always get an answer from someone who knows more than you and personally I know very little here! They are all aware that we must want to learn a lot, so they put themselves to our/my service when we wish it or when they think it would be a good thing. There is no time wasting, we always do useful and pleasant things, it's great! I must say that talking with them is one of my favourite occupations! They are all so kind and are so knowledgeable...

There are different people. They look 'normal' you know, like Earth people, but as soon as we talk to them, we realise their great knowledge is far wider than we would think. They always have something intelligent to say. Or, since they can read our thoughts (in the same way as we can feel/see theirs), they often have the answer to what I was just going to ask them, before I do it! That's quite amusing! So I don't often have questions to ask, since they've replied to it before I start thinking to formulate one! There is so much to discuss, so much to marvel at, so much to understand! There must be enough to last an eternity I reckon...

Yet I must also do my 'exercises'. It's of no use to learn

one 'should' do such things to improve oneself, yet not practise it, is it! So I have to stroll towards water, the lake, the rivers, the gardens and other beautiful places I have here. I don't always need to actually move of course. I can just think of it and it takes me there at once, I see myself there! That way I have a peaceful and serene place where I feel good. I then can go deeper into what I've just heard or practise as much as possible if I can manage it. Sometimes it's difficult to know how to do things well. So, as soon as I say to myself: "Blast! I can't manage it!" someone appears at my side as if he knew I had a problem... Obviously he must know it, but this instantaneous transmission of thought feels strange!

There are always pleasant things to do, no more chores, nightmares, worries...what a happy place! It is Paradise indeed for me...and no work either, unless one wants some! Those who wish to do what I would call 'work', do it for the pleasure of it, so they can't complain! Some do gardening or build houses or buildings to welcome other people, because newcomers to this world need to find themselves 'somewhere'.

BR- Do they build by hand or by using Thought power?

There are different ways to do it here. If they want to have fun building brick by brick, they will do it 'by hand'. They imagine they have bricks and they give themselves the work to build brick by brick! But if they know how to use their thoughts, they visualise the building, imagine it complete and it appears! The longer they think of it and put finishing touches to it, the longer it will stay for those who need or will need it. There are always people who enjoy doing things like that.

Personally I prefer learning and learning about myself, I mean to get to know myself, since I discovered I am not really acquainted with that unknown Me, hidden within for such a long time and whom I didn't know existed somewhere 'over there'! It feels strange to go and search for one's 'Lost Me'. (Nearly like Marcel Proust's title, *'The Search for Lost Time'* isn't it?!). But do make a note that I don't lose and never have lost or wasted my time!

BR- Yes I know, you were right to do so! So, happy search!

Next time I speak with you I hope I shall have found someone interesting within me, to tell you about which of my 'facets' I have met! But it could perhaps be awful of course, who knows!

BR- That would surprise me!

I have already seen one or two individuals but there are more I am sure. So we'll be able to gather them all, piece and 'paste' together that final 'parcel' in order to see what it ends up as!

BR- Ask your friends about the interesting topics my Spirit communicator, 'River Man', dictates to me, about the creation of the world…

It will be worth writing books about the adventure of your feats in acquiring spiritual knowledge; why don't you do it too?

BR- Did you understand what I have just told you?

Of course I have heard what you said! That is why between what I recount to you about my life and what you learn from elsewhere, there will be plenty enough to fill lots of books!

BR- I do hope so!

My friends told me you have a <u>very</u> good teacher from here, who has started to tell you fascinating facts and you'll never be bored with it, as you love it! So they seem to be right, don't they? You must keep going, you must not give up! It is always useful to learn more, if one progresses by seeing further than one did before.

Darling I shall let you get on now as you are bound to have things to do. But I am very glad you came to talk to me. I feel happier when you do so and we have been able to share each other's lives… We feel closer that way.

BR- Do you know about Jim getting a job as a recording engineer in a big recording studio in Wales? I hope you heard me properly?

Of course I did understand. You explained to me what your Jim does. I am very pleased for him and proud of him, tell him! He tried so hard to succeed, it feels good to know he is more settled now. If he's happy, that's all that matters in the end, isn't it?

All my love and kisses Sweetheart. I wish you all a good day and life until you and I talk again. Your mum who always loves you.

BR- I am proud of you Darling Mum! You are doing so well!

***

CHAPTER 11
Spirit warning - Floating above bed - Spirit 'video' of funeral - Dave speaks from Beyond

13th July 2004 - *Unexpectedly, during the home practice circle. The pen starts slowly, making loops, then words are shaped, in French:*

Grandma here, my granddaughter. You are my granddaughter! I lived on Earth a long time ago, yet I did not really get to know you because you were very young. You've spoken to me since, however we were not able to talk of anything else but the matter which preoccupied you at the time (*She's referring to baby Angélique*).

Now all that is solved, I would like to tell you <u>I often look after you</u>! I am near you when you have worries or when you think of cats and animals, because I love them too, just like you. I have always loved animals and I am so happy you do! I was always close to you, in order to encourage you, when you had problems or when you were making efforts or doing difficult things. This is why I would like you to know I am often near you...

BR- Thank you ever so much! You are very kind. Please tell me more about yourself?

My life here is very different from the one I had on Earth. I had a good rest after arriving here as I wanted to be able to tackle this new environment with a clear mind. <u>I had been so scared of dying that I had to rest for some time in order to recover from the fear and the pain</u>, because I had been very ill before leaving the Earth. I was wrong to be afraid, as everyone had looked after me well when I arrived here- there were lots of people to welcome me. My husband had, unfortunately, passed over before me, that's why I was so unhappy on Earth after his departure. My daughter had obviously not gone yet (My second daughter of course - I know that you are aware the first one was already here).

476

So the arrival was not too hard or shocking because I saw again all my family and friends, but my father and mother, though present, were more distant than I was hoping... Perhaps because we had that terrible business between us all throughout my life and I had told them I would hate them forever?! But they were there when I arrived, without doing much more. We did see each other later on, then gradually we understood there was no longer any need for arguments or hatred, since the solution to this problem had long been found! But it had indeed caused a break between us - we had to learn to repair it gradually. Now it's done and we have a more normal relationship. Yet we each go and do what we want at our own level of thinking.

BR- What do you do and learn?

When I arrived I didn't know much about this life here, because I had never been before! But I was helped to understand gradually everything one can do by concentrating. I learnt fast, as I wanted to be able to achieve what I was shown! My mother had told me (when on Earth) that if one could live happily in Paradise, one would never have to work or do anything whatsoever! I think she was wrong in a way - there were and there are heaps of things to do! But it is not work in the sense of 'work'. They are interesting activities that teach you new stuff.

I did my best to learn as much as possible to be able to cope. Then I learnt to no longer worry about the Earth, as I was concerned about our 'Suzon' whom I'd left alone, so far away, to struggle with life. She had been perfectly capable to do what she had to before and will certainly be able to do so afterwards. But it was worrying to know one's child is alone on Earth when she has problems.

My life here is comfortable now. I only do pleasant things. I learnt to use the power of thought to travel and to talk to others. I know one can make things come simply by thinking of it! We have many animals around us here, if we love them,

477

so all this suits me! I look after them a lot as some arrive, feeling rather lost when passing from one world to the other...I help reassure them when they arrive, so that they understand they have nothing to fear.

BR- What do you do for that?

They arrive terrified sometimes, so what is needed is to calm them down. I hug them and kiss them, receive them, give them something to eat so that they feel like on Earth. Then gradually they learn all they have to do is make a wish for it to happen. My friends here taught me how to speak to them by thinking of them and communicating... *(Just then my cat Princess interrupted us and I was unable to tune in again afterwards).*

21st July 2004 - *During the weekly home practice group. While I was trying to transmit 'messages' for the group members, I unexpectedly received one myself directly, in French!:*

Léonie Moleux present! Wishing to speak with her granddaughter once more...I'd like to tell you our last conversation *(8 days ago!)* had been very interesting in my opinion, as I had not often done this kind of communication before. Now I am getting a taste for it! I find it amusing to be able to link up with the Earth and not be harmed by it. The 'publicity' (let's call it) done by the Church on this subject was so bad and baneful that I had always been wary of it...but I realise now it was nonsense and one cannot believe their labelling it as 'bad and doom'.

So I come back to the fact that I am delighted to be able to talk to you. You have always been my favourite little one in a way, as you are my second daughter's daughter. My second daughter was always a good child and a good mother in spite of all her setbacks. So I do love you, without having had the joy to know you well when I was amongst you all, as we lived so far away. Then I left myself to come over and rejoin my husband Léon. Now we are all together here and there are lots of things to do as your mum has told you, I think. I realise I have not explained properly what I do during my 'free time'. I have a lot of free time here, there is no compulsory work, but if one wishes to learn something new, there are always opportunities and new avenues.

I have been here a 'long time' in Earthly terms, but it took me quite a while to get acclimatised. I simply wanted to rest at the beginning. I did not want to think deeply or try anything new.

Now that I am well settled, I have learnt to look after those needing help. The mind of a child or of an animal is the same in a way. They are all young, loving and ready to love you and be loved. Yet some have suffered so much on Earth that when they arrive here, they are very frightened and are still trying to escape those who attacked them! Therefore I do like to welcome them and show them they can be loved without being harmed. As they gradually settle here, they are shown they can have fun and trust those they meet. I talk to the children but also to the animals. <u>Both need to regain their trust</u> in other people as their Souls have been so hurt, sometimes they take a long time to trust again: they are scared to be injured or attacked...

You have some photos of me, haven't you? It is such a pity we cannot recall when we met while on Earth, but never mind. You know me a little and I know you more in fact, as I had news of you as a child from your mum. Finally I came here <u>and I started obtaining some information about you and yours</u> of course, when I realised one could do it fairly easily!

My life here was still agitated at the beginning, because my Earthly life was filled with worries and also lots of regrets since the departure of my first little one who never had the love of her real mum. That is what I regretted all my life, you see.

479

Therefore 'my inside' was always very restless and perturbed, even if I appeared happy on the outside.

My arrival here changed a lot of things and finally I got used to this new environment. My little one was here when I arrived and for a long time I never left her side in order to catch up with what I had lost. My love for my little girl had never diminished and I needed to show her and let her know I had not really abandoned her, certainly not willingly!

So there we are. Now that I am free from my problems of conscience and worries, I would like to help you more with your life, if I can do anything there.

BR- It's very kind of you Grandma. What do you suggest?

Your children have grown up, haven't they? There will now be less concern on that score, I am told. They will find their path and will have good and interesting lives. You will need more time for your work with our information and your mum who is dictating a book, if I understand correctly.

BR- That's correct.

My friends here tell me you wish to publish all this information. This goal is commendable but you will perhaps have problems being accepted sometimes. There will be days when life will appear harder than before, because the public does not always know what is good for them!

"We shall do our best from here", they say. "But you will need a lot of courage and trust in yourself and us here". This is the message I pass on to you. You will need the strength to face the public if people criticise you, but there will not be any catastrophe, do not worry, everything will go well...

My darling granddaughter, may I call you so? I would love to be your 'guide' in the sense of guardian of your working life. You have decided to help others with your knowledge and I would like to help you say what is needed when necessary.

BR- Many thanks! What exactly?

Earthly people's opinion is not always correct, sometimes

they have twisted ideas. So I would like to help you prove to them they are wrong!

BR- How? Through teaching, or by passing on 'messages' from Spirit?

Let us do it, we'll help you and there will be plenty of work for you. You will start wanting to help people on Earth but we shall help you from here. *(I asked her for more precise details as to the kind of help, but the reply came at once in English! Therefore my guide must have stepped in).*

Putting words in your mouth will be the first step and then we'll help you guide them towards their own goal. You can give them proof of our existence by being yourself and letting them know we are here. Let us work with and for you, it will happen easily, you'll see. Try and trust us and you'll see all will fall into place.

BR- It is important I can pass on evidential messages ...

Let us do the work through you. You'll be pleased with the result. You can rest assured we'll help you do as you suggest. We'll tell you more later. You'll be able to do as asked but you have to work more at it...

27th July 2004 - *The pen makes a few loops then words come in French. It's Mum:*

The problem is always the lack of peaceful time for communication. It is necessary to be calm for it to be a success! Put yourself in our place and realise how much effort we need to put into it so that it works if we have to cross some fog and a storm at the same time! That's what it feels like...

The last time we spoke, Darling, it was to tell you I had encountered different people and those I met had not had the same experiences as I had. I would like to expand on this. They had been here much longer than me, yet they know less than I do concerning the seeing from a distance, travelling into the past and perhaps even the future (though I do not have much

481

experience with that and it is more difficult). They surprised me as I used to think everyone learnt the same things at the same rate, at the same stage of their stay. I would say to myself: "The longer one is here, the more one learns." Not so! There are some people who don't bother to try to acquire any new knowledge. They are quite content to keep doing the same things as they've always done! My friends here explained to me it is the desire to learn which makes you progress here. The more you want to know, the more you will be told and be helped to experience or understand. As for me I like nothing better than learning, not only because it is interesting, but it allows me to tell you things you probably did not know about. Anyway, even if you knew it, it is a confirmation of what you learnt or read elsewhere, isn't it? As I actually live it now and so do Dad and all the others here...

BR- Do you know your mum came to talk to me?

The moment you asked me your question, it made me lose the thread of what I was telling you...

BR- Oh, I am so sorry!

The best is to listen, not interrupt and wait till the end to ask a question.

BR- Ok I'll be more careful...

The thread is 'repairing itself' now... I was telling you I am glad to learn more and more because I can relay it to you. We shall publish this book, shan't we? Or at least you will. It will be great, successful, you'll see, because people will have something new and interesting to read. It is not every day one communicates with the 'Dead' and the Great Beyond and they relate everything they do there, is it?

My biggest pleasure is to be able to talk to you Darling, because you do realise, don't you, that I too have 'lost' you all, in a way?! I too grieve the 'death' of my family, because a 'death' is simply a long lasting parting. So that is what I endure! My life on Earth has been devoted to you, all the time and my life here now is for you too in a way - to tell you I am not 'dead' at all, nor is Dad! We are all in excellent health here, morally and 'physically', but not in the Earthy way. You have so much work to do yet I have so much to do to have fun somehow! It's not fair, is it? You will all *(my brothers and my children)* have to start to learn to listen like R-*(my nickname)* does. That way I shall be able to speak with all of you! If not, the next time I talk to you might be here when we are face to face! So you should really try to listen before that, shouldn't you?!?

3rd August 2004 - *In French. It's Mum:*

The pleasure of your company is always great Darling. Please do not deprive me of it, if you can avoid it - yet do not worry if you have not got the time, because I know how busy you must be!

I don't have much to tell you at the moment. I am still working on my little exercises of self-improvement. They say I need to do some more profound self-study in order to know myself better. It's not easy to do but it must make me concentrate on myself, as they tell me I have, like everyone else apparently, a big journey to do within myself to discover the 'Me' I do not know, that is to say, my Soul. It sounds very grand to say this, but that's what I was told to do!

I must say the idea to have oneself elsewhere seems bizarre in a way. I have not grasped all the explanations, but I can see <u>we are not simply what we think we are</u> - we have far <u>more scope</u> than that! <u>It must be</u> **what reincarnation and all that stuff is about,** because if one has many more aspects which we do not know, it must mean we have lived elsewhere and differently.

It amuses me to think I have been someone else on several occasions. This feels strange, when I tell myself I am Touky's, R-'s and Michou's Mum! But I have got to get used to it if I want to be a good pupil and manage to understand better what is taught here… Therefore I do my best to learn, so that I don't 'get told off ' (I was going to say!) but it's not true, we are not told off! We are surrounded with people with infinite and incredible patience. They never seem to get irritated or impatient, nothing appears to upset them. So why would I worry? *(Short silence then…)* Last time we spoke I think I told you I was shown tricks to make my life easier. I also saw <u>some people here who do not understand we all are 'Spirits' and we no longer have a solid flesh body</u>!.. We had to explain to them and make them grasp there was no longer any need to bother with the idea of a flesh body. We also informed them it is much better to comprehend this as soon as possible; that way we make our life easier and much more pleasant!

If I had worried like they are doing, I would not have enjoyed all the things which I had fun with. I would also have had far too much to do to be able to find the time and the peace needed in order to talk to you! We have to learn to relax and be very calm to <u>concentrate on one 'batch' of thoughts at a time</u>, but it's not always easy to concentrate when one has to do it for quite a long time.

So that is what I've got to show to the people who arrive here. This 'job' was suggested to me because I had noticed this fact myself. I was surprised they were not as happy as I am and were missing out on the discoveries I had made and still make now! Therefore I talk to them, explain things, we go for strolls together and chat. I am now doing something a little like what the others had done for me when I arrived here! We help each other you see, the more we learn ourselves, the more we can help others. It does us good to feel useful, especially when we know how miserable one is on arrival here, having left loved ones on Earth! The hardest moments have always been to remember the past and not being able to go back towards you, in order to be able to carry on loving you like before. To find a new way to help you is rather difficult when one has done it in a different way, if you see what I mean. There is so much difference between kissing someone physically and doing it 'mentally', isn't there!

So I have to learn this and get used to this new system. I suppose it must take some time but I comprehend how newcomers feel... They too have those problems and this inner wrench, they too want to be able to go back to kiss their relatives and tell them they still love them, even from this side of Life which carries on invisibly!

I put myself in their place because I do understand. We chat, I tell them what I have just been taught. If there is something I don't know well, I am helped at once as there are always helpers near me who can give a hand as soon as I have a little problem or some questions.

I know my helping other people already is strange, but I think I have been given this task to show me that what I learnt can indeed assist others and it had helped those who in turn gave me a hand when I arrived! Therefore, in a way, we are passing tips along and in the end it does everybody good. The impression it gives me is to be a teacher again. It's amusing. It's no longer of French or English but about experiments in a new world, which is invisible to my children and the 'Earthlings'.

I have to start explaining to those who arrive where I have just come from! It's very weird as I still feel like a novice yet I am asked to act as a tutor, whereas I think of myself as a beginner and not advanced enough for that role! However, I must admit I manage to talk to those newcomers. I make them understand we feel as we feel because our mind is turned towards the Earth as old ideas, regrets and thoughts don't leave you...

But if one manages to detach oneself from that and see things differently, by understanding we can no longer do things 'the old way' and why we must do them in another way, well, it begins to be clearer for them and for me too somehow, because by explaining to others, one also learns better oneself.

So, this is where I am up to with my 'work'. After this I don't know what they will invent again to make me 'progress' more! Now I'll say goodnight Darling, have a good rest to feel in better shape tomorrow and less stressed out or tired.

BR- How do you know I am or not?

You must be, so I am guessing! Lots of kisses from your mum.

21st September 2004 - *Last Sunday 19th, Dave had to go back to hospital for the fifth time! Today is my father's birthday - he would have been 101 yrs old...and tomorrow will be Mum's who would have been 96 yrs old. I remind them mentally, just in case... The pen starts in French at once:*

Oh indeed it would be far too old! Just picture being 100 years old or nearly - one must look awful! Imagine what kind of body one would have if one lived that long! As for me now, I do not live for my 'body', as you know. I am ignoring it completely because the body (of flesh of course) does not exist in reality. We <u>invent one</u> mentally and it appears as we've imagined it. Yet after a while, we realise <u>it is of no importance whatsoever to have a body</u>. It is just to feel 'right'. After all it's difficult to imagine oneself as a light!..

However I still see <u>some people here who think they have to look after their body</u> and go to bed and cook themselves meals! That is because they<u> have not understood that life here is very different</u> from the one they had on Earth. It's only a question of getting used to not thinking like on Earth.

(I briefly tell her Dave was in hospital and I spend most of my time there, as much as is allowed... As I relax deeper to listen better, it makes me doze off... I wake up one hour later, with the feeling of having had a long conversation during that

time, but nothing had been written of course. Retrospectively, I am sure Mum and 'all the others' will have done their best then to talk directly to my own Soul, to warn and prepare me for the impending tragedy…)

Thursday 23rd September - *Diagnosis of Dave's condition: The tumour has grown so much it blocks the stomach!*

Monday 27th September - *Surgeon Mr W. subjects Dave to an enormous and horrendous double by-pass of the stomach and gallbladder, declaring it is 'to enable him to eat'… A week later, Dave still cannot keep down any food whatsoever and often vomits a very dark liquid. An awful time for him, all the more as he is in the High Dependency Unit in York where he cannot sleep because of the noise from others around and the constant medical attention. Jim buys him a portable DVD player and lots of comic films to try to soften and brighten his dad's life, but sleep deprivation wears Dave out… In the end my poor husband begs the nurses to give him a private room, a rare thing for him to do as he is usually so reserved and modest! He had never been really ill in his life and never been in hospital!*

Friday 8th October - *Private room at last! But Dave is literally nailed to his bed, facing depressing bare walls, hooked on to all the tubes which need to drain, 24hours a day, the plasma flowing unceasingly from the horrendous wound cut right across his whole torso, a flow no one seems able to halt! The operation was useless - he is still totally unable to eat and is as skinny as the prisoners in Hitler's concentration camps!*

Monday 11th October - *On the eve of Dave's 69th birthday, Anne-France brings her dear dad the rambler, enormous and superb posters to entirely cover the wall facing the hospital* *bed - South Pacific sandy beaches, sunset by the sea, Canadian mountains and rivers. Also multicoloured balloons to decorate his room for his birthday. All the nurses found excuses to come and glance at the new décor...*

14th October 2004 - *23.50hrs- Late but I try to link up just in case. (Today Dave seemed dazed, dozing off, could not keep his eyes open. At 21.15hr he swallowed a little of a chocolate drink. Within a few minutes, he admitted he was suffering awful stomach pains! It had been his first 'food' for 17days!) The pen starts in French:*

Mum here. Last time we spoke we discussed my life here. Now I shall talk to you about your life, as I am told to tell you from here. The pleasure to please is always more important than the pleasure one has when receiving something oneself. So you all gave a lot of pleasure to Dave and I hope that would have pleased you. The idea of modernising his wall and improving his 'landscape' was of course excellent! I do have to give you some bad news: The waiting for his death will not last long, you know. It will be soon, unfortunately. There may be a short respite then <u>he will fall asleep for good. We shall be here to wait for him and welcome him</u>, you do know that. You will all need a lot of courage and we'll send you some, but your poor children will suffer from it, believe me! You will have to do everything you can to help them. There will be days when they will feel very lonely and you'll need to be there for them. The end will not be hard for him- in fact, he will not really be in pain as the medication will help him... You must be there for him, very close to him. It will help him. He is afraid of being alone when he dies, because he does not really know where he is going or what is going to happen. He does need you all, therefore you'll have to organise yourselves to be there.

BR- Of course! But we do need a more precise warning...

Anne-France had to go back down to Kent for work, his sister and brother are in Norfolk...so when?..

Just a moment... I'll ask... In autumn there will always be leaves falling, in the same way as there will always be people leaving the Earth at any moment. In September you had a message saying 'about two months', so that would make it near November, but the chosen <u>moment will depend upon his state of mind at that time</u>...

If he can be kept fairly cheerful, he will last longer. If he loses courage and strength, he will escape from his physical body to come and rest here, then live happily and normally, though he will certainly be unhappy to have left you all!

There will be days when he will be better and you'll all feel hopeful, but on others he will feel unwell and you'll all be worried. You'll need to remain optimistic even when he is not well, in order to help him last longer if the dates for his departure are not right for everyone to be there... But there is also the organisation of our 'reception' here which will help us tell you more precisely. It does not depend on us, we are only a 'reception committee' don't forget! <u>The date will only be really 'fixed'</u> ***when HE decides he can no longer stand it and wants to leave - then that will be the end...***

We shall only know it when it is much nearer... You'll have to listen to us more often.

(Over the next days I frantically had to convince Dave's sister to bring forward by one week the visit to York she and her husband planned. I could not tell them Spirit had told me the end was much nearer - they would not understand how I knew!

I also tried desperately to organise for Dave to be brought home to sleep in his own bedroom, but with Macmillan nurses at hand in the hope it may be more pleasant for him. Unfortunately the paperwork and red tape were frustrating and they talked of one week to fix this. I knew there would not be time!

Even more frustrating was the surgeon Mr W. taking me aside to tell me unexpectedly: "You do understand why I decided to do that complicated operation: So that he could enjoy your French cuisine!.. It's good if he can go home…"!!!

Enjoy my French cuisine?! For several weeks my poor Dave had not even been able to swallow a single sip of drink without vomiting it! I was too worn out to tell that man I knew perfectly well that he knew he was talking what I'd call nonsense. Dave was paying the price… by being starved and pointlessly crucified on a bed, him the tennis and football player, the rambler, the gardener!

Dave's brother and his wife happened to be journeying back from a holiday, so, unknown to me, briefly called in on the way to see him that Saturday… His sister arrived that weekend, disguising the reason for her unexpected appearance with the excuse of a 'delayed birthday surprise'. They watched together a televised match with Norwich City football, their life-long favourite team. His sister joked and chatted, bravely and successfully hiding her tears. Now and then we would leave the room to let Dave rest quietly.

__18th October__ - I had spent the past nights trying to sleep on an armchair near Dave. There is no room for anything else. Tonight I lay down on a sheet on the hospital floor in a corner, to be able to stretch out more. I was just dozing off after midnight when I suddenly heard gurgling and realised poor Dave, nailed on his back, was literally choking, as dark green gunge was regurgitated. He could not move at all nor hold a bowl! I rushed to lift his head up with one hand, trying to tuck a bowl under his chin and at the same time I desperately tried to reach the bell (on the other side of the bed) to call the nurses. No one came for a long time and only until after the crisis was over! What would have happened if I had not been there to catch him in time?..)

Tuesday 19th October 2004 - *Most of the time Dave is quiet, looking around his bedroom in an inquisitive manner, but he is obviously not examining the decor at all, instead <u>he seems to look at 'thin air'</u> around him! Yet when a nurse comes in, he refocuses on what is being done to him or near him. Anne-France came back by train today at noon. She is therefore with me as we sit quietly by the bed in the afternoon. As Dave is peering at the 'thin air' around him, he suddenly stares wide-eyed at 'space' in front of him <u>and exclaims in a very surprised but clear voice</u>: "Mum??!!" Anne-France and I look at each other. Yes, we'd <u>both heard it</u>! We have no doubt he had actually seen his 'deceased' mother whom he was so fond of. Since he'd never really grasped the idea of an 'Afterlife', it is understandable he looked so surprised to see her appear!*

His long standing and very best friend from Norwich, David B., warned by Dave's sister, does a day return journey to spend a while with him today. He even sings him their favourite Norwich supporters' anthem! By then Dave does not have the strength to speak but squeezed his hand. As the rest of the day passes, he becomes drowsier...

Tonight <u>our Dave passes to Spirit World</u> at 23.02hrs... We (Jim, Anne-France and myself) were with him by his bed-side all the time...sending him loving, healing thoughts so that he had peace of mind and was not frightened. Right to the last minutes we spoke to assure Dave of our constant love, reassuring him he was not to think he was abandoning us. I told him again I would look after the children and he could fly away to get rid of the pain and of that poor body, diseased and mangled by surgery, to go to his family waiting for him. Anne-France and Jim, courageously facing him, made sure they held back any tears in case he could see their face, so that their Dad did not get distraught by their grief. Only once he'd flown away did the flood gates open...

491

26th October 2004 - *During group practice, my guide came unexpectedly to announce this:*

We are all around you. We have been waiting so long to be able to let you know he is all right now. You have done a good job. He had been frightened to leave you, to let you down, but you told him it was ok so he has come, relieved to be free from pain! We can vouch for this. He has accepted the fact that he has no solid body now and that it can be discarded like a dirty garment. His had definitely seen better days, so he is happier now.

We had a few tears of course, because he saw the children before he went and knew they'll be heartbroken, but he knew there was no going back when his body gave up - he felt himself float above it. He had a few gasps of amazement at seeing himself above every one, but he soon learnt to tackle it as his family came close to him.

The hardest part, he said, was to leave you all behind accepting he had gone because he was so ill, but not wanting to lose him of course. That's what upset him: To know you'd all be bearing the pain and the grief on your own - you and his brother and sister of course. He says: "Please let them know I love them all dearly. We did not always talk about that before, but lately I had learnt it was important to say it, to make sure it was not too late for others to know how one felt..."

All over him is a glow of happiness for not being ill anymore, but inside him lots of sadness for not being with you all. That spoils it for him unfortunately. Make sure the children understand he has not gone away. They must understand he is still alive and certainly well - they need not worry at all about him. He is fine! He has not suffered when he passed over - he just slipped over here by sliding out of his body painlessly, softly and silently.

You were all with him and that helped him have the courage to go, because he knew you would not let him have

492

any pain or problems if you could help it. So he felt reassured to have you near him and he slipped out as fast, or rather as easily, as could be done. He did not really notice he was coming out of his body until he became aware he was above the bed and all around him were his loved ones, his family, his animals, his friends. He said "Am I dead then? That's strange to think I am dead and I don't feel any different! I am dead, yet I am alive. What a contrast to be in!"

By the time he'd slipped out completely, there was no hold of his body onto his Spirit and he felt so free, so free he could fly, he said, having been bed bound for weeks!.. It made him so happy to be able to move at last! That was his first and main joy - to move about freely, not to be tied down anymore. "No restriction" he kept saying, "no restriction, how wonderful!"

That's how it happened. You were all there unaware of it, but we could see it because we were all close to all of you to give you support and encouragement, to help you bear the pain and grief.

You've done wonderfully well, all of you, to bear it and see to his funeral in such a positive, active way. You'll bear the fruit of it later. It will have done you some good to do it that way, you'll see. So do not regret to have had to do it. All will be well, you'll be helped. Do not worry.

29th October 2004 - *The frantic work over the past days aimed at organising a 'Celebration' of Dave's life and a Woodlands Burial today. Neither my children nor I could bear the thought of a cremation. Dave loves Nature, so his Earthly body will rest among trees. 13 miles north of York, Terrington offers a lovely Garden of Rest where a tree of one's choice is planted on the grave. We did not want the meaningless (to us) waffle of a religious service.*

We hired the attractive rooms of the Village Hall which Anne-France's artistic talent and imagination decorated beautifully and tastefully, while Jim organised the soft lighting and meaningful music. The large crowd of mourners was amazed and moved when faced with large displays of Dave's various facets. Large frames with scores of photos and even more of his own landscape paintings brought alive and revealed Dave the University language lecturer, the tennis and football player, the rambler, the gardener and Flower Show prize winner, the Art Society painter, but also the loving dad and husband. Speeches and songs from those sharing memories brought tears and laughter. Everybody accompanied Dave to his haven in the Woodlands a short walk away, each planting a daffodil bulb on his resting place. Our holly tree with berries is the emblem of Dave the birdwatcher and nature lover. He is now surrounded by young and older trees growing around him, thus creating a lovely little wood, home to birds, rabbits and deer. No bad taste paraphernalia of stony tombs and other mis-matching constructions! Beautiful nature, just as Dave loves it!

30th October 2004 - *In 'Automatic', in English. My Guide is online:*

'Mum' makes sure he is all right.

BR- What do you mean?

Your mum is making sure Dave understands where he is. He has been shocked to discover that all you said was true... and he wishes he had read what you'd asked him to read! Now he is here he has to adjust, a bit dazed by it all! He kind of understands what it is about, but he is amazed by so much that he does not seem able to take it all in. <u>He has learnt of your big efforts to give him a suitable send off.</u>

BR- How did he hear of it?

<u>He has been told all the details of what you have done</u>, all of you, because we knew you wanted him to know it so much. **So we organised our main helpers to tune in to your world and see what you did so that they could relate it all to**

494

him. He has thus learnt you had fantastic ideas to see him off, as he is not really there but is here. He loves the idea of being in the countryside as a body surrounded by plants and trees. "You have chosen a good tree", he says, "because the frost won't get it and it will remain green all year round". Also you loved the idea of berries for the birds and so does he! That's what he told us as we were relating various details. That ceremony not in a church gave him a few laughs, because he knew people would want to talk a lot and say much about him! But no one seemed to know he was not in that box though!

He says: "Thank you very much for <u>giving my body</u> a decent burial... It was mighty interesting indeed!" That's what he wants to put across. We use our words but his were of the same idea. He has no time or knowledge to communicate himself directly yet, because he has to settle gradually and learn so much, as we go along acclimatising him to his new surroundings.

BR- What are they like?

He has a piece of land around him on which he likes to walk. He had been so confined in bed for the last part of his days that he wanted freedom of movement. So we helped him by <u>constructing with our mind, and using his,</u> a place looking like the places where he'd walked with his friends as we knew <u>that would be beneficial to him to release the frustration</u> of the confinement in bed. He has accepted the idea that he is now in this world of ours and not in the other. He has lots of sad thoughts regarding having to leave his children without their dad. The son he loves was to have his Degree Day, he said and "I've let him down by leaving too early". That is one of his main regrets - not to have been able to be there in person, as promised and hoped for. He knew you'd want him there, so he will no doubt try to make a mental effort to attend as we'll try to explain to him he could visualise it and see or sense it. We'll have to work at it with him, because it is a bit early to expect him to do everything himself.

495

You'll have to be patient with him in as much as he has to learn a lot from scratch, you see? Your mother had had a lot of tuition from you as she was still on Earth. Your husband had not discussed the subject for long enough to be able to cope in the same way as your mother did. But you are not to worry about him, as we are here to help him along and he is doing fine. We have his interest at heart. All of us gather to help him accept, understand, discover and most of all heal his mind from the sadness of the bereavement caused by his bodily death and by the shock of being somewhere unusual and unexpected.

We still have plenty to tell you. You had a hard time lately as we saw. It was to your credit that you'd managed to look after him as much as you could so that he did not feel alone. You have earned a lot of respect and love from our side for this, not that you needed to because we knew you could do that easily enough, since we know your strengths and weaknesses. So we'd like to say thank you in a way you are not expecting.

BR- No need at all for thanks! It was only normal.

Say what you like, we know you could have walked away and not bothered!

BR- There is no way I would ever have done that!

Therefore we can assure you that you will be given a great helping hand with the next stage of your development. The matter is in hand and we will reveal it as it comes gradually. You'll have to be prepared for more work on Earth than you think...but if you are prepared to do it, you will be pleased to see results thanks to our linking to you more easily than before.

BR- Er...you know I am wary of promises...

My little one, we have never made promises we would not be able to keep! Our promise is you will become a better medium than you have been.We have used your inner ears so far. You could learn to use your inner eyes now. That will take some time, lots of practice and many hours of patience, but if you want to do it you can now as we have set up the process.

BR- Please can you explain it?

That would be difficult to explain in details but you can imagine a wheel in motion, a big water wheel turning slowly. As the water gathers in the scoops, some is left, lots falls out. As you'll learn to receive the information, you'll be able to scoop some vision and lose a lot of what is shown, unfortunately. But as you learn to tune in your senses better and better to a more refined level, then you will see more.

That is a promise which will not always cause pleasure, because you'll feel obliged to tell people what you see... That will cause you to have to work for them, as they'll want you to help them!

BR- Well, that's fine...

My little one, you have been a hard worker and we are not afraid of making you work hard. You will have to try to find time for your mum's book and all the other things involved, but if you are willing, 'we are game' as you say on Earth! We know a lot of these modern words, as you call them. We learn them to be up-to-date with you all, you see! As you learn, you will enrich your own life with the satisfaction of helping others even more. You will be asked to speak in public, for this is what you like doing, you will be asked to do services! No need to doubt my friend - you are not being conned or tricked. We are offering you the opportunity to do services or other gatherings, so that you can round up your gift in spreading the word of eternal life.

We are only interested in helping you achieve what you've always wanted to do - help others. Learn all you can teach them. You have achieved quite a lot in the latter years. You have learnt to trust us and learnt certain things. We have to keep your trust and we have your interest at heart. You can also be trusted to do some pure link work, you want to pass on the truth; no one can fool you with fake facts if you can help it! So, we will do our best to help you become a 'purer link' as much as we can. Not that you are not 'pure', but by that we mean 'crystal clear' compared to being easily distracted or tired. So you will be even more precise in details given.

BR- Many thanks, that's great.

You'll certainly have to work hard at it, you know...we cannot make you a visual medium overnight. You'll have to practise and practise until you cannot fit in any more. You can always say 'no' if you want to.

BR- 'No' to what?

To our offer. You can refuse. You are not obliged to do it. You can stay as you are and that will be fine. But we had the feeling you wanted to be able to do more. That's why we are offering you this opportunity of seeing those you hear, because you will still be able to hear us if you tune in quietly. So, the vision of those there will simply be added to your original gift and that will be our little 'birthday on Earth' present!

BR- It took me all those years just to be where I am now!

You cannot expect to be a perfect medium overnight or at birth. That is rare and meant to be. Others have to work at it! You can start simply by being quiet now and then, not worrying about hearing or listening, simply quiet...so that the mind, which moves so fast all the time, stands still for a second or two...then more as you go along. That will allow us to send pictures to your 'mind processing system' and you will eventually be able to pick up the details of what we are sending. We will thus be able to send you more and you'll receive more and everything will be well on the way. All you have to do is be still, for a short while at a time, without worrying whether you are seeing or not, all right? You won't get anything at first probably so don't worry. It takes some polishing from our part too. We are willing to work for you and with you. That's what will happen if you say yes to our offer.

BR- Do you think I am going to say no to this?!

You cannot expect a miracle, that's all we want to make sure, because we don't want you disappointed at first and possibly giving up! <u>It will have to be practised!</u> You've always been guided as much as we can without interfering with your own life. You can rest assured we'll be there all the way, to give you what you asked more of - the Truth all the time, so that should reassure you about not being 'conned or tricked'!

You can ask us questions, you can enquire, you can ask for help, you can <u>tell us what works and what does not</u>. It will have to be a partnership, you understand. <u>We cannot be sure of what you see</u>. So <u>let us know</u> if and when you do and when you don't, so that we can rectify things from this end.

BR- How do you do that?

Leave it to us, we'll do it and then we may explain a little what you are experiencing, coming from our end. All will be revealed as much as can be explained, considering the two worlds are far apart, as far as dimensions are concerned. You can now enjoy the rest of your evening, thinking about what we said and see whether you think it's a good idea.

BR- Come on! You know I'll love it!

Are you quite prepared to work for all those people knocking on your door, asking for help, proof etc?..

BR- (jokingly) - Well, I can charge them, that may reduce the flow!

No objection to this of course. You have a career to have some money, you can change career by teaching others what you know of our world, as we teach you what to tell them. They'll want proof; you'll show them that you can see their loved ones...and less loved ones! They should believe what you say. Having said that, you'll have lots queuing...but you'll have the right to say no if your health starts suffering from it. You cannot wear yourself out by opening the door 24 hours a day, you see?

So be sensible, have limits and people will have to fit in with you, so that the link remains clear and good all the time. We cannot work with tired people who are no less clear than a foggy night! You can test it yourself: If you cannot hear us it's because we cannot come through. That's so simple! As the public asks for you, will you please remember all the time that the <u>link</u> is the main thing! If you cannot get the link, you won't see or hear anything and will not get information. So <u>you</u> have to work at your link. For that <u>you</u> have to be calm and precise in what you hear and see. For that <u>you</u> have to be constantly calm and serene to be able to pick things when they arrive or you may miss them altogether! So <u>you</u> will have to learn to fit in two minutes a day to start with. Then more as you wish to give us a plain background on which to work, i.e. to project our thoughts and pictures for you to receive, then transmit perfectly, if you can! That's all we ask of you...

BR- (joking) - Why not add psychic art, apports, direct voice?..

You can joke, we don't mind. You have accepted and that's all that matters now. We can get started. We love the idea of doing so. You can rest assured you won't be disappointed by the results as they progress. May your remaining days be numerous and happy with the knowledge you'll help thousands of people.

BR- Come on! That's a bit of an exaggeration, isn't it?!

Yes, you will. Because it will be what your new life will become - a helper of Spirits directly involved. A day in a medium's life is very hard indeed, believe me.

BR- I have sometimes problems relaxing and concentrating...

You will have to train for that, as we said...

2nd November 2004. *Home practice group. The pen draws loops then words come in English:*

One day you'll be able to see us more than you do now, you will, I promise. Then you'll be even more aware when we are near you and you won't worry about not being in tune. All you need to know now is that your Dave is doing fine. He is slowly settling down to his new life. No, he is not lonely, he has all his family around him; his father, mother and others are there. She had to be there first of course, being his mum, but he did not take it all in at once. He had such a shock to think he was 'dead' and yet feeling whole. It threw him off balance a bit as he kept saying: "I can't believe I am supposed to be dead!" "That was the same for me when I came" said his mother. "I knew I was alive yet I was told I was not. That was a confusing state of affairs indeed! My first reaction was to think I was asleep and dreaming it all…but I was not unfortunately, because I would have liked to go back to kiss the children one last time, to say goodbye instead of slipping away".

BR- Was it him or her saying this?

That was said by Dave's mother. She was telling him how she had felt. That way he knew that it was normal to feel bewildered and a bit confused. "My son, you cannot go wrong here' she said, 'you'll be looked after".

BR- What is done for that?

Making sure he understands where he is, what he can do with his Mind is the main thing. He has to concentrate on what he is doing at the moment to control his thoughts…

7th November 2004 - *(19 days after Dave's departure). From the quick notes I jotted down: During the service at the Spiritualist Centre, medium B. N. was giving, successfully, very short messages (Short so as to reach more people in the room) round the hall, to many people in the congregation. Suddenly she said:*

501

I have a link with a gentleman now in Spirit World who has not been gone long at all. He passed <u>very</u> recently. I get the name David. I feel he became quite poorly and not himself at all. Does anyone understand this?

(I waited but since <u>no one else</u> put their hand up, I said "I may be able to understand this". She carried on) He gives you a hug. You must have talked to him about Spirit. He says you gave him healing too: "Healing worked wonders; it helped me 'crossing over'. Everything you said was true!" He used to think 'all that stuff' was rubbish... There is a mother link - a strong person, she puts her arm around him and says: "We manage very well, thank you". He says you organised some very nice 'easy listening music' at the funeral. It was uplifting, not doom and gloom or depressing and I hear the famous tune 'Thank you for the Music'! He wants to thank you for everything."

All this was obviously correct. Wonderful he managed to send a message so soon via someone else!

9th **November 2004** - *Once more, unexpectedly during the practice group. The pen started but I could not decipher the words clearly. I asked for it to be repeated. It did, in French, then I heard Mum's words too:*

Darling we are all ready to talk to you to tell you what happened the day you all said goodbye to your 'dad' in a lovely way. I would like to thank you for thinking of including us in your speech. You could have avoided it. It pleased your dad to know you spoke about it, would you believe!

You must be told and know <u>we were all there to welcome</u> your poor Dave, who had suffered so much from being immobilised! He is so happy indeed to have fled from that and now he is very glad not to have any more problems or trouble! You all did your best so that it was a good day and the people who came are very pleased to have been there. Everything was impressive and interesting I gather, <u>according to what I saw and was told</u>.

BR- (Stunned)- You actually <u>saw</u> what took place?! How come?!

I saw it because I looked into what the 'great friend of everyone'*(?)* who came to see you, brought back and reported when he came back, to tell us about it.

He <u>saw</u> everything you did and <u>showed it to us by thinking</u> about it very hard. That way we were able to read/see his thoughts and his report, his tale. It gave us great pleasure to see what you did! At the end the idea to have a tree on a grave is so lovely and fantastic! What a great idea to celebrate the life of somebody one loved!

BR- I am so sorry not to have been able to do the same for you!

My life was not as interesting and lively as his, so you would not have had much to say, believe me!

BR- Can you tell me what happened before and after his passing?

We hope you have all recovered from the shock and you can accept and understand he is not suffering any more. His life amongst you all has been very useful and respected. Everybody loved and still loves him obviously. There are times when he is sad because he knows he will not see the children again until their arrival here, one very distant day. But at other times he is so happy to be free at last, freed from that bed where he was 'nailed like a corpse' he said. He could not bear it anymore...and all that vomiting happening at any time without any warning!.. It weakened him and made him ever so miserable! He wanted to flee from it all and he came here!

We knew he was going to arrive, as we had been warned by the droves of those who looked after him. We knew we could be there to encourage him to make the leap towards the Great Beyond (as we used to call it) and to welcome him.

503

Also to reassure him as it is always a little, or quite, frightening to discover one is 'dead' when one knows one has people who love us, who are left behind on the Earth!

He has moments of joy...and moments of sadness, but we explain to him what he has to do to get rid of those and transform them into good times for you all. So, he will soon know how to do it by himself. Before long you will have even more news from him, when he is able to communicate directly on his own. He will have to learn to do it, but I am sure he will accept to make the effort, so that his children are no longer alone and 'abandoned' as he has the impression they are... We have told him repeatedly they are in good hands and they are safe, since he did his utmost so that everything was sorted out and organised...but he still has that sadness when thinking he won't see them again for a long time.

Sometimes he went off for a walk to 'stretch his legs mentally' because he needed to do it, to free himself of those times of immobilisation. He is able to walk here and to enjoy himself like he used to...

We have spent a lot of time with him so that he is not alone - he knows what to do. It is only a question of practice now - and patience on your side! The first time we spoke to you was to reassure you everything was fine, he had not lost his bearings! He knew where he was as <u>he had been helped by all your prayers and your love</u> guiding him towards us waiting for him...

<u>When he saw himself in mid-air, he was nearly scared because he thought he was going to fall!</u> But his mother and the rest of his family reassured him it was normal to come out of one's body when one no longer inhabits it!

The most interesting aspect is that he has understood at once we were there to welcome him; therefore he was 'dead' as he said! But he did find it difficult to accept, because he probably had a weird idea of what being 'dead' meant, since he kept saying to himself: "How can I be dead yet feel so alive and light?!"

It was hard for him to get used to for a little while but in the end he did. His mother talked to him at length and he listened to her, so happy to have found her and see her again after being apart for so long! I must tell you he had tears of joy when being with them all once more, as he did love them very, very much and cried when they died… So his joy soon showed itself when he came over and saw them here, whole and happy to have him with them at long last! My own mother never knew him so she was not present, but my dad came to help me speak to Dave and make him understand what he wanted to know. So we all met up and he learnt we had always loved him and we thanked him for being such a good dad to your and his children. I must tell you he was touched by this… The rest was only a question of learning to become acclimatised to this new world, where there are so many joys and pleasures if only one knows how to settle in it! We are going to help him and are helping him. He will have no problems, do not worry! He will have plenty to do indeed!

You can carry on (*with this conversation*) later on if you wish. But we wanted to let you know everything was fine and he was well surrounded. He will never have any problems. We all love him and he will gradually learn what he is shown, so all is well!

15th November 2004 - *The conversation starts in French:*

Mum wants to speak to you Darling. I have tried several times to let you know everything is fine here. There are times when Dave is upset to have left you, but he knows it's no use doing this now. I think he has understood the best thing is to send you good loving thoughts so that all goes well for all of you. He does remember indeed what happened when he left!

505

He told the story many a time to lots of people because he is amazed about what took place, not having really ever grasped previously what could happen when one dies because he used to not want to discuss it before! So now he enjoys being able to say: "I am dead and yet I can talk! How incredible this is!"

There are times when he has very clear memories and others when he is less sure...but they are only temporary moments. Overall he feels right in <u>his new body of a young man, fairly young but not too much</u>. He feels good like he did when he was at his favourite age. He is pleased to be fit again, not ill, not suffering, no tubes, no hospital! <u>He has regained his freedom and he rejoices</u>! Now he has to learn to communicate by himself, so that everybody on Earth believes him.

Dave knows who he is, where he is and he wants you to know it too. This is why he must teach himself to communicate on his own, in order to give details which will help those who doubt, believe and understand there is a life after 'death', a fact he was not too sure of himself... before coming over here!

"Down there", he says, "I thought it was of no interest or importance to talk about it. Now I see why she kept wanting to discuss it - to teach me what I would have to do or to face... Now it does not matter because I have understood. I did well not to ignore what she was telling me as I was leaving. I was scared to leave but she was telling me to let go and not to fear anything whatsoever. Now it's done and she was right.

I am embarrassed to have doubted her knowledge - my folly not hers! But I shall make up for it and will help her prove to others she was right indeed..." That's what he wants you to know.

Most people wonder what happens when one dies. It is very <u>different from one person to another</u> of course! We have here lots of people who have come out of it. They have gone through it and all have a story to tell. For them it is one of the most extraordinary moments of their life, as you can guess. It is interesting and amusing to hear them talk and <u>tell each other the kind of experiences they had</u>! It's a bit like a cinema - each one has his little film to see or show, but it's not too sad. Sometimes it is, there are big tears because they've lost a large part of their family who are not all here yet. They have either left their loved ones behind on Earth or committed suicide or similar - so it makes them very sad. But if <u>they had fun when passing from one world to the other, it's when they had a strange experience. For example, floating above the people who thought them to be 'dead'</u>...and who had no idea their <u>loved one was hovering above them and heard every word they said</u>!.. Things like that can be amusing because it shows once more Earth people's ignorance and their great need to learn something.

So that's what is talked about around us at times. Newcomers let us know what they feel and we explain to them how to cope and enjoy being here without having too many regrets or remorseful feelings. After all, let us not forget <u>life on Earth is only a school, an experience we were not obliged to have</u>. If one has really 'botched' it, it's because one was not very skilled for that particular life, it's not exactly the end of the world, is it? After all, the end of the world does not exist... There is not any end to anything since life is eternal!

One of the best things I heard here was: "The life we lived has not been useless. We have learnt everything we wanted to learn and the life we had was quite pleasant, so we were lucky..." It was not so much 'luck' they had than 'practice' of what they <u>chose to do</u>, because after all, one does choose what one wishes to try...(*Short silence then the pen starts again...*)

The experience Dave has lived recently has shaken him a lot but did him some good. He has understood that what you had told him was true. If he has grasped it and accepts it now, it is a very 'good mark' in his favour to recognise he was wrong to mock you and those who believe in it. So he says he wants to help you do what you have to do, because you have been putting all your heart in it for a long time and he did not help you. He understands that now. He did not help and caused problems by depriving you of the understanding you needed. Now that he has no longer any doubts on the subject (for a good reason!), he made the decision to settle properly here and when he has grasped everything he has to do and learn, he expresses the desire to help you, in order to 'pay back' having doubted you and 'fought' in a way...

Yet he was doing his best in those days, so he should not be blamed too much. He did not know as much as you, therefore he can't be judged as 'guilty', can he, and he should not feel guilty.

BR- Of course not! I had long resigned myself to simply plant a few 'seeds' in his mind for his own good, even if he did not want to discuss the subject!

That was what he said. Now all he has to do is learn, then we'll see... According to him, he had been wondering for years what 'all that stuff', as he called it, was about! But he could not start asking you because he 'did not want to look a fool', he says... He was afraid of looking daft to have changed his mind!

BR- He would never have! I would have been pleased and would have admired him for doing so! If only I had known he wanted to!

So we reassure him all is fine on your side of life too and he will only receive praise for everything he did well for all of you. It has put him at ease in a way, yet I think he still wants to feel you all forgive him for having doubted so much and caused problems...

BR- Of course! There is no need to 'ask for forgiveness'; it's understandable he could not get his head round it...

My darling daughter I'll let you sleep now as your 'hour of beauty' has long gone! Once more you stayed up to speak to us, but I am pleased to be able to let you know all that, because it's not just my own experiences we talk to you about, but also your Dave's too! So they come from two different people, man and woman, moreover there are very big differences! I give you a big kiss from me but also from him! He says he wanted to do it better for a long time but he did not dare, knowing he was due to die soon. He did not want to make you suffer from even more regrets and all that...

"I wanted to tell her I have always loved her", he is saying now, "but I did not dare to say it in words. I think she has understood it, hasn't she?"

BR- *Oh yes, indeed...*

"That's right", he says, "we both knew but neither of us said it clearly. We knew, that was enough and is enough for me to think she still did love me after all. After all. That's what matters now. I can rest happy to know it did not make a difference. We still loved each other in the end... Have faith in me, I promise I will help you communicate what I have to say, like your mother does. You'll have two communicators when I've learnt what to do. Good job, hey?! Lapses never meant there was no love, remember that, lapses were lapses not hatred. Look out for my work. Lots of love to all of you, my kids and my little wife who had so much courage on the last days of my life. I'll never forget what she did for me, tell her. All my love to all of you left behind, remember that. All my love is still there, not going."

BR- *Have some fun! Enjoy where you are! Don't torture yourself... The children are all right, everything considered, because they know you are well and not suffering anymore. So this helps them overcome the grief caused by your disappearance. Learn to communicate more, that will be wonderful!*

"Place your hand on my heart, know that I am still alive, that's what I wish I could tell you clearly in your head.

You will be told elsewhere. Place your hand on my heart and you'll know it's me talking to you."

BR- All right.

All has been said for now. Be quiet in your mind and you will receive more as you go along. Do not fret, he'll be all right.

BR- I am not fretting...

You will be recompensed for your efforts. Be quiet within and you will see what we mean. All will be well. That's it for now. A good night's sleep to you! We are sending peace of mind and our love to you all.

7th December 2004 *- 20.00hrs - Alone at home. I relax and wonder whether anyone wants to come on line. The pen starts in English:*

People want to talk to you. You could be a good receiver if your mind could be quieter at times. Let us begin then with the first person who is in the queue...there are so many people! ..."My Mum is there..."

BR- Who? Whose Mum?

"My Mum is there", declares Dave, "to say hello at last, she says". She did not really want to say hello to you before, but "now all is well" she announces. She's understood more what had happened, as I explained we both had our differences... Anyway I was not holy either, so all is well and forgotten...

BR- (Sending her a thought) - Hello Nana. Thank you for talking to me. It's a nice surprise.

We could have a party here if you were all with me! We have met so many people...

BR- Who are 'we'?

My parents and I. They made me meet so many people I had known before and now we keep talking and reminiscing. That's quite fun because I never thought we could do that sort of thing! I am most surprised and amused by it. If you could tell the children I am all right, absolutely all right now - no more pain, suffering, misery! I've forgotten all that because I want to forget it! It was awful and had no purpose in the end. Why do all that for nothing? I can't understand it. Still I suppose they thought they were doing their best...

I've got to tell you something: If you think I am talking to you directly, no I am not, because I've not been taught how to control my mind to reach yours. So I've learnt to talk to you in my head and (they say) <u>my mind is 'picked' by someone else who transmits</u> it to you. How they do that I've no idea, but if it works am quite happy with it!

I remember the last thing I did on Earth was to sick up some stuff, then I felt very weak and even weaker... I wanted out! <u>I wanted to clear off, I could not stand it anymore</u>. All I could think of was to get rid of that sickly feeling in my guts. My mind was numb with that horrid feeling of being trapped and gunged inside. I wanted to go out, out of all that, out of the hospital, out in the country. *I wanted to cry, to be free, to release all the pent-up frustration...and suddenly I felt I was lifting...I was being lifted, I floated,* I could not believe it! I felt as if I was floating...and then I saw you and Jim and Anne-France and 'me' on the bed, the three of you around it - and there was another person too...*(A friend)*. But I also saw my mum and dad and the others! I thought "If I go any higher I'll fall off"! I laughed when they said: "Welcome to our world son!" They actually said 'our world'...and I thought: "How can it be their world, they are dead!"

But then I realised I was with them and I then must be 'dead' too! ... and that was such a strange feeling to think: "You are dead" yet feel as alive as before! In fact <u>more alive</u> than before, because I was not feeling alive in that hospital! My mother came up first and said: "You can relax now my son, it is all over. We've been watching you and over you, we've been waiting for you for several days, you had such a bad time!

You can relax now. They are all right on the Earth, we've checked, they are all right because they knew you were going and they thought it was the best thing for you to do. So they encouraged you to go, not because they don't love you, but because you'd suffered too much. You had to be free, that's why you are here. You could be free then, they told you."... Last night you came to meet me at my new home, you know...

BR- Did I?

You did indeed! You came all alone and said you were here to see whether I was all right, as you were concerned I may still be upset to have left you all. Of course I am upset! I could not get over that easily! But you know here they have a good system of protection for 'new arrivals'; they look after you as if you were going to fall at each step! They really pamper you!

My parents were there of course but there are other people who came and talked to me. At first it was the ones I knew. Your mum was there first of course...she had to come and said: "Bonjour Dave, you've made it! Congratulations!"

I am surprised she could still speak French or English, but that's what this world is about, it's full of surprises! I thought she might have forgotten about me since she died long ago! But you see I did not know anything about this world, so I must have had a lot of erroneous ideas, I guess... Now I realise why you were getting so upset and frustrated when I did not want to listen to you. You must have thought I was such an idiot, hey?

BR- Not at all! It was just frustrating...

I used to think you were an idiot, wasting time with such fallacies and highfalutin ideas, but now I am very repentant! You had it right to a 'T' and I am the one who has got to learn to start from the bottom line, because all this stuff is bewildering!

My parents have understood I need a lot of help, because they required a lot themselves when they first came

512

and they know how confusing all this is! So they came to make sure I realised there was no need to panic and no going back "because the body had lost touch with the Spirit' they said. That's what 'death' is about, when your body is no longer in contact with your Spirit".

That rather threw me, as I had hoped to be able to go back quickly to say: "Hello, am back, am all right, you have not lost me..." But Mum said: "No, you can't go back there, it's over Son! You have come to us now and we'll look after you. You can rest assured they will be all right, because they have the knowledge they need to help them fight off the grief they will no doubt feel. It has to be done. So you listen to us, we are 'old hands' at this Son! You can trust us, we know what we are saying... You can rest assured the level of understanding your children have is no way near yours, you lagged behind by leagues...and they've overtaken you ages ago! Now they are reaping the benefits from their knowledge, they can cope with a parting which will only last during their own life time on Earth. As there is no definite end to that parting, it's only temporary... We've seen it done and you are proof of it, aren't you? We 'died' and now you are here with us...isn't that proof of the pudding? (As my mum used to say). So we are here to help you and you can be sure we will not let you fall on the way. You can rest if you want or you can try to understand a bit more how to cope here".

It has to be seen Darling, this place really has to be seen! You cannot believe how beautiful it is! Think of the most beautiful landscape you've ever seen and multiply it by thousands, that will give you an idea of what I see!

My mind is overjoyed and blown by the beauty and the colours of these landscapes. I've never seen such mountains or lakes or seas. It's so wonderful! But I am not travelling all the time! I had a time for walking when I arrived, that's what I wanted most and above all. I needed to stretch my legs, I've been so stuck in that bloody bed! But now I can stretch my legs at will and gallop all over the place!

My favourite place is a little pond-like lake with fish in it. It has flowers on it, like water lilies, but they are not like the water lilies you and I know! They are fabulous...sort of multi-facetted petals with colours you have never seen before. Can't describe them! And the birds all around have songs you've never heard in your whole life!

My lovely trip around that 'region' felt great because I walked alone for a while, just to get my mind around all this. I wanted to understand what was going on in my head and my new legs, because it's quite something, you know, to find your-self suddenly walking freely after you've been stuck on your bed for weeks...out of the blue...without any warning! One minute you are sick to death (literally!) in a hospital bed, next you are near the ceiling looking down, then you are surrounded by your dead parents and families, then you can walk around the country without having to put any clobber on!

That walk did me good. I had to go alone because I had to talk to myself first before talking to others more. They'd had their say. I needed to think quietly. So that's what I did. I went out and strolled around, amazed... I saw what I seemed to recognise - a nice little lane I used to walk along and trees I knew and plants, so I felt "That's the life at last! All normal and beautiful". Yet as I walked further, I began to notice different landscapes and that surprised me, because I thought "I didn't know that place existed nearby!" But the thought created a new place! I wondered: "Why is there something different?" and that seemed to make a new place appear! I don't know why or how, but it did!

That's what I did when I first arrived after being greeted by everybody. My mum wanted you to know she had changed her mind about you now... That's all I was going to say today, because I was not sure how much I could tell you, since I could not really talk to you like on Earth, but now it feels quite normal actually. I can think aloud and you seem to pick it up...

BR- What do you do nowadays? What kind of place are you in?

You said you wanted me to tell you about my life here, so I started, but now it's more to do with understanding what is going on here. If one thinks of something strongly, it makes it happen you know...of course you know, I am sure! So it's something one has to get used to, isn't it? One can't just come from the Earth and be thinking normally and expect the same result as 'down there'... or is it 'over there' or 'under there'? I don't know where you all are in relation to me! But I know you have understood I am all right and not 'dead' and that's all that matters, hey?

My life has been useful to you all, I hope, so that you are well settled now or will be eventually. We can always look back at mistakes, I am told, but it is not a good thing to do it soon after your arrival here as it makes them appear in front of you and you don't really want to see bad times or errors... So I am told to look forward and ahead of me - that is, at the moment, to concentrate on what I am doing as I go along 'day by day'. If you have a day on Earth as long as I have a 'day' here, you'll have plenty of time to do things you've got to do!

You would need to want to sleep to make it change to 'night', but if you don't think of sleep or rest and want it to be daylight, it stays as 'daylight'! You understand that?! Isn't it amazing! You can alter the length of day at will! I wish I'd had that gift on Earth! I could have gardened and painted all 'long days'!

My life here has many purposes - to look for what's new, handle it, cope with it and practise it. But it's not all work. It's also enjoying it as much as you can because there is no hassle, no pressure here. You do what you want, when you want to do it. That's my type of life! No more bills, no more hassles,

515

phone calls pestering me out of my greenhouse or chasing me out of the bath! Now I am free from all that! Life has definitely changed, hasn't it?

But there is a dark cloud over it because you people are not in it yet... You'll have to be 'dead' to be here - but I know that <u>I can also see you if you are asleep and 'your Spirit' comes here</u>, they say. I thought it was the whole of you coming, but they say it is 'the Spirit', whatever that is...because obviously I am a 'Spirit' but <u>I feel whole,</u> like before, so it must be a different type of perception, that's all, I assume. Anyway you are not here all of you, so it will take me some time not to feel like phoning you to see whether you are all right... My mother told me you would come at night and I hope you all will. I have seen you R-, I told you before...

(Suddenly the phone rang then someone came in... So I went upstairs to escape, wondering whether the link had snapped off...but after about 10 minutes relaxing and trying to tune in again, the pen started the first words automatically as I heard the words)... Last night you came to see me. You said you'd be in touch again, because we need to talk to keep me informed of what goes on in your lives.

They said I could talk to you more easily because <u>you</u> had 'lots of experience and practice in talking to us', but you must tell me what to do to talk to Jim and Anne-France. I know I'll have to learn to do more than I do now, but it will no doubt take some time.

BR- You said I came 'at night'. So you have nights?

My 'nights' don't really exist now because you have no doubt learnt one does not need to sleep here... I had some sleep and rest at the beginning, I was so tired of being exhausted! But after my refreshing walks all around and my talks with my friends and family and your mum, then I realised that was not necessary.

So I decided not to waste time sleeping since I don't

516

have a body that needs to rest...and that has made a lot of difference in the end, because it restructures your 'day' in a different way. You think you have restrictions when you have hours set for doing this or that on Earth. If you have to sleep at night, it makes you shorten your day to fit that in. Whereas now I don't bother. I simply get on with what I am doing at the time and if the sun does not set, it's simply because *I* do not need the sun to set!

BR- *You see a sun?*

There is beautiful sunlight around. I don't know exactly where the sun is... I suppose there is one...or maybe it is a 'Spirit sun' too?! Everything is 'Spirit' here so there might be a 'Spirit sun'? You'll tell me no doubt!

But the constantly lasting, <u>overall impression I have is one of peaceful rest, longing to find my way round, have peace of mind, no need to worry about anything else at all</u>. I've had so many worries lately...but I realise it's not 'lately', it's at the end of my life on Earth... So it feels so good not to be concerned with health, food, pills, bills, payments, phone calls, all those pests which spoil life!

Now I have sunlight, shorts on, walk about, enjoy my views and talk to nice people including my own beloved parents. That feels really good because I had missed them so much when they died that I feared you'd all cry too when I go - but I know now that if you don't cry too much, it is because you know more than I did when they died!.. That's Education, Knowledge for you! Does wonders to those who have it, doesn't it?! *(Short silence then...)* My life has not got a pattern now. I don't want any pattern and restriction. I will not have any more rules, patterns, restrictions or decisions to make! I want to feel free, to fly like a bird or float like a fish! No more do's and don'ts. No more of all that! Now it's free Dave roaming the hills, up the mounts and down the valleys...yee ha! And that's the cowboy coming out! I'll gallop on my own legs not a horse, and will see lovely places without 'having to do' this or that. I'll do what I want when I want until I've had enough, then I'll change! Does that sound good to you? Does to me! You can see me in your mind's eye, can't you, galloping over fields and meadows, painting or taking pictures, swimming or walking, no more restrictions! Yippee! Me free, me free! Yeah! That's the life, kiddos!

Join me when you have finished your trek on Earth and we'll gallop over the hills together. I'll be there for you when you arrive - but I know that won't be for quite some time indeed, so no worry, I am not telling you you'll kick the bucket soon! Am just telling you I'll be there for you.

Now Life has some meaning for me. It makes sense to be free and to fill your mind and soul with the beauty of Nature, because until you are here you don't know what freedom is! I thought holidays were freedom but there were so often some hiccup or sickness or accident or delay or cost... and that spoilt it all! Whereas here, now, can you be sick if you don't have a flesh body, hey? Can't for the life of you! Because the life of you on Earth has gone and now it is the new life of you 'Spirit'... Yeah!

I am a Spirit, me Dave Rix am a Spirit! Write a song about that Jim-Bo! Me, your dad is a Spirit who did not know he had a Spirit in the first place! My mind goes round and round over these things. You have to understand, all of you, that it's all new to me. It's all right for you guys, you'd seen it or heard it before! Me, I had to experience it to learn the hard way! *I had to 'die' to be alive again!* That's something, isn't it? Am going to ramble on all 'night' (for you) if you keep asking what I am doing *(I was not asking anything at this point...)* because I am doing just that - loving every minute of my freedom!

But thinking of you has not disappeared you know. I am thinking of you and I have to be strong-minded to understand I must not feel bad for leaving you all, not feel 'down', because that does not help me at all. In fact instead of feeling better, it makes me feel worse! I have to be positive and think of you in a positive way, I was told. That means they said, "to think of them as if they were near you and you wanted to give them a lot of love and affection. That way your thoughts gather round them and create a lot of good energy to make things happen" (That's a quote from them, talking to me).

I had no idea that I could create energy to that extent! That's one more thing to add to my list of what I can do happily: Fill your lives with positive energy and that way I'll feel good because that will help you at distance even if I am not near you. Quite clever stuff actually, isn't it?

BR- You are doing very well. Congratulations! Is there still an 'intermediary' or are you talking directly to me?

Our thoughts must begin to join each other as I think I am hearing what you are saying when you ask a question... That's what it feels like. I think I 'sense' your question or comment in my head and I was told that's how it feels to you too. So we must be linking up somehow? I thought I was talking to that man in front of me who said he would help me with communicating to you, but now I think I may be going off his mind and to yours somehow? We'll have to see, won't we? Do you think you hear me?

BR- Yes I do, in my head. You are doing really well considering it's only 6 weeks since your passing over! (I relaxed even more deeply, but on top of having concentrated on listening for so long it was 'fatal' - I dozed off...)

14th December 2004 - *At my small home circle. The pen writes the first 7 words in English - it is my guide:*
One day you will see us better, but you need to practise more. The best way is to wait for the pictures to come in front of your eyes and not look for them. Just wait quietly so that you do not expect one thing or the other. As you wait your

mind calms down and waits too, then you will see. If you think too much, no picture can come because we cannot send it. It is a process of thought transference, you see. As we send the thought of a face or an object, the picture of it has to travel to your mind and the brain has to register it, but it won't be seen by the eyes of flesh so it will not be the usual brain pattern at work, it will be a different type of work. It has to be imprinted onto your Mind's eye, that is to say your 'inner eyes', the spiritual equivalent of your flesh sight. But the sight is not from the flesh patterns and reactions, it comes from the 'spiritual eyes' which can see beyond the flesh. That's how we do it. Therefore we need a very clear and quiet mind to have good reception of what we send. That way you'll be able to see more than you ever have.

Last time we spoke you had the visit from a gentleman you are very fond of, who has just arrived recently! We have him here again, wanting to talk to you to say: "Hello, I am all right. You have not had time to tell our two kids of my talk, have you? I'll be pleased when you can tell them as I'd like to keep in touch with them through you, if you don't mind".

BR- Of course!

He has a little weep now and then regarding the fact he misses them very much and wishes he could talk to them directly. It is a pity they haven't learnt to receive yet but they no doubt will one day. They have to understand it is a question of practice and practice takes time… He does accept it, he knows one can't learn to be a medium overnight and that's what he wishes he had done before.

"Why didn't I accept what you were saying' he keeps saying, 'We could have talked more about it. I would have understood so much more if I'd tried to learn. We were meant to be together obviously but I messed it up by not listening enough. You could have helped me learn what I am learning now"…

520

(I then give Dave the latest news about Jim and Anne-France)

All well received, he says. You have made him happy by giving him some news. He likes to know what's going on. He has not learnt yet to go straight to the source of news. He has to be told what's happening. We have your interest at heart, all of you, so we do look out for what's going on and what feelings you all have. But yourself coming to tell him what's taking place makes him happy. It's as if you were phoning him with the news, he said.

BR- What's the process? How does it reach him?

You told him the news. I heard it too so I passed it on to him. He has to have an <u>intermediary</u> to '<u>sieve' the thoughts one at a time</u>. It has to be done very slowly and clearly for the ***thought process to be <u>dissected</u> into little segments of electronic signals which can be <u>reprocessed</u> this end.***

BR- Could you explain more please?

Thoughts are like light signals which have to be decoded. <u>Your thoughts are slower than ours and they have a 'weight'</u> ours don't have.

BR- Really?!

You people on Earth have to think slowly to be able to understand something. Your thoughts do not have the lightness and speed ours have, yet thoughts are the same in a way. So what we mean is: Your speed of thought is not the same as ours and if we do not reconnect together, ourselves, the bits which we receive, they may not fit the pattern we are used to...

As we are here to help, we'll explain more clearly if possible: The <u>light</u> coming to us <u>from your mind</u> <u>carries little signals</u> which have a life of their own - they mean to be little transporters of information <u>which we have to decipher on our side</u>. To do this we need to be able to catch each little bit of information, look at it, and ***make it fit in the 'pattern-receiver-thought-processing-method' we have here.*** This is not a

521

machine but a way of receiving information that we all have here ***built-in within us***. We can receive without thinking and we can send without thinking.

As we do this automatically, all thoughts have to be very clear and concise; otherwise the pattern sent will be so mixed up we cannot read it, or others won't be able to read it. That way the decoding takes place at the bottom level upwards, so that each little bit of thought comes, gets cut up, looked at, processed and put in its right/correct category. When there is enough of it to make sense or give an idea of what is being said, the little bits get looked at, analysed, understood and processed more.

We can always understand something but if we get confused bits of information, we cannot piece it together. It has to be clear and concise. So please speak/think in a clear way so that we can receive it clearly and then Dave will be happy to have his latest news... "Without having to turn the telly on or lift the phone up" he says. All is needed now is to keep going, doing it.

Last time, you helped him by listening for a long time and he was very happy. He had to learn to send his thoughts via someone else for now. But he will soon be able to concentrate enough to reach your own mind and be able to send his own thoughts in your mind. That way he will feel he is really in contact for good. So far he is thrilled to have some link with the Earth and with you as he is still fond of you and would not want to lose your love and friendship, but most of all he wants you to know you have been a good mother to his children. He loves them so much and loves you for looking after them as best as you could and can. You have never left his heart, he says, but you had to be apart because Life made it so. As you grew up together, you had to know sides of each other which were not always compatible maybe and that's why there were differences, but that does not mean Love had died. That's his message, he says, his had not died and he hoped yours had not either. Now all is over, all life on Earth side of things has gone, but the new life he has may prove to be interesting and he hopes he can help you learn even more from his side, *(just as your mother told you things...*

(As there is a silence I send the thought that I'll need to stop because the circle members had things to share aloud- so my guide sent a quick reply)

Make time later please, if you can.

26th December 2004 - *It takes me quite some time to relax and tune in. After a while the pen draws across the page 8 horizontal lines of various designs made of loops... Eventually it forms words, in English:*

All is well now, you have calmed down. We were trying to keep your mind quiet while your hand wrote to keep the two separate, in as much as you need to have us writing. It is difficult because we need the part of the mind which helps with the writing but not the part which does the thinking. It is awkward to do. All is well, you have a quiet Mind and we'd like to tell you your loved ones are here...it's only a question of who speaks first! You could start with your mum if you like. Otherwise Dave is here with his own family. They have gathered because you had Christmas on Earth. They think Christmas is a special time and he has not been able to wish 'Merry Xmas' to his children, so he's doing it through you now.

We do not need Christmas here unless we want it; it is only a matter of taste and wishes. Everyone has their own views about this. What we want to say is that it was a special time for him because he had his children home with him and he enjoyed making them a special meal with all the trimmings, hors d'oeuvre, sweets etc. He had learnt to cook quite well, he reckons, "after studying Delia's book" he says. Not before, but after a while he could do quite well and got to enjoy it. *(I give him our latest news and mention I received a Xmas call from Dave's sister and brother)* Lots of people wanted to phone but we did not always respond to theirs.

BR- *What do you mean?*

I did not always phone people, just my own family for Xmas, that was most of my phoning...but we could pretend we are phoning each other now!

BR- *I miss our games of Scrabble together!*

Albert *(Probably one of his own friends?)* and a few others... We don't know many people who would play Scrabble...we could not find you many players nowadays!

BR- *I am not asking you to do so!*

Alfred is here with me, my dad's brother. He had left long ago but he was here to welcome me... I had not seen him for such a long time! Looking as good as ever, with his plants, as he used to grow them. We had that in common.

I'll let you rest now. Goodnight Darling.

27 December 2004 -The pen starts in English: my guide is online:

Everything is all right. Dave is fine. He has had a lot to learn as you can guess and he is still learning of course! He'll have plenty to do for quite a while. He is not too worried about you people, because he knows we look after you from here and he did his best (for you) on Earth. Although he does miss you and the children, especially the children of course, because they were his main point of reference in his Earthly life. He lived for them, always making sure they were all right. Now he has a big task to tackle: To learn more about his mind, his way of thinking, the power of it all. He is tackling things one by one. He is doing well, but you must not call out to him too often so that he can concentrate on what he is doing.

BR- *Can you explain this please?*

He is doing fine at the moment. He has his tasks to

524

cope with, so do not worry about him. He knows you are all okay. We mean for example, do not 'pray' to him, do not call him for help. That distracts him from what he is thinking or doing and may distress him if he thinks you are unhappy without him. <u>Just send him your loving and encouraging thoughts and that will help him in his new venture.</u>

Your family have their activities to deal with. Your mum is very busy indeed! She has undertaken to protect and help all those arriving here in great need. They are souls coming back who are lost because their passing was so sudden. She has chosen to join the team of helpers who welcome new arrivals. She helps them understand the reality of where they now are. She tries to lessen their confusion and panic at no longer being on Earth.

So if you need something, I am sure she will oblige. But if you just want a chat, could you wait a little longer while she finishes her tasks of rescuing and comforting those who have problems on arrival here?

Therefore all is well this side. We hope you are using your mind power to make your life easier in your world... All is needed is faith in it, applying it. You do not apply it enough you see. You could try more often, then you would see results... then you would not doubt! Practise what you have learnt. Do what you've been told to do to improve the power of your mind and your gifts within. All it takes is a bit of discipline and faith in what you can achieve. If you don't believe in it, of course you won't get any results. If you understand you can achieve a lot, the results will come of their own accord without any efforts.

(This last conversation at the end of a tumultuous and tragic year seems a suitable one to finish this <u>first</u> book of the on-going series of dialogues with those loved ones and my guide, living out of our Earthly sight if we are not clairvoyant, but fortunately for me, as a clairaudient, within earshot!

Volume 2 has already been dictated by my mother and all the others joining her, since it is a journal of her and their discoveries and progress. It will soon be ready for publication, to help interested readers find out even more and understand how the so-called 'deceased' can feel more alive than Earthlings do... yet they do not need a body!)

FINAL PAUSE FOR THOUGHT - From my mother

I remind you that what I tell you is the truth, because I never wanted to tell lies during my life on Earth either. It served and helped me well as I saw myself as an 'honest woman' when, once here, I had to glance at my life.

BR- Which life are you talking about?

As your mum of course, didn't you realise? The best part of one's life is often spoilt by troubles one gives oneself by not always doing what one should, either by stupidity or ignorance, or else because one is nasty. Yet if one thought more about it, one would see indeed that there is only one path to follow: The path of Truth! To have Truth, all that is needed is to listen to the inner voice guiding you in Life. That voice is the one you must hear and recognise as the 'Voice of Wisdom'. Sometimes wisdom from your own Soul. Sometimes wisdom from another Being who chose to help and guide you on Earthwhen you have problems and you can't see your way out of them.

The solution? Inner life, which should have precedence over 'external life', if one wants to progress on the spiritual path. Once you have 'made your life' on Earth to the point when you think: "I have done the bulk of what I wanted to learn down here", well, you can let yourself enjoy the pleasure of joining in thoughts (even more?) with those who want to talk to you from the Great Beyond. In this case that 'vibrational world beyond the Earth' which the Spirit World is. It is invisible to the majority of humans, who are insensitive to the vibrations of those Beings who surround you with love and kindness to help and inspire you...

The solution is to <u>listen and apply what they tell you</u> so that it's worth transforming your life into a calmer, smoother one, in order to achieve some progress on Earth, since that includes work for the world of Spirits and at the same time, work to help humans on Earth...

*** **<u>END of Volume 1</u>** ***

Please visit my website for furthur knowledge:
www.Italkwithspirits.com